Urban Innovation Abroad

Problem Cities in Search of Solutions

Urban Innovation Abroad

Problem Cities in Search of Solutions

Edited by
Thomas L. Blair
The Polytechnic of Central London
London, England

PLENUM PRESS • NEW YORK AND LONDON

Library of Congress Cataloging in Publication Data

Main entry under title:

Urban innovation abroad.

Includes bibliographical references and index.
1. City planning — Case studies. 2. Urbanization — Case studies. 3. New towns — Case studies. 4. Poor — Social conditions. 5. Poor — Economic conditions. I. Blair, Thomas Lucien Vincent.

HT166.U736 1983	307.7'6	83-19263

ISBN 0-306-41492-9

© 1984 Plenum Press, New York
A Division of Plenum Publishing Corporation
233 Spring Street, New York, N.Y. 10013

Printed in the United States of America

Preface

This book focuses on the response to City Poverty by public institutions responsible for urban affairs and offers a timely record of the achievements, failures and prospects for effective urban management, development and plan implementation.

The idea for the book emerged during the period 1976 to 1983 from the annual courses and conferences on "Urban Habitat: A Decade of Plan Implementation" organised for urban managers and planners from developing countries by the Habitat Forum Centre for Human Settlements, School of Environment, the Polytechnic of Central London.

The views and proposals offered by our contributors establish a firm basis for the exchange of information, knowledge and experiences among a growing international cadre of planners concerned with the provision of housing, jobs, services and healthy environments in developing countries. In addition, the new perspectives gained will assist public officials, legislators, and international aid agencies in making effective improvements in public policy and planning action for urban settlements in the coming era of relentless pressures.

Our work will be of immediate interest to the urban development planning and design practitioner, and urban manager, who may be faced with similar or analagous problems; to the student and teacher who require detailed urban studies material and data for discussion, research and instruction; to the geographer, sociologist, economist and specialist in public administration and Third World studies who see their responsibilities as part of the settlement improvement and development process; and to the concerned individual, community planner and member of voluntary, non-governmental organisations working on behalf of low-income families in slums and squatters settlements.

Grateful acknowledgement is given to the support of the Polytechnic and its Rector, Dr Colin Adamson, and to the bodies which over the years have contributed to the Habitat Forum activities, these include the British Council, the Commonwealth Foundation and the German Foundation for International Development.

Thanks are due to the contributors, many of whom were guest lecturers or fellows at the Habitat Forum, whose generosity of time and effort made the book possible. In addition, much has been gained from colleagues at the Polytechnic and from course and conference participants who helped define the reality and validity of Third World urban development planning. I am equally indebted to the principal organisations at which I have been privileged to speak and share ideas: the International School Committee of the Royal Town Planning Institute, London; the International Division of the American Planning Association, Chicago and Washington, D.C.; the International Union of Local Authorities, The Hague; and the United Nations Centre for Human Settlements, Nairobi. My secretary, Iris Grayson, was of invaluable assistance in organising and typing the first drafts of the manuscript. Finally, acknowledgement is given to the authors, firms, organisations and agencies whose works are quoted or used herein, and to publishers for use of material and illustrations from their work.

Thomas L. Blair
Professor of Social and
Environmental Planning
and Director,
Habitat Forum,
School of Environment,
The Polytechnic of
Central London

London, April 1983

Contents

CONTENTS

Urban innovation abroad
problem cities in search of solutions
Introduction

Thomas L. Blair

Cities, with their industries and commerce, cash wages, and bright lights are focal points of attraction in all parts of the world. In many developing countries, however, massive urbanisation has led to the explosive growth of large urban centres, an unprecedented world phenomenon.

Thirty years ago, 20 per cent of the population in developing countries lived in the urban areas, cities and towns. Fifteen years ago this proportion had reached 31 per cent. By the year 2000 it will be 45 per cent. And the big cities are growing bigger - a trend which is vividly apparent in the rapidly growing concentrations of populations in metropolitan centres. Mexico City, Manila, Jakarta, Calcutta, Bogota, Sao Paulo and Khartoum have tripled or quadrupled their numbers and many sub-Saharan African cities have increased more than seven-fold since independence.

In effect, the Static city of colonial days has become the Dynamic City of today. Yet many of the most productive large urban centres are in a critical condition as successive waves of population growth and economic change have increased the gap between the demand for satisfactory living and working environments and the capacity of the public sector to deliver the required services.

Central institutions responsible for urban affairs encounter serious difficulties in responding to the mounting pressures of rapid urbanisation, economic and technological changes, and cultural transformation. They fail to comprehend that the sprawling slums and squatters areas are not

1

isolated or temporary phenomena, or marginal appendages to
the "real city" - they are the city, the Urban Majority.

National politicians and international aid agencies find
it difficult to agree on the necessary public policies and
planning actions. Land use planning approaches, such as
master plans, zoning, and development control, and more
recent attempts at slum clearance, expanded and satellite
towns, urban renewal and upgrading of slums and squatter
areas, have proved of limited use in the face of the rapidly
growing agglomerations where tens or even hundreds of thousands of people are added to the population every year.

As a result, the Dynamic City of developmental dreams is
a Problem City in search of solutions to a range of critical
and interrelated factors:

i   unbalanced population, spatial and economic growth;
ii   large-scale deprivation and unmet provision of land,
      housing, employment and transportation needs;
iii   deteriorating environments and inadequate basic ser-
      vices;
iv   shortages of public fiscal resources and qualified man-
      power for effective plan implementation and management;
v   uncoordinated national and municipal urban policies and
      inadequate organisational structures;
vi   costly imported finance and inappropriate planning ideas
      and technology;
vii   the absence of meaningful public participation in the
      planning and development process.

Together these problems constitute a measure of City
Poverty, the gap which remains between the reality of under-
development and the goal of balanced social, economic and
physical development. But how well have these problems been
dealt with by policymakers and planners, government, the
private sector and international aid agencies? And what are
the prospects for the future?

The contributors, drawn from many countries and differing professional and administrative backgrounds, take a close
look at the experience of Third World cities, and contrasting
world situations, in formulating, implementing and evaluating
policies for improving urban settlements, especially low-
income communities. Their papers, based on years of dedicated
work in the field often anticipate new problems and suggest

new directions, thereby providing correctives for immediate application and insights for innovative policy changes.

Five key questions facing Problem Cities in all parts of the world provide a unifying perspective for the book.

1. Urban Policies and Settlement Planning

Can we identify successful examples of public policies, strategies and guidelines for meeting urban settlement needs, particularly in the related areas of housing, employment, improved basic services, and resource-generating activities?

2. Urban Management and Finance

Are there some successful least-cost departures from conventional urban planning, management and financial practices which are capable of wider application?

3. Urban Plan Implementation and Public Participation

What are the prospects for an integrated approach to urban plan implementation, one which involves community participation, local resources, and appropriate technology?

4. Education and Training

How can new innovations in training, education and research be of use to planners, managers and the communities they serve?

5. National and International Action for Settlement Development

Can we identify appropriate changes in public policy and international action, aid and investment activities, which are required to implement development and the effective improvement of settlements, especially low-income communities?

This introduction offers a commentary on selected aspects of the contributors' papers to highlight recurrent themes, issues and policy proposals, and to guide the reader in assessing emerging patterns of Urban Innovation.

CITY STUDIES

In Kingston, capital of Jamaica, planned management of urban growth is considered an essential element of national and metropolitan policies to counter the adverse effects of rapid urbanisation. Current strategies, described by Gloria Knight, an urban administrator, seek to reduce rural to urban migration, contain city growth, improve living and working environments, restructure population densities, and create new centres of economic growth and employment supportive of national development requirements.

It is increasingly apparent, however, that provision of shelter and services for the large mass of Kingston's urban dwellers living in sub-standard housing areas and squatters settlements is a key issue for immediate direct action. Consideration should be given says Knight, to strategies for housing the poor providing access to a wider variety of shelter options within a planned programme, at standards which are affordable and safe, and assisted by innovative cost-reducing building techniques and financing schemes. Strategies for improving the delivery of public services, presently under study, include a range of new approaches:

- Government provision of land for sale as serviced plots to encourage self-help building;
- Granting security of tenure to tenants and squatters to stimulate their improvement efforts;
- Encouraging trading commercial and industrial development in designated residential areas to broaden the local tax, employment and resource-generating base;
- Introducing a "betterment" taxation system so that Government can recapture costs of land use development redistribution to poorer areas;
- Rationalising public service networks and provision of utilities in areas of greatest social need.

Kingston's experience portrays a richness, intensity and variety of planning strategies, but limited implementation possibilities, at least in the short-term. There is an urgent need to strengthen the Kingston local authority's fiscal powers and its ability to generate resources and direct their allocation to projects benefiting low-income communities and the unemployed. The authority must also be enabled to play a more strategic role in urban and national development, guiding the growth of urban investment pro-

ductivity and incomes, coordination of the overlapping and
often conflicting activities of public service agencies, and
education and training of qualified personnel in urban management, development operations and policy implementation.

A major task ahead, it would appear, is to create a
centralised development agency within local government which
is action-oriented, flexible in outlook, sensitive to human
and material resource issues, and based on realistic assess-
ments of achievable objectives. Its institutional management
style and activities would be enhanced by a commitment to
integrated planning and implementation in the crucial fields
of housing and services, employment, the informal sector and
public participation. To be effective it would require a
chief executive with demonstrable diplomatic skills; a management organisation with prestige, links with major sectoral
public agencies and private enterprises, and ready access to
decision-makers; trained staff of multi-professional backgrounds working together toward common solutions; and the
involvement of client communities as an essential component
of all urban projects. In this regard, lessons can be learned
from the success of the Urban Development Corporation, a
special-purpose agency initiated by the Jamaican government,
to act "as a developer in the public interest and to make
development happen in designated areas."

A broad set of unresolved issues impede the progress of
metropolitan planning and management in Delhi, the first
Indian city to have a plan guiding its growth. According to
recent investigations by Professor Abhijit Datta and his
associate at the Indian Institute of Public Administration
these issues have to do with defining the nature, focus and
role of planning, governance and institution-building.

While noting some achievements in architecture, landscape design and environmental improvement during the first
plan decade, the authors carefully document the failure of
municipal administration and the metropolitan Delhi Development Authority (DDA) to respond adequately to the city's
explosive population growth, urban sprawl, slums and squatters settlements and resulting pressures on housing and
public services.

It is imperative therefore that in the preparation of
the second plan solutions to shelter and urban poverty should
be a central focus of interest. The emphasis should be

shifted away from insensitive physical master plans and costly urban design schemes to practical projects providing employment, shelter and services for the poor. This would require, as well, strengthening the urban economy, including the informal sector catering to low-income communities, and relating it to national development efforts.

Creating appropriate and innovative plan-making and plan implementation agencies remains a critical task, and the authors highlight the inadequacies of the new metro-authorities created by central government. In Delhi, the DDA is divorced from the populace and municipal and private economic interests in terms of governance and resource-raising capability. It has no effective command over the urban development process and the multiplicity of agencies providing public services, or the resolution of conflicts between states, jurisdictions and governmental agencies. Under these conditions the needs of the urban poor will continue to be unmet and the achievement of overall urban improvement and development will be further retarded.

New policy perspectives and planning actions are required which:

- Accept the need for trans-sectoral integration and coordination of the social aspects of settlement planning with the spatial structure of the economy;
- Seek to optimise public and private initiatives and intergovernmental arrangements to finance and manage plan implementation;
- Relate the formulation and implementation of public programmes to the needs and involvement of the poorest communities;
- Undertake the reorganisation and reorientation of public institutions, planners and administrators to carry out these unfamiliar tasks.

In many Third World cities dramatic changes in direction and emphasis have taken place in official policies for planning and managing the improvement of housing and socio-economic conditions of low-income communities. Nairobi City Council and its policies, described by Gilbert Njau, a housing development director, is one significant example.

Njau outlines the difficulties faced by a post-independence city administration aspiring to provide new housing at conventional "modern" standards for the majority of African urban inhabitants. Housing provision lagged far behind need due to massive rural to urban migration, the growth of slums and unauthorised squatters settlements, increased costs of building construction, and the inadequacy of the Council's policies in regard to low-income communities.

In the worsening economic climate of the mid-1970s a new sense of resource-realism prevailed. There was a greater readiness to accept "non-conventional" strategies involving popular participation in housing construction through site and service schemes as a means of reducing costs, increasing employment, and ensuring that the facilities provided were affordable by the urban poor.

Njau highlights the successes and failures of the Dandora Site and Service Project, co-funded by the World Bank and the Kenya Government, which marked a turning point in the evolution of Council policies. The Project components included self-help housing building with Council support; market sale of plots to generate new sources of revenues; and the formation of a special department for project implementation and management. Furthermore, the Council was encouraged to review and improve its administrative, fiscal and management structure for the coordinated implementation of policies.

Dandora's self-help building groups are, in Njau's view a commendable example of cooperation between the Council and plot-holders, and a measure of the untapped reservoir of mutuality that exists in slum and squatter areas. In contrast to the typical urban voluntary associations formed by low income groups to assist their survival, which are generally founded on common bonds of ethnicity, religion or place of birth, the housing groups in Dandora were consolidated at supervised orientation meetings and based on a common desire to collectively build new homes in a new environment. The groups, many of them including women plot-holders, have varied in their performance but it is hoped that more guidance and assistance from the project unit will increase their changes of success. In Njau's opinion, collective self-help organisations can make a major contribution to resolving Nairobi's housing problems and should be accorded a prominent role in official policies.

Dandora's successes have been translated into Kenya's Second Urban Project, and the project department is now a

fully fledged Housing Development Department within the
Council's structure. Njau notes however that strengthening
the capability of the Council to plan and implement settlement improvement is a key issue. He calls for a central
planning and coordinating unit within the local authority to
ensure that planning is carried out on a comprehensive and
continuous basis and that resources are allocated in a
rational manner. Consideration should be given to formulating practical proposals for project implementation: devising techniques for allocating plots, and identifying and
selecting beneficiaries; providing employment facilities in
or near project areas; and creating strategies for reducing
conflicts between the Council, its technical experts and the
community. On a broader level, policies are required to
decentralise urbanisation and employment opportunities to
stimulate national regional development and reduce migration
to the capital city.

Management is one neglected factor in the achievement of
improved housing and service provision in rapidly growing
cities in development countries; institution-building is
another, and David Pasteur examines both these factors in his
paper evaluating the implementation of the Lusaka squatter
upgrading and site and services prcject.

At the outset Pasteur establishes the dual and complementary role of management: to implement projects and
programmes, and to improve and adapt institutional structures
for the ongoing tasks of settlement development. He then
describes the Lusaka Project, one of the first generation of
recent World Bank-sponsored and co-financed approaches to
urban low-income housing in developing countries. Its distinctive characteristics include: a major public sector
involvement in a large-scale attempt to meet shelter needs;
the important role accorded to the local political party
leadership in the organisation of community efforts; and the
formation of a special Housing Project Unit (HPU) which
assumed the leading role within the City Council, integrating
all the components and functions in the upgrading project in
a single agency.

In evaluating the Lusaka Project it can be claimed, as
Pasteur points out, that the squatter upgrading process calls
for structures, procedures, and styles of management which
are different from conventional forms of municipal project
management. Therefore the creation of a special project

organisation, like that of HPU, is a justifiable and adequate approach to project implementation.

However, as Pasteur rightly suggests, there are important points that should be raised before concluding that a special project organisation is the best solution for achieving both rapid housing provision and long-term institution-building. The HPU did achieve large-scale housing development in a fairly short time-scale. This advantage was attained however at the expense of the long-term requirements of institution-building as it was not firmly based within the overall existing administrative machinery of the relevant local and central government plan-making and plan implementation authorities. On the other hand, it is also quite clear that had an alternative "matrix" approach been used, one which enabled the HPU to gradually create formal linking arrangements within established government structures, the results may have strengthened the institutional capacity and capability for project implementation but proved less innovative, slower in achieving results and perhaps less sensitive to grassroots needs. This dilemma of choice of organisation and management for the implementation of squatter upgrading in the short and long-term, and Pasteur's implicit hypothesis that rapid housing development matching the growth of problem cities is inconsistent with institution-building, obviously requires much further study and research.

New methods of organising and managing the improvement of low-income urban communities call for new skills and learning experiences. Elpidius Mpolokoso, a housing administrator and educator, explores this issue and proposes an innovative means of responding to the education and training needs of policymakers, professionals and communities involved in the settlement development process in Zambia.

Mpolokoso briefly surveys the unprecedented rapid movement of population from rural to urban areas, and notes the importance of an additional dimension of migratory behaviour, the "right to move freely," which is an aspiration deeply-held by many ex-colonial peoples and enshrined in the Zambian constitution. He examines the scale of growth of urban squatter areas and the new self-help and upgrading policies introduced to cope with the demand for housing and basic services.

To implement these policies, says Mpolokoso, the nation must create the requisite manpower, at all levels, to integrate the social, economic and physical aspects of settlement improvement and development. Three main target groups are identified – policymakers, professionals, and implementors at the community level – and he outlines the specific types and methods of training required, for example, sensitising experiences, process learning, skill development and self-help learning. Multi-disciplinary, trans-sectoral patterns of thinking and acting should be encouraged so that participants can relate specific project requirements to the broader process of urban development. Existing courses in the national educational system cannot be expected in the short term to meet these objectives, they are too ivory-towered and sectoral in the inherited western tradition, hence different ways of providing appropriate education and training for action now must be found.

In Zambia the National Housing Authority (NHA) has the statutory obligation to enhance the capability of persons and organisations involved in housing provision and construction, and to assist them in obtaining facilities for training, education and research. Mpolokoso proposes that the NHA become the leading agency for the promotion of integrated human settlements planning education and help local authorities, teaching institutions and the building industry in mounting required courses, especially at mid-career levels. The NHA itself should establish a human resources centre related to low-income settlement development, which he feels would gain the support of international funding agencies.

In Bangladesh, a poor nation of 71 million people, where six million live in urban areas and are expected to increase ten-fold by the the year 2000, urban planning is of recent origin and there are only a few dozen planners in the whole country. Nevertheless work has begun on a National Physical Plan outlining a spatial urban system and a Regional Plan for Dacca Metropolitan Area. Both planning exercises highlight critical institutional and financial problems and policy challenges, according to a recent evaluation research study by Charles Choguill.

Acknowledging a substantial contribution from administrators and professionals actually involved in day to day planning activities, Choguill offers an extensive coverage of major problems and challenges. Chief among these are:

-   Reducing population concentration in ill-sited unauthorised slums and squatters settlements; provision of land

and services in flood-free locations; improvement of public transit efficiency and reducing the long travel distances to workplaces; and constructing low-cost housing units that are more than temporary migrant camps;

- Coordinating the delivery of public services - a problem dramatically illustrated by the volume of payments to the Dacca Municipal Corporation by water, sewerage, telephone and electric power agencies for damage caused by cutting through existing roads;

- Deciding what type of Regional Plan would be most compatible with the National Physical Plan, as well as of greatest benefit to the future of Dacca;

- Incorporating spatial and human settlement strategies into national economic development plans;

- Balancing industrial development and high-priority housing and service needs in the allocation of land, but also conserving scarce land resources and preventing encroachment on good agricultural land;

- Training qualified staff to plan and implement the Dacca Plan (tasks presently performed by expatriate consultants) and involving relevant government departments, local authorities and the Dacca public in the planning process.

Choguill draws attention to the need for a central agency combining widespread popular support, planning expertise and operational capability. Why, not, he speculates, create an integrated Development Planning Organisation for Dacca Metropolitan Area to cover the entire development and planning process with powers of implementation in reference to local, regional and national planning needs. Above all, he concludes, good plans are not enough. Plan implementation requires appropriate legal, fiscal and participatory structures and a greater degree of political commitment to institutional change by decisionmakers at the highest levels of government.

Planned urban development in new oil-rich Third World countries has not been an easy process, contrary to earlier predictions. Progress has been limited by domestic institutional and political factors and further frustrated by international economic forces and the unexpected decline in foreign earnings from oil. When countries like Nigeria and

Mexico struck oil popular expectations rose, governments
embarked on ambitious and expensive projects and increased
their borrowing abroad to pay for imported goods and equipment. However, the onset of the world economic recession and
the oil-glut sent prices tumbling and national dreams of
rapid urban-industrial development became a nightmare of
indebtedness. Inevitably, cuts in government spending and the
wholesale abandonment of scheduled urban projects followed.
In retrospect, according to recent reports, during the good
times too little attention was paid to creating national
urban-industrial policies and organisations supportive of the
integrated implementation of affordable programmes and projects; and during the subsequent recession meeting the needs
of cities and their populations was curtailed by belt-tight-
ening fiscal measures.

Nigeria is a case in point. In the past, Lagos, the
nation's bustling migrant-attracting, sprawling capital,
received the lion's share of planning interest - with little
observable success. Subsequent military and civilian governments endorsed the benign neglect of problem-ridden Lagos and
the spread of urbanisation across the country. But what are
the pitfalls of this strategy; and is Nigeria, Africa's most
populous nation, well-prepared for implementation of planned
urban growth? In his contribution, Ukwa Ejionye, a university
sociologist, focuses attention on Nigeria's new system of
government and the urban and national planning policies which
will have immense and untold effects beyond Lagos. The
designation of a new Federal capital and 19 state capitals
and scores of local government headquarters, new towns and
industrial centres will generate a phenomenal growth of urban
areas. He notes a disturbing emphasis on economic planning,
and an assumed unlimited economic growth rate and supply of
fiscal resources, to the neglect of social, physical and
environment planning. This is an oversight which even in the
best of times would place heavy pressure on both existing and
future urban settlements and strain the national capability
for planning and implementation.

Specific attention is given to policies creating the new
federal capital at Abuja, the Federal Housing Programme, and
the World Bank-assisted Nigerian States Urban Development
Programme. He finds an uneasy combination of conflicting
interests: national and state governments, local authorities, external aid agencies and the private sector, and a
lack of definition, clarity and harmonisation of their roles.

Major constraints identified include the lack of: and appropriate institutional framework and coordination of urban
policies and programmes that can be adopted simultaneously by
the Federal, State and Local governments; mandatory legal
controls and regulation of public and private urban development agencies; education and training of specially-qualified
personnel and effective manpower utilisation and inter-professional cooperation.

Ejionye's recommendations, which merit serious study in
governmental circles, include:

- Creation of a new authority to coordinate all settlement
  planning and development efforts, and determine the
  appropriate institutional and legal structures for
  integration and implementation of policies;

- Basic research studies of national housing, industrial
  location, and urban development policies and programmes;

- Broad surveys of education and training facilities, and
  formulation of guidelines for training the required
  settlement planners, urban managers and allied personnel.

These corrective proposals may themselves prove too
expensive in a climate of economic recession, but they are
certainly points for consideration and analysis. The goal
is, according to Ejionye, to set the stage for future development by strengthening institutional capacity in urban
settlement planning and implementation.

Mexico's contribution to world awareness of settlement
problems is by now quite well-known. Its government played a
key role in the United Nations Habitat Conference at
Vancouver 1976 and established one of the first national
agencies for human settlements. Yet finding solutions to the
intractable difficulties of Mexico City, the nation's capital
and economic giant, has continued to elude policy makers and
planners despite the advent of oil.

Mexico City is now the third largest city in the world,
after New York and Tokyo, and may become the most populous
metropolitan area by the year 2000, containing 25 to 30
million people. Its problems read like a litany of despair:
rapid annual population growth (3.5 per cent) at a faster
rate than the country as a whole (2.5 per cent); lack of
dwelling units and land to house the massive increase in slum

and squatter populations; high levels of pollution and
serious traffic congestion; high costs of supplying water,
sewerage, and electric power; serious problems of urban
governance and lack of public financial resources; and the
city has been sinking at a rate of 35 feet over the past 70
years.

Recent observations by senior administrators, DeCarmona
and Renfrew, trace the city's evolution from pre-colonial to
modern times and analyse the ecological aspects of managing
urban growth. The authors provide some valid insights into
specific problems, and the difficulties of the organisational
structures and policies introduced to deal with them.

The new Secretariat for Human Settlements and Public
Works initiated a self-help building programme to tackle the
housing deficit in Mexico City, but it lacks the financial
resources to make a definite impact. Urban decongestion, a
major goal of the National Urban Development Plan, has not
been attained, thereby worsening the pressures on housing and
public services.

Modest success in the long struggle against flooding has
been accomplished by construction of a deep-drainage system.
New hydraulic projects have been introduced to provide more
drinking water. However, sectoral environmental initiatives
have achieved little improvement in the quality of life.
There is as yet no comprehensive view of the ecological
problems of the city and its region, and proposals for an
Urban Ecology Plan for the Federal District have been shelved
for lack of money. Anti-pollution measures have not been as
successful as expected, mainly because of inadequate control
mechanisms and the lack of the economic and technical capabilities to treat water. The Metro Master Plan and schemes
to promote use of public mass transport have made little
impact on the city's daily commuting problems and traffic
congestion caused by widespread ownership and use of private
cars.

Mexico City, like many other large Third World cities,
has experimented with slum and squatter upgrading and site
and services projects. Perhaps the most interesting innovation, with effects at the city and local level, is the
legalisation of landowning rights and tenure for squatters
which, it is said has led to greater civic identity and pride
in building and homemaking. This has not gone unchallenged
however. Legalisation of the illegal occupation of land by

giving the squatters security of tenure may work against the
interests of the families concerned. Legalisation will bring
the properties into the commercial urban land market and
hence ownership is likely to pass into the hands of specu-
lators and the more wealthy and powerful middle class.

Alternatively, however, the Mexican authorities might
well argue that though this market "transference" takes place
in some cases, it should not be used as a reason for depriving squatters of the right to security of tenure. Abuses
could be prevented by a strict system of registration and
control over land transaction, though it is acknowledged that
this would be expensive and difficult to administer. Better
ways to overcome speculation should be explored, among these,
the granting of tenure on a collective basis (to an association of residents, for example) rather than on a individual
family basis, and introduction of a tax to recapture unearned
increments in land value.

The authors observe that every improvement of public
services attracts more people to the city, and further ex-
acerbates an already difficult situation. Much work remains
to be done in terms of policy formulation and identification
of key issues of future urban development. Yet to be worked
out are the frameworks for appropriate environmental management, planning and implementation, the procedures for project
financing and cost recovery, public education and participation programmes and support services, and incentives to
facilitate project success.

Mexico City is an illustrative case of too many people
and too many activities competing for scarce resources in the
wrong place. Its primacy in the national economy inhibits
development elsewhere and thereby constrains overall national
development. Hence consideration has been given to formulating alternative strategies for urban and regional development. For example, Deconcentration Strategies to divert
investment, jobs and people to the surrounding metropolitan
region and to assist the development of peripheral zones up
to 100 kilometres from Mexico City. Consideration should
also be given to Decentralisation Strategies which identify
potential growth centres with good prospects for sustained
and rapid growth in Mexico's less-developed regions. These
would be complementary ways of meeting in the long-term, some
of the problems of Mexico City as well as assisting national
economic development. Whether these strategies are affordable
in the present economic climate is in question, but that they
are unavoidable in the long-term cannot be in doubt.

CONTRASTING EXPERIENCES IN URBANISATION AND MANAGEMENT

The widespread exchange of urban information taking place within and between world regions today has highlighted a range of contrasting views and experiences in urbanisation management and planning. In Africa, for example, concern is with not only the practical problems of managing rapid and massive urbanisation but also with redefining the inappropriate functions of cities inherited from the colonial era. The Dual City remains - one modern, the other deprived - and there are major policy and planning issues stemming from maldistribution of economic opportunities, cultural deracination and the poverty of underdevelopment and continental exploitation. These points are discussed in a contribution by T.L. Blair.

In China, and increasingly between China and America, there is a growing interest in understanding and modifying the social, political and economic constraints on urban planning administration, implementation and management. New insights into these matters have emerged from a recent visit and report of a delegation of American planners. The US delegation noted the major concern of Chinese government and planning officials with controlling the urbanisation process, especially in the crowded eastern cities where more than two-thirds of the nation's urban population live. Current policies include setting city population and economic growth limits, discouraging in-migration and industrial expansion in central areas, and diverting growth in economic activity and employment to surrounding areas and satellite new towns. City planning is considered an essential element of urban development, with an emphasis on efficient management and economy of construction, environmental improvement, enhanced civil defence, and large-scale public participation through neighbourhood committees.

In all these activities fundamental questions arise. How to adhere to national planning policies and standards and allow for individual city needs and differences? How to programme new building construction and conserve the environment and existing usable housing stock? What are the requirements for strengthening the legal, organisational and leadership base for the planning process? What should be the role of new towns? What types of planners and planning education are required for plan implementation and management? And, there is the over-arching question: How to enable the universal provision of basic settlement facilities, even in limited amounts?

The visit also unearthed information, previously unavailable to western planners, on the most recent reorganisation of national and municipal agencies within which urban policy is formulated and implementation decisions taken. Sectoral national commissions for planning, economics, and construction each have their counterparts at municipal level where disagreements are adjudicated by city government. A special Beijing Urban Planning and Administrative Bureau derives its planning powers from its responsibility for selecting sites and designing all approved construction projects.

Of more than passing interest was the widespread devolution of autonomy and responsibility to the neighbourhood level, the basic social unit and lowest level of official government in Chinese cities, and the way in which this makes the delivery of local public services more personal, direct, unbureaucratic and cheap than in the majority of western countries. In addition insights were gained about the sociology of slums. Why, for example, is there less socio-pathic behaviour and social disorganisation in deprived urban communities in China than would be predicted from western experience with slums and the "culture of poverty?" Is the explanation for urban cohesion and social control to be found in the pattern of familial relations, civic pride, the all-pervasive influence of the disciplined Communist party, or aspects of the historic centuries-old cultural organisation of Chinese cities?

At first contact it is apparent that contemporary China is a centralised socialist state committed to "modernisation within marxism". Hence, it must come as a shock to most visiting western planners that broadly the urban system works. There is no "free economy," real estate developers and land market; few shopping centres, private cars or private toilets; but many bicycles, public meetings and highly organised forms of public participation. What one tends to forget however are the underlying historical imperatives for understanding urban China. China, with 5,000 years of continuity, has the oldest and most extensive system of cities of any society in the world. The Chinese people have built more big cities and managed them longer than possibly any other peoples in the world. The result is a broad and diverse

experience with urban management, administration and social
organisation, and regional and town and country planning and
development from which much can be learned.

Nevertheless, as China faces the future, it seeks to
find ways to raise the standard of living of urban, as well
as rural, peoples and meet the national goals of modernisation, self-sufficiency and increased economic productivity. Hence the key areas identified for further joint
exchanges and cooperation include:

- Evaluation of master planning, urban and housing design,
  and the limits to city growth and new towns approach as
  decision making tools;
- Techniques of capital improvement programmes, systems
  planning, construction, transportation planning, environmental conservation and preservation, neighbourhood
  renewal and self-help housing;
- Education and training in all areas associated with
  planning, design, plan implementation and management.

Sharing information and experiences about urban management and plan implementation also takes place within Europe,
and involves local authorities and governments of less-developed, but rapidly urbanising countries, and those of highly-
industrialised countries further along the path of urbanisation. In his paper David Rushforth discusses the ways in
which the "joint activities" of the Organisation for Economic
Cooperation and Development (OECD) assist information exchange to meet the changing needs and special problems of
urban managers.

Rushforth identifies a broad set of ideas derived from
an OECD study group. Urban management encompasses the organisation and carrying out of essential tasks of city government, administration, planning and governance. It involves
participation of political decision-makers, professional
advisors and citizens, and requires an awareness of, and
relationship to, national policies and local needs. In
meeting the pressures of urbanisation its emphasis is less on
physical planning per se, and more on shaping the whole
pattern and complexity of urban change and improving the
capability and adaptability of institutions responsible for
urban affairs.

It should be noted that an important stage in the evolution of these ideas took place at a seminar on "Aspects of

Urban Management" convened in Izmir, Turkey 1972 at the behest of the governments of Greece, Portugal, Spain, Turkey and Yugoslavia. The serious administrative difficulties and ineffectiveness of local government caused by rapid urbanisation over the past quarter of a century were discussed. Background papers described how the social, economic and physical changes taking place were creating imbalances between existing structures of city government and the needs of society. In the search for solutions, it was widely recognised however that policies and solutions evolved in highly urbanised and industrialised nations may not be appropriate without careful thought and modification, to countries at different stages of development. For southern Europe therefore, interest focused on the need for greater international cooperation to share knowledge and experiences about innovative practices, and the transfer of proven methods to new areas. Hard-pressed urban managers would then be able to discover and evaluate the organisational frameworks, information networks, and training systems for urban management and implementation which could help them overcome existing institutional constraints.

Further elaboration of these ideas occurred at the 1977 Athens symposium which focused on problems of plan implementation, and the 1979 Milton Keynes symposium which concentrated on an assessment of policy making experiences and the role of research. Rushforth's paper gives details about these meetings and notes the lack of plan implementation theory, good case studies and documented examples which embrace an awareness of the whole policy execution and decision implementation process. He highlights the commonality of many problems such as land use control and land ownership, rising costs and their implications for standards and procedures, and the increasing demand for public participation and decentralisation of decision-making.

He calls attention to the frustrations felt by many persons about the intrinsic irrationality of a planning process which isolates plan-making from plan-implementation, and proposes the development of a checklist of procedures by which inter-relationships can be identified and the robustness of plans improved. Finally, he underlines the importance which should be given to the human aspects of urban management, namely the motivations, skills and attitudes of individuals at all levels of responsibility, which help determine successful implementation.

NEW TOWNS - PRINCIPLES IN PRACTICE

The significance of new towns became internationally recognised in the 1960's and 1970's, and the new towns experience in developing countries, largely imported from Britain and Europe, now constitutes an important chapter in post-colonial history. Government policies stress the role of new towns in the transformation of less-developed regions and peoples. They advocate new capitals in more central locations, new satellite towns around congested older cities, new towns for housing workers near large industrial and port development, and new urban growth centres in virgin lands. Today, new town building extends to every continent and is a major component of a fast-growing urban development industry highly prized by national governments, international banks, aid and lending agencies and planning consortia.

Adapted to differing purposes and fast-changing conditions, new towns in developing countries are a fertile laboratory of ideas about future urbanisation policies, development strategies and settlement planning. Selected examples from contrasting world situations, Nigeria, Tanzania, Malaysia and Britain, provide a useful reference point for discussions about the relevance and validity of new town principles in practice in developing countries. Broadly, answers are sought to such questions as: What are the opinions, record and potential of new towns as a solution to urbanisation and modernisation in developing countries? What can be learned from a comparative and retrospective view of the recent British experience and the export of new town planning abroad?

Specific aspects of new town planning and development are highlighted: national goals and strategies; legislative and financial instruments; administrative and management organisation; development corporations and authorities; master plans; the politics of planned migration and resource exploitation; land acquisition and land use; industrial promotion; large-scale programming and planning; social, economic, physical, environmental and cultural components; low-income housing and community development; design costs, and standards of infrastructure; and plan implementation.

Abuja is the largest newly-planned city in the world, and as Nigeria's new Federal Capital it will be a monumental emblem of the largest black nation and leading political

force in independent Africa. But, why Abuja - carved at
great expense from the vast virgin territory of Niger,
Plateau and Kwara states in Nigeria's heartland? Government's political and administrative reasons are three-fold:
a desire to escape the explosive and chaotic growth of Lagos,
to assist regional and national development, and to relocate
the capital in a central and ethnically-neutral area where no
Nigerian will be regarded as a "Native Foreigner." Abuja is
planned as a government administrative centre with minimum
industry. Relocation of government offices, now underway, is
to be completed by 1986/87 when the projected population will
be 250,000. Thereafter the city is expected to grow to 1.6
million by the year 2000, later reaching an optimum population of 3 million.

Stephen Lockwood served as resident general manager for
the Master Plan of the new Federal Capital City and Capital
Territory, and writes authoritatively about the policy issues
and problems of creating a new city appropriate to a developing country. The goal was to design an "affordable city,"
namely a city development process, urban forms and system
technologies which would husband scarce resources of the
public sector and households in terms of money, materials,
time, management and energy. Two major elements make up the
city: the Central Area of Government, national institutions,
business and commerce extending in two directions, and the
Development Corridors of residences and employment-service
sub-centres built in linear fashion to allow staged growth
along the major infrastructure system.

Estimating growth and variation in future population and
economic activities were major sources of uncertainty in the
planning exercise. Hence, the consultants sought to avoid
extremes of rigidity or vagueness which are all too characteristic of capital city and new town master planning.
Lockwood outlines the sequence of planning decisions,
options, choices and methods chosen to reduce the degree of
programmatic, technical and resource uncertainty. At the
residential community level, however, they chose a "loose-
fit" approach encouraging maximum flexibility in design
because "experience has shown that attempts to impose a high
degree of design control in a fast growth context may limit
legal development, but not population growth, resulting in
over-crowding, peripheral squatter development, and other
unintentional effects."

Lockwood's contribution has the additional merit of highlighting key urban policy and implementation issues facing Nigeria and developing countries. He sees the Abuja planning exercise as an opportunity to search for solutions that can be generally applied as part of a national response to urbanisation. A choice exists, for example, between second-best strategies for problems-in-cities to be attacked through project by project additions, upgradings and retro-fits, and strategies dealing with problems-of-cities which seek to "harness the unique potentials of cities to provide the most cost-effective context for alleviating the problems of the poor through capitalising on the economies of scale and agglomeration of firms, public services, and households alike." There is a need, he says, for a broader frame of reference for urban Nigeria – encompassing a portfolio of national policies and actions ranging from urban renewal, to urban extensions, satellite growth centres and new towns. In this context, he would argue, Abuja is less a unique symbol and more a potentially useful urban prototype.

The planning and future of Abuja will of course engender continuing discussion and debate within and external to Nigeria. Further consideration should, in my view, be given to such questions as:

Management. What are the realistic manpower limitations in Nigerian administrative capacity for urban development management?

New Towns Experience. To what extent has the planning of Abuja benefited from, and avoided the pitfalls of, the international and Third World new towns experience?

Peoples Livelihood. How are ordinary citizens of Abuja to gain their livelihood without a greater emphasis on indus-trial, commercial and informal sector economic activities?

Squatters. What are the short- and long-term estimates for the growth of low-income communities and squatters set-tlements in or near Abuja, and how will they be dealt with?

Relocation. What plans are there for the relocation of displaced villages, estimated at 50,000 people residing in the rural areas of the Federal Capital Territory? What will be the resource flows and reciprocal relations between Abuja and its rural hinter-land?

African City.   Recognising that Nigeria has a renowned
heritage of urban cultures and a strong architectural and
planning tradition at collegiate and professional levels,
what are the proposals for the involvement of Nigerian professionals and institutions in the planning, design, building
and management of Abuja?

Resource Realism.   In the post-oil boom era a new attitude of resource realism will be recognised as an important
constraint on building Abuja.   Already according to government sources 722.5 million <u>naira</u> has been spent (guesstimates
rise to several billion) and, if current trends prevail,
these expenditure/costs will escalate rapidly due to inflation, higher costs of materials and transport, and wage
increases.   Therefore, it may prove prudent to build Abuja on
a less grand scale and at a pace consistent with reduced
national resources, with an alternative emphasis on providing
modest and decent human settlement provision in older cities
and designated state capitals on the verge of a crisis of
urbanisation.

In Tanzania, government policies support the revival and
preservation of indigenous arts and crafts within the
national goal of self-reliant socialism.   Richard May, an
urban planner, looks at how these cultural policies and
political idealologies relate to the planned location of the
new national capital at Dodoma.

Dodoma was designated in 1973 and strategically placed
in one of the least advantaged regions in the centre of the
country intersected by major rail and road routes.   Its
development is the responsibility of the Capital Development
Authority guided by the Master Plan for Dodoma and the Urban
Design for the National Capital Centre prepared by foreign
consultants.   The new town will include the National Capital
Centre as the seat of government, linked by a modern commercial centre to existing Old Dodoma, and have an urban
infrastructure capable of serving the city and surrounding
region.   The expected residential population of 350,000
people, rising eventually to 800,000, will live in small
communities connected to the central area by transit loops
and arterial roads.   Moving the national capital to Dodoma
from Dar-es-Salaam on the coast is intended as a means of
modernising Tanzanian society. That is, improving its pivotal
position in governing and directing national and regional
development from a predominantly rural to an urbanising/

industrialising society with greater social and economic
opportunities.

Dodoma must also exhibit within the plan framework
settlement patterns expressing the nation's traditional
cultures and goal of socialism and self-reliance. This
requirement has far-reaching implications in economy and
design terms. In the formal areas, for example, Dodoma must
achieve a certain urban monumentality associated with centres
of government, but be sensitive to varied landscapes and
cultures, and built at minimum capital and maintenance costs.
In the residential areas, it must give full opportunity for
people to participate in the cost-saving construction of
their homes and enable them to augment their food supplies
and incomes with produce from their shambas and trading
activities. As President Julius Nyerere says in the Plan
foreword, "While the Master Plan incorporates positive features and values of other cities in the world, it should
result in the growth of a Tanzanian and African city which
will allow the future generations to develop in the spirit of
the contemporary Tanzanian nation".

Richard May acknowledges the consultants' attempts to
embody the overall planning concepts. For example, they
reflected the varied landscape features and designed low-
density human scale communities. Ample open spaces are
provided as stages for national symbols, and the low-rise
building forms are in keeping with the topography and limited
national budget. Nevertheless, other than general references
to galleries, museums and the like, there is little mention
in the Master Plan or the National Capital Centre plan report
on the role of Tanzania's African culture in Dodoma's development.

In his view, provision for the continuity of indigenous
cultural patterns - arts, crafts, dance, ritual - should be
considered an essential aspect of urban planning in developing countries. They help ease the transition to urban life
for new migrants and can, through the use of local skills and
materials, make a contribution to building a new and satisfying environment and broadening income-earning opportunities.
May recognises that indigenous culture is not easily adapted
to the western design forms and institutions inherent in new
town plans. However, achieving maximum success in the integration of indigenous culture calls for more detail than is
found in most plans and requires supportive governmental and

social organisations and resources, based on widespread popular participation.

Some practical steps that can be taken in Dodoma include:

- organising the local manufacture of requisite building materials, and aiding and training people in self-help construction on sites with services provided by the development authority;

- promoting local community development efforts with the cooperation of the national political party and relevant government agencies responsible for social welfare and foreign assistance in this field;

- identifying community leadership to help transfer the responsibility for carrying out and managing programmes to the new citizens themselves;

- preserving traditional cultures in new town development by planning the national cultural facilities to be built in the capital, providing training in arts and crafts, especially those related to building and decoration, and establishing the pattern of national pageants, theatrical and musical presentations.

The Dodoma project provides some interesting questions for study and debate at the interface of planning, culture and politics. New Modern/Self-Reliant/African City? What are the inherent contradictions when government chooses planning consultants (in this case neither nationals nor socialists) with the conscious intent of building a modern world capital emulating non-African urban forms, but stresses the need to accommodate the basic values of traditional society and support the national cultural and political ideology? How can urban designers transcend goal conflicts and achieve a balance between indigenous culture and imported borrowings within the built environment? What is transferable, compatible and appropriate, and what is not? And, more importantly, how to create and integrate the required national manpower and counterpart staff, institutional forms, management structures and popular participation to implement the cultural, economic, political and design aspects of settlement plans?

Rapid urban growth in Malaysia exposed widespread imbalances in social, economic and physical development and heightened tensions between competing races and social classes in a pluralist society. In the 1970s the government proposed a New Economic Policy to rectify these imbalances and give disadvantaged groups a greater share in national development. Planned urbanisation and the building of new towns or growth centres formed part of this strategy. The contribution by Haji Abdul Rahman, general manager of Johore Bahru, provides some insights into the issue of redistributive urban and regional development planning and the problems and achievements of new towns in Malaysia.

At the outset Rahman outlines the historical factors placing Malays, the bulk of the rural poor and deprived city slum dwellers, at a disadvantage by comparison with the urban Chinese, Indians, Europeans and Malay elites who derived major benefits from postwar development. He notes the concern of government to resolve the race/class/regional conflicts which often erupted in violent confrontation.

In response government adopted strategies to decelerate rural exodus to congested cities and direct urban growth and industry to less-developed rural regions. Of central importance was the planned migration of Malays to agro-industrial new towns as a significant step in bringing them into a modernising society. Adaptation to urban-type living and working environments would give them the "know-how" to compete successfully with other ethnic/economic groups. Implementation of these strategies would demonstrate the government's commitment to the New Economic Policy and achieve national unity through the eradication of poverty and the identification of race with economic function and geographical location.

Rahman describes and discusses the pattern of social, economic and physical planning at regional, town and neighbourhood levels. Reference is made to British new town concepts which served as a model for Malaysia, and consideration is given to the limitations and inappropriateness of this model as applied in developing countries with different conditions and problems. He notes that new town goals of self-containment, self-sufficiency and social balance were not achieved in the case of Petaling Jaya near Kuala Lumpur; that new town development was not undertaken by separate, quasi-autonomous development corporations but by technocratic government departments; and that coordinated planning and administrative control, and public participation, remains to be achieved.

Cultural factors require special attention in planning new towns for Malaysia, he says, especially the potential contribution of traditional self-help organisation (<u>gotong-royong</u>) in aiding adaptation to urban life. Guidelines are necessary however to ensure an appropriate balance between recreating the traditional village environment in the new town and the installation of modern structures, activities and facilities.

New town agro-industrial development in resource-rich virgin territories is now firmly embodied in Malaysian law and guided by regional master plans and development authorities. Whether Maylaysian new town planning can be successful as the primary means of overcoming deep-rooted socio-economic inequities is of course a question for which answers are enthusiastically sought. Nevertheless, much has been learned about the relationship of regional planning to national and urban planning. It is clear however, that success or failure of new town strategies <u>per se</u> does not hinge on proclaimed national goals and physical plans alone. Many countries have sought to establish growth centres in new locations through agro-industry, new towns, population migration and resettlement programmes etc. While these have proved of limited use in some areas, there have been general problems of inconsistency, non-replicability and limited impact. They are too often grand "monuments in the desert" - expensive projects providing too few jobs and surrounded by the poverty they attempt to alleviate. The new towns in Malaysia and elsewhere should make provision not only for large-scale government agro-industrial projects, population migration and resource exploitation (with due consideration of disruptive side-effects), but also meet the basic and emerging needs of pioneering communities. Furthermore, creating the new Urban Man within effective functioning new towns requires skilled and socially-sensitive management teams, coordinated social, as well as physical and economic planning actions, citizen participation, continuous monitoring of achieved results, uninterrupted government and private sector support, and the long-term commitment of populations and policy-makers to societal change.

Creating a framework for the implementation and management of planned urban development in changing societies is not a uniquely Third World problem. Many developed industrial nations and those at intermediate levels of technololgy face serious difficulties as well. Britain and its latest new

town, Milton Keynes, provide a comparative example. In their
contribution Lee Shostak and David Lock delineate and analyse
characteristics of the British approach to new town development which they believe are critical to a successful implementation process, namely the institutional instruments or
framework of legislative, administrative and financial powers
created for the construction of new towns. They stress the
key role of the new town development corporation in securing,
laying out and developing the land. Specifically, they place
great emphasis on the "Milton Keynes factor": the implementability or strategic flexibility of the Plan for Milton
Keynes, and the nature of the development philosophy and
style adopted by the Milton Keynes Development Corporation to
balance political considerations, commercial profitability
and social and environmental concerns.

The authors do not argue that the British new towns
model is in any way appropriate for use in rapidly developing
countries in the Third World. Instead it is suggested that a
review of the strengths and weaknesses of the process used to
develop Milton Keynes aids the identification of criteria
with which other approaches to plan implementation can be
evaluated. Some of the important criteria for evaluation
include:

-   Is a steady flow of capital investment likely to be
    available for infra-structure, housing, industry and
    community facilities?
-   Will the "real" increase in land value resulting from
    the urban development be used to offset the costs of
    basic infrastructure and community facilities?
-   Does a public or private agency exist which is respon-
    sible for guiding rapid urban development and is this
    agency sufficiently powerful to perform this task?
-   Is there a national or regional industrial location
    policy which ensures that new employment generating
    enterprises are encouraged to locate in the new urban
    development?
-   Is the strategic development plan sufficiently flexible
    to allow detailed changes in response to different
    economic, financial, social, or political pressures?

Milton Keynes, located between London and Birmingham, is
one of thirty-two new towns which have been designated since
1946 and nearly a million people have gone to live in them.
Clearly, this is not the occasion to debate the inadequacies

of British new town policies in dealing with the dispersal of industry and population from congested cities to new towns, nor to proclaim the manifest need for an emergent sociology of planned migration.   Ray Thomas, a research director, chooses in his paper to accept that the new towns represent one of the most successful achievements of recent British planning, but speculates on the desirability of uncritically exporting Britain's new town strategies, organisation and experience elsewhere.

His concern is with questions of the transferability of planning knowledge, ideas and action by implementors and managers, at two levels.   One is international, namely the export of new town knowledge from Britain and the industrialised nations to the Third World; and the other is internal within a Third World country and relates to the transference of knowledge of building new towns to the benefit of other forms of urbanisation and planned urban development.   In many cases it is the prestige aspects of new towns which have been exported and seized upon by developing countries - as evidenced in the new towns and capital cities, New Delhi, Brasilia, Chandigarh, Islamabad, Dodoma, and Abuja - at the expense of any serious consideration of new town ideas as a solution to the main urbanisation problems of these countries.

The main issue, says Thomas, is not new towns and their management but how can the new town approach be used in appropriate circumstances as a means of redistributing income and wealth.   He reminds us of the requirement for income redistribution inherent in the original new town social philosophy of Ebenezer Howard, and questions whether the sole test of the management an implementation process should be the use of "unearned income" to write off the costs of providing serviced sites, or in the Howardian sense should it be used to free the new residents, the people from deprived areas, of the economic and social burdens they have suffered for generations.

Ray Thomas is equally critical of the active profitable "new towns industry" exporting new town projects and techniques from western to Third World countries, and the silent educational establishments which reject the new town experience (presumably for its lack of a theoretical base) in their teaching and research programmes.   There is a vast area for discussion between these extremes, and he calls for multi-

lateral exchanges of information about new towns which are
not limited to government, commerce, and trade and aid agreements, nor to restrictive academic planning curricula, but
open to a wider range of opinion including concerned planners
and individuals, non-governmental organisations, and the
developing countries themselves. This broadened exchange,
enriched by research, particularly on the economics and
sociology of new towns, and the monitoring and review of the
implementation process, would help to identify those aspects
of the new town experience which are transferable from one
national context to another, or internally from a new town
situation to other forms of urbanisation.

Issues of international transferability and the validity
of new town principles for the developing countries are
clearly outlined in the concluding paper by Professor Gideon
Golany. They are examined by reference to three clusters of
elements and questions:

i Distinctions between the developed countries where new
towns have been highly advanced, and the developing
countries where the new town movement is beginning. For
example, differences in stages of development, social
and economic values, technology, commuting patterns and
public urban policy.

ii Traditional new town principles, as envisaged by
Ebenezer Howard and later practiced in the United Kingdom. For example, public or unified land ownership,
strong planning control, sound economic base with self-
contained and balanced self-sustained community, proximity of work to place of residence, combined green belt
and town and country atmosphere, and emphasis on implementation, maintenance and management.

iii Major questions of transferability of new town concepts.
For example, are the western new town principles and
policies valid in the developing countries, and to what
degree? What are the prime national and regional problems to be solved? Is there a serious danger of importing the new town concept without proper adjustments to
suit the needs of a developing society and economy. He
then formulates a series of assumptions and recommendations for planning policies and actions in regard to
national settlement and urban growth policies, site
selection, land ownership and land-use control, private
and public enterprise, economic base, urban design,
transportation, open space, community and neighbourhood
units, implementation, maintenance and management.

Professor Golany concludes from his schematic analysis that new town principles have general applicability in developing countries. New towns in urban and rural locations can help improve the conditions of low-income groups, generate employment opportunities, and serve as effective tools for implementation of national urbanisation and economic growth policies. Modifications and adjustments to the demands of unique social, economic and cultural settings are required. For example, the scale and size of projects should reflect prevailing limited resources and management skills. As developing countries begin to seek solutions based on their local roots and increasing self-reliance they may evolve their own unique design and management systems, thereby contributing to an emerging body of knowledge and practice concerning urban development planning.

CONCLUSION

What emerges from the experience described by the contributors is a picture, with varied components, of how the Third World is seeking to shape its own history through distinctive forms of post-colonial responses to urban planning and management, and changing definitions of urban growth, development and social equity. Clearly, meeting the challenge of Problem Cities has given a healthy stimulus to Urban Innovation in developing countries.

Emerging Points of View

Despite the enormous diversity of the cities and nations examined, there are comparable circumstances and areas of concern. The reports help to identify and stimulate debate on key urban and development issues, illustrate the energy and diversity of current approaches, and suggest modes of further study and action. There is a general feeling expressed that urban innovation in developing countries requires a new dedication to the mobilisation of efforts to overcome the burdens of the past and to preview a better common future; to curb inequities and encourage redistributive justice; to achieve comprehensive and integrated solutions to urban problems; and to democratise the planning process and ensure maximum choice and access by all citizens to an enhanced quality of life.

Practical Implications for Urban Projects

These views have implications for specific policy and planning actions which can be undertaken by national and municipal authorities responsible for urban affairs.

Urban Majority.   Recognise that the urban poor in developing countries are not marginal populations, they are the Urban Majority, and that to assist their access to life-enhancing living and working environment within the framework of urban and national development is the crucial test of all innovation in urban management, planning and implementation.

Urban Land.   Allocate an adequate and regulated supply of land for residential developments in order to provide realistic alternatives to squatting; give squatters security of tenure and ownership; ensure that the unearned increment resulting from the rise in land values can be recaptured by the community and public bodies; protect food growing land from urban and other uses.

Spatial Integration. Encourage innovative and efficient patterns of spatial integration and distribution of peoples and activities, especially in regard to the poorest who can least afford spatial isolation; capture large-scale economies of urban form and design through coordinated transport, employment, land use and locational factors.

Urban Systems Design. Assist the creation of urban systems and institutions which support the fiscal economy through efficient use of scarce resources such as land, energy, capital and technology, and harness abundant resources such as labour and the creative potential of the poor.

Evolutionary Housing Practices.   Review housing strategies and encourage a variety of shelter options, and include upgrading and sites and services projects as an alternative to slum clearance; seek evolutionary solutions through:

i   phased introduction of infrastructure in slum and
     squatter communities (upgrading) or on vacant land
     (sites and services) as residents become willing and
     able to pay
ii   provide legal tenure to resident plot-holders and
     to encourage them in the improvement and construction
     of their dwellings

iii organise and assist mutual help in housing construction
     and environmental improvement
 iv introduce flexibility in standards, housing design,
     completion time, and materials to support the efforts
     of low-income communities
  v encourage affordable projects which are cheap enough to
     be accessible to a large number of targeted
     beneficiaries
 vi introduce cross-subsidisation through land-use pricing
     methods and inter-sectoral subsidies to achieve minimum
     cost burdens for plot-holders and tenants and encourage
     formation of balanced self-sustaining communities.
vii monitor and review the existing planning process to
     identify and modify those aspects which produce
     negative consequences to targeted beneficiaries and
     impede the attainment of planned objectives.

     Community Organisation and Cultural Factors. Relate pro-
jects to the implementation possibilities at and within
community-level informal associations, youth and women's
groups, and unemployed job-seekers; ensure that the project
highlights the continuity of culture by balancing indigenous
cultural traditions with the new requirements of urban structure and organisation.

     Public-Private Sector Cooperation.   Define appropriate
roles for public and private sector cooperation and establish
guidelines for directing private funds and investment in
urban development; give particular attention to measures
qualifying firms for tax credits, e.g. by employing local
residents, assisting with street paving, lighting, services,
etc., and aid to neglected fields such as health and environmental planning, workers' and consumer education and protection, energy requirements and conservation, locally-based
community organisations undertaking development projects.

Agenda of Urban Policy Objectives

Understandably there is no general consensus about the universal applicability of specific policies and solutions,
without modification, in widely differing contexts. Nevertheless, the search for successful examples within the framework of the five key questions posed earlier does point
toward the formulation of an Agenda of Urban Policy Objectives for improving public policies and planning actions in
developing countries. These are:

1.   Formulating national urban policies which define and
      harmonise at all levels of government the inter-related
      goals of economic and physical land use planning with
      social equity and better living and working conditions,
      particularly for the poorest communities;

2.   Organising, strengthening and coordinating public and
      private institutional, financial, legislative and
      administrative management systems for plan
      implementation;

3.   Designing integrated affordable and implementable
      programmes and projects which utilise the initiatives,
      resources and creative energies of local communities,
      individuals and non-governmental organisations;

4.   Creating broad education and training programmes for
      policymakers, professionals, project personnel and
      community implementations;

5.   Establishing appropriate and cost-effective national
      and international arrangements for technical cooper-
      ation, information transfer, and trade and aid
      which take into account the needs and priorities of
      urbanisation in developing countries.

Urban Project Financing

     In the coming era of pressures on cities and city
governments many administrators will look to external aid for
financial assistance to overcome City Poverty. It seems
clear however that at a time of increased need the volume and
flow of financial resources from donor nations, international
agencies and private lending banks to less-developed regions
and countries is demonstrably inadequate. This is especially
true in the fields of potential direct impact on settlements,
e.g. housing and urbanisation, water supply and waste disposal, and building materials, and in education and health,
infrastructure and tourism, and technical assistance. Given
this situation, it seems reasonable to expect that the fiscal
requirements of Problem Cities will not be met in the foreseeable future except as they begin to give attention to
mobilising additional conventional sources of city revenue
and exploring possible options for generating new resources
in the formal and informal sectors of the urban economy.

The slow and gradual evolution toward Urban Innovation will require aid and assistance from the international community. To make this transition more effective lessons must be learned from the past success and failures of lending strategies. There is a necessity to re-evaluate the objectives and impact of the past two decades of multi-billion dollar urban project funding by international lending agencies. This retrospective review should be undertaken with collaboration between donors, and non-governmental organisations, and should include examination of the following crucial aspects:

1.   The effects of lending strategies on housing stock and socio-economic conditions, culture and life styles; the provision of basic needs and services and their relationship to urban growth and development.

2.   The impact of lending strategies on national, municipal and local policies in the urban sector; on project formulation, design, and implementation; on urban management institutions, planning and investment programming; and on the development of national, municipal and community institutional capabilities for self-reliance.

3.   The record of implementation experience in terms of site location choices; land acquisition and tenure; standards and procedures; project management and attainment of completion deadlines; impact on the housing market and related sectors of employment, services and facilities.

4.   Urban development operations in terms of project management; staff development and training; internal procedures; performance indicators; and compatability with assumed and actual needs of the targeted populations.

5.   Accessibility and affordability of projects; cost recovery and direct benefits to beneficiaries; interest charges and economic rates of return; number of urban households affected; percentage of project costs providing direct benefits to the urban poor.

6.   Project replicability, based on use of locally-generated financial resources and local materials and strengthened plan implementation agencies.

GLOBAL LABORATORY

Finally, because the burgeoning metropolises of the

Third World are an unprecedented phenomenon our knowledge of
their responses to the problems of urban planning and management is incomplete and inadequate. The need for exchange of
information and more studies in this area is therefore
urgent; especially studies which exhibit a pattern of critical thinking, a wide ranging global perspective, and a systematic search for valid alternative views, policies and
strategies. And, because Third World cities will provide
tomorrow's living and working environment, the Urban Habitat,
for an increasingly larger proportion of the world's population it is equally urgent that action on a priority basis
be undertaken at all levels of government to improve urban
management and plan implementation if City Poverty is to be
alleviated and the goal of economic and physical development,
namely social betterment, achieved.

There is an additional validity to these views, which
highlight the purposes and utility of this book, namely that
the cities of the Third World provide a global laboratory of
urban experiments whose successes and failures offer invaluable lessons for academics, planners, urban managers and
decision makers in the developed as well as the developing
world. In many ways urban western society suffers from a
chronic deficit in the international balance of knowledge
about cities. Urban problems are, in contrast to prevailing
conventional wisdom, long-term multi-sectoral, national and
world-wide in scope, and require national and international
involvement in the search for solutions. More systematic
observation of cities throughout the world, with different
types of government and at different stages of technological
and cultural evolution, could reveal recurring themes, and
might suggest ways in which urban planning and governance
might find new directions. Though definitive solutions
cannot be found in any one city, collectively in all cities
it is clear that proposed solutions to problems need to be
viewed more broadly in relation to the growing interdependence of national and international economic systems.

City Studies

Kingston, Jamaica: Strategies for managing urban growth and development

Gloria Knight

KINGSTON - THE RANGE OF PROBLEMS

The rapid growth of urban areas has adversely affected the quality of life available in most cities in the developing world. Many urban citizens lack access to employment, shelter, infrastructure and community facilities and services. Increasingly they gravitate to squatter settlements, transitional settlements, favelas, bidonvilles, ranchos; as Barbara Ward said "the name changes, the desolation remains the same."[1]

Accordingly, urban plans should provide a strategy for ensuring that urban citizens have access to essential facilities and services:-

i   suitably priced land to be used for shelters;
ii   employment opportunities located near to their houses so as to reduce transportation costs;
iii   properly maintained road networks with suitably priced transportation systems;
iv   potable water;
v   efficient solid waste disposal systems;
vi   electricity;
vii   effective communications systems such as postal services and telephone systems;
viii educational facilities at primary, secondary and tertiary levels;
ix   health services, particularly primary health care;
x   banking and shopping services, especially markets

through which cheap food supplies can be obtained;
xi   recreational facilities and community centres.

These services and facilities are available to some extent in
third world cities, - but in many cases they are not readily
accessible to the poor. The example of Kingston, Jamaica,
may be indicative of the situation in other similar cities.

The size of the population in the Kingston Metropolitan
Area (KMA) as at 1978, was in the region of 700,000 people,
ten times larger than the island's second city, Montego Bay.
It has increased steadily due to improved communication links
and the inability of agriculture to absorb the population
increase in the rural areas resulting in rural/urban migration and in a fairly high rate of natural increase. Thus
while overall population growth is in the region of 1.78% per
annum, the KMA is growing at approximately 3% per annum. As
in many other primate cities in the developing world, this
unprecedented population growth has created severe problems
of unemployment, poor housing, poor access to services and
amenities within a rapidly expanding metropolitan area (see
map).

The problem of unemployment is particularly difficult to
solve or to ameliorate. Some 24% of the population of the
Kingston Metropolitan Area is estimated to be unemployed.
But in some slums and squatter settlements the percentage is
believed to extend as high as 60%. Although succeeding
governments have tried to reduce unemployment by means of
"special employment" projects, and this has had some effect,
success has been limited by the larger numbers of unemployed
in relation to the funds available. Accordingly, the problem
of unemployment, together with a high rate of underemployment, continues to be one of the most critical matters to be
addressed in the KMA.

Approximately 45% of the population live in squatter
settlements. In addition, 28.7% of the population live in
high density "old" residential areas in which facilities are
also sub-standard or non-existent.[2] Thus, 74% of the urban
population occupies only 33% of the residential area living
at average densities of 2 persons per room and over 5 persons
per toilet. Of five shanty towns examined by Ann Norton, it
was noted that in three water was available only from stand-
pipes and in the remaining two, only 14% and 13% of the
houses had a piped water supply.[3] Those areas using a

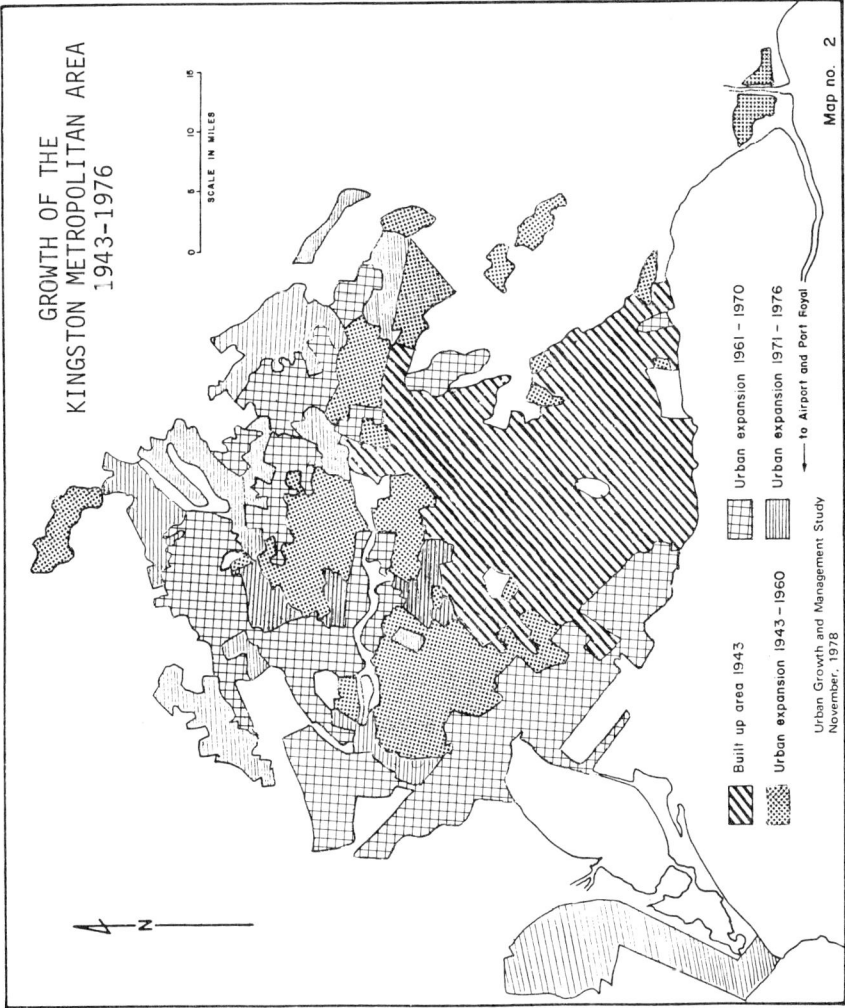

GROWTH OF THE
KINGSTON METROPOLITAN AREA
1943-1976

SCALE IN MILES
0   5   10   15

N

Built up area 1943

Urban expansion 1943-1960

Urban expansion 1961-1970

Urban expansion 1971-1976

→ to Airport and Port Royal

Urban Growth and Management Study
November, 1978

Map no. 2

stand-pipe are often at a further disadvantage in that the
size of the pipe carrying the supply is small, and sufficient
water is never available for the residents' needs. In slum
areas where tenement yards are the major residential pattern,
water is also generally supplied by stand-pipe. Here the
supply is metered, and, due to the pricing policy which im-
poses a higher charge as more water is used, tenement families are penalised by having to pay higher rates for poor
services and reduced availability of water. Further, there
are sections of the urban population which do not have access
to potable water at all, and it is estimated by the Urban
Growth and Management Study that in order to deal with these
sections 56 stand-pipes should be erected at a cost of
J$56,000.[4] Thus, although 91.5% of the population of the
Kingston Metropolitan Area has access to water, the distribution system needs urgently to be improved, particularly in
relation to high density areas.

The rapid growth of the Kingston Metropolitan Area has
exacerbated the limited access to central sewerage facilities
and the Liguanea aquifer on which the city is located is now
in danger of pollution. It has been recognised that a comprehensive sewerage system is critically needed for high
density areas of the city, and such a system is being implemented in stages. Meanwhile, however, the high incidence of
premises with defective toilets in slums and squatter settlements indicates the urgent need for quicker implementation of
an overall system and utilisation of techniques which ensure
that the new facilities are efficiently operated.

Solid waste disposal in these areas is at best erratic.
The local authority has installed large concrete bins in some
areas, but regrettably the evidence indicates that these are
not cleared regularly and they have become a health hazard
rather than a technique for improving the system.

Electricity is present to a surprising degree in many
slums and squatter settlements. The evidence indicates,
however, that the majority of the connections in these areas
are illegal. This is not surprising when it is recalled that
a supply cannot be legally obtained unless there is evidence
of right of tenure. Further, the pricing policy which requires the Jamaica Public Service Company to be economically
viable means that electricity is expensive and the population
in these areas often successfully use considerable ingenuity
to obtain the facility without payment.

Public transportation is used by the majority of people in slums and squatter settlements. Access to such transportation is available. The quality of service to these areas is, however, extremely poor. Lack of reliable transportation to a population which cannot afford the marginally higher prices for the privately-operated mini-bus is, therefore, a real disadvantage. The reason for the poorer service given by the bus company is the relatively high level of crime and violence associated with these areas. At the slightest sign of violence bus services, together with garbage collection services, are the first to be reduced.

Educational and health facilities in slum areas are in short supply and are of worse quality than in other areas. Overcrowding and under-staffing are the major problems, and until the number of facilities is increased, the effective operation of those in place will continue to be severely curtailed. The need for recreational facilities is urgent in all these high density areas, but it is perhaps even more urgent in slum and high density "old" residential areas where play fields are desperately needed for the youth, and where there is only 1.98 acres of play field per school. The squatter areas are slightly better off in this regard as there is generally more land available per household unit. Nevertheless, the need for organised facilities is great.

Housing need in the KMA for the period 1978-1983 was estimated as follows:-

Unacceptable units	- 9,100	
Units needed to reduce overcrowding	- 7,734	
sub-total of backlog as at 1978		16,834
Future households 1978-1983	- 8,047	
Replacement due to dilapidation	- 6,035	
sub-total of future needs		14,082
Total housing need 1978-1983		30,916

Source: National Planning Agency, Urban Growth and Management Study, 1978.

But the identification of need is only part of the problem. The difference between need and effective demand is critical. For example, in 1978 the cheapest fully built house being offered on the market was J$15,000. However, 80% of households could not afford to pay more than $5,500 for a house. The criteria of affordability therefore become ex-

tremely important in the equation of identifying housing
demand as against housing need. Further, inflation over the
succeeding years has widened the gap between housing costs
and the amount which can be afforded by households.

Altogether, access to infrastructure and community services and facilities is quantitatively and qualitatively less
for the poor in the Kingston Metropolitan Area even though,
as in the case of potable water and transportation, overall
access appears to be of a reasonable standard. The question
which arises from the foregoing therefore is what strategies
should be devised to speak to the problems of the poor?

KINGSTON – SOME STRATEGIES FOR IMPROVEMENT

Population Growth and Rapid Urbanisation

Attempts to reduce the rate of population growth and to
ameliorate the problems resulting from rapid urbanisation in
the Kingston Metropolitan area have centred around three
strategies.

The first is to facilitate access to family planning
services in order to reduce the rate of natural increase.
These services are provided through the Family Planning Board
which works closely with and reports to the Ministry of
Health. The question of teenage mothers receives special
consideration and the provision of assistance and advice to
these young girls is a focus of the programme as it is also
of special programmes operated by the Women's Bureaux, and a
number of voluntary organisations.

The second strategy is to create alternative growth
points so as to reduce rural/urban migration. Creation of
employment opportunities by way of industrial development has
in the past formed part of this strategy and the growth of
towns such as Mandeville and Santa Cruz has in part resulted
from the establishment of bauxite mining plants. In many
cases, however, the families of employees of such enterprises, have moved to or continued to live in Kingston because of easier access to required services and facilities.
Small industrial estates have also been established in a few
rural towns as part of this strategy. Most of these have
failed due to a number of reasons, chief among them the recession in the economy in the past four years, and the lack

of supporting services and facilities. The tourist industry has also provided an important component of this strategy, and the Ocho Rios development project which was planning in a comprehensive manner has become a growth point.

Examination of the shortcomings of using employment creation by itself as a tool for reducing rural/urban migration has led government to take a decision to establish a Rural Township Development Project. This project, which is now in its planning stage, is aimed at upgrading the quality of life and the fabric of development in the network of towns at the sub-regional and district levels, as identified in the 20-Year National Physical Plan 1978-1998.[5] The project requires that concurrently:

1   The potential for improving and increasing the economic base of the towns be identified. This will permit special emphasis to be placed on employment creation, utilising local resources wherever possible, to increase production, especially for the export market. Sub-projects may include one or more of the following:- agriculture and forestry products, aquaculture, livestock rearing, floriculture, agro-industry, manufacturing industry, mining, construction industry, cottage industry, craft industry, commerce and tourism.

2   The basic needs of the communities are met and that services and facilities are provided at the level needed. Planning for these services and facilities will take full account of environmental factors, including risk emanating from natural disasters, as well as the use of alternative sources of energy.

The outline planning of this project will be concluded during 1982 and detailed planning and implementation will take place over a ten year period. Two ingredients are essential to the success of this project. They are:-

a) the involvement of the local communities throughout the entire exercise.

b) the involvement of the local authorities, the various sector ministries and other relevant organisations.

It is expected that this project will lead to increased productivity, new job opportunities in a variety of agricul-

tural agro-industrial and service enterprises in rural towns
and will enable the government to take rational medium and
long-term decisions on expenditure relating to provision of
services and facilities not only in the towns themselves, but
also in the KMA.

The third strategy is to facilitate the expansion of
Kingston into planned areas to the west on lands which have
no potential for agriculture. Portmore, a satellite town,
west of Kingston of approximately 85,000 people was developed
by private enterprise over the period 1970-1980. Bracton, an
area immediately west of Portmore is in the process of being
developed by the Ministry of Construction (Housing Section).
Both areas have an acceptable level of infrastructure services, but the first plan of social services have only recently been planned and implemented by the Urban Development
Corporation, located south-west of Bracton, is being compre-
hensively planned as a new town and will provide employment
opportunities together with the required services and housing
for all income levels.

Slums and Squatter Settlements

In regard to slums and squatter settlements, a number of
strategies have been devised relating to the need for shelter
and for infrastructure services. In the area of shelter,
government has introduced three strategies to grapple with
the problem:

National Housing Trust. A national housing bank called
the National Housing Trust was established in 1976. It is
financed by contributions from all employed persons, and its
policy is to finance the provision of housing mainly for the
lowest paid of its contributors. With a 4% interest rate, a
family earning J$25. per week can afford a unit costing
J$13,000 payable over 30 years.

Sites and Service Projects. Three sites and services
projects have been located in the KMA, one of which has been
completed. These projects are geared towards a lower income
group than that catered to by the Housing Trust. Services
are provided, and part of a core. The beneficiary is required
to complete the unit over time with materials bought in bulk
and available for purchase on the site. Each site was designed to include an employment component. Some problems

which are emerging from the existing projects need to be addressed. First of all, the employment component has not materialised. Secondly, the projects are large by Jamaican standards, and social problems are beginning to appear. Thirdly, if the project is to accommodate households at and below the minimum wage of J$32.00 per week, the difficulty experienced by that group in completing their units while living and paying rent elsewhere needs to be examined. The validity and applicability of the principle of the sites and services approach in Kingston is clear. However, there is a variety of methods by which this approach can be utilised. These should be examined and assessed in relation to the client population for which the projects are designed. The completion of a habitable core unit is one option which is now being implemented in the incomplete projects.

Squatter Upgrading Projects. These projects are geared to an even lower income group than Sites and Services. The aim of these projects is to upgrade areas in which squatters presently live, by provision of roads, water and suitable drainage and sewerage systems. Every effort is made to retain the maximum number of residents and block plans are prepared in such a way that existing units are not disturbed, unless it is absolutely necessary. An important facet of these projects is that residents are given tenure to their lots, and are therefore better able to improve their shelters. Government also ensures that ready access to social infrastructure such as health centres, schools, community centres is available.

These three strategies are intended to be self-financing. All are valuable, but need to be expanded if any attempt is to be made to meet the housing needs set out above. This is illustrated by the following:[6]

a)	Number of units awarded by National Housing Trust 1978–June 1982 to families earning a minimum of J$24.00 weekly	3,039
b)	Number of units allocated in Sites and Services projects 1978–1981	1,338
c)	Number of beneficiaries from Squatter Upgrading Projects 1978–1981	3,393
	Total	7,770

What seems most important is that the poor in the Kingston Metropolitan Area should have access to a wider variety of options from which to choose their mode of shelter, within a planned programme, ranging from:

1   lots of relatively low standard of services (ie. standpipes only, pit latrines allowable, and roads surfaced with tar and chip). Residents should have good access to transportation and to social services. Land size should be as generous as possible. Tenure whether by lease or by sale should be assured.

2   lots with a higher quality of services (and at a higher cost than 1).

3   serviced lots as at 2 with shell unit consisting of external walls and sanitary core.

4   high density town house type project in city centre.

5   high density three and four story apartment buildings in city centre.

Lots 1, 2 and 3 should be offered at the periphery of the KMA as well as within the easily accessible suburban areas, reflecting the variety in land costs. Housing at 4 and 5 could range from shell units with sanitary core to fully built three-room units, with those at 4 being expandable.

These options would provide shelter at varying costs and simultaneously every effort needs to be made to use standards which are affordable but safe. Building techniques which can assist in reducing costs should be investigated. The establishment of a Building Research Unit which is now being finalised with the assistance of the UN Centre for Human Settlements will be useful in this regard. Further, there is urgent need for innovative financing strategies which can help to bring housing demand closer to housing need.

Delivery of Services

In 1978 the National Planning Agency produced an Urban Growth and Management Study for the Kingston Metropolitan Region, which includes the KMA, and which set out clearly the strategies to be pursued to improve the delivery of services, especially to the poor.

The terms of reference for the Study were:-

a)   to establish current and feasible patterns of
        population growth for both old and new areas of
        urbanisation in the Kingston Metropolitan Region;

b)   to determine the type, volume, cost and ease of
        availability of urban services required by each
        of these actual and feasible growth patterns,
        both according to the service standards now pre-
        vailing and those suggested by the government as
        being more suitable for the future;

c)   to specify means and areas of experimentation for
        the systematic upgrading of the quality and quan-
        tity of public service delivered for each dollar
        invested in the operations of municipal, parish,
        and national government in the region;

d)   to incorporate the results in a draft capital
        budget for the region.

The Study was guided by a multi-sectoral and multi-disciplinary team.

    In regard to a) above, the study identified areas for
future urban expansion. Recommendations were made for the
Kingston Development Order to be revised so as to reflect
more sensitively the need for higher density of population
distribution in areas not now zoned for such purposes; for
Government to acquire and sub-divide lands for sale as serviced lots to low-income groups so that they can house themselves; for security of tenure to be provided to urban
dwellers in squatter settlements to enable them to upgrade
and improve their housing. A particularly important recommendation was that to institute a "betterment" taxation
system, which would allow Government to recapture some of the
costs of sub-division, servicing and enabling it to redis-
tribute some of the benefits to the poorer areas. The study
highlighted the need to allow certain commercial and industrial uses in residential areas where changes of use were
already taking place, and to identify more land for the
establishment of small industries complexes.

    In respect of the service network referred to at b) and
c), the recommendations aimed at rationalising responsibility

for operating the network among the many agencies involved, and suggested that a Public Utilities Council should be set up to give consumers a voice in the setting of rates for utilities.

With regard to housing and open spaces, again the question of rationalising responsibility for programmes was addressed, and a strong plea was made for the selection of areas to be upgraded to be dealt with on the basis of need. The provision of parks and playgrounds was recommended with the admirable proviso that playgrounds of schools should be used by members of the community where open space was limited.

In the case of health care, great emphasis was placed on the need for an efficient primary health care system, and again the question of rationalising responsibility along functional lines was addressed.

In respect of utilities, the requirement to serve areas of greatest social need formed the crux of recommendations, and it was suggested that Government purchase electricity in bulk for resale to low-income households, that public call boxes be made the priority of the telephone system, that exchanges in areas of greatest social need be expanded.

All the recommendations reflect the structural problems of urban management in Jamaica which is described on p.22 of the study as follows:-

> "It is notable, first of all, that the network is
> characterised by a proliferation of agencies and
> splintering in the provision of a service. His-
> torically, new additions and structural changes
> have been made in the ad hoc manner and have been
> grafted onto the previously existed system without
> sufficient adaption. Partly as a result of this
> failing, a second characteristic of the network is
> that agencies tend to have "isolationist" policies
> more oriented to zealously defending "kingdoms"
> than co-operation in order to achieve broadly de-
> fined goals. These two characteristics of the
> institutional framework have naturally resulted in
> an overall lack of cohesion in the network. On the
> other side of the coin is the lack of any single
> controlling body to give direction to various as-

pects of the system. Thus, uncertainty and confusion prevail which must have adverse effects on
planning for growth and long term expansion."

The structural adjustments recommended call for the
local authorities to receive all property tax revenue, for
them to become involved in the management of service agencies
- specifically the National Water Authority, for their training budget to be greatly expanded, and for them to have
access to technical assistance through the Ministry of Local
Government.

Finally, the study recommends the establishment of a
5-year budget for basic services - particularly those required by the poor.

These recommendations are all logical and worth considering. Some of them are in the process of implementation.
A revised Kingston Metropolitan Plan is being prepared by the
Town Planning Department. A Housing Policy is now being
finalised by the relevant ministry which will attempt inter
alia to tackle the fundamental problem of housing for the
poor in the Metropolitan Area. A programme of primary health
care is being pursued. The recommendations which so far are
not being implemented are the ones which deal with the funding and powers of the Local Authorities and the implementation of the 5-year budget for basic services. Both these
recommendations were adversely affected by the grave recession in the economy. When the economic situation improves, it is hoped that these two recommendations, which are
vital if the quality of services delivered to the poor is to
be improved, will be implemented.

Employment

The Kingston Metropolitan Area has been fortunate in
having the problems and responsibilities of managing urban
growth set out in such clear terms. The National Planning
Agency study successfully fulfilled its terms of reference.
Nevertheless, further work needs to be done to encourage
employment creation and increased productivity, through the
provision of necessary infrastructure services. The same
structural problems which exist in regard to provision of
services in residential areas exist in the coordination and
servicing of economic enterprises. The local authority needs

to establish systematic linkages with such enterprises in both public and private sectors. This will ensure its capability to service the requirements of these enterprises and enable it to look at the costs and benefits of alternatives, in a way which enhances access by the poor to employment and income opportunities.

Meanwhile, a number of strategies are being pursued so as to facilitate industrial and commercial development. First, in view of the shortage of venture capital, the government has established a special agency, the Jamaica National Investment Promotion Co Ltd, to promote job-producing industry and investment activities and to provide a link between foreign and local businessmen who may wish to implement projects singly or in joint ventures.

A second strategy is being pursued by the Jemen Industrial Development Corporate. In this case, emphasis is being placed on the garment industry because of its capacity to employ large numbers of women. Old factories are being refurbished, new ones are being built, and arrangements to market the products overseas are being finalised.

A third strategy is to revitalise the construction industry. During the recession, employment in this industry was greatly reduced. All agencies dealing with housing in both the public and private sector, are in the process of examining the market possibilities for a wide range of buildings. In addition a J$50 million project for the construction of interim facilities for the International Sea Bed Authority will require the employment of approximately 800 persons per day at peak.

A fourth strategy involves a project aimed at assisting the informal sector. Over the years, the area surrounding the largest market in the island, a hub for both wholesale and retail food marketing, has become highly congested mainly because the informal sector, concentrating on trading opportunities, understandably opted to locate themselves as near as possible to the market. The result is that within approximately one mile of the centre of the city, street vendors inhabit the sidewalks and sometimes the road itself, selling the most varied array of goods which can be found anywhere on the island.

The project proposes to provide separate wholesale and retail market facilities for all vendors in the area, to rationalise the existing road network, provide adequate off-street termini for rural and urban buses, mini-buses, taxis and allow for easy linkages to the railway system. The project is also seen as the starting point for the rehabilitation and reconstruction of West Kingston, one of the most deprived areas in the Kingston Metropolitan Area.

It consists of six main packages: Land acquisitions; improvements to road network and other infrastructures; new retail markets and upgrading of the existing market; rural and municipal bus termini; wholesale market; and relocation of 211 households.

The population in 1970 was 1357 persons. The area is characterised by intense economic activity, centred around the market complex, where thousands of people congregate on a daily basis to buy and sell a wide range of goods and produce. In addition, there exists a number of wholesale and retail business establishments, together with pockets of inhabited derelict housing.

The area is served by a social services complex called Operation Friendship, which houses the following facilities: a nursery; basic school; health clinic; dental clinic; dispensary; and an adult education centre.

The overall condition of the buildings is characterised as poor with 42% of all buildings slated for demolition.

Building Conditions

Good	11.02%
Medium	15.59%
Poor-improvable	6.98%
Poor-expensive	18.27%
Demolition	42.2%
Ruins	5.9%

The existing land use of the area is quantified as follows:

Land Use

Activity	Land coverage (in acres)
Markets	8.7
Education	1.5
Public Assembly	1
Commercial	17
Vacant lands	5.5
Residential	9
Industrial	7.5
Public Utility	2.5
Office	0.25
Vacant buildings	0.25
Transport	23
Ruin	7.5

It is estimated that approximately 12,000 higglers (street and market sellers) and in excess of 50,000 persons shop and use the transportation facilities in the area. The development plan provides for 871,200 sq ft (20 acres) of market space and the following amenities:

i   a new wholesale market
ii   a new retail market with an open square which
     would entail pedestrianising part of Spanish
     Town Road and West Queen Street
iii rationalising and widening the existing road
     network system
iv   improvement of existing infrastructure (lighting,
     sewer, water, telephone and drainage and
     engineering services)
v   a new municipal bus terminal for the Jamaica
     Omnibus Service, mini-buses and taxis, and a new
     rural transportation centre
vi   additional housing and neighbourhood centre
     adjacent to the project area
vii preserving and upgrading of existing retail and
     commercial buildings.

The benefit of this project is that it attempts to combine the enthusiasm and business acumen of the informal sector with the formal food marketing and small commercial business sectors. This is being done by providing the physical requirements for efficient operation and maintenance of the required services and facilities.

Are these strategies proving successful? Improvement in the quality of life is occurring but at too slow a rate to make a real impact in the large numbers of people living in deprived circumstances. There is urgent need for labour intensive projects which add to the reliable projects of the country, and for these to be located in such a manner and designed in such a way that the poor can benefit. Some of the new initiatives described above are being designed with this goal in mind.

Kingston – Managing Urban Growth

The degree of success which attends strategies to im-prove the quality of life of the poor is dependent on the capacity of government to manage the regional projects and programmes. The references made to the Urban Growth and Management Study earlier, have already indicated that urban growth in Kingston is managed by a variety of organisations. The Local Authority, the Kingston and St. Andrew Corporation (KSAC), is responsible for: the road network except for roads identified as national highways; solid waste collection and disposal; public health; public assistance programmes; markets; and planning and building approvals.

A variety of central government agencies are responsible for: the transportation system; production and delivering of potable water; the communications systems; the utilities; education; health care and family planning (excluding public health); housing; and preparation of development plans. The Ministry of Local Government, to which the KSAC reports, is responsible for both transportation and potable water.

By law, the KSAC has the authority to take a comprehen-sive approach to development within the city. However, lack of qualified staff, lack of money, and the fact that the national government is located in its city weakens the ability of the Corporation to operate in this way. Many of the decisions regarding the quality of life in the KMA are therefore taken and implemented by a multiplicity of organis-ations.

It is not surprising, therefore, that in Kingston as in other cities of the developing world, government has had to establish special purpose institutions for planning and im-plementing projects that facilitate integration at both the

national and local levels. The Urban Development Corporation
of Jamaica is such an institution.[7] Established in 1968,
it is a Statutory Corporation set up to act as a developer in
the public interest, and to make development happen in designated areas. An additional function is the creation of productive employment opportunities especially through use of
the construction industry. The Corporation undertakes projects which are too large or complex for the Jamaican private
sector to handle, or projects which are desirable but which
do not provide the profit margin required by private sector
enterprises. The Corporation is directed by a Board of
Directors appointed by the Minister responsible, presently
the Prime Minister and also Minister of Finance and Planning.
The Corporation relates to the Prime Minister and Ministry at
two levels. Operational matters are dealt with through a
Deputy Financial Secretary while matters of policy are handled in meetings with the Prime Minister. The relationship is
set out in Figure 1. This is in accordance with the Law
which states that the Minister responsible may, after consultation with the Chairman, direct the Corporation in matters
of policy, that annual reports including audited accounts
must be presented to the Minister within 4 months of the end
of each financial year, and that all borrowings must have the
approval of the Minister of Finance.

The Board of the Corporation is selected in a manner
which combines the dynamism of the private sector with the
public conscience of the public sector. At present it consists of the following type of members nominated as individuals:

Private Sector

Chairman   Director of Sales for one of the largest
                  private sector enterprises. Formerly an
                  entrepreneur in the housing industry.
Vice-Chairman   Senior partner in one of the largest archi-
                  tectural firms.
Businessman   Entrepreneur
Lawyer
Representative   of Jamaica National Investment Promotions
                  Company Ltd. - a Government Company estab-
                  lished to facilitate project development in
                  the private sector.

Public Sector

Government Town Planner
Permanent Secretary, Ministry of Construction (Housing)
Permanent Secretary, Ministry of Agriculture
Permanent Secretary, Ministry of Mining and Energy
Deputy Financial Secretary, Ministry of Finance and
  planning

There is also a Staff Representative, elected by the Staff, and the General Manager is a member of the Board.

The Board meets monthly, receives progress reports and policy papers from the Secretariat, and guides the Corporation in its policy and operations. The wide range of skills freely available to the Secretariat from this source has been

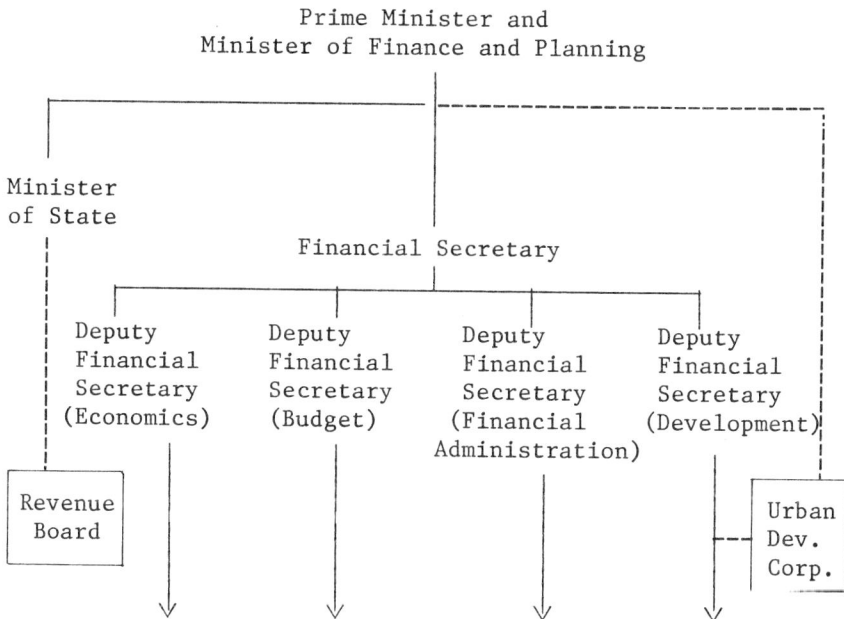

Prime Minister and
Minister of Finance and Planning

Minister
of State

Financial Secretary

Deputy
Financial
Secretary
(Economics)

Deputy
Financial
Secretary
(Budget)

Deputy
Financial
Secretary
(Financial
Administration)

Deputy
Financial
Secretary
(Development)

Revenue
Board

Urban
Dev.
Corp.

Fig. 1. Position of the Urban Development Corporation in the Governmental System. ☐ Statutory Enterprises; ——— Central Government Links; ----- Special Purpose Institutions Links. Source: Ministry of Finance and Planning, Jamaica, March 1982.

Table 1.   Relationship Between Planning Agencies and the
           Urban Development Corporation.

Macro Level: Agency		Relationship with UDC
National Planning Agency (Economic and Social Planning)	–	Represented at local level when required
Town Planning Department (Physical Planning)	–	Represented at National and local boards
Scientific Research Council (Scientific and Technological Planning)	–	Liaison established by Secretariat
Department of Statistics (Responsible for collection and collation of national statistical information)	–	Liaison established by Secretariat
Micro Level: Agency		Relationship with UDC
Local Planning Authorities	–	Represented at local level
Government Ministries	–	Represented at National and local levels as required

and continues to be of great value. This technique is repeated at the local level for every UDC project. Each major
project therefore has its own Board or Advisory Committee
which includes representatives of the local Authority and
other knowledgeable local people from the private sector,
together with representatives of public agencies whose involvement is of importance to the project.

The UDC operates in designated areas. Whether the area
is a small section of a city as in the small town of
Oracabessa or is an entire New Town as in the 45 square miles
that make up Hellshire, the main principle used in all the
projects is comprehensive planning and integrated implementation. The way in which the Corporation fits into the planning system is therefore important, and is shown in Table 1.
In the past, a closer relationship has existed with the
National Planning Agency, the Chief Technical Director of
which used to be a member of the UDC Board. At present a
close relationship is still maintained, but on an informal
basis.

The linkages in Table 1 are carefully nurtured so that the Corporation is aware of and indeed often participates in planning at both levels, especially in the case of the Town Planning Department. Indeed the Town Planning Department and the Corporation collaborate on specific projects from time to time.

It should be noted that when an area is designated, the Corporation takes the place of the Local Authority in the granting of planning and building permission. The UDC law requires that a plan of development for the designated area be prepared and referred to the Local Authority for comment. This plan, together with such comments, is submitted to the Minister responsible for UDC for his approval. If there is a disagreement between the Local Authority and the Corporation, the Minister puts the proposals and comments before the Cabinet for a decision. In fact the plans are discussed with the Local Authority while in the process of preparation, and by the time they are submitted for formal comment, they have been agreed. On one occasion when agreement was not forthcoming, the plan was not finalised. When the project has been implemented, the area reverts to the guidance of the Local Authority.

The Corporation has always been careful to build up rather than reduce the status of the local authorities in its decision-taking processes. It has never forgotten that the towns belong to the people who live in them. The Corporation, therefore, regards itself privileged to plan, to learn, to help to implement and in the final analysis to hand over to the local authority and to withdraw, hopefully having added to the economic stock and improved the quality of life of people in the area.

The Secretariat of the UDC reflects the comprehensive approach to planning. Figure 2 shows the structure of the Corporation, but not how it works. The organisation is project oriented, and each project is dealt with from conception to implementation by a team drawn from all the skills in the various departments. A multi-disciplinary project team is established from the beginning to liaise with the client population, and proceeding through four stages they conceptualise the project, define it, plan it and finally implement it. This team seeks the advice of the local community, initiates contacts with the government bureaucracy as required, and pulls in people and skills that are essential to the

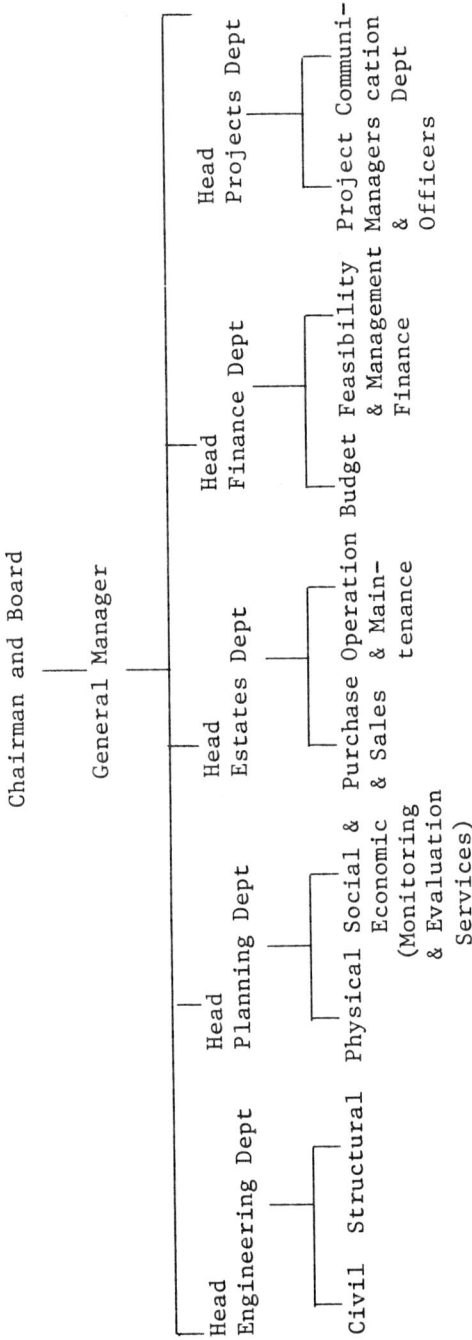

Fig. 2. Urban Development Corporation Formal Organisation.

project at the earliest stage possible. They make recommendations to the Area and UDC Branch, but these are first examined by an Executive Management Board, an internal board
consisting of the General Manager and the five heads of departments and the Company Secretary.   The same document,
amended if and where necessary is then sent to the Area
Board, and subsequently to the UDC Board.   It should be noted
that at each of these points the document is viewed by a
multi-disciplinary team varying in levels of experience.
Each project is reported on at least once a month, - more
frequently if required.   This system enables the management
team of the Corporation to use the initiatives and innovations of junior and middle level members of staff, to guide
them in their work, and to be up to date on the position
regarding each project with a minimum of paper work. Further,
this system encourages commitment to a particular project
which appears to help to find solutions more readily when
difficulties arise.

The multi-disciplinary approach is vital to this exercise.   It should be borne in mind however that an important
aspect of its success is the ability to manage conflict, for
conflict does arise when different disciplines meet to discuss details of development projects.   As long as the goals
are clear-cut, and the need to use the conflict effectively
is realised, the project benefits, and is better able to meet
the needs of the people who after all, do not divide their
lives into sectors, or into the categories of the various
technical and professional disciplines.

The need to involve the client community in the entire
exercise cannot be overemphasised.   Suffice it to say that on
one occasion when the client community could not agree among
themselves as to what was best, the project was not implemented.

The Corporation's projects are financed from a variety
of sources as shown in Table 2.   The costs of staff and overheads are met from 12½% of project costs, of which 10% is
related to technical and professional services, and 2½% to
overheads.   If consultants are used, their costs are included
in the 10% related to technical and professional services.
As a result of this, the Corporation's staff is not paid from
the Government's budget, and it therefore has more flexibility in regard to levels of salaries and prerequisites
offered to staff.

Table 2. Urban Development Corporation - Sources of Finance.

Item		Source
Land	-	Government Loan
Infrastructure	-	Government Loan Institutional Financing*
Secondary Development	-	Commercial Banks Institutional Financing
Operations	-	Commercial Bank

* eg. World Bank, Inter-American Bank, Caribbean Development
  Bank, Commonwealth Development Corporation.

The Corporation is presently implementing 8 projects,
dealing with a variety of purposes, eg. city-centre renewal,
town expansion, upgrading of rural townships, development of
resort towns, and development of new town. It holds assets,
as of 1981, of $358.7 million with debts of $325.2 million.
In each of its project areas, it has made investments in
office buildings, hotels, shopping centres, the income from
which will, in future years, enable it to meet its debts, and
to undertake additional projects. Meanwhile, it has established two companies to own its commercial properties. One,
National Hotels and Properties Ltd owns hotels and operates
them when necessary. The other, Turtle Beach Developments
Ltd, owns apartments in Ocho Rios which are rented to tourists. Consideration now has to be given to the management
techniques to be used for these and future investments.
Examination of this aspect of the Corporation's work is in
process, and recommendations on this matter will be made to
the Board and to the Government during 1982/83.

CONCLUSIONS

The problems which are faced by the poor in the Kingston
Metropolitan Area are appalling. Strategies are being implemented by Government to ameliorate or solve these problems, but their success is limited by lack of funds, lack of
skills, and particularly management skills. This is exacerbated by the fragmented approach to development. Special
purpose institutions such as the Urban Development Corporation can be useful when they use a comprehensive approach
and implement projects in an integrated manner.

Jamaica is a poor country, and although assistance can be and is being obtained from international agencies and through bilateral agreements, it is imperative that the country increases its productivity and income. Increased income will be able to finance improved delivery of services and improved and new training schemes, thus enabling the country, and its main city Kingston, to gain maximum benefit from one of its major resources - its people.

REFERENCES

1. Barbara Ward, Human Settlements: Crisis and Opportunity, an official report based on a meeting of experts preparing for the United Nations Habitat Conference on Human Settlements, Vancouver, Canada, published by Information Canada. Cat.No.SU31-7/1974, p.11 (1976).
2. Gloria Knight, Urban Infrastructure and Community Facilities and Services: the Caribbean Experience, prepared for the Inter-American Meeting of the United Nations Habitat and Human Settlements Foundation on Finance and Management of Human Settlements, Mexico City, 27 Nov-1 Dec(1978).
3. Ann Norton, Shanties and Skyscrapers: Growth and Structure of Modern Kingston, University of The West Indies, Institute of Social and Economic Research, Jamaica (1978).
4. Jamaica, Ministry of Finance and Planning, National Planning Agency, Urban Growth and Management Study, Final Report, NPA, Nov.(1978).
5. Jamaica, Ministry of Finance and Planning, Town and Country Planning Department, National Physical Plan: 1978-1998, Vol. 1 (1982).
6. Jamaica, National Planning Agency, Economic and Social Survey, 4 volumes (1978-1981).
7. The Urban Development Corporation Act, Kingston: Government Printer (1968).

Delhi: Two decades of plan implementation

Abhijit Datta and Gangadhar Jha

After a fairly long period of spontaneous and haphazard growth and sprawl, Delhi became the first Indian city to have a blueprint for planned development, the Master Plan for Delhi 1961-81. This timely review of the achievements and failures of the implementation and administration of the plan provides some useful points for consideration by urban and regional development planners, and suggestions for redefining the planning system, resource mobilisation and public participation.

DELHI AND ITS GROWTH

Delhi is in fact several cities - a legacy inherited from the legendary Mahabharat days of 900 BC. As many as nine Delhi's were built on various sites according to the whims and fancies of the rulers.[1] It is now the seat of the national government and a prime centre of distributive trade for the north and north-west India. It has acquired this status because of a host of socioeconomic and historical factors. Delhi today consists of Shahjahanabad walled city built by the Moghul Emperor Shahjahan in 1638, its outgrowth - old Delhi, now noticeably a slum area, and modern New Delhi, born with the transfer of the capital by the British from Calcutta to Delhi in 1912. The expansion of these two settlements has by now enveloped the sequestered sites of earlier settlements which came up and vanished in the annals of history. Besides these, there are about 500 colonies with a population of about 0.6 million developed unauthorisedly after the initiation of planned development. Then there are

villages, about 100 in number, which have been brought into
the fold of urban areas by the extension of the city's urban
limits over the years. The urban areas apart, Delhi as a
Union Territory, spreads in an area of 1485 sq kms with rural
segments having an area of 1038.7 sq kms (Table 1).

The urban segment of 446.39 sq kms experienced an ex-
ploding rate of population growth from about 0.7 million in
1941 to 3.6 million in 1971 (Table 2) brought about by the
huge influx of about half-a-million refugees after the political partition of India in the late forties.[2]   The increase is due to net migration at the rate of around 60 per
cent[3] during 1941-51, about 34 per cent during 1951-61,[4]
and about 51 per cent during 1961-71.[5] Delhi receives an
estimated 150 thousand immigrants every year, and the un-
abated flow of migrants has now swelled the present population of Delhi to an estimated 5.5 million.

Table 1. Area and Population of Local Bodies within the
Union Territory of Delhi - 1971.

Local Bodies		Area in Sq Kms	Population	Density of Population per Sq Kms
I.	Municipal Corporation of Delhi	1,399.3	3,706,558	2,649
	(a) Rural	1,038.7	418,675	403
	(b) Urban	360.6	3,287,883	9,118
II	New Delhi Municipal Committee	42.7	301,801	7,068
III	Delhi Cantonment Board	43.0	57,339	1,333
IV	Total Urban (Ib+II+III)	446.3	3,647,023	8,172
V	Total Delhi Union Territory	1,485.0	4,065,698	2,738

Source: Census of India, Delhi District Census Handbook, 1971

Table 2. Growth of Population in Delhi 1901-1971.

Sl. No. (1)	Year (2)	Total Population (3)	Urban (4)	Rural (5)	Percentage Variation over the previous decade		
					Total (6)	Urban (7)	Rural (8)
1	1901	405,819 (100.00)	208,575 (51.40)	197,244 (48.60)	—	—	—
2	1911	413,851 (100.00)	232,837 (56.26)	181,014 (43.74)	+ 2.0	+ 11.7	- 8.2
3	1921	488,452 (100.00)	304,420 (62.32)	184,032 (37.68)	+18.0	+ 30.7	+ 1.7
4	1931	636,246 (100.00)	447,442 (70.33)	188,804 (29.67)	+30.3	+ 47.0	+ 2.6
5	1941	917,939 (100.00)	695,686 (75.79)	222,253 (24.21)	+44.3	+ 55.5	+17.7
6	1951	1,744,072 (100.00)	1,437,134 (82.40)	306,938 (17.60)	+90.0	+106.6	+38.1
7	1961	2,658,612 (100.00)	2,359,408 (88.75)	299,204 (11.25)	+52.4	+ 64.2	- 2.5
8	1971	4,065,698 (100.00)	3,647,023 (89.70)	418,675 10.30)	+52.9	+ 54.6	+39.9

Source: Delhi Administration, Bureau of Economics and Statistics, Delhi Statistical Handbook, 1974.

THE DELHI PLAN

Rapid population growth and urban sprawl placed great pressure on urban services and Delhi became a city of blight, squalor and epidemics. The increasing influx of immigrants from various Indian states in search of work opportunities further accentuated the problems of housing and services and led to encroachment on public lands and the formation of large squatter areas.

In order to redeem Delhi from his worsening situation an Interim General Plan and then the final Master Plan were prepared. Approved by the Government of India in 1962, the Master Plan intended to correct the haphazard growth of the past and to promote planned growth during its life span - 1961-81. The plan was conceived in a regional context wherein urban Delhi formed the core of a larger metropolitan region within a radius of about 25 sq miles. Development of seven 'Ring Towns'[6] around Delhi was envisaged as the instrument to secure balanced development of the region which could ultimately redirect growth and relieve pressures on Delhi.

The Master Plan, prepared with the assistance of a Ford Foundation team from America headed by Gerald Breese and Bert Hoselitz, also included a Land Use Plan for urban Delhi to find solutions for the entire complex of inter-related urban problems, social, economic and governmental. It aimed at "balanced and integrated development" to take care of both present and future growth up to 1981. The planners felt confident that: "Since the land requirement for the next ten years or so has been notified for acquisition by the Delhi Administration, all future land use can be regulated by the Master Plan and land sub-division controlled by zonal development plans". The planning strategy was in essence, to translate into physical form planning policies and principles based on the contemporary realities of the dynamic but rather unregulated and chaotic conditions in the Metropolis.[7]

Urban Delhi was intended to be planned for a population of 4.6 million up to 1981; the additional population (out of a projected population of 5.5 million for 1981) was proposed to be decanted to the Ring Towns. At the city level, the land-use plan sought to promote a spatial pattern having a positive relationship between the workplace and residence. With this end in view, urban Delhi was divided into eight

68   A. DATTA AND G. JHA

planning divisions, each to be self-contained in matters of
workplaces, residences, recreational areas, shopping and
other requirements. These were to be functional units reflecting their own patterns of development and land use, and
individual physical characteristics, social and cultural
values. Population was to be distributed in the planning
divisions through de-densification of old and congested
areas, like, the walled city of Shahjahanabad, and re-
densification of sparsely populated areas. Positive relationship between work place and residence was to be established by deconcentration of employment centres within urban
Delhi. In order to achieve this, district centres, subdistrict centres and flatted factories were given pivotal
roles.

    The Plan also proposed to equalise services and ameni-
ties in the whole of Delhi and suggested several useful
proposals for the renewal of older and congested parts of the
city. The urban limit conceived for the year 1981 was to be
contained by an "inviolable" green belt and acquisition of
the entire land within the urban limit was recommended. The
plan also outlined the staging of land development and provided a policy frame for its administration.

    Soon after its preparation the plan received strong
policy support. For the first time in the history of urban
development in India a progressive urban land policy was
announced by the Union Government indicating modalities of
the scheme of 'large scale acquisition, development and disposal of land' in Delhi.[8] It was decided to acquire the
entire land within the urban limits of 1981 excluding those
already urbanised. A seed capital of Rs 50 million was
raised by the Union Government to facilitate the operation of
the scheme and the Delhi Development Authority (DDA), con-
stituted under the Delhi Development Act, 1957, was given
authority to oversee the implementation of the plan by various action agencies.

REVIEW OF PLAN IMPLEMENTATION

    Initiation of planned development has had visible impact
in many spheres. The city has a wholesome environment; it
looks clean, green with widened roads and a chain of local,
district and regional parks. The city has extended to the
urbanised areas of the adjoining States of Haryana in the

south and west, and in the east has touched the urban areas
of Uttar Pradesh. A number of new residential colonies
(13,412 acres), industrial estates (2,350 acres), commercial
centres (330 acres) and relocation colonies (2516 acres) have
come up, thus augmenting the housing stock and adding shelter
and work opportunities for the city dwellers. About a million
squatters have been relocated in 43 planned re-settlement
colonies. Substantial improvement has occurred in about 71
'urban villages'. The old city has been decongested to some
extent by shifting the wholesale vegetable market and cycle
market to new planned sites. In order to impart a wholesome
environment to the city, and also to minimise traffic
hazards, city dairies with about 12,000 cattle have been
relocated on three new dairy farms. Planning of a new township for 0.9 million people - Rohini - within the city of
Delhi has just been announced containing an area of 2,497
hectares, with provision for housing, work places, recreational and civic needs.

But these achievements notwithstanding, there have been
lapses and failures also. Unprecedented in-migration overwhelmed the plan implementation authorities. Furthermore
development of Delhi was based upon the assumption of development of alternative job opportunities for migrants in the
Metro Region and the larger National Capital Region (NCR);
however, these regions covered an inter-state jurisdiction
and thus could not set up a well integrated and coordinated
administrative mechanism to effectuate the plan.

Some critical lapses and failures can be illustrated by
reviewing land use development. The urban land policy was
intended to support the broader objectives of the Delhi plan
which identified the 'urbanisable limits' in Delhi till 1981,
including the areas already built-up. It was envisaged to
develop additional areas of 30,000 acres of land for residential use, 4,800 acres for industrial use, 1,900 acres for
commercial use, 500 acres for government offices and 25,000
acres for recreational use.[9] Thus an additional total of
62,200 acres was supposed to be acquired, developed and disposed of for various land uses.

Achievement of these goals, however, has not proceeded
according to plan targets. By April 1980 about 42.5 thousand
acres of land were acquired,[10] some 19.7 thousand acres
short of requirements. Development of land for residential,
industrial and commercial uses was substantially below targeted requirements. (See Table 3).

Table 3. Development of Land for Residential, Industrial and
          Commercial Uses in Delhi, 1977-78 (Area in Acres).

Use	Envisaged in the Delhi Plan	Developed actually	Short Fall (%)
Residential	30,000	13,412	55.30
Industrial	4,800	2,350	51.90
Commercial	1,900	330	82.60

Source: Master Plan for Delhi, Table 5, p.43

    The figures for residential land development merit
further consideration. 13,412 acres of land for residential
use include 5,820 acres developed by the DDA as residential
plots, 1,276 acres for group housing schemes, and 2,516 acres
for squatters' relocation scheme, 2,300 acres developed by
the Central Public Works Department (CPWD) and the Municipal
Corporation of Delhi (MCD), and 1500 acres developed by the
House Building Cooperative Societies. Thus the land developed for residential purposes falls short of the targeted
development by about 55 per cent. The shortfall, in fact,
would be more since out of the total land developed for the
relocation of squatters about 839 acres of land is located in
the green belt which is beyond the Master Plan projected
urban limits and was supposed to be 'inviolable'.[11]

    The slow pace of development and disposal of acquired
land, coupled with an accelerated rate of immigration, led to
the rise of unauthorised colonies on a large scale. About
0.6 million people are presently residing in such colonies
which occupy an area of 7,500 acres.[12] Unauthorised development in industrial and commercial sectors also occurred. A
major industrial policy objective of the plan was to relocate
the noxious and non-conforming units on new planned locations. But over the years, these units have in fact increased from 9,363 in 1962 to about 24,000 in 1978.[13]
Inadequate augmentation of commercial space has also led to
conversion of residential houses into business use, and unauthorised development of shops and establishments.

    It is worth recapitulating that the district centres,
conceived in the plan as having a mix of shops and commercial
offices, were assigned the role of effectuating the plan's
prime objective of self-contained planning districts. However, even as the plan period ended only two such centres
were developed of the sixteen envisaged in the plan.

Another severe lapse pertains to the old built-up areas where no positive impact could be made in all these years of plan implementation. The walled city of Delhi, the central business district and major wholesale trade centre for cloth, hardware, foodgrains, paper, dry fruits and spices, has been losing its population by way of conversion of residential houses into shops and makeshift storehouses. This has aggravated the problems of congestion, traffic jams and deterioration of the living environment. The affluent population has moved out to the suburbs, leaving behind low income people in the core city. The situation was further aggravated by declaring the entire walled city a slum area and freezing reconstruction of the dilapidated houses. At the same time, however, no recourse was taken to stop the conversion of residences into commercial use, even though adequate instruments to prevent this were available under the Shops and Establishments Act and licensing procedure. In spite of the avowed objective of shifting of noxious and hazardous industries, no step could be taken in this regard and in fact their number has proliferated over the years.

The most conspicuous failure of plan implementation in the national capital is the distorted development, rather than the proposed balanced development, of the eight planning districts. Planned effort seems to have been entirely directed to the development of south Delhi - an affluent locality of the capital, leaving the settlement across the river Yamuna unattended to. The situation in trans-Yamuna areas, having a population of about a million, still continues to be grim with unplanned unauthorised colonies, lack of basic services and amenities, like access roads, drinking water, draining and sewerage. Only towards the end of the plan period were efforts started to initiate planned growth and regularisation of unauthorised colonies.

The way in which the urban land policy and its scheme of large scale land acquisition, development and disposal operated in practice further illustrates the pattern of distorted development. Between 1960-61 and 1970-71, Delhi's high income groups were given as much as 49.8 per cent of the total plots of land through auction. Those whose land was acquired (alternative allottees) were given 14 per cent, and the middle income group and the low income group were allotted only 24.7 per cent and 11.5 per cent of the total plots respectively.[14] The proportion of land given to the low-income group actually declined from 55 per cent in 1961-62 to

3.2 per cent and 1.9 per cent in 1969-70 and 1970-71 respectively. Yet, the urban land policy had envisaged keeping a
suitable proportion of land for low-income persons.

Lapses in plan implementation were primarily due to two
factors: the basic premises of the plan could not hold good;
and development activities could not be properly organised to
effectuate the planned intentions. Inaction at the metro-
regional level completely overwhelmed the development effort
at the city level. No attempt was made to spell out the plan
proposals for urban Delhi into specific time-bound packages
of programmes and schemes. Monitoring, feedback, control and
periodical review of implementation could not inform the
administration of plan at any stage even in a rudimentary
form. Even though the plan was reviewed in 1973 by the Town
and Country Planning Organisation, a central government
agency, no follow up action could be initiated to set it
right.[15] The DDA, which was supposed to bring about effective coordination among the various action agencies having
forgotten its role, became just one of the many.

REDEFINING THE PLAN AND PLANNING SYSTEM

Many of the problems in Delhi's development have arisen
because of the approach of planning itself. A master plan is
essentially a single-shot long range exercise. It has some
built-in deficiencies brought about by its attempt to foresee
purposes, needs and the situation of a complicated organism -
the city - some twenty or twenty-five years ahead. It proceeds with a tacit assumption that no unexpected event or
emerging situation would occur to alter the perspective as
visualised by the plan. It is because of this rigid and very
long term approach that the master plan becomes incapable of
delivering the goods, especially in a dynamic situation like
Delhi. The combined explosive demographic growth, swift
physical sprawl and the pressure for civic services completely overwhelmed the static frame of the Master Plan.

Further, the master plan is basically a land-use plan
concerned with city-form. Its concern for economic growth of
the city is almost minimal. Providing a solution to the
problems of shelter and urban poverty, so rampant in the
Third World cities, is not an objective of a master plan, and
consequently, urban planning as practised in Delhi so far has
been elitist in nature.

The second plan for Delhi is presently being formulated spanning up to the year 2001. The new plan has to have a better appreciation of the realities of the situation and has also to subserve national objectives of fulfilling the minimum needs and creation of equal opportunities for all the urban dwellers. This calls for adopting altogether a new approach to urban planning. It must have a long run perspective of the city's growth in the next 10 to 15 years in terms of various elements of the city, namely demography, economy, housing, shelter and service needs and an action programme on a short run basis properly dovetailed with the national five year plan. The emphasis has to shift from city-form and structure to provision of employment and shelter by strengthening of the urban economy and relating it to the national development efforts.

At macro-level, it would require an identification of Delhi's function and linkages in the region. The plan then must enable Delhi to perform that function by utilising its comparative advantages, skills and resources. This needs to be reinforced by key sectoral programmes and policies to strengthen the urban economy. Land-use planning has only to subserve this broader objective by earmarking of locations for various activities in different sectors.

The walled city of Shahjahanabad is presently the centre of distributive trade in several commodities. Its functioning is immensely encumbered by congestion, physical blight and decay. It has, therefore, to be revitalised, preferably by shifting some of the wholesale trades and relocating them on new planned locations.[16]

Predominance of low income urbanites is going to be a Third World imperative in years to come. The housing policy, therefore, has to be attuned to a suitable shelter strategy based on incremental housing, with built-in scope for improvement for future rise in income and located in proper relationship with the work centres.

In order to contain the problems in urban Delhi, coherent policy and planned efforts are urgently required at the regional level to develop the Metro Region and the National Capital Region which could provide job opportunities to the immigrants flocking to the city of Delhi. This itself inevitably depends on how effectively development effects are organised and coordinated both at the regional and city level.

RESOURCE MOBILISATION

Resource availability for plan implementation in Delhi
has been quite generous by Indian standards. During the five
year period 1970-71 to 1974-75 the per capital annual expenditure on urban development was highest in Delhi (Rs 131),
compared to the other three metropolitan centres, Bombay (Rs
125), Madras (Rs 117) and Calcutta (Rs 102).[17]   On the
average this comes to around £6-7 (£1 = Rs 18 approx.), a
paltry figure by western standards!

Yet it is unlikely that urban development will be accorded a higher priority by the Indian Planning Commission to
substantially alter this level of investment outlay.   In
future, this may even be lower, given the rural bias in
Indian planning and a shift of urban development efforts
towards the small and medium towns and away from the metropolitan centres. Moreover, the contribution of national
funding for Delhi's development cannot be directly related to
settlement planning as such, since the territory's five year
plan finances development expenditure for education, road,
public health and medical facilities only.

There are, of course, the five year plan allocations
available under the Central Plan undertaken directly by the
central ministries and a part of such funds is being spent on
Delhi. For instance, more than half of the central public
works department's plan funds is spent on Delhi alone; this
proportion would be much smaller in the case of the plan
outlays of the railways and the telephone. However, there
are some investments on central undertakings operating in
Delhi, like transport and milk supply, that would be additional to the Territory's five year plan. The major pro-
viders of the investments on shelter, utilities and commercial projects are the DDA and the two municipal authorities
in Delhi and New Delhi.

Therefore, the main funding agencies for urban development function outside of the five year plan allocations and
it is a curious assumption that Delhi's urban development
needs can be met from the internal resources of the local
authorities in Delhi. Furthermore, the major plan implementation agency, DDA, relies almost exclusively for financing
its development scheme through a 'revolving fund' which can
take up only financially viable and attractive schemes in
order to recover the seed capital and roll it back to finance

further investment; hence its organisational survival is
dependent on maximising return on acquired public land sold
to the highest bidder. DDA has been striving hard to plough
back a part of its profits for common amenities and low-
income housing; but this is constrained by the compulsions of
the revolving fund strategy. Urban development for the poor
in this context becomes the first casualty.

PUBLIC PARTICIPATION

Urban planning in Delhi must also address a larger question about the scope of settlement development itself: is it
to be viewed only in terms of physical structures and their
location or in terms of the social, economic and human needs
of the population that constitute it? If it is to be related
to the people that inhabit settlements, then one has to re-
fashion the existing planning, implementation and financing
systems that have operated so far.

The scope of public participation in settlement development is linked with the status of the lead agency: is this
an organisation accountable to the people that benefit from
its endeavour, or is it an organisation foisted on the people
by a remote central government? In Delhi, the development
authority is a creature of the central government to plan and
develop through the operation of a revolving fund, meaning
that it is devoid of the mandate from the beneficiaries of
its efforts either in terms of governance or resource raising. Being a sterile organisation in political and fiscal
terms, DDA is constrained in mobilising public support or
participation in plan implementation.

Among the local government authorities in Delhi, only
the New Delhi municipality has an operating surplus to be
deployed on urban development projects. Here too the municipality has a nominated board and, therefore, its rapport with
its constituency is not direct.

If one views public participation in programmatic terms,
it is possible to identify a number of schemes and projects
undertaken by the various public authorities in Delhi where
opportunities exist for direct participation at the client-
level. However, the tradition of the public authorities in
India, including Delhi - both central and local - is so
insular and bureaucratic that an open dialogue between the

official agencies and their clients is almost unthinkable.
Take the case of plan preparation; here the official planners
would satisfy the requirements of public participation by
following the legal formalities of inviting objections and
their summary disposal, until someone challenges the proposal
in a court on technical grounds. The concept of an open-ended
dialogue with the citizens, both at the plan preparation and
at the plan implementation stages, is absent. On top of it,
if the development authority itself is divorced from any
popular sanction, the result could be stifling in terms of
people's aspirations and unrealistic in terms of their requirements.

SUMMARY VIEW

We have recounted the experience of Delhi and its metropolitan authority, DDA, during the two decades of plan administration and implementation. Some of the deficiencies highlighted, in terms of approach, policies, organisation,
financing and the nature of development, are unique to the
city being the national capital. Yet many of the basic issues
identified: the nature of planning, institution-building,
fulfilling minimum human needs, the role of economic and
social development in settlement planning, the role of public
participation and decision-making, and resource financing
methods are all common issues of urban development in Third
World countries, India in particular. The achievements of
Delhi's development are substantial in architecture and landscape design, but in terms of priorities these must take a
residual position and conform to the overall human objectives
of settlement development.

REFERENCES

1. Gerald Breese, "Urban and Regional Planning for Delhi -
      New Delhi Area, Capital for Conquerors and Country,"
      Princeton, New Jersey (1974).
2. Government of India, Town and Country Planning Organis-
      ation (TCPO), "A Diagnostic Study of Migration to
      Delhi," mimeo November, p.2 (1969).
3. N. Bhaskar Rao, "Estimates of Migration to Metropolitan
      Cities of India 1941-1951 and 1951-1961". Demographic
      Training and Research Centre, Bombay, mimeo, n.d.

4. Town and Country Planning Organisation, "Metropolitan City Centre of Delhi, Studies on the Working Force and Population Aspects," mimeo, New Delhi Redevelopment Advisory Committee, New Delhi, n.d.
5. Town and Country Planning Organisation, "Migration to Delhi, A National Capital Regional Study," mimeo (1975).
6. Delhi Development Authority (DDA), "Work Studies Relating to the Preparation of the Master Plan for Delhi," Vol.I. pp. 16–17, n.d.
7. Delhi Development Authority, "Master Plan for Delhi" (1961).
8. Government of India, Ministry of Home Affairs, No. F.37/16/60-Delhi, dated 2 May 1961.
9. Delhi Development Authority, Work Studies, op.cit. p. 404.
10. Data from the Land and Development Department, Delhi Administration.
11. Delhi Development Authority, "Resettlement Colonies – Review of the Problems," mimeo (1977).
12. Report of Committee of Experts on the Working of Delhi Development Authority, Government of India, Ministry of Water and Housing, p. 45 (1978).
13. Report of Committee of Experts on the Working of Delhi Development Authority, Government of India, Ministry of Water and Housing, p. 55–56 (1978).
14. Government of India, Ministry of Works and Housing, First Report of the Working Group on Mid-term Appraisal of the Delhi Master Plan and its Implementation, mimeo, New Delhi, p. 3, n.d.
15. Town and Country Planning Organisation, Review of Master Plan for Delhi: Some Recommendations for Future Development, mimeo (1973).
16. See Abhijit Datta and Gangadhar Jha, "Improvement of Living and Livelihood in Delhi's Walled City", Nagarlok, vol.XII, No. 4, October–December (1980).
17. Abhijit Datta and Bappaditya Chakravarty, "Organising Metropolitan Development," final report of a study completed for the Indian Institute of Public Administration, Centre for Urban Studies, New Delhi and the Indian Institute of Management, Regional Development Group, Calcutta, October (1979).

Nairobi: Evolution of a housing planning and management policy for low-income communities

Gilbert J. Njau

Nairobi's policies for planning and managing the improvement of housing and socio-economic conditions of low-income communities have undergone an evolution in direction and emphasis from the late colonial period to the present. An important turning point occurred in the mid-1970's with the design and implementation of the Dandora sites and services project financed from the World Bank, from which many lessons have been learned of great relevance to planners and decision-makers.

NAIROBI: PROBLEMS OF INHERITANCE AND INDEPENDENCE

The City of Nairobi, like many other cities in the developing world, is faced with severe socio-economic and development problems which have their root in the rapid rate of growth coupled with a relatively meagre resource base. Although the Government and civic authorities have been concerned with this state of affairs, they were slow in devising appropriate policies and programmes to deal with the issues involved. Official policy was characterised by inherent contradictions which inevitably inhibited action, and was heavily influenced by pre-conceived, conventional approaches which preclude a realistic assessment of a fairly fast changing situation.

Urbanisation and City Growth

During the colonial period, Nairobi's population growth was very modest mainly due to artificial restrictions on

movement of the African population. A balance was therefore
maintained between population and jobs available. The city
was well planned and very high standards of infrastructure
and services, including housing, were vigorously enforced.
These, however, were geared to meet the needs of European and
Asian residents of the city.

The African population was accorded no say in the conduct of the city's affairs. Decisions on matters affecting
their welfare were made by the dominant immigrant communities. Thus a relative disparity in the provision of housing
and services existed with Africans getting least priority.

The African population, which was predominantly male,
was considered temporary in the city as they were expected to
return to their respective places of origin if out of work or
retired. Housing that was provided for this sector of population was mainly single room units with shared facilities in
which individuals were allocated bed spaces. Family units
were discouraged from settling in the city and as such only
very few dwellings were constructed which could accommodate
them. It is, however, important to note that rents were low
and could easily be afforded by low-income populations.

The City Council constructed a number of housing estates
close to the industrial area for Africans, and the other
racial groups, with only a few exceptions, were accommodated
in privately developed housing. In addition, other institutions such as the Government and the Railways constructed
housing for their own employees of all categories. A not-
able feature during this period was the provision by employers of housing for their low-income workers. This made a
great deal of sense under circumstances prevailing at the
time. It is evidently clear that during this period provision of low-cost housing was geared to employment opportunities, and the burden was shared by all major institutions
both public and private. The demand and number of completions
was essentially low and was not a strain on available resources. The policy served the limited objectives of the day
fairly well but did not take into account likely long term
changes which could upset the balance.

In the late fifties there was a change in policy regarding movement of population. The East Africa Royal Commission
1953-1955 strongly advocated creation of a stable African
urban population among other things. The implementation of

this recommendation resulted in slight relaxation of controls on movement as well as provision of modest self-contained family units.

This trend accelerated in the sixties. All restrictions were removed on the eve of Independence in 1963 thus ushering an era of rapid population growth in urban areas, and Nairobi absorbed the bulk of this increase. There were high rates of population growth into the seventies with a peak being experienced in 1973 when growth was estimated at a rate of 7.3% per annum. Towards the end of the seventies, the rate appears to have declined giving an overall intercensal rate of growth of approximately 5% (see Table 1).

Table 1. Nairobi's Estimated and Recorded Population

Year	Total Pop.	No. of Households(2)	Rate of Increase
1948	118,976 (1)	29,750	
1957	221,700	52,920	
1962	347,431 (1)	86,860	6.2%
1969	509,286 (1)	127,350	7.1%
1979	834,549 (1)	214,100	5%
1985	1,186,000	296,500	

(1) Population census
(2) Based on family size of between 3.8 to 4.3

Nairobi's population is fairly young and has a relatively higher proportion of females than is normally the case. There is also evidence that household size is a declining factor which suggests a higher rate of household formation than the one that pertained in the past. This has meant that demand for housing and urban services is equally higher.

Migration into the city accounted for the bulk of the population increase in the sixties and early seventies. It is estimated that between 1962 and 1969 migration accounted for 4.3% of the annual increase. The natural rate of increase has tended to rise due to the special demographic characteristics of the population, and it is estimated that this now approximates the national level of 3.8% per annum. This therefore leads to the conclusion that the rate of migration into the city has declined considerably, but despite this the actual numbers flocking into the city are still very high and poses problems to the city authorities.

Incomes and Housing Affordability

The growth in population has not been matched by the growth of the economy and employment opportunities, however. Worsening economic conditions were largely to blame. In the sixties the national economy grew at a relatively high rate of between 6.7% and 7.8% per annum. However, in the Seventies the global economic recession had a toll on Kenya's economy. High rates of growth were unattainable and in fact the economy experienced a considerable decline. In 1980 for instance the real growth in the GDP was only 2%.

In Nairobi a substantial proportion of the labour force is outside the range of gainful employment either in the modern sector or the informal sector. Unemployment tends to be higher among low-income groups whose incomes are in any case rather unstable and fluctuate over time; and it is estimated that 40% of Nairobi's households have incomes below the poverty level of Kenya shs.700 per month per household of seven persons.

Given the dramatic decline in the rate of economic growth and continued high level of migration into Nairobi, per capital incomes have fallen significantly. According to income projections made in 1976, no improvement in household incomes were expected over the next decade. Therefore the proportion of households requiring inexpensive forms of housing was expected to remain very high (see Table 2).

To highlight the housing implications of this date, the estimates of affordable capital costs can be related to the 1975 costs of:

(a)   Housing built by self-help methods or direct employment of labour: which were K£1000/1300; and

(b)   Contractor-built housing: which were K£1350 for a one-room house with shower and w.c.; K£1575 for a two-room house; K£1750 for a three-room house.

Thus it can be demonstrated that most of the households in the lowest two quintiles, 40% of Nairobi's households,

Table 2. Estimated (1975) and Projected (1985) Household Incomes, Affordable Monthly Expenditure, and Capital Cost of Housing (1975 prices).

	Cumulative % of Households	Average Income per household (K£ pa)		Affordable Exp. On Housing, at 20% of Income (Ksh per month)		Affordable Capital Cost at 10% interest, 20 years repayment (K£)	
		1975 Est.	1985 Proj.	1975 Est.	1985 Proj.	1975 Est.	1985 Proj.
Lowest	0 – 20	208	206	69	64	359	357
Low-middle	21 – 40	400	134	134	134	693	691
Middle	41 – 60	760	766	254	255	1313	1323
Middle-upper	61 – 80	1250	1254	416	418	2159	2166
Highest	81 – 100	3529	3263	1086	1196	5928	6200

Source: Nairobi's Housing Needs: Meeting the Challenge, 1976, Vol.III.

would be unable to afford single family occupancy for a complete house built by either self-help or contractor-built
methods.

Housing Problems and Policies

The very high rates of population growth experienced
within a short period posed a number of problems to the city,
overcrowding, congestion and deterioration of the environment, which required a major capital outlay that was not
available. In housing, due to the growth in households, the
annual need for housing was estimated at 9,000 units in 1972
and was expected to rise to 17,000 units in 1985. In addition, a major expansion in the provision of water, drainage, road network and community facilities was necessary.
Although the city was faced by such problems, it is significant to note that there were no appropriate policies and
programmes to deal with them. Official action as outlined
below proved to be irrelevant to the issues at hand and made
little impact.

Soon after independence, the new administration was
determined to remove the disparities that existed before
especially in respect of the African population. Major improvements were made to the low-cost housing areas. Old
housing was provided with individual services and in some
cases was converted from single rooms into family units of
two rooms with amenities. Slum clearance was embarked upon
but the first scheme that the Council tackled presented so
many problems that the attempt was dropped. Although this
still remains the policy of the Council, very little has been
done.

The Council planned ambitious new housing construction
programmes, purportedly for low-income population. The housing was to be constructed of permanent materials and was
intended to be of fairly high standard. Indeed the new administration aspired to build housing that was superior to
that provided during the colonial era.

The effect of this policy was that very little housing
was completed. Between 1962 and 1970 only 7,400 units were
provided which represented an annual average of less than
1000 units per year. This compares very unfavourably with
the estimated demand of approximately 33,000 units over this

period. After 1970 very few units were completed but the
rate of housing production started picking up towards the end
of the seventies. Thus the housing shortfall continued to
grow and by 1972 it had reached a level of 60,000 with approximately 48,000 units falling within the two lowest income
categories. Allied to the number of units produced is the
cost of such housing. Due to the high standards that were
advocated at the time the units completed were relatively
high in cost and could only be afforded by medium income
families. This to a very large extent explains the low turn-
over of housing completed as well as the large shortfall in
the low-income sector.

Acute shortage of housing resulted in overcrowding in
the existing estates and gave rise to growth of unplanned and
squatter settlements. Such settlements are typified by structures of simple and usually low quality construction, often
in poor state of repair with elementary or no supply of piped
water or adequate sewerage disposal facilities. In addition
the settlements have no roads of access or security lighting
and densities are extremely high.

The Mathare Valley area of Nairobi clearly illustrates
the problem. In 1964 its population was estimated at 4,000.
In 1969 the population had risen to 19,000 and to 53,000 in
1971. Other squatter areas of the city experienced a similar
rapid growth pattern. Thus in 1971 an estimated 30% of the
city's population lived in uncontrolled and unauthorised
settlements. By 1978, housing units in all such areas had
increased to a figure of 65,000 and comprised 38% of the
city's total housing stock. The authorities were not happy
with this turn of events. Attempts were made to curb the
growth of these settlements by demolition but without any
success. Demolition of a squatter village only forced the
population to relocate somewhere else.

In the field of social and community facilities the
Council was also faced with a burden of catering for an ever
increasing population. The facilities provided during the
colonial period soon proved to be inadequate, and a major
expansion of existing facilities and provision of new ones
was required. The burden therefore was not only in terms of
capital outlay but also in recurrent cost which now accounts
for a major proportion of the annual budget. (Education and
health alone make up approximately 60% of the Council's
annual recurrent budget).

Meeting housing and community needs has placed a severe strain on the Council's finances. All accumulated reserves have been utilised and for a number of years the city has operated on a deficit. Thus Council's ability to mount major programmes has been drastically impaired, and inevitably affected the rate of development.

DANDORA: THE TURNING POINT

In the seventies, Nairobi realised the futility of the housing policy being pursued. Although a substantial number of housing units had been constructed, no impact had been made in the solution of the housing problem and the situation had grown worse for the lower income groups. A solution had to be found that would provide a large number of houses at low enough costs that could be afforded by people earning Shs.200 to Shs.800 ($26-104) per month. The site and services approach was therefore accepted as an answer to the problem.

The World Bank did a lot to sell the idea of a site and services scheme to the City Council. Right from the beginning, an agreement was reached that the scheme was to consist of a large number of plots in order to make an impact. Agreement was also reached on basic principles to be adopted, namely:

(a)   normal building standards were to be relaxed in order to achieve cost savings.

(b)   the Council was to confine itself to provision of infrastructural services and sanitary facilities on the plot leaving the construction of houses to the allottees.

(c)   the Council was to provide materials for construction of an initial two rooms as well as technical guidance and supervision during the consolidation phase of the development.

(d)   allottees were not required to make a down payment in order to accommodate those with no accumulated capital; however all costs for the project were to be recovered from the allottees where possible.

(e)   allocation was to be fair, with eligibility confined to
      heads of households earning between Shs.280 to Shs.650
      per month, having evidence of residence in Nairobi for a
      period of two years, and not owning any other residen-
      tial property in the city.

(f)   the scheme, in addition to housing, would provide the
      necessary community facilities as well as employment
      opportunities within the site.

(g)   the Council was required to set up a project department
      adequately staffed with skilled personnel and reporting
      through a Committee of Council vested with plenary
      powers. Government was to be represented in the Commit-
      tee by the Permanent Secretaries of the relevant minis-
      tries.

(h)   a separate body was to be set up to continuously monitor
      the process of implementation and consolidation.

Dandora Described

     The project was to be sited at Dandora on the eastern
side of Nairobi on a site, 350 hectares in area, approximately 11 km from the central business district. It was
mainly chosen because it was the only large uncommitted
parcel of land owned by Government and the Council. In addition, the site could be easily serviced by extension of
trunk mains from the adjacent housing areas.

     A good road connecting the site with the city centre and
industrial area existed and therefore the Council was satisfied that employment would be accessible from the site. As
this was going to be costly to the allottees a decision was
made to develop employment centres within walking distance
from the scheme at Dandora and Ruaraka industrial areas.
(The problem of physical accessibility to jobs still remains.
The development of industrial estates close to Dandora has
lagged behind housing development, and the provision of jobs
within the scheme has not materialised yet).

     The Dandora scheme consists of 6000 plots and related
community services, and is funded jointly by the World Bank
(55%) and the Kenya Government (45%). Financing is a mixture
of a normal Bank loan ($ 8m) and International Development

Association credit ($ 8m). The borrower is the Kenya Govern-
ment who in turn on-lends the total amount to the Council.
The usual interest rates for Bank loans and IDA credits apply
but the Government did not pass the same benefits to the
Council. Instead the interest rate of 6½% is charged for
part of the money to be used for he shelter component while
(8½% is charged for money used to finance the other components. An elaborate system of cost apportionment was devised to ensure that as much of the cost is recovered from
the allottees. However, due to the normal city-wide practice
some elements such as schools and health centres were to be
recovered from the rate fund.

The first phase consisting of 1000 plots was designed by
Council staff while a consultant was hired to design the
rest. This first phase was designed with very low standards,
a factor which caused a big controversy when bye-law approval
was sought. As the scheme had advanced to a point of no
return a compromise was reached which enabled the first phase
of the scheme to be completed. However, the standards for
phase two had to be raised. A substantial delay did occur as
design of the project had to stop while a new brief was being
drawn. This coupled with higher standards of infrastructure
provision raised the cost of phase two by about 40%. The
allottees in this latter phase are expected to pay approximately 30% more than those in phase one. A higher element of
subsidy from money made on the market sale of a limited
number of plots has slightly reduced the actual cost to the
allottees.

As a part of the project, the Bank agreed to finance a
number of studies. The first, was concerned with the review
of Local Government finances, and was carried out by a team
from the International Monetary Fund (IMF) which examined the
allocation of responsibilities between Central and Local
Governments, inter-governmental relations, including revenue
sharing and the scope for new sources of local government
revenue. Before the implementation of the study's recommendations, the Government was required to keep the local authorities viable by maintaining the existing levels of grants.
Although the study team reported in 1977, no action has yet
been taken by the Government.

The second study was connected with low cost housing and
squatter upgrading. The study objective was to prepare proposals for providing a large number of site and service plots

as well as improvement proposals for squatter settlements in
Nairobi, Mombasa and Kisumu. This study formed the basis of
Kenya/World Bank Second Urban Project.

The third study was concerned with Nairobi City Council's housing operations. During appraisal of Dandora project it became evident that the Council's administrative
arrangements for housing delivery were seriously deficient.
An agreement had been reached that an integrated housing
agency for Nairobi was urgently required. The study therefore was required to define the tasks of the proposed agency
and its mode of operation.

Dandora Project is a unique case in Nairobi's experience. It has been the turning point in the Council's housing
policy. The scale of the project was large enough to make a
sizeable contribution to the housing stock for low income
populations. The project is popular with the allottees, a
factor which has helped to erase the stigma previously attached to sites and services. According to independent observers, the project has catered for the target population
with relatively few exceptions.

An added advantage is the improvement of the city's
administrative structure in the field of housing implementation. The project department was a successful experiment
and a considerable improvement on the previous system, and
has led to the transformation of the project department into
a fully fledged Housing Development Department within the
Council's structure. Certain weaknesses in financial management and control in the City Council, as well as in the other
local authorities, were brought into focus. Although only
short term corrective measures were introduced, a commitment
was made by the Government to find long term solutions to the
problems.

Kenya's Second Urban Project is a continuation of the
first project, but its scope was extended to cover, in addition to Nairobi, two other main towns, Mombasa and Kisumu.
In addition the project addressed itself to the question of
squatter settlements which have continued to grow in spite of
police action by the authorities.

The approach adopted in the Second Urban Project was an
improvement on the first project. Project preparation was
undertaken by a consultant hired and supervised by the Min-

istry of Housing and Social Services. The standards used in the sites and services component of the project were at the higher level accepted in phase two of Dandora as a result of the insistence of the City Council of Nairobi, and though Kisumu and Mombasa were willing to accept lower standards no exception was made. In upgrading areas the level of service differs from city to city. Nairobi is only to provide primary infrastructure services while the private land owners are left to upgrade the structures or redevelop the area. In the other two towns grouped communal facilities are provided in addition to the basic primary infrastructure.

The total project cost is approximately US $69.4 million with the Bank/IDA contributing US $50 million which is about 72% of the project cost. Of this amount approximately US $ 37.1 million will be spent in Nairobi. This represents a very high proportion of the project cost, a factor which shows Nairobi's dominance over other urban centres. The money will be on-lent to the local authorities on the same terms as in the first project.

Technical assistance financed through the scheme was designed, in line with the National Development Plan, to strengthen institutional capabilities of both central Government and local authorities in project implementation, organisation and financial management. Major areas covered include: consultancy services to assist the Government in restructuring of the relevant ministries and agencies; review of housing bye-laws; monitoring and evaluation; preparation of the third project and the establishment of a transportation planning unit in Nairobi City Council.

In brief, the Nairobi component of the Second Urban Project covers the following main aspects:

(a) Site and Services Plots - out of 11,770 plots to be financed under this scheme 9000 are to be located in Nairobi. These are spread in three main sites, Kayole, Mathare and Villa Franca.

(b) Settlement Upgrading - provision of basic infrastructure in three areas of unplanned and uncontrolled settlements, Mathare Valley, Riruta, and Baba Defo Area.

(c) Settlement Plots - preparation of about 2,500 surveyed plots with public water and sanitary facilities and unpaved roads. These plots would be used to cater for squatters displaced by upgrading activities in Mathare Valley. The standards stipulated in this component are extremely low and they have led to a controversy within the Council which is affecting the progress of the project.

(d) Community Facilities - provision of social education and health facilities, including nutrition and family planning support.

(e) Employment Opportunities - provision of commercial activities and small scale industries within the project areas.

(f) Housing and Improvement Loans - provision of housing loans for new housing construction, and extension of the terms of reference to cover house improvement in squatter upgrading areas.

There are major differences between the first and second projects in Nairobi. The number of site and service plots is much higher in the second project. These plots, unlike in Dandora, will not have any superstructure (including sanitary core) before allocation is made. This was done in order to allow maximum flexibility for self-help housing consolidation. Allottees are expected to build their own houses with increased material loans offered under the project. The settlement plot is an added innovation to take care of the squatter and low-income renting families dislocated by upgrading activities in Mathare Valley. These groups of people represent the very poor stratum of Nairobi's population.

In the first project an attempt was made at cross-subsidisation through market sale of plots, but the number of plots reserved for this purpose (300) was too low to make any impact on allottees repayments. The number of market sale plots has been increased considerably. While the surplus realised in the sale of these plots will be used for cross-subsidisation in Mombasa and Kisumu, in Nairobi it will be utilised in creating a separate housing fund for construction of more housing units. Thus the project will fund the construction of the first phase and preparation of the second phase of a four year programme. In the other towns the market sale plots will be financed fully by the project.

The second project, accepted the main recommendation of the study of the Council's housing operations, namely to provide the basis for setting up new Housing Development Departments patterned after the Dandora Project Department. The department has the same status within each city council as other departments. Dandora Project Department formed the nucleus of the new department into which it was merged. Manpower skills required by the department in the implementation and management of the project will be provided on a full-time basis. In future the department will be the principal agency through which the city will design and implement low-income housing developments. Its role therefore will be expanded to include all housing development activities of the Council. Management of completed housing will still remain the responsibility of the Social Services Department.

SELF-HELP BUILDING: THE UNTAPPED RESERVOIR

The Dandora sites and services project is remarkable not only in the way it attempts to bridge the gap between shelter needs and planned housing production, and influenced subsequent urban projects, but in the manner in which it recognised the resourcefulness of poor urban communities and managed the formation and operation of supportive social networks, especially mutual self-help building groups among the low-income former residents of squatters areas.

The Dandora settlers were selected from within families earning between Shs.280-650 per month, ie. within the second quintile of the income scale. The Council planned and prepared the plots. The on-plot development consisted of a sanitary core (toilet and shower) for type A plots and a sanitary core plus one room for type B. They were required to construct an additional room for type B or two rooms for type A within a period of 18 months using a building materials loan of Shs.2880 (Shs.3200 in Phase II) per room provided by the project. In addition the project provided technical assistance, supervision and help with community development to guide the settlement of allottees and the consolidation process.

The materials loan is available to all allottees on application, and disbursed in stages after a certain amount of construction work is completed and valued. Thus an allottee is required to have some capital to start off otherwise

he would not be able to commence construction and draw his
materials loan entitlement. The building groups were formed
therefore to enable the poorer allottees to pool their meagre
resources to develop their plots. To facilitate the operation
of these groups, members were given preference in releasing
the initial instalment of the materials loans.

Building groups were formed on the initiative of the
Community Development Division of the project unit. The idea
is based on the traditional African mutual help practice
prevalent in the rural villages but modified to suit urban
conditions. In this case, the groups are not based on common
backgrounds of origin, ethnicity, religious affiliation or
prior social contacts. This is more so in Phase I of the
project since allottees who had been selected on random basis
from applicants from the whole city had very little time to
make contacts. The groups were therefore formed during the
orientation meetings which were organised by the community
development officers. In Phase II, however, there are cases
of groups formed whose members are either employees of the
same company or resided in the same squatter area, eg.
Mathare Valley. Even in such instances, ethnicity has not
been a factor. This Development in Phase II is explained by
the long delay in settling the allottees who actually were
selected in 1976 but started to be settled on their plots in
1980. In these cases the groups were formed prior to the
allottees taking possession of their plots.

All building groups are legal entities registered under
the Societies Act and all have a legal constitution. A fee
of Shs.20 is payable for registration to the Registrar of
Societies. These groups are voluntary and members join after
realising the advantages of group association. The size of
the group is not limited but small groups are preferred as
they are manageable. There is an added advantage in that it
would not be an unnecessarily long time before all group
members get their houses constructed. In Dandora the size of
the group membership ranges between 10 and 16 persons.

In Phase I there are 15 groups with a total membership
of 158 which is approximately 16% of all the allottees in
this Phase. The department is in the process of group formation in Phase II and 12 groups with membership of 102 have
been formed and are in operation. Experience in Phase I does
show that there are more female allottee members (58%) than
males (42%). This sex composition of the groups may be attributed to the fact that many females are unemployed or
self-employed in the informal sector and that their incomes

are generally low relative to their male counterparts. Thus group membership would improve their chances of completing their houses and in addition they tend to have ample time to participate in meetings and actual development of their plots.

Each group elects its office bearers in accordance with the constitution. They hold meetings regularly every month and decisions are made by the group as a whole. In exceptional cases, office bearers can make decisions on behalf of the groups after consultation with some members and the departmental staff.

All groups are assigned to a member of the community development staff who is expected to work very closely with the groups. The role of such staff is as follows:

- assistance in registration of the group with the Registrar of Societies
- assistance in management of their monthly contributions and materials loans
- training of group leaders in leadership skills, record maintenance and simple book-keeping
- assist in the day to day management of their affairs
- attendance of group meetings and rendering advice on matters under discussion
- helping in purchasing of materials and giving advice and guidance.

The groups, like all other allottees, receive technical advice from the department. This includes selection of a suitable type plan, fitting the plan on site, setting out the building including advice and supervision during construction. The community development officer in charge of the group is also very much involved in this process.

Although materials loans are advanced by the project, the labour is expected to be provided by the allottees or hired by them at their own cost. Since the loan given is not sufficient to cover the full cost of material, and extra money is required to pay for the labour, the group members made monthly contributions to a collective fund. These contributions are based on the estimated building cost as well as the ability of members to pay. In practice contributions range between Shs.50 and Shs.150 per month. There have been instances where groups have decided to lower the level of their contributions which had been set at a level that they could not sustain. Group members are expected to supervise

construction work on their own plots. This means that employed group members would have to take leave during construction on their own plot. In a few cases in Phase I group
members provided unskilled labour but many allottees have not
been able to do so for a variety of reasons. Hired labour
therefore has been extensively used. Current daily rates
range between Shs.20-30 per day for unskilled labour and
Shs.50-60 per day for skilled artisans. In spite of these
costs it was found a more effective method. However, the
member whose plot would be under construction provides the
organisation, management, supervision, selection, and purchasing of the necessary materials.

As indicated above, the number of allottees organised in
groups is relatively small. However, their performance in
general is much better than in the project as a whole. By
the middle of 1979 a total of Shs.250,000 had been contributed by group members. A total of 244 rooms out of 257
planned had been completed. This represents approximately
95% success rate and compares favourably with the overall
Phase I completion rate of 75% at the same time. All of the
groups are on their way to completion and several did complete the initial development (at least two rooms) within the
stipulated period of 18 months. In terms of cost the groups
have done very well. They rank together with individual
allottees and are far ahead of contractor built units in this
respect.

In addition to advantages cited above, groups have provided a very good base for fostering community cohesion and
spirit. Members get to know one another well and friendships
are developed into other forms of cooperation. A clear manifestation of this fact is that many of these members have
continued some form of cooperation after completion of their
planned house construction, eg. group monthly contributions
which are given to members in rotation.

The performance by groups is indeed satisfactory and has
enabled poor allottees to complete their houses. In spite of
many advantages which this approach offers to low-income
families, it is surprising that only a small number of allottees have shown an interest in forming groups. This can be
attributed to a number of reasons some of which have been
observed in Dandora. These include:

(a) Allocation was confined to people with an income either
     from wage employment or business operation including the
     informal sector. Time available for housing construction
     was very scarce.

(b) Failure by some members to contribute regularly mainly
     due to their meagre and irregular income.

(c) Management of completed units by owners hence depriving
     the group of the income derived from renting. Of late
     the groups require that the completed units be managed
     by the groups and not by individuals.

(d) Differences in plans and site characteristics which
     meant groups had to spend unequal amounts in developing
     individual plots.

(e) Internal conflicts arising from (b), (c) and (d) above.

(f) Poor management provided by mainly untrained and inex-
     perienced allottees. There is need for the department to
     move beyond their advisory role and provide the manage-
     ment skills that the group cannot provide, eg. finance,
     records, etc. Training of group members should be in-
     tensified and the department staff should try to win the
     confidence of group members.

(g) Misuse of group funds by their elected officials. This
     can be avoided if the department's involvement in man-
     agement of groups is extended.

The building groups in Dandora represent the first large
scale experiment of this kind in the country. Although a
wide measure of success has been achieved improvements need
to be made in light of experience gained. In particular
management of group operations and finances require streamlining through greater direct involvement of the project
department. Groups should retain their decision-making
powers and should continue to run their affairs on a day to
day basis otherwise initiative and drive may be seriously
impaired. The department is reviewing the progress of these
groups with a view to strengthening them and making them
effective tools for development and improvement of the environment in general.

Nairobi, like many cities in the developing world, has
adopted the sites and services approach as a major element of
their housing policy. Experience has shown that this combined
with aided self-help greatly enhances the effectiveness of
low-income housing programmes. It successfully combines
private and public resourcefulness. In particular it taps
private capital and provides incentives for savings by the
lower income groups. These are resources which otherwise
would not have been deployed towards improved housing. There
is conclusive evidence especially in Dandora that individual
families are able to acquire housing cheaper through this
approach than any other.

The approach has much promise and therefore efforts to
improve it should be intensified. The few problems experienced can be resolved and should not be used as an excuse for
discontinuing with this experiment. In planning of projects,
this approach should be incorporated as a central feature
with assurance that standards, building designs and procedures, etc. are simple enough to enable relatively unskilled and inexperienced group members to cope with them.
The potential of the system is wide and is capable of being
developed into a major housing movement for low-income
groups. This is therefore a challenge to housing planners,
administrators and policymakers.

THE WAY FORWARD

Nairobi entered the 1980's confronted with many problems
and issues. The prospects for the foreseeable future are not
very bright. The overall rate of inflation currently stands
at 15% pa and in the construction sector it is estimated at
25% pa. A city whose revenue base is not expanding at such
rates is therefore bound to have severe difficulties. The
Council, as a matter of necessity, is required to devise
rational policies and programmes in order to contain the
situation. Although in the late seventies some progress was
made in this direction it was not enough.

The national planning machinery has recognised the need
to slow down the growth of major urban centres including
Nairobi. In an attempt to reduce the level of migration to
these centres, the Government has adopted a policy of rural
development. This calls for intensification of agriculture,
expansion of arable land by irrigation and provision of ser-

vices in certain designated market centres. Industries that are agro-based are encouraged to locate in the rural areas. By raising rural incomes and by improvement in accessibility to services it is hoped that more people will be encouraged to remain in the rural areas. Associated with this is the policy of development of secondary towns which would take some population that would otherwise go to Nairobi. The fact that the rate of population increase for Nairobi appears to be declining may be true but the numbers that come to the city are still very high and need to be provided for.

Although there is awareness of the issues confronting the city at the local level, official response requires a great deal of streamlining. The local administrative machinery needs to be restructured in order to enhance planning. Overall planning is haphazard, a fact which is attributable to lack of a central planning and coordinating unit. In a situation where needs far exceed the resources available such a unit would be of immense value. The role of such a unit would be:

i   to monitor the growth of the city and provide the necessary information and statistics required by decision makers.

ii to assess the needs of the city and to identify resources required to meet them.

iii to formulate appropriate policies and programmes that are consistent with resources available.

iv to propose projects within agreed policies and programmes and to prepare briefs for the design of these projects.

v   to monitor and evaluate these policies and programmes and constantly adjust them in the light of experience.

vi to set targets that must be achieved and prepare the required development budgets.

vii to order priorities for the city both between various sectors and between specific projects.

The central planning and coordinating unit advocated here should be a permanent feature of local authority struc-

ture and should be placed very high in the administrative
hierarchy. It will ensure that planning is carried out on a
comprehensive and continuous basis and that resources are
allocated in a rational manner. Interdepartmental rivalries
will be avoided and decisions will be rationalised thus ensuring effectiveness. Emphasis should be placed on the provision of housing in a way which is not limited to shelter
only but is extended to cover the associated community facilities for education, health, recreation and well-being.

A realistic housing programme must fully recognise the
scarcity of resources which is critical to its success. It
must be based on the principles of affordability (people's
ability to pay) and replicability (the generation of sur-
pluses to be used for financing new projects). The basic
objective of such a programme would be to spread the benefits
to the maximum number of people so that lower income groups
will not be placed at a disadvantage vis-a-vis the higher
income groups.

In the past housing constructed was of a very high standard, hence relatively costly. This meant that it could not
be afforded by a vast majority of the city's population, and
especially low income families. Such housing ended up being
subdivided but this did not succeed in eliminating the disparity. Besides the increase in housing stock was very low.
As a matter of policy the authorities must emphasise full
cost recovery to ensure that the available funds are recircu-
lated to the benefit of all.

To be able to recover the cost, housing must be designed
to standards that can be afforded by any of the target population. Standards therefore must be modest and appropriate
for the respective groups. They must also be capable of
being improved over time.

As housing problems impact more on the low income group
public action should give high priority to this sector.
Assuming that the private sector will be encouraged to provide for higher income groups, then site and service programmes including aided self-help should be the main thrust
of our housing implementation policy. This approach has
definite advantages and has proved effective in a number of
countries. It must be realised that this will not solve
housing problems overnight and therefore attempts must be
made to preserve as many of the existing units as possible.

In line with this policy demolition of squatter settlements should be replaced with a policy of progressive improvement of existing structures and environments.

For aided self-help and sites and services schemes to succeed there must be full participation of the affected groups. There are problems of their participation at the planning stage but full and effective participation can be ensured during construction stages without any problems. Effective community participation is achieved when strong and close social ties are created and the attitudes and traditions of the people are taken into account. Community development officers have an important role to play in creating social cohesion. In addition, the level of technology and procedures required must be simple so that they can be mastered by fairly unskilled populations.

To make a major impact in the field of housing, more resources will have to be channelled to this sector. The Urban Study Group reported that capital investment in housing was about 3.3% of Nairobi's GDP in 1971. If the estimated need was to be met the level of investment would have to be raised to 7.25%. In order to achieve this level of investment all sources of finance must be tapped. These include direct government financing, private financial institutions and investment, credit unions and, above all, informal sector resources.

Administration and management are important factors which are often ignored. A sound administrative structure, adequately staffed with skilled and experienced personnel, ensures efficiency and eliminates costly delays. Development and strengthening of institutions should therefore be accorded high priority.

High unemployment and underemployment together with meagre and unstable incomes are still major problems; and the prospects of substantially raising the incomes of the bottom sector of the population remain bleak. However, further deterioration of the situation can be arrested by pursuing a pragmatic industrialisation policy. Such a policy should give priority to labour-intensive industries which have the potential of substantially increasing employment. In addition the recommendation by the ILO/UNDP Employment Mission to Kenya (1972) that the informal sector should be promoted and encouraged should be vigorously pursued. This recommendation,

although accepted by Government, has not been translated into
a programme of action. The Council is very well placed in
promotion of the informal sector through the sponsorship of
appropriate local industries and possibly providing a market
for their products directly linked with housing development.

LESSONS FROM EXPERIENCE SHARED

    Nairobi's experience does illustrate the evolution of
housing policy through trial and error. Nairobi has experimented with a number of approaches to housing without being
able to come to grips with the problem. Frustrations arising
out of failure in meeting the challenge persuaded a reluctant
City Council to adopt a site and service approach. While
this approach is not a panacea to the city's housing problem,
it provides an answer to the low-income population. Through
this method meagre public finances are made to provide for a
relatively large number of people. Private resources are
mobilised through self-help, thus bringing housing within
reach of those at the bottom of the income scale.

    The projects have forced the city to review its adminis-
trative structure and make improvements. In particular, the
creating of the Housing Development Department has stream-
lined implementation of housing projects. The staffing of
the department and the new committee structure has eliminated
bottlenecks in the implementation process. The Government
has also been forced to pay greater attention to the problems
of local authorities especially in the field of finance. The
World Bank has played a major role in this change of attitude.

    In the past the Council housing programme concerned
itself with the provision of shelter. Community services
were never conceived as a necessary part of housing development. It was not uncommon to have houses completed and
occupied before any consideration was given for schools,
health centres, etc. In the site and services programme
these services were considered an essential part of a housing
scheme and the necessary finance was provided.

    For a long time the Council had a negative attitude
towards unplanned and squatter settlements. A policy of
demolition of such settlements was pursued even though this
had no effect on their growth. The policy is now sympathetic

towards these settlements and the emphasis has shifted from demolition to upgrading. The second project has allocated a fair proportion of finances for this purpose.

The emphasis has rightly been placed on low-income popu-lations. Public funds are to be channelled to this sector while the private sector is to be entrusted with the pro-vision of housing for medium and high-income groups. In the higher income housing sector, market forces influence costs much more so than in the low-income housing provided by the public bodies. There is the danger therefore that housing may become too expensive for the higher income groups forcing them to take housing intended for the low-income families. There are signs that this is beginning to happen to Nairobi.

The real threat is that the policy may produce ghettos where the low-income population is confined to these large site and service areas. The Council is aware of this possi-bility and therefore the introduction market sale plots and deliberate reservation of land for higher income groups in project areas is intended to attract people of higher income.

Nairobi's experience may have certain weaknesses but it has something to offer to cities in a similar situation. The experience is transferable and can be easily adapted to a variety of administrative systems. Comments from visitors are very encouraging and indeed some countries in Africa have sent their experts to learn from our experience. We have also sent people to observe management of projects in other countries. In this respect therefore Nairobi has become a part of an information exchange and experience sharing net-work.

REFERENCES

Bibliography on Human Settlements, with Emphasis on House-
        holds and Residential Environment - Kenya, compiled by
        Carin Boalt, Suzanne Grant Lewis and Dorothy Myers,
        Housing Research and Development Unit, University of
        Nairobi, Kenya; Department of Building Function Analy-
        sis, School of Architecture, University of Lund,
        Sweden, Document D13 (1982).
East Africa Royal Commission 1953-55 Report, HMSO London
        (1955).

Peter Gutkind, Social Organisation of Unemployed in Lagos and
    Nairobi, in "African Social Studies: A Radical
    Reader," P. Gutkind and P. Waterman, eds., Heinemann,
    London (1977).
Andrew Hake, "African Metropolis: Nairobi's Self-Help City,"
    Chatto and Windus for Sussex University Press, London
    (1977).
Human Settlements in Kenya, A Strategy for Urban and Rural
    Development, Physical Planning Department, Ministry of
    Lands and Settlement, Nairobi, Kenya (1978).
International Bank for Reconstruction and Development,
    "Appraisal of a Site and Service Project-Kenya," World
    Bank, IBRD Report No. 607a-KE, Washington DC.
International Labour Organisation, Employment, Incomes and
    Equality: A Strategy for Increasing Productive Employ-
    ment in Kenya, ILO, Geneva (1972).
M S Muller, Local Authority Housing in Kenya, Housing
    Research and Development Unit, University of Nairobi,
    Kenya, Dec (1979).
Nairobi Metropolitan Growth Strategy, Nairobi Urban Study
    Group, Town Planning Section, Nairobi City Council, 2
    vols. (1973).
Nairobi's Housing Needs: Meeting the Challenge, A Report to
    Nairobi City Council, April 1976, Coopers and Lybrand
    Associates Limited in association with Institute of
    Local Government Studies, University of Birmingham, 3
    vols.
Republic of Kenya, Ministry of Economic Planning and
    Community Affairs, Development Plan 1979-1983, Govern-
    ment Printer, Nairobi (1979).
United Nations Mission to Kenya on Housing, Prepared for the
    Government of Kenya, by Lawrence N. Bloomberg and
    Charles Abrams, United Nations, Commission for Techni-
    cal Assistance, Department of Economic and Social
    Affairs, Printed by the Government of Kenya, Dec
    (1964).
World Bank, Kenya Staff Appraisal Report, Second Urban
    Project, Urban Projects Department, World Bank,
    Washington DC (1978).

APPENDIX

MODEL CONSTITUTION FOR BUILDING GROUPS
Dandora Project, Nairobi, Kenya

1 NAME

The name of the society shall be.................
(in this constitution referred to as "the society")

2 OBJECTS (to be stated)

3 MEMBERSHIP

a) Any allottee in Phase 1 of Dandora Scheme over
the age of eighteen years shall, be eligible for
membership of the society and shall, subject to
the approval of the committee, become a member on
payment of an entrance fee of Sh.........

b) Every member shall pay a monthly subscription of
Sh........ not later than the 15th day of each
month.

c) Any member desiring to resign from the society
shall submit his resignation to the secretary,
which shall take effect from the date of receipt
by the secretary of such notice, subject to the
approval of the group and there being no
financial loss to the group.

d) Any member may be expelled from membership if the
Committee so recommends and if a general meeting
of the society shall resolve by a two-thirds
majority of the members present that such a
member should be expelled on the grounds that his
conduct has adversely affected the reputation or
dignity of the society, or that he has contra-
vened any of the provisions of constitution of
the society. The Committee shall have power to
suspend a member from his membership until the
next general meeting of the society following
such suspension but not withstanding such suspension a member whose expulsion is proposed shall
have the right to address the general meeting at
which his expulsion is to be considered.

e)   Any person who resigns or is removed from member-
     ship shall not be entitled to a refund of his
     subscription or any part thereof or any monies
     contributed by him at any time.

f)   Any member who falls into arrears with his
     monthly subscription for more than two months
     shall automatically cease to be a member of the
     society and his name shall be struck off the
     register of members. The committee may, however,
     at its discretion, reinstate such member on pay-
     ment of the total amount of subscription out-
     standing.

4   OFFICE BEARERS

a)   The office bearers of the society shall be:-
     (indicate)

     all of whom shall be members of the society and
     shall be elected at the annual general meeting to
     be held in each year (see also rule 6b below).

b)   All office bearers shall hold office from the
     date of election until the succeeding annual
     general meeting subject to the conditions con-
     tained in sub-paragraphs c and d of this rule but
     shall be eligible for re-election.

c)   Any office bearer who ceases to be a member of
     the society shall automatically cease to be an
     office bearer thereof.

d)   Office bearers may be removed from office in the
     same way as is laid down for the expulsion of
     members in rule 3d and vacancies thus created
     shall be filled by persons elected at the general
     meeting resolving the expulsion.

5   DUTIES OF OFFICE BEARERS

a)   Chairman - The Chairman shall, unless prevented
     by illness or other sufficient cause, preside
     over all meetings of the committee and at all
     general meetings.

b)   Vice-Chairman - The Vice-Chairman shall perform
        any duties of the Chairman in his absence.

c)   Secretary - the Secretary shall deal with all the
        correspondence of the society under the general
        supervision of the Committee. In cases of urgent
        matters where the committee cannot be consulted,
        he shall consult the Chairman or if he is not
        available, the Vice-Chairman. The decisions
        reached shall be subject to ratification or
        otherwise at the next committee meeting. He
        shall issue notices convening all meetings of the
        society and shall be responsible for keeping
        minutes of all such meetings and for the preser-
        vation of all records of proceedings of the
        society and of the committee.

d)   Treasurer - The Treasurer shall receive and shall
        also disburse, under the directions of the com-
        mittee all monies belonging to the society and
        shall issue receipts for all monies received by
        him and preserve vouchers for all monies paid to
        him. The treasurer is responsible to the commit-
        tee and to the members that proper books of
        account of all monies received and paid by the
        society are written up, preserved and available
        for inspection.

6   THE COMMITTEE

a)   The Committee shall consist of all the office
        bearers of the society and........ other mem-
        bers elected at the annual general meeting in
        each year: such committee members shall hold
        office until the following general meeting. The
        committee shall meet at such times and places as
        it shall resolve but shall meet not less than
        once in any three months.

b)   Any casual vacancies for members of the committee
        caused by death or resignation shall be filled by
        the committee until the next annual general meet-
        ing of the society. Vacancies caused by members
        of the committee removed from office will be
        dealt with as shown in rule 4d.

7   DUTIES OF THE COMMITTEE

a)   The Committee shall be responsible for the man-
        agement of the society and for that purpose may
        give directions to the office bearers as to the
        manner in which within the law, they shall per-
        form their duties. The committee shall have
        power to appoint sub sub-committees as it may
        deem desirable to make reports to the committee
        upon which such action shall be taken as seems to
        the committee desirable.

b)   All monies disbursed on behalf of the society
        shall be authorised by the committee except as
        specified in rule 12d.

c)   The quorum for meetings of the committee shall be
        not less than............ members.

8   GENERAL MEETINGS

a)   There shall be two classes of general meetings –
        annual general meetings and special general meet-
        ings.

b) i   The annual general meeting shall be held not
        later than..................... in each year.
        Notice in writing of such annual general meeting,
        accompanied by the annual statement of account
        (see rule 11b and the agenda for the meeting
        shall be sent to all members not less than 21
        days before the date of the meeting and, where
        practicable, press advertisement not less than 14
        days before the date of the meeting.

   ii   The agenda for any annual general meeting shall
        consist of the following:

        a) Confirmation of the minutes of the previous
           annual general meeting.

        b) Consideration of the accounts.

        c) Election of office bearers and the committee
           members.

      d) Such other matter as the committee may decide or as to which notice shall have been given in writing by a member or members to the secretary at least four weeks before the date of the meeting.

      e) Any other business with the approval of the Chairman.

c)   A special general meeting may be called for any specific purpose by the committee. Notice in writing of such meeting shall be sent to all members not less than 7 days before the date thereof and where practicable by press advertisement not less than 7 days before the date of such meeting.

d)   Quorum for general meetings shall be not less than....... of the registered members of the society.

9   PROCEDURE AT MEETINGS

a)   At all meetings of the society the Chairman, or in his absence, the Vice-Chairman, or in the absence of both these officers, a member selected by the meeting shall take the Chair.

b)   The Chairman may at his discretion limit the number of persons permitted to speak in favour of or against any motion.

c)   Resolutions shall be decided by simple voting by a show of hands. In the case of quality of votes, the Chairman shall have a second or casting vote.

10   AUDITOR

Community Development Staff responsible for the group will be inspecting the books at least once a month.

11   FUNDS

a)   The funds of the society may only be used for the following purposes: (indicate)

b)   All monies and funds shall be received by and
        paid to the Treasurer and shall be deposited by
        him in the name of the society in any bank or
        banks approved by the committee within 2 days.

c)   No payments shall be made out of the bank account
        without a resolution of the committee authorising
        such payment and all cheques on such bank account
        shall be signed by the Treasurer or the Assistant
        Treasurer and two other office bearers of the
        society who shall be appointed by the committee.

d)   A sum not exceeding Sh.100 may be kept by the
        Treasurer for petty disbursements of which proper
        account shall be kept.

e)   The committee shall have power to suspend any
        office bearer who it has reasonable cause to
        believe is not properly accounting for any of the
        funds or property of the society and shall have
        power to appoint another person in his place.
        Such suspension shall be reported to a general
        meeting to be convened on a date not later than
        two months from the date of such suspension and
        the general meeting shall have full power to
        decide what further action should be taken in the
        matter.

        The financial year of the society shall be
        from..........

12   AMENDMENTS TO THE CONSTITUTION

     Amendments to the constitution of the society must be
     approved by at least a two-thirds majority of members at
     a general meeting of the society. They cannot, however,
     be implemented without the prior consent in writing of
     the Registrar, obtained upon application to him made in
     writing and signed by three of the office bearers.

13   DISSOLUTION

     a)   The society shall not be dissolved except by a
             resolution passed at a general meeting of members
             by a vote of two-thirds of the members present.
             The quorum at the meeting shall be shown in rule

8e. If no quorum is obtained, the proposal to dissolve the society shall be submitted to a further general meeting which shall be held one month later. Notice of this meeting shall be given to all members of the society at least 14 days before the date of the meeting. The quorum for this second meeting shall be the number of members present.

b) Provided, however, that no dissolution shall be effected without prior permission in writing of the Registrar, obtained upon application to him made in writing and signed by three of the office bearers.

c) When the dissolution of the society has been approved by the Registrar, no further action shall be taken by the committee or any office bearer of the society in connection with the aims of the society other than to get in and liquidate for cash all the assets of the society. Subject to the payment of all the debts of the society, the balance thereof shall be distributed in such other manner as may be resolved by the meeting at which the resolution for dissolution is passed.

14 INSPECTION OF ACCOUNTS AND LIST OF MEMBERS

The books of account and all documents relating thereto and a list of members of the society shall be available for inspection at the registered office of the society by any officer or member of the society on giving not less than seven days notice in writing to the society. (This rule applies to registered societies only).

15 MEMBERS RESPONSIBILITY TO HIS/HER PLOT

a) It shall be the members responsibility to be paying the City Council all monetary charges until the society shall have finished two rooms (which include the kitchen) ready for renting in the month following after completion.

b) The society shall not undertake any development in a members plot who may be in any outstanding arrears, either to the City Council or to the

society. In case this happens to any member, the
society shall have to develop the next member's
plot in the list. If the member so affected
however clears the arrears, the society shall
start the development after finishing the plot
currently under construction at the time of
payment of the said arrears.

16   SURRENDERING OF THE PLOT TO THE SOCIETY FOR RENTING

On the society's wish to start development of the rooms
in a member's plot, the member shall be called upon to
surrender his/her plot identity card to the society.
The society shall hand over the card to the Community
Development Officer in charge, who shall be the custod-
ian of the card on behalf of the society. The card
shall be kept in the Community Development Offices of
the City Council's Housing Development Department. This
process shall continue until all the members shall have
benefited equally from the society. The rent collected
from the plots shall be used in paying monthly charges
for the plots and the balances shall be added to
society's finance.

On doing this the member shall sign an agreement form to
this effect in presence of at least 3 society officials
and the CD officer in-charge.

17   LOANS ENTITLEMENT AND COLLECTION

Any materials loan entitled to every member's plot shall
belong to the society. The society shall collect this
money whenever it may wish, after reaching mature stages
of construction which may warrant collection provided it
shall be used only in developing members' plots.

18   MEMBERS AVAILABILITY

Any society's member shall be availing himself/herself
to the society and to the Council, when required from
time to time to sign:

1 Application for a plan
2 Application for loan when needed by society plus
3 Any other duty the member would be required to do on
   behalf of the society in connection with the members'
   plots.

19* PLOT DEVELOPMENT SUCCEEDING ORDER

    a)   Ballot position sequence to determine who would get a plot earlier than the other. The society shall follow the same procedure in determining the order of succession in developing the members' plots.

or

    b)   All the members shall be called upon to conduct a secret ballot method to determine the order of succession.

* delete either a or b whichever is not applicable.

Lusaka: Management and institution-building for squatter upgrading

David Pasteur

INTRODUCTION

Lusaka and its large-scale squatter upgrading and site and services project provide one example of the growing acceptance during the 1970's of a range of aided self-help housing strategies and policies directed at dealing with the problems of urban growth in developing countries. The broad context involves a major public sector project, undertaken with shared external financing by the World Bank and local community participation, which offered the hope of improving living conditions for large numbers of people and reducing the backlog of housing and services provision.

Recognising that the formulation of appropriate strategies and policies at the international or nation levels does not guarantee successful implementation on the ground, this brief report focuses on a "neglected factor" in the preparation of plans and projects, namely the municipal management of project implementation, a crucial problem area responsible for so much of the gap between objectives or aspirations and the final results.

The Importance of Management

It is hardly necessary to stress the importance of management especially as it relates to the implementation and delivery of projects and programmes, in order to meet massive and urgent needs. The end objectives of management can be summarised as efficiency (output), effectiveness (impact on objectives and clientele), integration of functions and delivery systems (internal and external coordination) and responsiveness to and partnership with the community (participation).

Institution-Building

Successful completion of projects is only one reason for the concern with management. Increasingly it is realised that the institutions and systems of management must be improved for the longer term beyond the life of the immediate project into continuing programmes and that this is one of the objectives of management.

Content of Management

The performance of a management system depends on three groups or clusters of factors:

i   Structural or organisational arrangements, roles, and relationships

ii   Management processes, procedures, techniques, operating systems, rules etc.

iii Organisational culture and values, management style, leadership, motivational factors.

The three sets are interrelated: account must be taken of all of them in discussing management, and progress must be made in all of them in improving management.

Responsibility for Management

The assumption tends to be that the public sector is responsible for management of human settlements projects and programmes. Yet in some cases the development of spontaneous settlements has been 'managed' by community structures and processes, and the public sector may be becoming newly involved as a partner, either major or minor. The Lusaka case is clearly one of a major public sector involvement with a high management content, but the management role of the community cannot be ignored, nor should the possibility of cases with a more even private/public sector balance be ignored.

Management Implications of Squatter Upgrading

What are the characteristics of the upgrading process
and environment which have implications for management? Some
of these characteristics are shared, at least to a degree by
other more conventional forms of human settlements development, but most are distinctive to upgrading. It is on this
distinction that the claim rests that squatter upgrading
calls for management arrangements (structure, procedures,
culture) that are different from conventional forms of municipal project and service management.

a) **Partnership in Management and Control.** Since the
settlement has been developed initially in an autonomous
fashion by the residents, the agency's involvement is external, and hence there emerges a partnership with the community
involving it in consultation and decision-making (management)
at most stages, as contrasted with a top-down intervention.

b) **Partnership in Physical Development.** Development action is a partnership with individuals and community groups
in house building and elements of infrastructure/community
services; this entails a particular type of extension activity, which must take account of the fact that involvement
is not optional as in a site and service scheme.

c) **Complexity and Uncertainty.** Due to the mixture and
interaction of physical, social, economic and financial components in project activity, and to the context of an established physical settlement (as opposed to a green-field
site), and an established social setting (as opposed to settlers moving individually to a new area), there are unusual
demands for coordination, and for an ability to respond to
uncertainty and change.

d) **Upgrading is Evolutionary and Continuous.** The development process has several components and stages each with
their own skill and staffing requirements, and the process
itself is not once-for-all, but continues or merges into the
maintenance phase incrementally both on physical and social
aspects.

Thus upgrading is an unconventional form of urban settlement development occurring in marginal areas of cities
usually on a large scale, in which the prospects of full
incorporation into the conventional city system of development and service provision are limited.

THE LUSAKA SQUATTER UPGRADING AND SITE AND SERVICES PROJECT

The project started implementation in 1974, and has provided basic infrastructure for the three largest squatter complexes totalling about 130,000 people or one third of the city, resettlement on adjacent overspill plots for those displaced by works, and housing improvement loans for those resettled and in existing settlements provided in kind through building materials stores. It has also developed 4,400 Site and Services plots at different standards: (the resettlement phase for these came after the study). It has provided schools, health centres, community centres, markets and small industry sites for these areas. Leasehold tenure is being granted. The project is jointly financed by the World Bank and the Government of Zambia.

It is also necessary to draw attention to the distinctive characteristics of the project and its environment so that its relevance to other situations can better be assessed:

- It is a large-scale project affecting one-third of the population of the capital city.
- It is a single-city project, not a nationwide one.
- It is a 'first project', at least as regards its main upgrading component, and therefore experimental.
- At the same time Zambia had in the early 1970's established a tradition of steady change in housing policy, and had quite extensive experience in site and services projects.
- Zambia is a one-party state, under UNIP (United National Independence Party), with intensive party organisation down to grass-roots level, especially in the squatter areas.
- Zambia has had a viable and stable system of urban local government.

Management Characteristics of the Lusaka Project

On what characteristics does the claim of the Lusaka project rest to be considered a successful example of management and institution-building? The management characteristics will first be summarised, and then assessed from the point of view of their long-term institution-building potential.

a) **Institutional Framework for Implementation.** Following pressure by the City Council, it was decided that implementation should be by a special Council Department, the Housing Project Unit (HPU), containing most of the necessary skills, and with minimal reliance on other departments (Fig. 1). HPU deals direct with the Council's Finance Committee, has generous staffing and certain preferential conditions of service, and the Director has delegated powers of appointment.

In a viable government system in a one-party state, association of the project with local government has been successful, and has enlisted the support of councillors. Responsibilities have been almost completely integrated in HPU; where initially they were separate they have brought problems. In the case of revenue collection this was taken over from the City Treasury: in the case of land acquisition this could not be taken over and was a continuous problem to the end of 1977.

d) **The Project Agency: Organisation, Staffing and Management.** With three Divisions, Engineering, Social Services and Finance and Procurement, HPU has given equal emphasis to the social/community activities as to physical/technical. Thus a traditional professional basis of divisions was used, but with a form of areal or field organisation at the second level (Fig. 2).

The main field staff cadres created were Community Development (CD) officers under Social Services drawn partly from the local government urban CD cadre at the senior level, but mainly newly recruited persons trained at the junior level, and Construction Advisers (Team Leaders and CA's) under Engineering drawn from building trades and local government, with initially no special training and with lower salary and status than the CD cadres. These cadres were specialised as to promotional/resettlement/self-help/community development work, and building advice and supervision respectively; but CD staff required knowledge of housing and building and CA staff had to be able to handle the social situation. It is arguable that a single cadre with different levels and training in all the skills would have been preferable. The CD cadre were latterly renamed Housing Officers. Specialised field cadres for stores management and revenue collection were also needed.

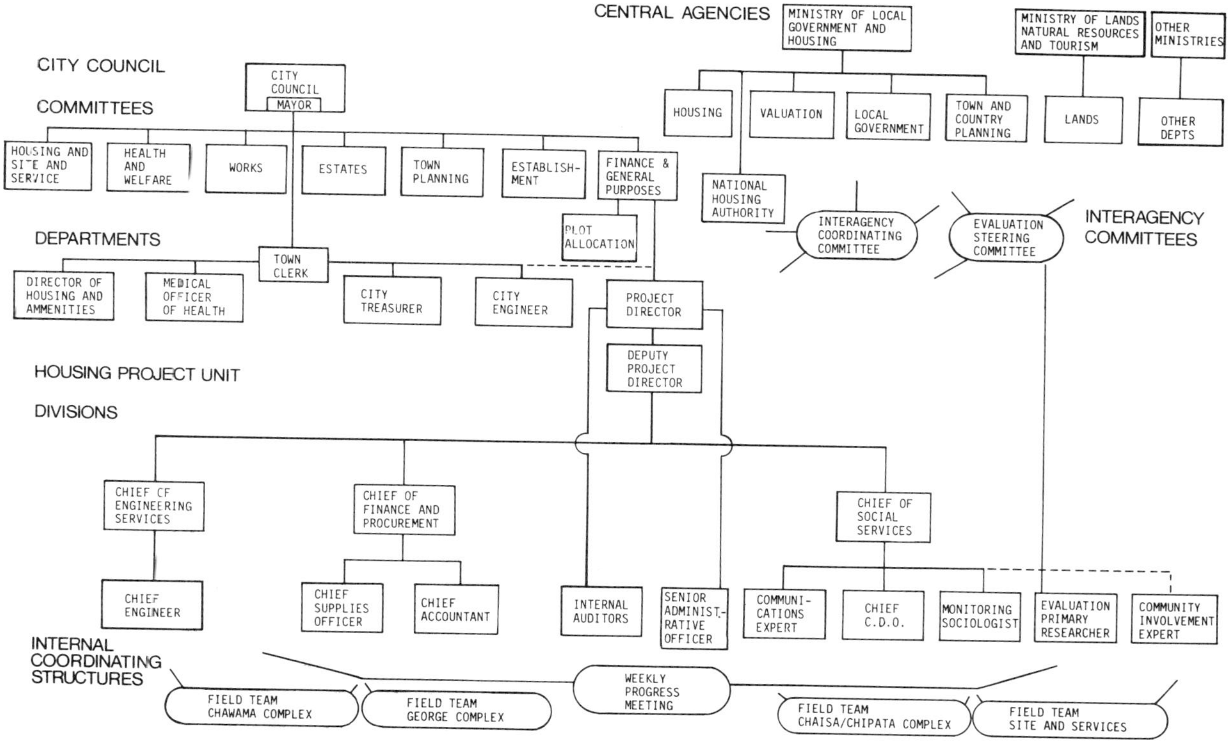

Fig. 1. Project Orangisation: City Council, Project Unit and Central Agencies. Source: Diagram supplied by the author from his book The Management of Squatter Upgrading, A case Study of Organisation, Procedures and Participation, Saxon House, Teakfield Ltd, England, 1979, pp.26-27.

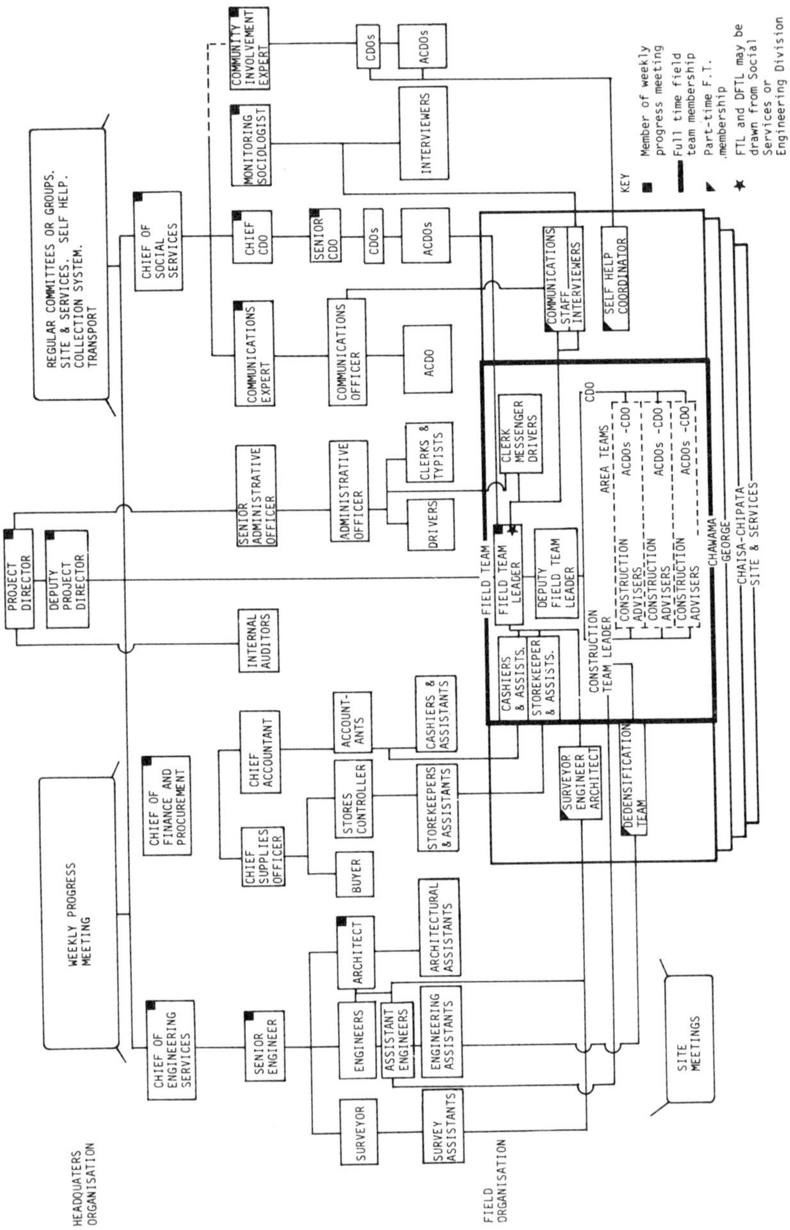

HEADQUATERS ORGANISATION

WEEKLY PROGRESS MEETING

PROJECT DIRECTOR

DEPUTY PROJECT DIRECTOR

CHIEF OF ENGINEERING SERVICES

CHIEF OF FINANCE AND PROCUREMENT

SENIOR ADMINISTRATIVE OFFICER

CHIEF OF SOCIAL SERVICES

REGULAR COMMITTEES OR GROUPS. SITE & SERVICES. SELF HELP. COLLECTION SYSTEM. TRANSPORT

COMMUNITY INVOLVEMENT EXPERT

MONITORING SOCIOLOGIST

CDOs

ACDOs

INTERVIEWERS

CHIEF CDO

SENIOR CDO

CDOs

ACDOs

COMMUNICATIONS EXPERT

COMMUNICATIONS OFFICER

ACDO

COMMUNICATIONS STAFF INTERVIEWERS

SELF HELP COORDINATOR

SENIOR ENGINEER

CHIEF ACCOUNTANT

INTERNAL AUDITORS

ADMINISTRATIVE OFFICER

CLERKS & TYPISTS

DRIVERS

CLERK MESSENGER DRIVERS

ENGINEERS

ACCOUNT-ANTS

CASHIERS & ASSISTANTS

FIELD TEAM LEADER

FIELD TEAM LEADER

DEPUTY FIELD TEAM LEADER

AREA TEAMS

ACDOs -CDO

ACDOs -CDO

ACDOs -CDO

ACDOs -CDO

CHIEF SUPPLIES OFFICER

ASSISTANT ENGINEERS

STORES CONTROLLER

CASHIERS & ASSISTS.

STOREKEEPER & ASSISTS.

CONSTRUCTION TEAM LEADER

CONSTRUCTION ADVISERS CONSTRUCTION ADVISERS CONSTRUCTION ADVISERS

CHAMAWA—GEORGE—CHAISA-CHIPATA—SITE & SERVICES

ARCHITECT

BUYER

STOREKEEPERS & ASSISTANTS

SURVEYOR ENGINEER ARCHITECT

DEDENSIFICATION TEAM

CDO

ENGINEERING ASSISTANTS

ARCHITECTURAL ASSISTANTS

SURVEYOR

SURVEY ASSISTANTS

FIELD ORGANISATION

SITE MEETINGS

KEY

■   Member of weekly progress meeting

—   Full time field team membership

----   Part-time F.T. membership

★   FTL and DFTL may be drawn from Social Services or Engineering Division

Fig. 2.   Project organisation: Project Unit internal structure.
Source: The Management of Squatter Upgrading, 1979, pp.28-29.

Field staffing was established at a level to match the scale of the project and the field staff of the three divisions tied together in a Field Team, based at a site office and with a Field Team Leader drawn from either Social Services or Engineering (usually the former), possessing authority to coordinate and control team members for operational purposes. There is a Field Team for each of the three upgrading complexes and for Site and Services. As the project developed, the Teams acquired identity and effectiveness in handling the implementation process in the field - mainly the communication, participation, resettlement, loan/stores and building supervision processes, but also coordination with the physical contract work, especially in its socially sensitive aspects where timing is important. The teams have lowered the 'centre of gravity' of the organisation with headquarters staff performing more of a supporting as opposed to a directing role.

A Weekly Progress Meeting was institutionalised for corporate coordination and progress monitoring. Initially limited to Division heads, it soon expanded to include most section heads and all the Field Team Leaders. A weekly meeting with a structured agenda scanning all aspects of the project fortnightly, and with a wide distribution of minutes has proved a very successful management device, the only disadvantage of which is the fact that it takes a full morning each week. Field Team meetings have been held fortnightly but there have still been weekly meetings of the main cadres in the team.

Note:

Though the original proposed project design, finalised by the World Bank, was detailed and specific in regard to such matters as the organisation of HPU, CD briefing procedures and training, nothing was said about management procedures, apart from the functions of monitoring and evaluation. An implicit assumption seems to have been made that management procedures are not a problem, and are readily available and adequate for the tasks of the organisation as soon as it starts to work. The HPU experience suggests that this is not the case; and the management process emerges in a much more trial and error method than the project itself. What in fact emerged was a management system which could or could not be seen as the product of a deliberate decision-making process about how a management system should work.

NATIONAL AGENCIES	CITY COUNCIL AND PROJECT UNIT	COMMUNITY

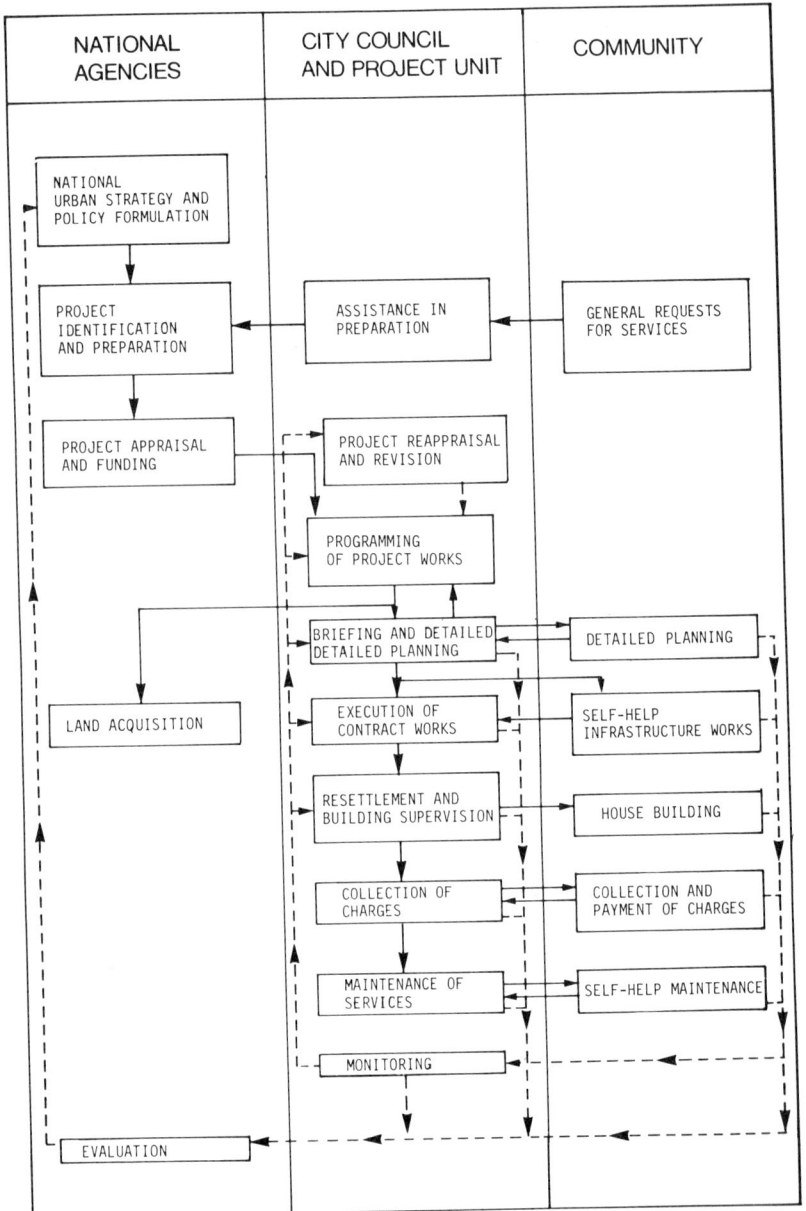

Fig. 3. Management sequences and feedback relationships.
Source: The Management of Squatter Upgrading, 1979,
p.3.

The management sequence and feedback relationships are illustrated in Fig. 3, in which the HPU's internal management processes appear in the central column.

An Inter-agency Coordinating Committee established at the beginning of the project never took root, and failed to assist in the crucial problem requiring coordination, namely land acquisition. The experience suggests that committees solve nothing unless special attention is paid to composition, leadership, purpose and powers.

HPU attempted a full-fledged Network Analysis at the beginning of the project, but was unsuccessful for two reasons: activity timings and interrelationships could not be forecast whilst doing things for the first time, and non-specialised or part-time borrowed specialist staff were not sufficient for the task. Simpler programming methods were then used for the community development/resettlement activities, but these did not integrate all elements of the project. It seemed unlikely that satisfactory programming techniques would develop unless there was a specialist on the staff (as there was for monitoring), and unless simpler and more flexible techniques were evolved. HPU were quite successful in developing simple work programming procedures for field staff to plan, jointly discuss, and review workload on a week to week basis.

c) Relationship Between the Community and the Project. HPU has given the highest possible priority to establishing a two-way relationship of communication and participation with the communities. Two types of community organisation were available with which it could deal, the official Ward Development Committees (WDC's) under the City Council, and the party machinery of UNIP. It was decided to use the latter because of its greater intensity of organisation at constituency, branch and section levels. WDC's performed only limited decision-making and ratification functions. Given the one-party system, the party structure is both pervasive and representative. The project has tended to strengthen and develop the role of the community and the party, and in later phases of the project the extent of consultation and decision-making has tended to increase.

HPU has employed an intensive method of briefing of leaders and participants at the three levels of party organisation in order to gain support for the project, largely

through oral communication supplemented by films, visual aids
and visits to completed phases of settlement. The process of
resettlement to overspill has also been highly organised and
closely supervised. The main structure for community decision-making has been the Road Planning Group (RPG), named
after its principal activity but also concerned with the
location of community facilities. An RPG was formed by each
main area, based mainly on the party leadership but including
representatives of other groups in some cases. A planning
methodology of Road Walks was evolved. Weekend planning
seminars were held to combine briefing and consultation
before the commencement of each complex. Lower level decisions, eg. on the layout of resettlement blocks and the
location of standpipes, have been made at section level. The
project has been instrumental in effecting a total revision
of party branch and section areas consequent on the movement
to overspill areas and the need to standardise the number of
families served by one standpipe. These procedures have
undoubtedly been staff-intensive and hence added to project
costs, but have been clear benefits in project effectiveness
and development of the communities. They have not apparently
caused any delay in the project because no physical contract
work has been held up because of them.

d) **Community Involvement in Implementation and Cost Recovery.** Contributions by the community to construction work
through 'mutual self-help' have been on a very minor scale,
and have not made a significant contribution to development
or cost savings, despite initial hopes to the contrary.

HPU took over cost recovery from the City Treasury after
early problems and created its own Collections Unit with
on-site cashiers, and incentive system to reward prompt payment, sanctions including turning off water supply and seeking the assistance of party section leaders to enforce payment. Early experience showed that recovery of materials
loans for which sanctions were lacking was less favourable
than for service charges, but in neither was a viable level
achieved.

Note:
    The estimated cost of the whole project, including the
larger Site and Services element, was in 1974 US $ 41.2m, of
which 48.5% was by loan from the World Bank and 51.5%
financed by the Government of Zambia. The principle of full
cost recovery by the City Council, without subsidy, at

interest rates comparable to mortgage rates has been adopted. Recovery includes all project components including project unit costs. Four methods of recovery were used:

i   Composite monthly service charge on beneficiaries cover-ing Site development costs at 7½% over 30 years, water charges, refuse collection charge, token sum for prop-erty rates (to be increased after 5 years) and 10% sur-charge against default.

ii   User charges for markets and community centres.

iii Building materials loan repayments at 7½% over 15 years.

iv   General city-wide property rate and personal taxation covering the project unit, and off side roads and street lighting.

Costs were allocated pro-rata to plot size in upgrading and site and services and there is no cross-subsidy. Elements covered by general rates entail a degree of cross-subsidy to project areas.

At the appraisal stage the project was expected to gen-erate a surplus for the City Council after 4 years, but pro-ject delays and collection shortfalls have affected this. There have been no community contributions to the project components apart from isolated instances of self-help trench digging, for which the financial value has been paid to the groups concerned, and a certain amount of market stall con-struction by cooperatives. Concerning the Project Agency, the cost of HPU was estimated to be 13.7% of project costs. Due to the extended period of execution this is likely to have risen.

THE INSTITUTION-BUILDING ACHIEVEMENT AND LESSONS OF EXPERIENCE

Lusaka is an example of the first-generation 'project' approach of the World Bank in the field of urban housing, in which it was assumed that a successful project would not only achieve project outputs but would also create new management systems. The institution-building objective was implicit rather than explicit. In retrospect the project can be as-sessed against four criteria:

a)   achievement of large-scale innovative development within
     a fairly short time-scale.

b)   the carry-over of that development into the continuing
     maintenance and further development stages.

c)   innovation and experimentation in management structures
     and procedures in the short term.

d)   long term and lasting improvements in management struc-
     tures and procedures (institution-building).

     The project has done well on a) and c) and less well on
b) and d). It is now quite fashionable to say that the project approach is self-defeating and is not the right way to
combine institution-building with project achievement. There
would appear to be a choice between the objectives of rapid
project achievement and institution-building. In the one
case the targets are achieved, but there remains a severe
problem of transition to maintenance and the next stage of
development. In the other there is a more firmly-based
institutional development, but targets are likely to take
significantly longer to achieve. Rapid development matching
the growth of cities is thus inconsistent with institution-
building.

     Before coming down on the side of the second alternative
and concluding that in the longer term HPU is likely to prove
a failure, let us have a closer look at the experience, both
during the project development phase, and at the current
handover to maintenance phase to see whether there is not a
'middle way'.

Project Development Phase

     HPU became more distinct and separated from the main
City Council than was probably intended at the design stage.
There was less secondment of city council staff, and fewer
functions were handled by the main Council departments than
expected. These could probably have been dispensed with,
though not those relating to personnel. Close attention was
given to the approach of the handover phase from 1977 on-
wards, but this had to bridge a gap which by then had opened
wider than it need have done.

The Handover Phase

As the end of the project period approached in 1979-80, the Council had to confront the issue of organisation for maintenance and further development, and has now made two significant structural responses.

The first is the Kalingalinga Project Unit in the Department of Housing and Social Services, which results from the Council's wish in 1977 to initiate upgrading in another settlement, following the example of HPU, but using the regular departmental machinery. Staff and operating methods have been taken over from HPU and are working within most of the constraints of the Council's structure and procedures, though with some special arrangements for decision-making and control.

The second is the Periurban Section of the Department of Housing and Social Services. Rather than absorbing HPU field staff into the regular sections of the department, an area-based section for upgrading and site and services areas has been created into which the four Field Teams have been absorbed ie. the housing/community development building advisory staff. The level of staffing recognises the need for continuing development as well as maintenance and revenue collection. Purely physical maintenance (roads, water, refuse) is in the hands of the relevant regular departments. The Field Team approach and the operating and management procedures of HPU are being preserved, but again the section has to work within the environment of the Council's regular personnel and financial procedures.

These structural responses are promising, but it will take time to show whether they will take root and receive sufficient top-level management support to secure the long-term retention of management innovations.

The Effect of the Size and Location of the Project

A large single-city project is unsuited to long-term institution-building, as there is almost bound to be a scaling down of activity in the next phase. In a more favourable economic climate there might have been a basis for retaining HPU as a permanent development department. As it was, the priority for a second national project was for other towns, for which a smaller scale of activity was proposed and a different institutional structure of central technical and financial functions in partnership with local implementation and community development by existing departments of local authorities. However these projects, though delayed, can still benefit from certain significant elements of the HPU experience such as field staffing and procedures and community involvement procedures.

CONCLUSION

The HPU experience in Lusaka represents a massive burst of management innovation which has created new and successful systems of management for squatter upgrading. This innovation is now being adopted and adapted in the parent institution, and the extent of the long term institution-building achievement that will result is still in the balance. The alternative would have been a gradual process of change within the existing machinery, building up to a similar end result. That result might have been more firmly rooted in the Council's structure and administrative culture, but it would certainly have been qualitatively less innovative and appropriate to the distinctive needs of upgrading.

REFERENCES AND RELATED LUSAKA EVALUATION STUDIES

David Pasteur, "The Management of Squatter Upgrading, A Case Study of Organisation, Procedures and Participation," Saxon House, Teakfield Ltd., Farnborough, England (1979).

David Pasteur, "The Management of Squatter Upgrading Phase 2: The Transition to Maintenance and Further Development," Development Administration Group, Institute of Local Government Studies, University of Birmingham (1982).

Ann Schlyter and Thomas Schlyter, "George - The Development of a Squatter Settlement in Lusaka," The Swedish Institute for Building Research, Gavle, Sweden (1979).

Carole Rakodi and Ann Schlyter, "Upgrading in Lusaka: Participation and Physical Changes," The National Swedish Institute for Building Research, Gavle, Sweden (1981).

Marja Hoek-Smit, "Community Participation in Squatter Upgrading in Zambia, The Role of the American Friends Service Committee in the Lusaka Housing Project,"

American Friends Service Committee, Philadelphia, Pa. (August 1982).

German Agency for Technical Cooperation, "Kalingalinga Integrated Upgrading," Report of the Preparatory Mission, Stephen Mulenga, Jurgen Oestereich, Peter Weiss, Eschborn/Frankfurt (November 1979).

Zambia: Urbanisation and training for settlement improvement

Elpidius Mpolokoso

The Government of the Republic of Zambia has adopted two policies as a means of improving low-income settlements in urban areas. These are, site and service schemes and upgrading of squatters areas. There is, however, an existing crisis in the training of personnel capable of launching a systematic, comprehensive and well-planned attack against the wide-ranging housing problems in urban settlements. Noting the historical background to rural/urban migration, and the limitations of the existing educational system to cope with the need for appropriately trained personnel, proposals are made for a new innovative role in education, training and research to be undertaken by the National Housing Authority to assist the resolution of the current housing situation.

HISTORICAL BACKGROUND

Zambia has a relatively long history of urbanisation. This started as early as 1906 when a complex of copper mines began in the north-western part of the country. Large population centres characteristic of pre-colonial West African countries or even Botswana were unknown in Zambia. With the growth of the mining industry population, centres developed along the railway link, with Lusaka, the capital and largest city, followed by the copper belt towns of Ndola, Kitwe, Mufulira, Swanshye and Chingola. The rapid growth of the urban population in relation to the entire country's population is so great that Zambia is considered to be one of the most urbanised African countries south of the Sahara, with the exception of South Africa. This has been largely due to migration from rural areas.

Apart from the industrial growth, another factor which has encouraged the rural/urban migration is the abolition of the colonial pass laws. The Colonial Government used two methods to control the urban influx, namely the registration of Africans and the pass system created by local authority bye-laws. Registration required all Africans to obtain an identity card known as a situpa, issued at the holder's village. The second control was the requirement that an African visitor to any urban centre, including those looking for employment, have a valid visitor's permit to be in a private location or African township. These pass regulations were enforced by the Northern Rhodesia police through night raids known as ifipekeni ('inspection'). In the very early morning hours, the police would encircle a number of houses, banging on walls to bring people out, to search for unauthorised persons. A person without an identity card would have to return to his home village to obtain one, while an unauthorised resident could be prosecuted. Between 1947 and 1956 there were 94858 convictions for violations of these pass laws which indicates on one hand how effective the migration control was, and on the other, how strong the rapid industrial growth was, and still is, as a rural/urban push factor.

The fight against colonial pass laws featured as an important manifesto in the independence struggle. Both the Independence and 1973 constitutions contain the following guarantee:

"No person shall be deprived of his freedom of movement, and for the purposes of this article the said freedom means the right to move freely throughout Zambia, the right to reside in any part of Zambia."

HOUSING SITUATION IN ZAMBIA TODAY

After the abolition of the Colonial Pass Laws, the urban influx from rural areas was rapid (see Table 1). It is believed that four out of five people live off the land in most African countries, and only one in 10 of the continent's population live in towns. Zambia's urban proportion of about 30% is well above the continental average. The annual growth rate of the population of Lusaka is 8.9%. This rate has put Lusaka at the top of the 20 capital cities in the Third World (see Table 2).

Table 1. Growth of Urban Population in Zambia

1963	1974	
2,843,000	3,039,000	rural
667,000	1,656,000	urban
3,510,000	4,965,000	total
123,000	401,000	Lusaka

Table 2. Population Growth in Third World Cities

Estimated Population 1975	Annual Growth Rate (%)	City
435,700	8.9	Lusaka
2,151,300	8.9	Kinshasa
3,610,000	7.2	Bogota
1,189,900	6.9	Lagos
1,657,100	5.8	Ankara
3,528,900	5.8	Chile
702,500	5.6	Nairobi
805,700	5.6	Dakar
2,842,600	5.5	Caracas
2,420,900	4.9	Baghdad
5,477,900	4.6	Jakarta
8,482,900	4.5	Mexico City
1,561,100	4.3	Manila
3,924,700	4.2	Karachi
6,064,900	3.7	Cairo
6,903,800	3.7	Bombay
3,654,500	3.5	Bangkok
1,810,500	3.3	Ahmedabad
4,857,900	2.7	Rio de Janeiro
9,200,000	2.3	Calcutta

The rural/urban migration since independence has been characterised by the rapid growth of squatter settlements where the residents are subjected to substandard living conditions. The main reason is due to the fact that the Government cannot provide accommodation for every town dweller due to acute shortage of financial resource: "To house Lusaka alone, we would have needed Kwacha 110m (£736m), between 1964 and 1974 to provide a two-bedroom house to all its citizens. But the money was just not there. This method would have cost 152% of the national budget," according to Richard Martin, Deputy Director, Lusaka Housing Project Unit.

The growth of urban population has not been matched by significant industrial expansion. It has occurred during a period of world-wide inflation, low copper prices and an unfavourable international political atmosphere. The urban centres therefore have been unable to assimulate the new migrants in terms of housing or health facilities, education, employment and various other social amenities. With the assistance of the World Bank loan of Kwacha 26.5m (£17m), the Government has embarked on developing human settlements through self-help schemes. This switch from providing housing by conventional methods to self-help and squatter upgrading is reflected in Table 3, which shows the distribution of Zambia's urban housing stock 1973 and 1974.

From this table it can be seen that the dwelling units provided by the self-help method, ie. serviced site units and squatter units, increased from 33.8% to 36.2%, while the high- and medium-cost housing remained static and the low-cost housing dropped from 50% to 47% of the total stock. The amount of overcrowding which is commonly found among the less-privileged urban dwellers can well be imagined if the total urban population shown in Table 1 is compared with the total housing stock in Table 2.

The question which arises from the existing housing situation in Zambia is: how are we going to cope with this serious human settlement problem? During the periods of scarce financial resources the true answer lies in the train-ing of personnel capable of applying a revolutionary system of approach. Residents in squatter settlements have demon-strated the willingness to improve their standard of living. This willingness to improve is a useful force which should be tapped through research and put to good use. With trained manpower a lot can be achieved in the implementation of poli-cies and in mobilising the masses for positive human settle-ment development.

THE ROLE OF THE NATIONAL HOUSING AUTHORITY

The National Housing Authority is the biggest Government agency with direct responsibilities for spearheading housing

Table 3. Distribution of Urban Housing Stock in Zambia, by
          Category of Dwellings, 1973 and 1974

| December 1973 | | December 1974 | | |
Number	Total Stock	Number	Total Stock	
27,398	11.2%	29,108	11.2%	High, medium cost
122,222	50.0	123,488	47.4	Low cost
12,226	5.0	13,533	5.2	Servants' quarters
16,580	6.8	18,579	7.1	Serviced site units
178,426	73.0	184,708	70.9	Total official stock
65,887	27.0	75,792	29.1	Squatters units
244,313	100.0	260,500	100.0	Total stock

programmes throughout the country. Besides advising the
Government on human settlements development and direct involvement in the construction of dwellings, the Authority is
empowered, by the 1971 National Housing Authority Act, Chapter 421, "...to do anything for the purpose of improving the
skill, knowledge or usefulness of persons employed in the
building industry and in that connection to provide or assist
other persons or local authorities in providing facilities
for training, education and research."

     With its locally-recruited staff, headed by expatriate
professionals, the National Housing Authority has, since
1971, provided high-, medium- and low-cost houses for the
capital city of Lusaka and for other township councils
throughout the country. In the field of training as required
by the Act, no significant steps have been taken especially
at the national level. The sum of Kwacha 15,000 (£9,500) is
annually budgeted for training purposes. This sum is spent
on mid-career training for the staff employed within the
organisation. Considering the problems of urban settlement
which the country is now facing, time has come for the
National Housing Authority to live up to the Government's
expectation by introducing a national training and research
centre for human settlements development.

LIMITATIONS OF THE CURRENT EDUCATIONAL SYSTEM

     Before deciding to establish a human resources training
centre, it is worthwhile to look at the existing educational

system and consider whether it is playing its required role. The present educational system has not provided enough Zambian personnel capable of carrying out responsibility for comprehensive planning, coordination and control. The few Zambians who are expensively trained at the University of Zambia and overseas are not easily absorbed in the national human settlements development fields. After satisfying their sponsor's bonding requirements, they resign to join private firms. Reasons for their resignations vary: they include lack of incentives in the Government institutions; uncooperative attitudes and mistrust of senior officials within an organisation; and failure to adjust their skills, which are in most cases insensitive to the needs of wide-ranging social groupings within which they are expected to work.

The present general Zambian educational system, which is undergoing vigorous reorganisation, has been likened to, 'a train which travels on a single track bound for one destination, but which ejects most of its passengers without stopping at several points along the route.' Only those who are most academically-able are favoured at the expense of the vast majority of others. This competitive spirit does not usually end at school but continues in one's employment, with disastrous consequences, when dealing with projects of an integrated nature.

The twelve years of primary and secondary school education have four stages of screening. The major ones are after the seventh grade and Form V, when between 80% and 90% of the total intake of students leave school to join teams of job seekers in urban areas. The post-seventh grade school leavers, who on the average account for 82% of the total intake, leave school at the age 13 to 15 years. At this stage, they are too young to be absorbed into any industry. Since the learning of English, which is the country's official language, takes most of the time on the school schedule, there is not sufficient time to train children in skills for human settlements development.

In the final year of the secondary school education students sit for the Cambridge School Certificate examinations. The secondary school syllabus and learning materials have to be geared to these examinations and have very little relevance to the cultural, social and economic needs of the Zambian society. The situation is aggravated by lack of Zambian teachers in the secondary schools. More than 75% of

the secondary school teachers are expatriates serving on
short contracts of not more than three years. There are four
trades institutes which enrol some secondary school leavers.
Their syllabus and learning materials have a foreign flavour
and are affiliated to the London City and Guilds standards.
The School of Engineering at the University of Zambia has not
developed sufficiently to produce enough physical planners,
land surveyors and architects. As long as the present system
of education is relied upon, there cannot be any hope of
rapid human settlements development in Zambia. The Government
has realised this. Already, new proposals and recommendations
for a new educational system have been prepared and published
by the Ministry of Education. Emphasis has been put on a
system which contributes to the economic and social development of the country. When these proposals and recommendations
are finally implemented, many government institutions, including the training and research centre which I am proposing
for the National Housing Authority, will greatly benefit from
the graduates of the new system.

PROPOSALS FOR THE NATIONAL HOUSING AUTHORITY

The National Housing Authority has to realise its statutory obligation to provide the nation with human resources,
capable of developing human settlements within the framework
of the Government's housing policies. It has also to be
aware of the plight of the less-privileged people for whom
the settlements are intended. The kind of training which the
authority should provide within its organisation is that
which will take into account the fact that housing is not
only shelter, but also touches upon many facets of economic
activity and development. The end result, therefore should
not only be the mobilisation of the low-income urban dwellers
in acquiring shelter through self-help methods, but also to
help and care for their social and economic well-being.

In the training of personnel for human settlements development, the question of who should be trained becomes very
crucial. Since the basis of the training operations has to
be at the community level, the main target areas should be
mid-career persons engaged in various political, social and
economic institutions. These should include policy-makers;
planners and technical staff; and implementors. The type of
training for policy-makers, who should include leading politicians, civic leaders and senior administrators, is that

Table 4. Training Target Groups, Types and Methods

Target Groups	Types of Training	Method of Training
Policymaker - leading politicians - civil leaders - senior administrators	- sensitising experiences - process learning	- short-term conferences, seminars, workshops, tours
Professionals - planners and technical staff - sociologists - economists - geographers - trainers	- sensitising experiences - process learning - skill development	- intensive medium training related to living improvement efforts
Implementors - project managers - field staff - party branch leaders - local chiefs - local tribal elders - school masters	- sensitising experiences - process learning - skill development - self-help learning	- intensive short-term workshops involving total field immersion and task simulation exercises

Source: Adapted from T.L. Blair, "Education for Habitat," Architectural Association Quarterly, London, Vol.12, No. 1, 1980.

which will make them sensitive to the situation prevailing in
low-income settlements. Most of our politicians have shown
tremendous ability in mobilising the masses to vote for them
in general elections. If similar efforts and ingenuity were
to be used in human settlements operations, a great deal
could be achieved. What this target group needs is a series
of sensitising experiences and process learning.

Professionals and technicians in planning and in social,
economic and cultural fields also need sensitisation experiences, in order to appreciate fully, the existing housing
problems in Zambia. Skills of planning with the people for
whom development programmes are intended, should be developed. Suggestions have to be made to the planners and technical staff to restructure their organisation in order to
cope with today's human settlement problems.

The third target group of implementors is a very important one. It includes people within the area of action such
as project managers, field staff, community coordinators,
community leaders and general local inhabitants. Local communities have demonstrated, in plain terms, their willingness
to improve their living standards by building their own housing and by earning a living one way or another. The proposed
resource centre should develop skills of the implementor in
channelling this willingness to improve, into properly-
designed development projects. Table 4 attempts to summarise
the target groups for human resources training.

A research department should grow as an integral part of
the human resources centre to act as an intelligence unit.
There is need to analyse the Zambian social groups from both
the historical and contemporary perspective. Methods of
steering change for the improvement of living standards for
the less-privileged people, need thorough research. Communication skills must be probed into and disseminated into all
training target groups. Another important field study for
the research unit should be the use of indigenous building
materials. Zambia depends largely on imported building
materials. The production of burnt bricks from the abundant
clay instead of cement blocks, and the use of Zambian timber
instead of the imported type, would reduce building costs
considerably.

A proposal for instituting a human resources training
and research centre would be incomplete without making reference to finance. In its capacity as a statutory parastatal

organisation, the National Housing Authority should be prepared to bear all the responsibilities of providing the
buildings for the centre and money for running it. There is
very keen interest among developed countries in funding projects related to low-income settlements development. The
training centre proposed in this paper would gain the support
of international agencies such as the World Bank, Development
Programme, African Development Bank and African Development
Fund.

CONCLUSION

In endeavouring to meet the deteriorating housing situation affecting the less-privileged persons, particularly in
the urban centres, Zambia will need a new brand of skilled
personnel, capable of utilising the limited financial resources in mobilising the masses for the general improvement
of their settlements, in urban as well as rural areas. By
introducing a training and research centre for human settlements development, the National Housing Authority will not
only be fulfilling its legal commitment, but will also be
laying a cornerstone for a meaningful social, economic and
cultural development of the nation.

REFERENCES

Human Settlements in Zambia, Report of the Workshop at the
        University of Zambia, 12-15 September 1975.
Ministry of Education, Educational Reform: Proposals and
        Recommendations, Lusaka, Zambia, October 1977.
Blair, T. L., Education for Habitat, Architectural
        Association Quarterly, London, Vol. 12, No. 1 (1980).
Blair, T. L., Training for Human Settlement Development,
        Habitat International Journal, Vol. 4, No. 1/2,
        Pergamon Press, Oxford (1979).
Heisler, H., Urbanisation and the Government of Migration:
        The Interrelationship of Urban and Rural Life in
        Zambia, London (1974).
Martin, R., Housing Project Unit: The Facts, Housing Project
        Unit Report, Lusaka, Zambia, n.d.

Dacca: An analysis of plan implementation, past and future

Charles L.Choguill

BACKGROUND

Bangladesh is probably the least urbanised major nation
in the world.[1]   According to the most recent census in
1974, Bangladesh had a population of 71.5 million, of which
6.3 million, or 8.8 per cent of the total population, lived
in urban areas defined as having at least 5,000 residents.[2]
Not surprisingly, the allocation of development funds under
the terms of the National Economic Plan has reflected this
situation.   The planned development of Bangladesh is expected
to be based on the economic growth which will occur in the
rural areas.*

---

* More formally, urban areas in Bangladesh are defined to
  "include places having a Municipality (Pourashava), a Town
  Committee (Shahar Committee) or a Cantonment Board.   In
  general, an urban area will be a concentration of population of a least 5,000 persons in continuous collection of
  houses where the community sense is well developed and the
  community maintains public utilities, such as roads, street
  lightings, water supply, sanitary arrangements, etc.   These
  places are generally centres of trade and commerce with a
  population substantially non-agricultural and having non-
  agricultural labour concentration and a high literacy rate.
  An area which has urban characteristics but has less than
  5,000 population may in special cases be treated as an
  urban area."

At the same time, such a strategy seems likely to lead to serious problems in the currently urbanised areas, problems for which early solutions must be found if what some might go so far as to call a disaster is to be avoided. The rural areas of Bangladesh can be characterised as areas of low productivity, high rates of population increase and a low man-to-land ratio. The total amount of land in Bangladesh is 34.5 million acres. Of this, 15 per cent is under forest and 17 per cent is not available for cultivation. A further 6 per cent is cultivable waste and the balance of about 63 per cent, or 22.5 million acres, is cultivated.[3] At the beginning of this century, the population to land ratio was 1.3 persons per acre of cultivated land. Today there are four persons per acre and it is estimated that by the end of this century, there will be eight persons per acre.[4] Even at present, it is estimated that nearly 38 per cent of rural families are landless.[5]

From this statistical overview, one must recognise that rural Bangladesh is already supersaturated with population and that although agricultural productivity can be increased, it would seem inevitable that over the coming years, a marked

---

Even the census data themselves are subject to error as it is estimated than an under-enumeration of 6 per cent occurred in all areas except the major cities of Dacca, narayanganj, Chittagong and Khulna where the estimated under-enumeration was 16 per cent. Hence, the population on 1st March 1974 is estimated at 76.2 million and given a 3 per cent annual rate of growth since then, the current population is about 80 million.

It is difficult to derive the precise allocation to rural projects as in addition to including the 'agriculture, water resources and rural development sector,' rural projects are included in other sector allocations, particularly in transport, power and communications, education, health and family planning. In the First Five Year Plan 1973-78, agriculture was allocated 26.3 per cent of the budget, while in the 'hardcore plan' for 1975-78 (which was designed when the First Plan ran into difficulties) it was allocated 29.7 per cent and in the Two Year Plan 1978-70, the allocation was 25 per cent. In each case, these were significantly larger than the next ranking sector allocation.

increase is likely to occur in the rate of urbanisation. The
Harvard University Population Centre has suggested that, even
if there is a drastic decline in the fertility rate, the
number of urban residents will increase by tenfold by
2003.[6] This is equivalent to adding 29 cities the size of
Dacca over the next 24 years.

The largest city in Bangladesh, as well as the capital,
Dacca is well located at the centre of the country. With an
estimated present population of about 2 million, compared to
the second city Chittagong's population of 900,000, it is
very much a primate city. Its regional hinterland of daily
influence is estimated to cover 4,000 square miles, extending
up to 80 miles in a single direction. Despite difficulties
in transport, the daily commuting distance extends up to 30
miles.[7]

Constrained from expansion on the west and south by the
Burhi Ganga River and on the east by the Lakhya River, the
increasing population of the city has expanded primarily in a
northerly direction.[8] Unfortunately, this northerly expansion on land above monsoon-flood level is impeded by the
military cantonment on the northern outskirts of the city and
by a new international airport which is being constructed
beyond that.

Dacca itself consists of areas of widely varying density
and congestion which reflect the development pattern of the
city. The original site of Dacca, on the Buri Ganga River
between the Chawk and Bangla Bazaar, became known as 'Old
Dacca.' At the beginning of the twentieth century, under
British influence, New Dacca developed in the Ramna area,
complete with a race track, spacious parks and new government
buildings. In 1962, work on the so-called Second Capital in
what is now Sher-E-Bangla Nagar, began to provide a legislative forum and administrative centre for the Government of
East Bengal, and eventually for the Government of Bangladesh
about 5 miles to the northwest of Ramna.

It is within this framework that the topic of implementation is being approached. As a result, not only will attention be directed to the reasons why implementation in Dacca
has encountered problems in the past, but also to what can be
done in the future to meet the challenges of a rapidly growing urban population. Necessarily, this look to the future
involves a consideration of factors beyond the simple carry-

ing out of projects included in a plan. In fact, this paper will examine three fundamental assumptions in the context of Dacca's experience.

1.   Success in implementation depends upon the establishment of an efficient organisational structure for planning;

2.   Implementation is dependent upon the ability to finance the projects proposed in a plan; and

3.   Once a sound project has been planned, finance arranged and execution of the project organised, successful implementation is not always just a simple matter of engineering.

In the review of what has happened in the past, a fairly gloomy picture is painted. Yet is is necessary to remember that the practice of urban planning in Bangladesh is of fairly recent origin. It has only been since Independence that the necessary institutions have been developed for the task. Even today, there are no more than 30 urban planners in all of Bangladesh. Although it is impossible to say with complete certainty that the errors of the past will be avoided in the future, judging from the enthusiasm and dedication of physical planners in Bangladesh today, the chances of success are far higher now than they were a decade ago.

ORGANISATIONAL STRUCTURE OF URBAN PLANNING IN DACCA

The organisational structure for planning in Dacca is complex by any criteria. There are at least 32 official organisations that have control over at least a part of the planning machinery. These range from the mainline bodies such as the Dacca Improvement Trust and the Bangladesh Urban Development Directorate who have fairly broad powers to more limited organisations, such as the Inland Water Transport Authority which is responsible for the expansion and maintenance of water transport.

The overall structure for planning within the Government of Bangladesh is highly centralised. The President of the Republic presides over the National Economic Council which in turn considers requests for financial allocations for the thirteen ministries. The Planning Commission separates the ministries from the National Economic Council. The Planning

Commission itself is divided into cells, one for each ministry, whose function is to review requests from ministries and
make recommendations to the National Economic Council. As a
result of this complex structure, there is an unavoidable
tendency toward following a sectoral approach and ministries
are pitted against one another in their quests for funds and
project approvals. Once approval is obtained, the project
activities and implementation are jealously guarded by each
ministry. The inevitable result is a lack of co-ordination
between ministries involved in inter-related projects.

Even at the local level, such as the Dacca Metropolitan
Area, the sectoral approach of the central government has
profound implications. unfortunately this division even
extends into the various departments within a single ministry. A brief examination of four of these agencies provides
some insight into the co-ordination problems that arise.

The most important national urban planning body is the
Urban Development Directorate (UDD). Created by government
order in 1965, the Directorate is organisationally a part of
the Ministry of Public Works and Urban Development. The
government order establishing the UDD listed the following
functions:

a.   "to advise the Government in matters of policy relating
      to urbanisation, land use and land development;

b.   to prepare and co-ordinate regional plans, master plans
      and detailed layout and site plans of the existing as
      well as new urban centres;

c.   to undertake socio-economic research and collection of
      data for determination of the location and pattern of
      future urban development;

d.   to prepare programmes for urban development regarding
      selection of sites, acquisition of land, reclamation of
      land;

e.   to secure approval of the preparation of plans and ob-
      tain necessary funds from the government or any other
      agency approved by the government;

f.   to advise the existing urban development authorities on
      their operations at their request."[9]

Despite an acute lack of qualified planners, the UDD has approached its tasks with vigour. Master plans have been prepared for Kanchan, Chorasal, Rangput, Rajshahi, Jessore, Sylhet, Cox's Bazaar, Rangamati and Mymensing. A National Physical Planning Project has been started (with United Nations Development Programme assistance) to provide linkages between physical and economic planning and to build up the training facilities for planners at the Bangladesh University of Engineering and Technology*. The UDD is also involved in the early stages of regional planning, including the preparation of a regional plan for the Dacca Metropolitan Region, an activity that will be discussed further below.

Despite some successes, there are serious problems. In the absence of legislation, none of its plans are considered to be legal documents and none of its suggestive measures are binding on anyone. It has no implementation powers itself. As a result, the plans prepared in the UDD have not been fully implemented by any authority. Further, despite the expertise that it is building up, Section f. of the establishment order precludes the UDD taking any initiative in Dacca due to the presence of an existing urban development organisation, the Dacca Improvement Trust.

The Dacca Improvement Trust (DIT) was established in 1956 within the legislative framework of the East Bengal Building Construction Act of 1952 and the Town Improvement Act of 1953. Whereas the 1952 Act is meant to control developments by private individuals, the 1953 legislation provides for planned development efforts. The former established the position of an 'authorised officer' while the latter gave this role to the DIT. As a result of the two acts, in matters of building control, the authorised officer and his staff examine planning applications. There are building by-laws to judge the nature of the applications and to guide building construction. The applications are not referred to the plan-

---

* This activity accounts for the interest in Bangladesh at the University of Sheffield. Under United Nations auspices, a Joint Master of Urban and Regional Planning Programme between the University of Sheffield and the Bangladesh University of Engineering and Technology was established in 1974. Selected students on the course study one year in Sheffield, a second year in Dacca and then join the Urban Development Directorate.

ners normally as this is not required by law. The DIT is also empowered to prepare a master plan and in all other matters concerned with improvement, rehousing and road construction schemes, the master plan is followed. In these matters, the planners are consulted. The final decision in cases of controversy lies in the hands of the Chairman of an eleven-member Board of Trustees. The Trustees themselves have control over the institution of major development works.

Organisationally, the DIT comes under the Ministry of Public Works and Urban Development. This means that it is financially dependent upon the National Economic Council and the Planning Commission in order to implement its projects. For almost all of these, loans are made to DIT from the Central Government and interest must be paid on these monies. Furthermore, DIT is prohibited from cross-subsidation of projects, a constraint that has serious implications in development activities aimed at the less fortunate members of society.

The accomplishments of the DIT include a Master Plan, prepared in 1959 [10] and never updated, a number of road improvement schemes, some parks, the development of certain industrial estates, housing projects (usually for the more wealthy members of society) and the establishment of a number of markets throughout the Dacca area.

The linkages between DIT and other organisations are complex. In the provision of services, DIT is dependent upon the Dacca Water Supply and Sewerage Authority and the Public Health and Engineering Directorate. To acquire land, approval is required from the District Land Allocation Committee. Finally the DIT performs planning services for the local authority as requested.

The local authority is the Dacca Municipal Corporation which is an elective body, with a mayor as head of the Corporation. The law governing the Corporation at present is the Pourshava Ordinance of 1977. This allows the Corporation to function in the areas of public health, water supply and sewerage, control of articles of food, maintenance of parks, gardens and forests, town planning, primary education, building control and development planning (prevention of pollution, improvement of the environment). The Corporation itself has not taken up all of these newly acquired functions. The major area of activity has been in the repair and maintenance of roads, with some efforts in market development and education.

As in the case of DIT, the Corporation needs approval from the National Economic Council and the Planning Commission to initiate major projects. As the local authority is administratively a part of the Ministry of Local Government, Rural Development and CO-operatives, problems associated with the sectoral approach remain. Almost all allocations are on a loan basis upon which interest is charged.

The fourth organisation to be considered here is the Roads and Highways Directorate (RHD) within the Ministry of Railways, Roads, Highways and Road Transport. As the name implies, this Directorate is an engineering agency. The Directorate has a simple but efficient process of operation. It can initiate projects on its own. Sometimes it follows up the initiatives of the politicians and decision-makers. However, for the purpose of project planning, the executive engineers undertake research and estimates under the guidance of the superior officers. In doing so, they follow the Project Evaluation Proforma circulated by the Planning Commission. The Chief Engineer as head of the organisation gives initial approval and makes arrangements for obtaining approval of the administrative Ministry and then the Planning Commission and the National Economic Council. For implementation of the projects the Executive Engineers have special powers which enable them to spend any sum of money for a project that is within the limits of their allocation from the Annual Development Plan. This delegation of power, which is unique among the four agencies examined, leads to a smoothly functioning Directorate. And given that engineers are seen to accomplish projects, this enhances their position in the eyes of the decision makers even though their projects may cause any number of problems at the local level.

The RHD is active in Dacca itself. Although precise data on expenditure is sketchy, it appears that the Directorate spends on average three times as much per year on roads in Dacca as the Dacca Municipal Corporation and about the same amount as the Dacca Improvement Trust.[11]

THE SYSTEM IN OPERATION

From this review of the organisation framework one can get a fairly accurate idea of the way the system operates in practice. The organisation most likely to be capable of making an impact on the problems of Dacca, the Urban Development Directorate, is excluded from working there. Even if permission were granted, the powers of implementation would have to be added to its mandate.

Two of these organisations have no planners at all, the Roads and Highway Directorate and the Dacca Municipal Corporation. Whereas the former can construct roads, the latter has more broadly based powers, including those of road construction, the examination of building applications and participation in town planning. The Dacca Improvement Trust, which currently has two planners, examines planning applications but restricts its planning staff to the task of preparing local improvement projects under the terms of a very outdated master plan.

Applications for permission to build or alter land use must be made to two agencies. The Dacca Municipal Corporation determines building applications which must then be submitted to the Dacca Improvement Trust for planning permission. Furthermore, the DIT itself has little power other than to restrict certain kind of building activities. As a result of these factors, between 1961 and 1974, no more than 4,000 building applications were submitted although the population of Dacca increased by over one million. The financial powers of the development agencies are inadequate to meet the needs. They are dependent upon loans and grants from the government. The DIT and the Corporation repay these loans with interest. The concentration of effort of the DIT, for example, is very much directed to earning as against non-earning schemes. Between 1965 and 1975, the DIT spent Taka 59.6 million (about £2 million, assuming 30 Taka = £1.00) on non-earning schemes such as road construction and improvements and parks but Taka 241.4 million on earning schemes, such as industrial estate and commercial development and the development of middle and upper income residential areas. Local taxation seems to offer no remedy as, for example, Dacca Municipal Corporation manages to collect no more than 39 per cent of its tax demands.[12]

An excellent example of the impact of financial constraints upon the DIT is found in the development of Tejaon Industrial Area, which is located in the mid-eastern part of the city and served by the Dacca-Narayanjanj Railway Line and the Dacca-Tongi-Mymensing Trunk Road. The industrial estate

was originally formulated in 1950 by the East Bengal Communication and Building Department, which at that time was responsible for co-ordinating and carrying out building in the
public sector. Due to severe financial constraints and lack
of interest by the Central Government in Karachi, the project
floundered until the establishment of DIT and the Master Plan
of 1959. The Master Plan included the development of the
industrial area on ground above flood level. A recommendation was also made for a local detailed plan to provide
housing areas for industrial workers adjacent to the site.
The DIT, constrained by its own financial situation, bought
the residential land and sold it to developers (at cost) for
the construction of upper income class housing at Gulshan and
Banani. Two interpretations of this action are possible.
One prefers to conclude that it was the financial constraints
that led to this solution rather than a complete disregard
for the lower income industrial workers. The effect is that
aside from those workers who are willing to risk crowding
into low-lying land that is subject to flooding, over half
must travel more than forty minutes to reach their place of
work in the industrial estate. Such a situation results in
loss of production and hence perpetuates the critical resource situation of the Bangladesh economy.[13]

Of the four mainline agencies examined, three have the
power to plan and construct elements of the road transport
system. Obviously some agencies, such as the Roads and Highways Directorate, have more independent power to do so than
others and do so in a more efficient manner. Although in
theory development is guided by the 1959 Master Plan, one
must not forget that in 1959 Dacca had a population of something in the vicinity of 500,000 compared to a current population four times that amount. The co-ordination problems in
the implementation sphere are apparent. An example of the
waste that occurs is found in the payments made by various
public utility agencies to the Dacca Municipal Corporation
for damage to roads in the laying of water, sewerage, telephone and power lines. Invariably there are separate
agencies for each of these services, but it is unfortunate
that they feel compelled to cut along and across the roads to
perform their respective tasks one after another. In two
divisions of the Dacca Municipal Corporation, during a six-
month period of 1978, a total of Taka 4.8 million was paid to
the Corporation by other agencies for damage caused by the
cutting of roads. (Table 1).

Table 1. Payments by Public Service Agencies to Dacca
         Municipal Corporation, East and West Division, 1978.

Agency	Payments to the West Division	Payments to the East Division
Period	2 Quarters ending October 1978	2 Quarters ending November 1978
Titas Gas	Tk. 16,808	Tk. 3,319,218
Dacca Water Supply and Sewerage Authority (Water)	10,365	373,308
Dacca Water Supply and Sewerage Authority (Sewerage)	12,000	–
Dacca Electricity Supply	18,921	34,245
Telegraph and Telephone	428,390	207,879
Public Works Department, Ministry of Works	60	–
Public Health Engineering Directorate	–	14,900
Private	31,290	248,694

Source: Dacca Municipal Corporation, Office of Engineering

Even when everything seems to be neatly organised, when
finance is approved and when the implementation is organised,
there is still no guarantee that everything will come to a
successful conclusion. In 1973, a significant proportion of
the population of Dacca was comprised of 'bustuharas,' or
'bastees,' squatters who had no legal claim to the land they
were occupying.[14] In January 1975, the military government
of Bangladesh moved in to 'solve' the problem, by force,
distributing about 150,000 bastees into three camps at Demra,
Tongi and Mirpur.

The original plan in each of these camps was to provide
a site and service scheme as soon as possible. At each area,

provision was made for about 4,000 housing plots (13' x 25' or 14' x 26'), tubewells, health, education, religious and shopping facilities as well as limited provision of employment opportunities*.

Whereas the creation of the settlements at Tongi and Demra went more or less according to plan, the camp at Mirpur has encountered severe problems. Built on paddy land below flood level, the settlement required a flood protection dike around the site of about 80 acres. Unfortunately, apparently someone forgot to do soil bearing tests before construction and the dike sank into seven feet of black loam mud, rupturing completely in six places. As a cost overrun has already occurred, the future of the project is in some doubt.

From the three initial assumptions then, one can conclude on the basis of Dacca's experience that both organisational structure and adequate finance are necessary conditions for successful implementation. Yet even with these two prerequisites, constant monitoring and feedback of information on the implementation process is required if success in this sphere is to be achieved.

PLANNING FOR IMPLEMENTATION IN THE FUTURE

Although it is impossible under existing Bangladesh conditions to forecast accurately the population of Dacca, it is apparent that by the year 2000, the city could well be several times its present size. Although the population planners are optimistic, there is little reason to believe that a significant drop in birth rates will occur in the near future.[15] If anything, the pressures on the rural areas will increase over the coming decades with the only escape valve available being rural-to-urban migration. More ominously, time does not stop in the year 2000 and it is the duty of the planners to look even beyond that date.

---

* The establishment of the new settlements up to fifteen miles from central Dacca caused severe economic disruption of the existing employment patterns as most residents earned their livelihood in Dacca as day labourers, rickshaw pullers, peddlers and servants. See S. R. Qadir, Bastees of Dacca, Dacca, 1975, p.37.

As noted previously, at the present time the Bangladesh Urban Development Directorate, with United Nations assistance, is involved with the preparation of a National Physical Plan. Although the project was originally formulated in 1972, it did not seriously begin until 1975 and it is still uncertain exactly what form the Plan will finally take. Obviously the plans already prepared by the UDD may need revision as the number of planners in the Directorate increases. Perhaps the most that can be hoped for, given the meagre planning resources available, are urban plans for the four urban areas that currently have planning authorities – Dacca, Chittagong, Khulna, Rajshahi, as well as plans for a few other rapidly growing district centres, such as Mymensingh, Jessore, Comilla, Bogra and Barisal. The Asian Development Bank has agreed to finance a regional plan for the Dacca Metropolitan Area, as well as feasibility studies for water supply expansion in the five district towns which may well become part of the National Physical Plan. Personnel from the Urban Development Directorate have already been dispatched to these five cities to begin preliminary work on the collection of data required for the study.

With these developments in mind, it may be of value to consider the type of plan that would be most compatible with the National Physical Plan effort as well as of greatest benefit to the future of Dacca. 'Benefit' in this sense hinges completely upon the ability to implement the plan. Although a glossy, optimistic paper plan would be relatively easy to prepare for Dacca, if it cannot be implemented under the existing severe financial constraints in Bangladesh, the preparation of such a plan would be a completely wasted effort.

The most important aspect of such a plan, and of the entire National Physical Plan effort, should be its integration with the National Economic Plans prepared by the Planning Commission. In fact, this effort to integrate the physical and economic sectoral investments of the various ministries in time and in place over the long run should have been done at the outset of the exercise. Such was not the case although remedial steps in this direction are to begin. This First Five Year Plan 1973-78, the 'Hardcore' Plan 1975-78 and the Two-Year Plan 1978-80 offer minimal guidance to the physical planners in that they contain no spatial strategy for the development effort. In a sense, the National Physical Plan, by designating certain district centres for

special attention has begun to fill this void. Yet if the
economic planners fail to follow this lead and to plan for an
expansion of employment opportunities in these district
centres, their potential for slowing down the migration flow
to Dacca from the rural areas will not be realised.

Once the spatial urban system for the nation is established, those charged with preparing the Dacca plan have a
framework within which to operate. The priorities for attention should fall within the sphere of the political decision
makers. Given the probable unpopularity of certain essential
measures, it is possible that these issues could be passed on
to a committee representing the mainline planning organisations concerned with Dacca. Although this would be unfortunate, it would not be serious if the political decision-
makers endorse the priorities, for without public support
from the government itself, even the best plan will never be
implemented. It is impossible to over-emphasise this point.
Certainly the existence of such a committee would expedite
the transmission of day-to-day decisions that would be required by the planning group preparing the plan.

So what should the priorities be? In terms of land use,
they probably involve a consideration of space for expansion
of employment opportunity through industry and commerce, the
continued improvement of the urban transport network as well
as provision for interurban links and the provision of public
utilities, such as water, sewer, telephone and electricity
lines. As we are dealing in terms of space requirements, the
provision of housing areas might have a higher priority than
the allocation of land for industrial estates. The reason
for this ordering is that the spatial requirements are
greater and although both activities require land that is
above flood level, the make-shift, low-investment housing
that is likely to result is far more vulnerable to the pressures of climate than the purpose-built industrial premises.
Furthermore, as we have seen, there appears to be a direct
link between higher productivity and nearness of workers'
residences to their places of work. Yet since a sizeable
majority of the population of the country cannot afford to
pay any rent at all for their housing, what is required here
is little more than the provision of land and services in a
flood-free location.

On the whole, however, those urban facilities which have
a high payoff in the short run, such as transport, utilities

and industrial space, are given a higher priority than those
which may lead to improvements in the longer term, such as
health care and education facilities. Yet even on the high
priority items, the standards that can be achieved in
Bangladesh are far different from those possible in more
developed countries. The 100-foot carriageways included in
the 1959 Master Plan simply are not feasible either in terms
of economics or in terms of land consumption. Even in residential areas, in order to conserve land, gross residential
densities in excess of 150 persons per acre must be attained.

The plan itself, if it is to be implemented at all, must
provide long-term guidance to the development of Dacca.
Historically, Dacca has expanded from south to north and
there is no reason to expect that this trend will change in
the future. Detailed allowance should be made in the plan
for the development of the priority items over at least the
next twenty years, with more general outline proposals for
further expansion that occurs after that. In the shorter
period, however, it may not be possible to rigidly delineate
the location of even the priority items. To incorporate
flexibility, some elements of the plan during the first
twenty-year period may need to be included in only outline
terms.

Of even greater importance than the plan itself, however, is the implementation policy. This should be ex-
plicitly spelled out in a policy document to accompany the
plan. Resources for the development of Dacca are scarce and
the resource situation is unlikely to improve. Functionally
inter-related and spatially clustered projects should be
scheduled for implementation at roughly the same time period.
In order to achieve this, what is required is the equivalent
to an 'annual development plan', a document giving a feasible
financial allowance of funds for a given period and suggestions as to the best ways to spend the money on groups of
inter-related projects.

An important requirement of this annual implementation
plan is that it be open-ended in the sense that it is capable
of linking up with other projects in subsequent annual plans
without wasting the resources that will be available at the
later dates. Whereas the overall urban plan integrates
activities through the spatial environment of the city, the
annual implementation plan integrates these activities
through time. An important element of the integration of

such a physical planning effort with the National Economic
Plan is the assurance by political decision-makers that the
annual allocation to this activity will not vary widely from
year to year. Some variation is inevitable which implies
that flexibility is required in the creation of the annual
plans.

The success in the implementation of even such a plan as
this requires an organisational structure that includes clearly defined and integrated activity areas for both the
planners and the engineers. The Dacca Regional Plan itself
is to be prepared by outside consultants, although hopefully,
government departments, local planners and the Dacca public
will be deeply involved in the process. Yet as noted, a
significant proportion of the plan, particularly in the more
distant time periods, will require detailed local plans for
specific areas if the plan is to be realised. This seems to
imply that the planning authority best suited to undertake
the work is one first, with popular support, second, with
demonstrated planning expertise and third, with the ability
actually to put in place the projects envisaged by the plan.
No existing organisation fulfills all these requirements.
The Dacca Municipal Corporation under the Ministry of Local
Government, Rural development and Co-operatives, has elected
assembly. The Urban Development Directorate, under the
Ministry of Public Works and Urban Development is without
doubt the leading planning organisation. The Roads and Highways Directorate, under the Ministry of Railways, Roads,
Highways and Transport, is perhaps the most efficient im-
plementation organisation.

It is tempting to suggest that the best solution to the
problem would be the creation of a new organisation and the
abolition of a large number of the existing ones. The logical
location for such a group would probably be in the Ministry
of Local Government and hence such a development would tend
to bring local planning into the rightful sphere of the local
authority. One solution would seem to be a transfer of a
consolidated Urban Development Directorate and most elements
of the Dacca Improvement Trust to the Ministry of Local
Government and an abolition of the constraints on the UDD for
operation in Dacca. Implementation would then become the
responsibility of the engineering elements of DIT with inter-
Departmental contracts for specific projects to other government bodies.

The very restrictive constraints on finance would necessarily require loosening as well. Although it is not unreasonable to expect such a planning organisation partially to pay its own way though the inclusion in its programme of some self-financing measures, most projects which are viewed as high priority in the present context are those which promote national economic goals and involve benefits which do not directly return to the planning organisation. Such projects require block grants from the Treasury rather than merely loans for which interest is charged. Cross-subsidation of projects is probably essential if any project is to be undertaken for the strata of the population with the lowest incomes unless grants are included for these as well. Given the resource situation in the nation, such grants should be restricted to those projects which contain demonstrated economic benefits in the productive sphere. Identification of these latter projects should be an integral part of the activities of the Planning Commission. Obviously, this is purely a speculative suggestion and would be dependent upon action by the political decision-makers in the Bangladesh Government. Yet without some sort of clearly cut, finely-tuned organisation that can incorporate the entire development process in Dacca from plan formulation to implementation to monitoring and review, success on this front is likely to remain elusive. And with the potential growth which could take place in Dacca over the coming years, achieving success may well be an inherent part of survival.

CONCLUSIONS

Based on the experience in Dacca, the following conclusions appear to be relevant:

1. Plans for the city are incapable of being implemented unless explicit account is taken of the limited resource availability for the projects that are proposed. The resources which must be conserved are not only money, but agricultural land as well. The only feasible solution to the Dacca problem is one that is inexpensive but involves minimum loss of valuable land from foodstuff production.

2. To some extent, the financial resource constraints can be partially alleviated by the inclusion of an annual plan for implementation in Dacca which is an integral

part of the long-term urban development strategy for Bangladesh and for the Dacca Metropolitan Region. In a similar manner, the plan must be closely linked to the National Economic Plan, which implies the inclusion of a spatial strategy in the latter plan.

3. It is unrealistic to expect an improvement in the amount of resources available for urban development in Dacca or any other urban area in the country. In fact, over the foreseeable future, as rural-to-urban migration accelerates, the real value of such resources, not only on a per capita basis, but possibly on an aggregate basis as well, is likely to decline.

4. The best use of the available funds is dependent upon a simple and efficient organisational structure, giving considerable powers to plan and implement to a single body.

5. To meet its responsibilities adequately, the planning organisations in Dacca must greatly increase the number of planners available in the country. This involves not only the further development of training institutions in Bangladesh but the inclusion of a very generous dose of foreign assistance as well.

6. Particularly in the case where there is scarcity of resources, as clearly illustrated by the Dacca experience, planning and implementation must be viewed as parts of the same activity. Plans that cannot be implemented are useless to the organised development of a city and the resources wasted in their preparation would be far better spent on alternative pursuits.

7. Finally, without the political commitment of the decision-makers within the government and their recognition of the importance of urban planning in the economic development of the country, it is unlikely that the urban planning efforts will be successful. The physical planners should take every opportunity to demonstrate the relationship between their projects and the growth in production and productivity within the nation. It is only through the acknowledgement by the general public that such activities are of value to the nation that the needed support for success in the field can be achieved.

ACKNOWLEDGEMENT

I wish to acknowledge Md. Khorshed Alam for permission to use certain examples included in his thesis, 'Proposal for an Integrated Development Planning Organisation for the Dacca Metropolitan Area," submitted in partial fulfillment of the requirements for the Joint Master's Degree in Urban and Regional Planning, University of Sheffield/Bangladesh University of Engineering and Technology, 1979. Much of the information included in the paper is based on conversations with Bangladesh planning officials, United Nations staff associated with the National Physical Plan for Bangladesh as well as academics and students from Bangladesh. In particular, I would like to acknowledge the help given by Emeritus Professor J. R. James in clarifying my own thoughts and ideas and for acting as my guide to Bangladesh over the last five years. Any errors in interpretation are, however, mine alone.

REFERENCES

1. B. L. C. Johnson, Bangladesh, London, 1975, p.77.
2. Census Commission, Bangladesh Census of Population -
    1974. Bulletin 2, Dacca, 1975.
3. J. R. James, 'A Discussion Paper on Some Aspects of Town
    and Country Planning in Bangladesh', Report prepared
    for the Ford Foundation, 1973.
4. J. Faaland and J. R. Parkinson, Bangladesh: Test Case for
    Development, Dacca, 1976, pp. 124-5.
5. A. Abdullah, et al., SIDA/ILO Report on IRDP, Appendix A,
    1974 .
6. Quoted in Some Aspects of Development Planning in
    Bangladesh, United Nations Relief Operation, Dacca,
    December 1972.
7. N. Islam and H. Hossain, 'The Relationship of Urban
    Centres with their Rural Hinterlands', National
    Report on Human Settlements: Bangladesh, Prepared for
    the United Nations Conference on Human Settlements,
    Dacca, 1976, p.73.
8. The official population figures for Dacca are 1951:
    338,460; 1961:550,000; 1974:1,604,796.
9. Government of East Pakistan, Water, Power and Irrigation
    Department, Government Order No. 464-E, dated Dacca 17
    July 1965. Dacca, 1976, p.73.
10. Spenceley Minoprio, and P. W. Macfarlane, Master Plan for
    Dacca, London, December 1959.

11. Estimates based on Project Evaluation Performa of the various agencies at different time periods.
12. M. S. Rahman, Bangladesh Pourashava Statistics, Dacca, 1977, Table 10A.
13. M. K. Alam, 'Proposal for an Integrated Development Planning Organisation for the Dacca Metropolitan Area,' Master's Thesis, Ch.2., Sheffield/Bangladesh University, 1979.
14. Estimates of the number of bastees vary widely from one half the population in S. R. Qadir, Bastees of Dacca, Dacca, 1975, pp. 3-5, to as few as 10.3 per cent of the population in R. H. Choudhury, N. R. Ahmed and S. Huda "Movement of Immigrants to Urban Regions of Bangladesh," in: "National Report of Human Settlements: Bangladesh," Op. Cit., p.88.
15. See, for example, Bangladesh Population Control and Family Planning Division, Bangladesh National Population Policy: An Outline, Dacca, June 1976.

Beyond Lagos: Problems of implementation and management of rapid urban growth and development in Nigeria

U.A.Ejionye

INTRODUCTION

Understanding and acting upon problems of implementation and management of rapid growth and development in Nigeria requires at the outset an appreciation of the cumulative effects of the country's new system of government and policies on urban and national development planning.

Under its presidential system of administration, Nigeria now operates a three-tier system of government, Federal, State and Local. As a result, in addition to the Federal Capital of Lagos (to be replaced shortly by Abuja), there are 19 state capitals, that is, one for each of the 19 states in the nation, as well as a large number of local government areas and headquarters within the states. Furthermore, when the second wave of new states, presently under discussion, are designated there will be more state capitals and more local government areas and headquarters. This trend will generate a phenomenal increase in the growth of urban areas.

At the same time, it is apparent that the Fourth National Development Plan 1981/85 continues the emphasis of earlier plans on economic growth to the almost total neglect of physical, social and environmental planning. This neglect places very heavy pressure on existing and future urban settlements, leading to outmoded settlement structures, poor planning layout and inadequate provision of housing, infrastructure and services. Everywhere in the country, in the older cities and the newly created state capitals and local government headquarters, there is rapid unplanned population growth and sprawl, increasing economic and administrative activities and accelerated urbanisation processes and problems. Unregulated and uncontrolled private developments which grow in response to rising demands for housing and office accommodation contribute to the disorderly spatial and environmental development in urban areas.

In these circumstances, unless new strategies and machinery are created for the integrated implementation and management of urban planning Nigeria will face massive problems, if not chaos, in human settlement development.

Following a brief review of recent urban and development planning trends, this paper explores and makes recommendations concerning the need for new institutional frameworks for integrated implementation and management; legal control and regulation; appropriate manpower utilisation and inter-professional cooperation.

TRENDS IN URBAN GROWTH AND DEVELOPMENT IN NIGERIA

The Development of New Towns

The new town idea as an instrument of planning and development has gained some measure of popularity in Nigeria. There are a few examples which provide an illustration.

Lagos New Towns. The population of Lagos, now estimated at about five million, has been gradually dispersed to what is now known as Lagos Satellite Towns built within the Festival of Arts and Culture (FESTAC) village between Lagos and Badagry. It is estimated that in 1979, 30,000 people moved to the Satellite towns from Lagos. At the moment, the population of Lagos new towns is about 75,000.

Ajoda New Town. The Ajoda new town under construction is designed to absorb some of the over-spill population of Ibadan.

Proposed New Towns in Bendel State. In Bendel State, there is a government programme which aims at building one new town in each of the nineteen local government areas in the State.

The proposed development is apparently based on the principle of town-expansion (expanding towns). Its aim how-

ever, seems closely related to the idea of linking the urban
with the rural in what has become popularly known as rural
and urban integrated development.

Abuja New Town. Perhaps one of the most advanced appli-
cations of the new town idea is in the development of the
Abuja New Town which will replace Lagos as Nigeria's Federal
Capital City. Abuja, in every respect is conceived, planned
and built as a new town, and compares, as a new capital city,
with Gaborone (Botswana), Dodoma (Tanzania), Islamabad
(Pakistan), New Delhi (India), Canberra (Australia) and
Brasilia (Brazil).

The choice of Abuja as Nigeria's future Federal Capital
City has very interesting political as well as urban planning
development implications. The criteria of choice are clearly
stated in the "Aguda Report" of 1975, shown here in Table 1,
and were duly weighted in terms of their significance to the
Federal Republic of Nigeria's future needs.

Centrality, ie. its location in the middle of the nation
and ease of accessibility from all states, is the predominant
criterion in the choice of Abuja as an alternative capital
city of the Federal Republic of Nigeria. It is also a fundamental factor, at least in the Nigerian situation, which
contributes significantly to urban development and planning.
In this direction, Abuja should be seen as a purposely-built,
self-contained new human settlement for work and living,
designed, among other things, to absorb the overspill population of Lagos in particular and other Nigerian cities in
general. Its construction is an experiment in urban development. Sponsored by the government and backed by a clear
policy and a commitment of a sizeable national resource, it
will, when completed, serve as an instrument of population
dispersal, and the decentralisation of industries, employment
and administration.

Industrial Location and Balanced Development

An essential policy objective and strategy in the implementation of the Fourth National Development Plan (1981-
85) is that of ensuring the achievement of better balance in
the development of not only the different sectors of the
economy but also the various geographical areas of the
country. This is being promoted through the Federal Govern-

Table 1. Significance Attached to Criterion in the
          Choice of Abuja as Federal Capital

Selected Criterion	Weighting (by percentage)
Centrality	22
Health and Climate	12
Land Availability and Use	10
Water Supply	10
Multi-Access Possibilities	7
Security	6
Existence of Building Materials Locally	6
Low Population Density	6
Power Resources	5
Drainage	5
Soil	4
Physical Planning Convenience	4
Ethnic Accord	3
	100 %

Source: "Aguda Report," Report of the Committee on
         the Location of the Federal Capital of
         Nigeria, Federal Republic of Nigeria,
         December, 1975, p.47.

ment's industrial location policy. Nigeria's major industries
(currently with emphasis on steel development) are, as far as
possible, being spread throughout all parts of the country,
such as the Aladja Steel Company (Bendel State); Ajeokuta
Steel Complex (Kwara State); The Steel Rolling Mills Oshogbo
(Oyo State); Jos (Plateau State); Petroleum Refineries
(Kaduna State, Rivers State, Bendel State and Cross River
State to be established shortly; Metallurgical Mill (Imo
State); Paper Mill (Ogun State) and other industries distributed around Lagos, Kano, Enugu, Warri, Port Harcourt,
Onitsha, Sokoto, and Mina. This list is by no means exhaus-
tive; it is merely indicative of the growing spread of industries. However, the pursuit of this industrial location
policy has very important implications for urban growth and
planning because the location of industries determines, among
other things, areas where we could expect growth centres and
areas of future population concentration. For example, the
location of the Aladja Steel Plant between Ughelli and Warri

has already laid the foundation for the development of a
steel industrial city; and the siting of the Ajeokuta Steel
Complex in Kwara State has already developed the nucleus of a
steel industry town in the area. It is becoming apparent
that distribution of Federal, State and private companies in
the manufacturing, commercial and distribution industries
will influence, in the near future, the development of
cities, which, in turn, will generate those physical and
social planning problems usually associated with new centres
of growth.

Private Development

     Private development in Nigeria's main industrial and
administrative centres are a response to the rising demand
for housing, industrial and commercial office accommodation
and play a crucial role in stimulating unplanned growth and
pressure for the provision of major infrastructural facilities. In some cases, houses and private housing estates for
rent, have been built in parts of the city where there are no
access roads and where such basic amenities as water and
electricity are not yet provided. Until recently, private
development hardly had any effective competition from governments and government functionaries having responsibility for
property development. Even at the moment, when government
housing programmes have been significantly stepped up, private development still plays a major role in urban development. In their efforts to exploit the ever-rising pressure
on public housing and the growing demand for office accommodation, many private developers erect buildings that are
sub-standard or have failed to meet planning regulations and
control.

Policy-Guided Trends

     Urban Planning and Development Policy. The main thrust
of this policy, outlined during the Third National Department
Plan (1975-1980), and re-emphasised in the Fourth National
Development Plan (1981-1985), is based on promoting improved
layout as means of (a) arresting the tendency to chaotic
urban growth and (b) intensifying efforts in providing essential amenities and services such as urban roads, water
supply, sewerage and drainage, refuse disposal, parks,
gardens and recreational facilities. A Town and Country

Planning Programme, now established, is devoted to surveying, mapping and the preparation of Master Plans for the development of major cities and towns. The basic policy objectives also include dealing with secondary environmental pollution (ie. industrial activities as they affect water, land, air), noise pollution and natural disaster. To enhance environmental planning as an integral part of project planning by all agencies concerned, an inspectorate unit will be established in the Environmental Planning Division of the Federal Ministry of Industries to coordinate this function with the Federal Ministry of Housing and Environmental Development.

Housing policies are also considered. The Third National Development Plan contains a Federal Government programme directed towards providing quarters for its workers, and to providing direct housing construction for the masses as a broad objective. It sets itself an initial target of building 60,000 (later increased to 200,000) housing units annually. To finance the project, and increase opportunities for housing loans, the Government created a Federal Mortgage Bank. Furthermore, during the Third Plan period a new Federal Ministry of Housing, Urban Development and Environment and the Federal Housing Authority were created to implement the housing policy. The Fourth National Development Plan pursues the policy objectives of the Third National Development Plan, but with some significant modifications. The Fourth Plan notes, for example, a number of problems in developing a realistic housing programme, such as maintenance of high quality of residential housing and the ability of owners to pay for such houses; and the need not to impose high standards on all sections of the society. It therefore follows a modified policy in housing guided by the need to produce housing units at prices that various sectors of the public could pay, especially the low-income groups. Emphasis is placed on:

i   Encouraging individual house ownership and partnership between Federal and State Government in providing adequate housing units for the masses in both urban and rural areas;

ii Reviewing the Land Use Decree in order to facilitate the allocation of land to private developers wishing to develop housing estates within the framework of government regulations;

iii Encouraging local manufacturers of building materials such as cement and clay bricks as a means of reducing costs.

The Federal Housing Programme. As noted earlier, a major
element of Nigeria's urban development policy is based on a
programme designed to bring about a substantial increase in
the supply of housing stock throughout the Federation, especially for low-income groups. The success of the programme
depends very much on cooperation between the Federal and
State governments on one hand, and on effective implementation by the Federal Ministry of Housing and Environment
through its agencies, on the other hand. For example, State
governments are requested to make land available to the Federal Government for purposes of housing construction in the
States. The building of houses and their allocation in the
States are the responsibility of the Federal Housing Authority, an arm of the Federal Ministry of Housing and Environment. In financing the construction of houses the Federal
Ministry of Housing and Environment, through the Federal
Mortgage Bank of Nigeria, also plays a vital role. But making
land available by the States is not mandatory but obligatory.
In cases where some States refuse to make land available, the
Federal Housing Programme may be jeopardised. Besides, implementation is rendered difficult because the planning process, in this case under the Town and Country Planning Programme, is divorced from the implementation process involving
a different set of authorities - the Housing Authority and
the Federal Mortgage Bank. Problems of coordination, delay
and demarcation of responsibility are bound to occur at both
planning and implementation levels.

The problems identified above are complicated by the
fact that urban planning and development is on the Concurrent
List. This is to say, both the state and federal governments
share the constitutional duty of planning for urban growth
and development. It is, therefore, not clear where the federal government's responsibility stops and the state's begin
in planning and development. This again clearly raises the
question of cooperation, coordination and the clarity in the
demarcation of responsibility and authority relationships.

The Nigerian States Urban Development Programme (NSUDP).
This programme was set up in 1977 through the assistance of
the World Bank to enable the Nigerian States to contribute to
the overall national housing need. As a project-oriented
programme, it seeks to provide a framework for a continuous
and systematic housing delivery development which will be
self-sustaining and self-financing. The major broad objectives are to ensure:

i   A substantial increase in housing supply for groups
     expressing the greatest needs.

ii   Provision of housing that is affordable by the targeted
     population with or without subsidy from public funds.

iii Project replicability within the states' and federal
     resources.

iv   A high level of cost recovery for the project to be
     self-sustaining.

v   An adequate control of the effects of urban sector in-
     vestment on national and state economies.

Projects which the programme can support include: sites
and services; slum and squatter settlement upgrading; integrated social services programme; employment generation and
training programme; credit delivery for home construction and
improvement; assistance to local authorities for training and
post-implementation maintenance; and provision of some
aspects of municipal infrastructure.

The following States were identified as the first to
benefit from this programme: Bauchi, Benue, Imo, Ogun, Ondo,
Gongola and Niger. Lagos was included as the eighth mainly
because of its special urban growth problems. Other states
not included in the list were nonetheless requested to indicate their need and interest to participate in the programme.

Choice of project depends on need and could involve a
single project or a combination of projects such as sites and
services and slum and squatter settlement upgrading at a
time. Implementation is based on the results of feasibility
studies and requires conformity with procedure laid down by
the World Bank. For example, any project implementation
involves the following organisations which have different
levels of input of service or responsibility under the same
process:

The World Bank - responsible for project evaluation and
appraisal and for project financing and monitoring.

The Federal Ministry of Housing and Environment - responsible for policy formulation, programme scheduling and
coordination, programme monitoring and recommendation for
external financing.

Federal Mortgage Bank of Nigeria: (Project Development Department) - responsible for project identification, preparation of planning guidelines, project supervision, monitoring and evaluation, credit facilities for home construction or improvement and on-lending of external funds and cost recovery.

The State - responsible for setting up or appointing the Project Authority or Agency, and for Policy formulation, project design and appraisal, project supervision and coordination and for project implementation.

By 1982, five years after the programme was initiated, no project had actually started in any of the Nigerian states. Feasibility studies only have so far been completed in Bauchi and Imo states; studies are still going on in Benue and Ogun states; no studies have been started as yet in Gongola and Niger states, and agreement on implementation is yet to be reached in Lagos state.

In addition, there are no indications of interest for participating in the programme by those other states not listed. The question then is: what went wrong? The description given above shows that the NSUDP is state based. It is the state that sets up a Project Agency which designs and implements the project. There is now confusion regarding who should control it - the Federal or the State government. However, since the World Bank provides the project money, it is usual for it to issue directives or guidelines on how the money will be released. Similarly, the Federal Government agencies which disburse the money also insist on conformity with World Bank directives and may impose other conditions to ensure accountability. As a result, implementation and management is impaired by the participation of too many interests and the development of cumbersome lines of communication. Moreover, emphasis by Federal Government functionaries on financial control relegates to the background the more urgent need to facilitate swift action by the project agency. There has, therefore, been a complete lack of definition, clarity and harmonisation of roles between the various agencies. In addition, without a central implementation authority, no continuous and effective dialogue has been maintained with the states. Consequently, uncertainty and drift from lack of advice and information have been indirectly encouraged. Lastly, lack of technical and managerial skills required in the implementation of projects led some of the states to either abandon the idea or rendered them unable to make any decisions at all.

PROBLEMS OF IMPLEMENTATION AND MANAGEMENT

It seems clearly apparent that there are pressing problems of implementation and management. The major problem areas are examined below.

Institutional Framework and Coordination

The implementation and management of settlement planning and development policies and programmes in Nigeria is a major problem because of a lack of an appropriate institutional framework which can be adopted simultaneously by the Federal, State and Local governments. Ideally, this would make the coordination of implementation and management efforts at these three levels easy and effective. However since planning is on the Concurrent List, it is carried on at these various levels independently. Experience shows that the states and local governments are invariably less financially able to establish the appropriate institutional structure for implementation. Whenever they do, levels of relationships between institutions and professionals are not usually defined either between the Federal and State governments, or between the state governments, and between state and local governments. Consequently, efforts, resources and services are duplicated and coordination is not achieved. Lack of coordination, in some cases, may mean loss of vital information and advice, or loss of technical and managerial assistance. Above all, some of the institutions set up for implementation of projects or policy objectives may fail to bring together the two vital aspects of planning and implementation.

What seems necessary is the development of an institutional framework which handles simultaneously the functions of planning and implementation on one hand, and coordinates the activities at Federal, State and Local Government levels on the other hand. This organisational framework must take into account clear definition of roles and responsibilities and a proper indication of relationships, chain of command and lines of communication, control and accountability.

Legal Control and Regulation

Implementation and management of Nigeria's urban planning and development is hampered by lack of mandatory legal regulations which impose some control over development agencies, public and private. Regulations and control must be backed by strong and comprehensive legislative measures passed by the National Assembly and observed simultaneously by both state and federal planning authorities and implementation agencies. In this way standards can be enforced and rules observed, provided that the appropriate legal institutions are set up to monitor the effects of the regulations and the controls and to enforce them.

In other words, legal regulations and control affecting planning and development must be made the constitutional responsibility of the Federal Government: that is, placed on the Exclusive List. Unless this is done, any federal authority that is proposed to take responsibility for planning and implementation, and coordination, may find its operations hampered by lack of cooperation from the states or local governments.

Manpower Shortage

Nigeria shares with other third world countries the common problem of a shortage in the supply of appropriate skills and training required both in settlement planning delivery and in the management of urban development programmes. The Federal Government's guidelines for the Fourth National Development Plan (1981-85) emphasises the need for manpower development and utilisation in the implementation of its various policies, including urban development. Substantial shortages in existing and required manpower for the achievement of Plan objectives are noted (see Table 2).

Major categories of shortage and need are further identified in the Study of Nigeria's Manpower Requirements, 1977 by the National Manpower Board, with a special emphasis on strengthening management in all sectors of the economy. That study showed, for example, a combined vacancy rate of 27.2% for General Managers and Managing Directors; Personnel Managers; and Assistant Managers, fields in which one notes a heavy expatriate presence. (It is unlikely however that these occupational categories are urban managers of the type

Table 2. Estimated Manpower Requirements of the Fourth Nigerian National Development Plan 1981–85

(1) Category of Manpower	(2) Estimated Current Stock 1980	(3) Requirement for meeting Existing Shortage	(4) Requirement for meeting 1985 Employment/ Population Target	(5) Requirement for meeting Wasteage, 1980–85	(6) Additional Requirements meeting 1980–85 (3)+(4)+ (5)−(2)
1 Architects	650	620	860	50	880
2 Accountants	6,000	2,650	8,500	465	5,615
3 Town Planners	300	350	400	25	475
4 Civil and Structural Engineers	4,000	4,700	6,000	310	7,010
5 Builders	300	240	500	25	465
6 Electrical and Electronic Engineers	3,500	2,070	5,000	270	3,840
7 Agricultural Engineers	350	260	600	30	540
8 Land Surveyors	600	350	800	50	600
9 Quantity Surveyors	400	220	500	30	350
10 Estate Surveyors	500	250	690	40	480
11 Geologists and Geophysicists	450	370	600	35	555
12 Architectural Technicians	1,080	1,220	1,500	85	1,725
13 Civil Engineering Technicians	9,800	5,950	12,300	760	9,210

Table 2. Continued

14	Electrical/Electronic Engineering Technicians	10,600	8,060	13,500	825	11,785
15	Medical Doctors	8,400	4,830	15,000	650	12,080
16	Dentists	400	286	900	30	816
17	Pharmacists	3,000	1,690	5,000	230	3,920
18	Veterinary Surgeons	1,000	505	3,000	80	2,585
19	Nurses and Midwives	50,000	21,430	90,000	3,880	65,310
20	Medical Laboratory Technologists	1,200	640	4,000	100	3,540
21	Radiographers	400	190	800	30	620
22	Agricultural Officers	2,500	1,440	4,000	195	3,135
23	Agricultural Assistants	6,300	2,040	10,300	490	6,530
24	Statisticians	500	370	500	40	410
25	Administrative Officer	4,500	2,370	6,500	350	4,720
26	Executive Officers	6,800	2,270	10,000	530	6,000
27	Librarians	1,000	850	3,000	80	2,930
28	Legal Practitioners	5,650	2,260	8,135	440	5,185

Source: Federal Republic of Nigeria, Federal Ministry of Planning, Guidelines for the Fourth National Development Plan 1981-85, Lagos, Nigeria 1980, p.89.

required to deal with settlement planning and management).
As far as physical plan implementation is concerned, the
study indicates serious shortages of architects, town planners, land and quantity surveyors, engineers, technicians and
teaching staff (see Table 3).

The major point to be emphasised here is that although
managerial skill is generally one of the areas of great need,
special effort is required in order to produce urban managers
and related personnel who are badly needed for the implementation and management of urban growth, development and planning.

Education and Training for Essential Skills

Nigeria is meeting the challenges of manpower shortage
by expanding her education opportunities programme. New
educational institutions and professional bodies for the
training and development of the most urgently required skills
are being established. In the 1981/82 academic year there
were 16 universities and by 1984, the total will be 20 universities. The universities offer courses ranging from
Management and Business Studies, Engineering and Technology,
Environmental Studies and Natural Science, to Medicine, Law
and the Social Sciences. These are universities established
by the State governments. Also, the Federal government proposes to establish in each of the 19 states a polytechnic
and/or a college of science and technology. At the same
time, there are many colleges of education and teacher training colleges, some of which are either owned by the Federal
government or by State governments. Finally, the Federal
Government has established a number of specialised institutions providing services and advice or training in special
areas of need. These include: The Centre for Management
Development (CMD), Administrative Staff College of Nigeria
(ASCON), and the Manpower Board. An independent body like
the Nigerian Association of Schools of Management Education
and Training is also very important.

A major question which requires further research and
analysis is: how adequate and appropriate is the expanded
opportunities programme in the fields relevant for the production of specially-qualified manpower to deal with integrated implementation and management of planning and develop
ment. The impact of the educational institutions on edu-

Table 3. Nigeria's Manpower Requirements in Selected
          Occupations

Occupational Categories	Vacancy Rate(%)	Expatriate as % Total Employees
Administrative Officers (Public Sector)	0.3	4.8
Executive Officers (General Duties)	23.9	0.2
Executive Officers (Accounts)	28.8	2.0
General Managers and Managing Directors	5.4	21.5
Other Managers (eg. Personnel, etc.)	12.0	12.2
Assistant Managers	9.8	6.6
Accounts and Auditors	30.5	9.6
Architects	49.4	34.7
Town Planners	53.9	12.6
Land Surveyors	36.7	11.0
Quantity Surveyors	35.8	17.8
Civil and Structural Engineers	54.3	4.5
Electrical and Electronic Engineers	37.2	30.5
Agricultural Engineers	42.8	9.4
Chemists	40.7	20.2
Physicists	40.9	38.5
Geologists	48.0	9.4
Meteorologists	64.7	-
Biologists	42.0	24.2
Statisticians	48.0	3.4
Systems Analysts and Programmers	41.9	2.0
ENT Specialists	81.1	20.0
Psychiatrists	55.0	25.0
Pathologists (medical)	50.4	22.4
Pathologists (Vet./Plant)	70.0	16.7
Anaesthetists	43.9	32.0
Dentists	42.0	41.7
Surgeons	33.9	23.5
Medical Health Doctors	36.4	11.8
Optometrists/Opticians	66.6	12.3
Architectural Technicians	53.1	3.8
Town Planning Technicians	45.1	2.3
Survey Technicians	35.1	3.1
Civil Engineering Technicians	37.8	10.6
Mining Engineering Technicians	50.9	-
Metallurgical Engineering Technicians	39.6	-
Draughtsmen	33.5	1.0
Vet Technicians	37.7	8.7
Dental Technicians	63.7	3.3

Table 3. Continued

Occupational Categories	Vacancy Rate(%)	Expatriate as % Total Employees
Medical Laboratory Technicians	43.2	2.0
Dieticians and Nutritionists	36.1	1.6
Pharmaceutical Assistants	41.8	0.9
Teaching Staff of the Universities Lecturers in:		
Statistics	56.4	11.8
Mathematics	38.0	37.2
Computer Science	35.0	15.4
Medicine	48.0	22.9
Architecture	49.4	57.5
Building	59.1	33.3
Environmental Design	90.0	–
Quantity Surveying	41.7	42.9
Actuarial Science (Insurance)	57.1	–
Food and Home Science	54.5	10.0
Teaching Staff of the Polytechnics Lecturers in:		
Civil .Engineering	53.3	19.2
Electrical and Electronic Engineering	48.1	18.2
Chemical Engineering	72.7	22.2
Mechanical Engineering	40.2	7.9
Land Surveying	50.0	20.0
Physics	36.7	–
Accountancy	65.2	24.0
Finance/Banking	27.5	–
Agriculture	51.3	5.3
Fine and Applied Arts	65.6	–

Source: Extracted from the report of the Study of Nigeria's
        Manpower Requirements, 1977. National Manpower
        Board, Lagos.

cation and training generally and in producing the much
needed skills could be measured, perhaps by reference to
student enrolment in Nigerian Universities by subject areas,
by Universities and Polytechnics, and by graduate outturn
from Universities and Polytechnics.

This apart, an area of institutional response in human settlement implementation programmes which will play a very innovative role in Nigeria is within the government established specialised institutions working closely with professional and independent associations and planners from the social sciences. Such professional associations as the Council of Registered Engineers of Nigeria (COREN), Architectural Registration Council of Nigeria (ARCON), and the Nigerian Institute of Town Planners (NITP), must be made aware of the relevance of urban managers to settlement planning and development. The various specialised management bodies need to have an urban management input included in their management training programmes. When proper links are developed with these bodies and institutions, the course content on urban management training developed with their cooperation would be much more realistic and valuable to trainees and practitioners alike. This cooperative effort needs to be explored against the background of a proper evaluative study of the courses offered in the universities, polytechnics, and colleges of education and technology in the related subject areas to human settlement planning in Nigeria. Such a survey would provide a clear indication of courses offered, levels of skills and expertise achieved, and the gaps that need to be filled, and what the specialised bodies and institutions can offer to push levels of competence much higher.

Manpower Utilisation and Inter-Professional Cooperation

There is a major problem in determining the role of social scientists and involving them effectively in human settlement planning and development in Nigeria. Perhaps this problem is universal and an integral part of the process of professionalisation. Sociologists, economists, geographers (until relatively recently), and psychologists, are hardly accepted as planners by architects, engineers, technicians, surveyors, and town planners. Often, social scientists are required to demonstrate what they can contribute to planning because, by historical conception, development planning means physical planning and directly involves engineering, architecture, design and construction, surveying, town planning, valuation, etc. And yet, human settlement planning and development involves planning for people. It needs a backing ideology and philosophy; it needs some guidelines and basic goals in human terms; it requires some rationalisation.

BEYOND LAGOS   175

Human needs and aspirations must be built into planning; and
a process of participation by the people for whom we are
planning is essential. These are some of the very vital
socio-cultural inputs which social scientists, especially
sociologists can provide. Economists cannot be ignored when
it comes to evaluation and costing, at least; and geographers
must be called in to advise on land-use, among other things.

A reconciliation of historically-based definitions of
professionalism with the reality of our time is necessary for
the link between the various bodies and established educational institutions is to be a reality. Planning for
people must be reconciled with architectural determinism and
design-solutions to human settlement planning and development. Experts from the traditional planning professions can
and ought to work with social scientists, because an inter-
disciplinary approach seems demonstrably necessary.

WHAT CAN BE DONE

Given the problems of implementation and management
outlined here, there are a number of recommendations that can
be made for further consideration:

1   Creation of a Human Settlement Planning Authority as an
independent Federal Government of Nigeria institution charged
with the responsibility of coordinating all settlement planning and development efforts, conducting research, proposing
legislation on planning regulation and control, and re-
commending the appropriate institutional structures for integration and implementation of policies.

2   Undertaking a survey of the education and training facilities and courses available in Nigerian Universities,
Polytechnics, Colleges of Education and Technology, and
Teacher Training Colleges of relevance to settlement planning
in order to determine the level of skills and expertise acquired, and how they are utilised, and to assess the current
vacancy rate.

3   Organising sustained links between the Human Settlement
Planning Authority, educational institutions, and the
specialised management bodies and advisory councils in order
to work together in the training of urban managers. Cooperative efforts will ensure that the course content for the
short courses on skills in urban management would be enriched.

4   Initiating regular seminars and conferences, bringing together traditional professional planners, engineers, architects, designers, town planners, surveyors, valuers, etc. and social scientists, to re-educate themselves on the wider concept and instruments of integrated planning and on the urgent need to work together.

5   An evaluative study of the achievements of the Federal Housing Authority in the implementation of the housing programme should be undertaken. Data will be needed on stock of houses built and allocated, facilities (loans, etc.) for housing purchases, criteria for housing need and qualification for allocation, behaviour of Nigerians towards public housing and new housing estates, the state of low-income group housing, etc.

6   A systematic study of the Federal Government's industrial location policy is required to determine its current and future implications for urban growth, planning and development, population distribution, and the provision of infrastructure and social services.

7   The implementation of the Nigerian States Urban Development Programme under the supervision of the proposed Human Settlement Planning Authority is strongly advocated.

8   The Federal Government, through the Human Settlement Planning Authority, should encourage urban development based on the new town idea as a major instrument of planning to reduce congestion, promote decentralisation of industries and office accommodation, and to facilitate population redistribution and regional planning.

9   The Federal Government, through the Human Settlement Planning Authority, should seek the support, cooperation and assistance of specialised international agencies and independent institutions in the financing and running of projects, in organising seminars and conferences, and in providing fellowship and short courses of education and training in urban management and human settlement planning and development.

REFERENCES

Federal Republic of Nigeria, Federal Ministry of National
        Planning and Development, Lagos, "Guidelines for the

Fourth National Development Plan 1981-85," (Lagos 1980).

Nigerian National Report (Interim Version) submitted to the United Nations Habitat: Conference on Human Settlements, Vancouver, Canada 31 May-11 June 1976 (New York: United Nations) A/CONF.70/NR/54.

Aguda Report, Federal Republic of Nigeria, Report of the Committee on the Location of the Federal Capital of Nigeria at Abuja, (Lagos: December 1975).

Study of Nigeria's Manpower Requirements, 1977 (Lagos: National Manpower Board).

Blair, T. L., "Training for Human Settlement Development," Habitat International, Vol.4, No. 1/2, pp.7-33 (1979).

Insights concerning the manpower requirements of the Fourth National Development Plan were gained from data presented to the Annual Seminar of the Committee of Vice-Chancellors, February 1982, at the University of Benin in a paper by Professor V.P. Diejomaoh, Director, Nigerian Institute of Social and Economic Research (NISER), Ibadan, and Chairman, Nigerian National Manpower Board.

Mexico City:
Ecological-environmental
dimensions of urban development
and planning

Luis Sanchez de Carmona
and Edwin Sours Renfrew

BRIEF ACCOUNT OF ECOLOGICAL-ENVIRONMENTAL PROBLEMS

City Origins and Growth. The settlement of what is now
Mexico City dates back to the 14th Century. In 1325, northern Mexicans guided by their god Huitzilopochtli to the
Mexico valley, founded an island-city, Tenochtitlan, capital
of a great empire on a lake east of Cahpultepec. Although
the conquistadors made it the capital of a vast territory
which included the Californias, Central America and the
Philippines, the city's area and population remained stable,
despite floods which brought plagues and epidemics.

Five hundred years later, in 1829, shortly after the
proclamation of the new republic of Mexico, Mexico City became the centre of a Federal District, covering an area of
200 square kilometers.

At the turn of the century, the metropolitan population
was 540,000, occupying 23 square kilometers. From 1900 to
1910 several residential suburbs were created; a tunnel was
pierced to Tequisquiac, which temporarily solved the flood
problem; main streets were paved; incandescent street-
lighting was installed; many foreign companies set up
offices; and the inhabited area increased to 33 square kilometers.

By the 1940's it was clear that Mexico City was in the
throes of a massive growth in area and population (see Table
1) which posed serious problems for the authorities.

Table 1. Urban Development and Population Increase (1)

Year	Populated Area (km²) (2)			Population (in thousands) (4)			Population Density (inhabitants/km²) (3)
	Fed.Dist.	Conurbations	Total	Fed.Dist.	Conurbations	Total	
1900	23	–	23	540	–	540	23,478.26
1930	86	–	86	1,288	–	1,288	14,976.74
1940	92	–	92	1,700	60	1,760	19,130.43
1950	200	42	242	3,000	100	3,100	12,809.91
1960	320	70	390	4,900	340	5,240	13,435.89
1970	432	128	560	7,000	1,900	8,900	15,892.85
1979	534	346	880	9,500	4,550	14,050	15,965.90

(1) Ingeniera Civil, Official organ of the Mexican College of Civil Engineers. July/August /August 1980, no. 214.

(2) Conurbations within the State of Mexico City.

(3) Includes the Federal District and conurbations within the State of Mexico City. Population density is calculated on the basis of the area occupied by the Federal District and that of its conurbations.

(4) There is a 5.4% annual population increase in the capital city, Revista Mexicana de Construccion, no. 297, July 1979.

Incomers, mostly unused to urban work, added to natural population growth, put demands on public services, such as housing, drinking water, removal of sewage, street-lighting, electricity supply, the police and security services, health, transport, roadworks and communications, much greater than could be provided. In this respect, between 1935 and 1946, 30% of the inhabitants were ill-provided for; in 1952, 60%; in 1962, 70%.

Housing. In 1970, the Federal District had 1,219,419 dwellings, 5.6 people to a house; 54.3% of the dwellings were in one or two quarters where 51.3% of the population lived; the housing deficit stood at 130,000, not counting dwellings badly needing replacement.

The Urban Development Commission states a current housing deficit of 97,000 dwellings, likely to become 101,000 in 1982, which means that 70% of the population have no access to the house market.

Water. In 1970 about 96% of dwellings had access to drinking-water, 65% in the home and the rest from public taps or hydrants (though the supply to some parts of the megalopolis is restricted in wet seasons). Also in 1970, about 25% of dwellings had drainage. Except for some small localities in south Mexico City, everyone has electricity. Street lighting is deficient and insufficient; since 1965 incandescent lamps have been replaced by mercury vapour lamps (between 1971 and 1975 about 44,000 new streetlamps were installed, i.e. 21% of the Federal District total). In 1978, San Rafael suburb got sodium-vapour lamps, cheaper and brighter than the mercury system; now, that entire district, and the city's main streets have this type of lighting.

Drainage. The problem of draining off rain and residual water, which have flooded the metropolitan zone since pre-colonial times, has been partly solved by the deep drainage system, introduced in 1975. The Mexico City drainage system draws off rainwater and residual (municipal and industrial) water to the two rivers (which cross the city from East to West) and the Grand Canal, built to serve a million inhabitants in the early 1900s. The Churubusco River discharges into Lake Tecxoco, the Piedad River into the Grand Canal, north-east of the city, which drains, via 2 tunnels, into the Moctezuma, a tributary of the Panuco, which flows into the Gulf of Mexico at Tampico.

The deep drainage system, built 1954-1975, is 68km long, 50km being the main channel (diameter 6.5 metres) and 18km of feeder-channels (diameter 5 metres); the capacity is 200m³ per second. Despite these installations, Mexico City still lacks drains, largely due to a combination of recent factors.

Refuse Disposal. Since Mexico City's foundation, the collection, transport and final disposal of solid refuse has been a problem for the authorities. In the metropolitan area, two open-air rubbish dumps have been used, one in Santa Fe, the other, recently closed, in Santa Cruz, Meyehualco. Rubbish has been simply dumped, with no earth covering, and with adverse environmental effects - bad smells from putrefying organic matter, and hydrosulphuric acid produced by sulphate decomposition. This acid, together with water, produces carbonic acid which can pollute soil and water. Rainwater percolates through the rubbish and produces various detrimental substances according to the physical, chemical and biological processes in the soil. Also, there are fire hazards from methane gas (produced by anaerobic decomposition) when it reaches 5% to 15% of total volume. The flies, mosquitos and rats which live on the dumps carry infectious diseases as well as degrading the environment.

Subsidence. The lacustrine earth below the city is liable to compression and subsidence, especially in view of the increasing paved and built-up area, currently 880 square kilometres, and an estimated 1,540 square kilometres by the year 2000. This is aggravated by rainwater, which infiltrates the soil and overtaxes the drainage system. The increasing urban infrastructure, especially the metro, has necessitated the installation of pumps throughout the system.

General subsidence (9 metres in the city centre, and increasing by 50cm a year during the 1950's) has affected the course of the canal and the two rivers, so that now their gravity discharges are choked, and are higher than the surrounding terrain.

The daily activities of Mexico City inhabitants are inimical to the environment- the average citizen generates ½ kilo of rubbish daily, ie. 7000 tonnes for the area as a whole. The Santa Fe dump receives 717 single-journey, 262 two-journey, and 22 three-journey trucks a day. A truckload varies between 0.8 and 8.7 tonnes (average, 4.14 tonnes a journey), so the dump receives about 3,000 tonnes a day, some of which (paper, hard and expanded plastics, ferrous metals, plain and coloured glass) is sold as by-products. As well as the Santa Fe dump there is an industrialised plant for refuse where, after recovering some materials, eg. cloth, glass, paper and metal, the remainder is made into a compost-type fertilizer, having a trade-name "Rico suelo" (rich soil). This plant, at San Juan de Aragon, receives 180 tonnes of rubbish a day, using 34 trucks with an average load of 4.4 tonnes.

Open Space. The need for green open space in Mexico City has still not been fully met; there are about 4,2000 hectares of parks and gardens (4.75 square metres per inhabitant), a figure which should be doubled to provide adequate rest and recreation areas for the populace.

As regards the police and security services, the police force has increased, but without a commensurate improvement in equipment.

Education. The increase in educational facilities in the Federal District has not kept pace with the increase in population. In 1974-75 there were 729 kindergartens for pre-school education, with 3,888 educational staff, catering for 133,000 children (only 20% of the 3.5 year old population); 2,322 primary schools with 32,000 teachers and 1,424,256 pupils (however, out of every 100 registered in first year, only 64 reach sixth year). In 1,032 lower intermediate schools, 438,000 pupils were taught by 26,000 teachers, the drop-out rate was 10%. The 223 higher intermediate schools had 8,000 teachers and 250,000 pupils, the registration in second year was 70% of that of the first year. Finally, there were 43 'escuelas normales' (secondary schools) with 1,317 teachers and 13,700 students, and 37 institutes of further education with 220,000 students, 60% of whom were at the National Autonomous University of Mexico and the Metropolitan Autonomous University.

Transport. The anarchic development of the city made the urban transport system, which grew along with the metropolis and its population, inefficient. The wastefulness of this sector became evident in 1965, when 4,000 units of urban passenger transport were circulating in the city centre, and when certain streets, such as Moneda and Hidalgo Avenue, served 18 urban transport routes; 150,000 cars entered the central zone daily and parked in the streets; added to which,

the same zone contained the terminuses for suburban and
country bus-routes. In such circumstances, buses and trams
often circulated at less than walking-pace, and in that year
transportation meant four million man-hours overtime for the
population.

The Mexico City road network consists of a large number
of main avenues, three rapid-transit highways and many cross-
routes. Several of the avenues stopped short at one end, and
some of them still do, especially those leading to the city
centre. Since 1965, the increase in registered vehicles in
the Federal District (Table 2) and in the number of passenger
journeys (Table 3) has sharply increased. Passenger transport was a major problem in 1965, and this led to the Metro
being built as the backbone of an integral transport system,
the only one capable of moving 60,000 passengers per hour.
Three underground lines were introduced in 1970, 41.5km long,
with 48 stations, but they have not noticeably improved the
situation.

SOLUTIONS TO THE URBAN ENVIRONMENTAL PROBLEM

Faced with the ecological-environmental problems of
Mexico City, the competent authorities took a series of
measures to solve specific problems, but without taking an
overall view of the situation.

In 1977, the Secretariat for Human Settlements and
Public Works created the Directorate-General of Technology
for Autoconstruction (Self-Helpbuilding), with the main aims
of setting up the technical, financial and social instruments, and of bringing about the necessary action, for making
autoconstruction an organised process to help solve the housing deficit in Mexico. The Directorate works with other
departments who allot a part of their resources to housing
construction.

Since its inception in 1971, the Federal District Deep-
drainage System, whose main aim is to stop the flooding which
has plagued the city for centuries, has embarked on new
projects for interceptors, reservoirs and pumping-stations to
contain and divert rainwater and the water brought in by the
two rivers and from the hills west of the city.

As regards solid waste, the present plan is to place a
sanitary covering over the Santa Fe dump; the Santa Cruz dump

Table 2. Number of Registered Vehicles in the Federal District (1)

Type of vehicle	1906	1925	1950(2)	1965	%	1979	%
Municipal buses	–	–		65,000	(1.4)	7,800	(0.39)
Electrical transport	–	–		492	(0.1)	435	(0.02)
(Trams & trolley buses)	–	–		15,400	(3.4)	37,500	(1.88)
Taxis	800	21,200	55,000	283,000	(63.0)	1,730,723	(87.00)
Private cars				–		882	(0.04)
Metro carriages				144,608	(32.1)	212,547	(10.67)
Other transport (3)				–			
Total	800	21,200	130,000	450,000	(100.0)	1,989,887	(100.00)

(1) Ingeniera Civil, Mexican College of Civil Engineers, July/August, 1980, no 214.

(2) The figures do not show the distribution of 75,000 units of the 130,000, which is given as a total.

(3) Includes: goods vehicles, private buses, official vehicles, trailers, motor-cycles and bicycles; but does not include vehicles in the urban zone of Mexico State, which totalled 470,000 units.

Table 3. Number of Journeys Per Person Per Day in the
          Federal District (1)

| Type of transport | Year | | | |
| | 1965 | | 1979 | |
	Passengers	%	Passengers	%
Municipal bus	5,720,000	68.20	9,347,200	50.80
Electrical transport	661,920	7.90	607,200	3.30
Private car	588,640	7.02	3,532,800	19.20
Hired car	1,386,000	16.50	2,392,000	13.00
Metro	–	–	2,097,600	11.40
Other	26,560	0.38	423,200	2.30
Total	8,383,120	100.00	18,400,000	100.00

(1) Ingenieria Civil, Mexican College of Civil Engineers,
     July/August 1980, no. 214

will, in the near future (when the methane produced by decom-
posing organic matter has diminished), become a garden.
There are plans to establish four refuse incinerators and a
sanitized dump in Ixtapalapa.

In 1979, the Federal Districts' Commission for Road
Services and Transport worked out a guide-plan for those
services and a master-plan for the Metro, mainly to promote
the use of public transport, especially the Metro, and to
improve road services in the metropolitan area. The intention is that of the 35,600,000 journeys per person per day in
the metropolitan zone estimated for the year 2000, 94.4% will
be by public transport (45.8% by Metro, 34.3% by bus, 4% by
tram or trolleybus, and 10.3% by taxi) and the 5.6% remainder
in private vehicles.

The Metro master-plan proposes 21 lines by the year
2000, with 807 trains running on 378.13km of track and with a
potential capacity of 24 million passengers per day. The
plan for road services and transport has designated a large
number of streets as "axial roads" in order to speed up
traffic, with an average speed of 40km.p.h. (previously
traffic only moved at 10km.p.h.).

Undoubtedly, the competent authorities have accomplished undertakings in the various development sectors, such as those mentioned above, which tend to help solve the ecological environmental problems of the Federal District. However, few of these actions have managed to improve the quality of life of Mexico City's inhabitants; some, indeed, have had adverse effects on other aspects of development. At present, no programme has been implemented which takes an overall view of the environmental problems of this region. It has not been possible to bring about such a view for lack of parameters for determining the quality of life of inhabitants of the Federal District, parameters which would help in evaluating the positive and negative aspects of implementing a project.

Faced with this situation, the Ecological Commission of the Federal District Department, together with the Directorate of Urban Ecology of the Secretariat for Human Settlements and Public Works have decided to make a study of the Integral Plan for Urban Ecology in the Federal District.

AFTER-THOUGHTS AND POINTS OF CLARIFICATION

1. Mexico City, as many urban concentrations in third world under-developed and developing countries, has a problem with slums and squatter areas, due to population migration towards the city. These people come looking for a better environment, in general for better economical conditions.

    This is not always true, because Mexico City is a very expensive place to live. Living quarters are scarce and expensive, so the density of people living per room is high, sometimes as much as 6-10 people per room.

    The areas where people concentrate are far away from working places, and the mean two-way transportation time ranges from 2 to 4 hours a day, with about 2 to 3 bus changes each way.

    Also services are scarce, mostly water, drainage, and recreational facilities.

    The Mexican national urban development plan calls for a deconcentration program. This program has the objective of stimulating growth in certain areas, in the effort to restrict growth in places like Mexico City. This program is now operating, but the effects will not be seen in the short to medium range, due to the difficult economical problem which this poses.

For Mexico City, and its metropolitan area, the slums and squatter areas are a complex problem. Although there has been an intensive program for building living quarters, these are usually occupied by the lower middle class.

The federal and local authorities have implemented a self-construction program, which is oriented towards the upgrading of slums and squatter areas, but it lacks a solid financing instrument which would permit the people to buy the materials for this. For this reason it has had a small impact on the quality of housing. In the long range, this self-construction program will have a greater impact than now.

One of the programs which has had a very positive impact on the housing problem in Mexico is the regularisation of land ownership. During the last decade, at least 80% of the irregular land ownership (mainly in slums and squatter areas) has been solved, giving the people the land ownership. This has created a sense of belonging to the City, and has brought on an effort to build better and more solid homes, that is, with more permanent materials such as cement, building-blocks, etc.

2. As mentioned, the deconcentration program is a long range one. The short-term programs for augmenting the quality of life (transportation, public services, etc) have functioned as a promoting factor for population attraction. Not only do the quality and quantity of public services attract people, but mostly the big building projects such as the subway system (Metro), the transportation roads, the water system and a boom in general building have this effect. These projects (building) have attracted people looking for work.

3. Mexico City, if seen as a system, is very complex, not only in the local context, but in the national context. What is done in the City, is felt over the nation, due

not only to the population factor, but mostly due to the fact that it is the political and economical centre of the country.

In this context, the improvement of the quality of life by various programs has not been able to keep up with the increment of population. Though it is true, for example, that we now have better roads and more efficient municipally run public transport system than ever before, this is not enough because we have more people. The subway and bus system are always over used (too many people per seat; during the day, there are 3 to 5 people per seat). This in itself 'forces' people who can, to buy an automobile for private transportation, which causes traffic jams, and more air contamination.

So we do not always have the positive effect we look for. Many times the improved services only act as a mitigating effect which keeps the environment from losing its quality but not making it better.

In a sense, we may recognise that Mexico City may be defined as a stagnant environment, not always going forward. We will not see the positive effects of improvements until the migration process slows down.

4. The best alternative is the deconcentration plan which is operating at a national level. By promoting work in other cities of Mexico, we expect to restrict the migratory process affecting Mexico City, but results will not be seen in the short range.

To help this plan to go through the city is charging more for services such as water and energy, which are cheaper in other places. Also taxes are higher, specially in the automobile industry.

We know that one of the greater problems in the metropolitan area, besides air pollution, is the water problem. This is caused by two main factors: The resource is scarce in the zone and the infrastructure is deficient.

The local authorities have undertaken a big hydraulic project to bring in water from the Cutzamala zone -

about 90km from the city, and at an altitude of 1,000 meters above sea level - to supply Mexico City which is sited at 3,2000 meters above sea level. Mexico City needs about 60 cubic meters/sec. of water to have the demand satisfied, but only has the resources to extract 31m³/sec. The rest comes from outside sources.

As far as pollution, Mexico City is ranked as one of the most polluted cities in the world. About 11,000 tons of emissions are disposed in the air every day. About 40,000 lt. of water without treatment are discharged into other areas, mostly towards the north-east. Close to 10,000 tons a day of solid wastes go to open waste land.

The actions taken to diminish these problems have not been successful. If factories are forced to undertake strict pollution controls, many of them may close down, creating an employment problem. We do not have the economical or technical capabilities to treat water. Solid waste disposal is expensive, and there is still a problem with solid waste collection. These points outline the complexity of the system.

5.   The Integral Plan for Urban Ecology in the Federal District was a proposal between the Federal District authorities and the Ministry for Human Settlements and Public Works. The first is local, and the second is federal. This plan, was not able to continue due to economical situations, and is still at the proposal stage. We hope it will be undertaken sometime next year.

BASIC INFORMATION

The Federal District (Distrito Federal or D.F.) is an entity of the Federation of Independent States of the Mexican Republic and the site of the Federal Government. The most important part of the City of Mexico, capital of the country, lies within the limits of the D.F. The rapid growth of the city has extended its urban area beyond the geographic boundaries of the Federal District. Thus at present, the city metropolitan area includes territory from the State of Mexico which circumscribes the D.F.

The Department of the Federal District (Departamento del Districto Federal of D.D.F) is the Government of the City of

Mexico. The President of Mexico governs the city through the Head of the D.D.F., the City Mayor. Among the multiple responsibilities of the D.D.F. in terms of the government of the city, are those of establishing policies and technical systems or mechanisms for planning, controlling and directing urban development in the City of Mexico.

Mexico City is a key centre of the nation's economic activities and therefore plays an important role in the national economy. It contributes nearly 42 per cent of the GNP, 48 per cent of industry, 52 per cent of services, 45 per cent of commerce, and 60 per cent of transportation. In addition, it now concentrates around 25 per cent of the national population, which is more than 14 million inhabitants in its metropolitan area.

Urban ecology and the environment are the subjects of general concern of the General Direction of Urban Ecology of the National Secretariat for Human Settlements and Public Works. It has assisted in the formulation of a national plan for urban development and urban ecology, and is engaged in a proposal for an integrated plan for urban ecology in the Federal District.

Of additional interest is the Program of Scientific Interchange and Technical Formation (PICYCATEC-D.D.F.) of the Department of the Federal District. It focuses on the formation of the D.D.F. human resources in science, technology and administration, and assists the diffusion of the knowledge and experience acquired by the D.D.F through its actions of government.

REFERENCES

Eco-Plan Del Valle De Mexico, Secretaria de Asentamientos
        Humanos Y Obras Publicas, Subsecretaria de
        Asentamientos Humanos, Direccion General De Ecologia
        Urbana, Mexico-City, Mexico, n.d.
National Plan for Urban Development--Urban Ecology, Informa-
        tive Synthesis/November 1979, produced by SAHOP,
        Secretaria De Asentamientos Humanos Y Obras Publicas,
        Subsecretaria De Asentamientos Humanos, Direccion
        General De Ecologia Urbana.

        (Translation from Spanish with assistance of Chris
        MacDonald, PCL-International Services).

Contrasting experiences in
urbanisation and management

Urbanisation, housing and human settlement planning in Africa south of the Sahara

Thomas L. Blair

Africa is an intriguing setting for the study of man in urban society and the problems of rapid urban growth in developing countries. Indeed, the historical emergence of African cities, their decline and recent resurgence is, like the shape of the continent itself, a question mark with many challenges to planners, policymakers and academics. One is reminded here of Daryll Forde's remarks in the monumental UNESCO study "Social Implications of Industrialisation and Urbanisation in Africa South of the Sahara": "... since the urban situation is one in which new social categories and relationships emerge and none of the variables are static, the understanding of the restructuring of African communities, both actual and possible, will be greatly advanced by enquiries that have as great a time depth as possible."[1] Our understanding of the complexity and resilience of African communities and the possibilities of social, economic, physical and cultural change in rapidly growing urban areas is therefore considerably enriched by parallel studies of the history of older pre-colonial African cities and the centres where European industry and commerce began.

HISTORICAL URBANISATION

The history of African cities reaches back to the threshold of man's urban experience. Capital cities were a main feature from 3500 BC to the late centuries BC of powerful kingdoms along the Nile, Egypt, Nubia and Kush, and Axum in the mountains along the Red Sea.

Later, between the 9th and 15th centuries AD, towns and
cities grew in response to increased inland and ocean trade,
especially the export of gold, ivory and copper and import of
textiles and metalware. Overseas traders of Red Sea and
Indian Ocean ports had vigorous contacts with Arabia, India
and China; and the overland traders of the interior did a
flourishing business southwards and to the north across the
Berber Sahara to the Mediterranean and Europe. Port cities,
trading markets and production centres, and the city-states
of centrally-governed kingdoms enclosed large densely populated permanent settlements within their boundaries.[2]

The Shona kingdoms of the central-southern plateau -
Zimbabwe, Khami and Dhlo-Dhlo - were large mining centres
with houses, palaces and shrines built of stone. Ancient
Ghana, Mali, Songhai, Kanem-Bornu, Hausa and Congo-Angola
were large inland empires with urban-based civilisations.
Timbuctu, Kumasi and Kano were affluent urban settlements and
powerful trading entrepots in western Africa. And, along the
muslim-influenced east coast in the 13th century, there were
thriving cities at Mogadishu, Mombassa, Zanzibar and Kilwa in
what are now Somalia, Kenya and Tanzania.

By 1400 AD cities like these were urban centres of prosperous pre-industrial societies characterised by innovative
agricultural practices such as hoe cultivation, pastoralism
and collective ownership of land, extractive industry and
metalworking, and a well-developed economy for the production
of food and commodities for consumption and trade. They had
a wide range of non-agricultural workers, especially craftsmen and tradesmen, and an embryonic class structure ranging
from nobles to commoners and dependent peoples.

Distinctive patterns of settlement and architecture
developed. Not long after 1000 AD in the Yoruba kingdoms of
west Africa the palace of the oba, the marketplace, and the
old quarters around them served as central areas of well-
planned cities like Ile-Ife, Ilesha and Ekiti. Radial road
systems extended out to neighbouring towns and villages and
newly-settled areas were laid out in a grid-iron pattern.
Families lived in large houses set within a walled compound;
and groups of compounds, administered by the family elders,
formed the basis of an urban council responsible to the town
ruler. Kinship patterns linked the rulers to the ruled in an
intricate web of culture and experience.

The Edo city and empire of Benin, which took shape around 1400 was remarked upon by the first European visitors for its trading wealth, political order and urban comfort. "As you enter it," wrote a Dutch visitor around 1600, "the town appears very great: you go into a great broad street, not paved, which seems to be seven or eight times broader than Warmoes Street in Amsterdam ... The houses in this town stand in good order, one close and even with the other, as the houses in Holland stand ..."[3]

House building practices in the densely-populated settlements along the Niger River were based on self-build techniques with communal assistance, and these were described in "The Interesting Narrative of Olaudah Equiano, or Gustavus Vasa, the African" published in London 1789. Equiano, an Edo Benin, was captured as a boy and sold into slavery in America; he later purchased his freedom and went to London where he wrote in his narrative: "In our buildings we study convenience rather than ornament. Each master of a family has a large square piece of ground, surrounded with a moat or fence, or enclosed with a wall made of red earth tempered, which, when dry, is as hard as brick. ...Houses so constructed and furnished require but little skill to erect them. Every man is a sufficient architect for the purpose. The whole neighbourhood afford their unanimous assistance in building them, and in return receive and expect no other recompense than a feast."[4]

Pre-colonial African cities and housing architecture were mentioned in the journals and commentaries of many visitors.[5] Francis Moore in "Travels into the Inland Parts of Africa" published in London 1738 describes the houses of the Mandingo of Gambia as "convenient and vermin-free." Fourteenth century Kilwa impressed the well-travelled Moroccan scholar Ibn Batuta as "one of the most beautiful and best constructed towns in the world." Later, in 1498 Vasco da Gama and subsequent Portugese sea captains found Kilwa "with many fair houses of stone and mortar, very well arranged streets ... with doors of wood, well-carved with excellent joinery." Timbuctu was described by Leo Africanus to an Italian audience early in the 16th century as a city of learning where the king, his army and courtiers, and many magistrates, doctors and religious scholars resided, and whose great market did a prosperous business in manuscripts from Berber countries. Dr. Heinrich Barth, a German ex-

plorer, geographer and author of "Travels and Discoveries in
North and Central Africa" printed in London, 1857, remarked
with undisguised favour upon the larger buildings and complexes of Kano, Katsina and Timbuctu, and sketched in considerable detail the smaller mud dwellings and their
interiors.

COLONIAL CITIES

The vitality of African cities declined during the
period of the Atlantic slave trade, from the 1440's to the
1880's. With the onset of European imperialism and col-
onialism in the later 19th century new tendencies for urban
growth occurred. The colonies became suppliers of strategic
mineral and agricultural resources and served as outlets for
European manufactures. Cities grew as peasants were forced
from the land and pushed toward employment centres: mines,
plantations, cash crop farms, transport depots and processing
industries. Segregation and cultural deracination barred the
widespread assimilation by Africans of western technology and
prevented African societies from creating new structures.
The effect, in urban areas, was "to produce large floating
populations with low and insecure incomes, little differentiation in skills and education, and very limited means for
material and social advance."[6] A crucial transformation
had taken place in which the organisation of the pre-colonial
African City based on evolving indigenous communal principles, gave way to a European-dominated Colonial City and
greater dependence on economic and cultural imperatives,
skills, materials, political structures and leadership imported from abroad.

Patterns of economic adaptation and human settlement
varied across the continent. In interior west Africa and
Sudanic states European agro-industrial enterprises adapted
to the pre-colonial settlement pattern of "urban villages."
But many old towns, bypassed by economic change languished
and declined. In colonial capitals and large export and
trading centres, central business and government districts
were modernised and planned in the image of Europe. In the
settler territories, north, east and south, the colonial
towns were new towns: European in initiative, segregated in
spatial and social organisation and life-styles, and serviced
by the tied-labour of an itinerant class of indigenous low-
paid workers living in temporary hutments in "native quarters." One consequence of low wages, noted in a recent his-

torical study of Lusaka, was that urban Africans were unable to accumulate the resources to provide their own permanent housing in towns.[7] Home ownership outside the native areas was, in addition, beyond their means for reasons of cost, custom, or exclusionary practices. Together these factors effectively enforced the prevailing system of racial segregation, landlessness, penury and deprived living environments.

Broadly, one can say that imported economic and planning values from colonial powers were translated into the physical, and hence social, form of the city. Specifically, the varied character and development of colonial industrial/ commercial centres and urban populations in different parts of Africa is crucial to our understanding of the historical dimension of contemporary urbanisation and today's problem cities. More comparative research studies are required of (i) the new urban areas created under western colonisation and the prior existing African towns, (ii) the patterns of urban social and spatial planning, structures and organisation engendered in both types of situations, and (iii) the economic relations between urban and rural communities, and between major urban centres and the European metropole and the international economic system. Such studies would be of great assistance in understanding how external economic imperatives created the urban landscape in African cities, which remains today as part of the troublesome legacy of problem cities.

POST-WAR URBAN GROWTH

Cities continued to grow in the late stages of colonial rule after World War II. The causes were two-fold. Industrial and commercial innovations, still largely based on labour intensive activities, expanded production to meet world markets and greater numbers of migrants from rural areas were attracted to the city. At the same time deteriorating rural conditions, famine and drought stimulated mass emigration. In the 1950's towns with more than 100,000 inhabitants grew at a rate of 9 per cent per annum or about four times the annual population growth, and over one and half times that of smaller towns. By 1960, 8 per cent of all Africans lived in cities of 100,000 or more and 13 per cent lived in places of 20,000 or more inhabitants.

In the twenty years from 1950 to 1970 a massive increase took place in urban concentration. Twenty-eight million or 12.8 per cent of the African population lived in urban places in 1950. Two decades later, according to the United Nations World Housing Survey 1974, 75.5 million or twenty per cent of the African population lived in urban places; of which 14.5 million were in cities of at least one million, 31.6 million in cities of 100,000-999,000, and 29.3 million in cities and towns smaller than 100,000. There were seven cities with more than one million inhabitants and forty-four with between 100,000-500,000 inhabitants.[8]

Africa is the least densely-populated and least urbanised major world region, but its urban growth rate of 5.5 per cent per annum or doubling about every 15 years, is among the highest in the world, ie. twice the world average. Furthermore, the world's fastest growth of million-cities takes place in Africa and it is expected that there will be a doubling of the population of major cities in Africa within 10 years.[9]

The speed of urbanisation had its greatest impact in the largest cities. Lagos, which had only 126,000 inhabitants in 1930, grew to 364,000 in 1964, and 1,200,000 in 1968. Kinshasa's population was a mere 34,000 in the 1930's, 208,000 in 1950, a seven-fold increase, 1,250,000 in 1963, and reached 2 million in 1970.

City growth rested largely upon in-migration from rural areas, and occurred at a frequency many times that of rural; population growth. Zambia in 1970, for example, had an urban growth rate of 8.58, per annum and a rural growth rate of only 0.82. Similarly in Ethiopia in 1970 the urban growth rate was 7.03 as compared with a rural growth rate of 1.43.

Rapid urbanisation is but one factor in the crisis of human settlements in Africa. Relatively high population growth rates, on the order of 2.8 per cent per annum in 1970, are an additional disturbing factor and with further increases it is estimated that the population of Africa will double in approximately 25 years. The impact of this growth in rural areas, which contain in many cases 80 per cent of the national population and labour force, will bring heavier pressures on food, land and shelter which cannot be met adequately with existing resources. Typically, across the entire continent, overall high population growth, due to falling

death rates, and the rapid shift of population from rural to
urban places heralds a crisis of human settlements which will
disastrously affect the quest of nations for social and economic transformation.

SLUMS AND SQUATTERS SETTLEMENTS

All over Africa millions of people are on the move
toward towns and large cities in search of wages and better
services. They pour into cities at a faster rate than local
industries, services and housing can absorb them and settle
in crowded quarters and slums. Many become squatters in
makeshift huts, dugouts, shanty-towns and bidon-villes or
"tin can cities." The slums of Nairobi, Lagos, Dakar, Lusaka
and other places, are much more than blemishes on the urban
landscape. They are symptoms of the housing shortage, high
rents, land speculation, inefficient municipal services and
bad land use planning.[10]

Slums and squatters settlements are not isolated or
temporary phenomena, or marginal unfortunate appendages to
the "real city" - they are the city. Furthermore, they are a
result of, and a manifest link between, forces of rural and
urban development and under-development stemming from policies of public and private authorities invoked without consideration of their consequences. The contributing causes
are, on the one hand, policies of increased investment in
city-based governmental and industrial activities which when
combined with urbanisation makes the urban region attractive,
and on the other hand the lack of rural development which
abets the inclination to migrate to the city. New roads and
cheap forms of truck and jitney bus transport aid this movement from rural to urban places.

The growth of huge areas of makeshift housing and "uncontrolled" settlements is phenomenal. In 1968, more than a
third of the 273,000 inhabitants of Dar-es-Salaam were in
slums in squatters settlements, and by 1970, when the city's
population had increased to 344,000, half were in slums and
squatters settlements. The squatter proportion of Lusaka,
probably the fastest growing city in Africa, grew from 8 per
cent in 1962 to 48 per cent in 1969, when the total city
population was estimated to have reached 762,000. And in at
least five smaller Zambian towns, squatters make up between
67 per cent and 90 per cent of the town population.

According to United Nations estimates squatters settlements constitute 90 per cent of Yaounde, 77 per cent of Mogadishu, 61 per cent of Accra, and 50 per cent of Monrovia. The proportion of squatters in Ibadan is 75 per cent; in Kinshasa 60 per cent; in Nairobi 33 per cent; and in Addis Ababa 90 per cent of its inhabitants live in mud and wattle chica houses.[11]

Slums and shanty towns are now a permanent aspect of African cities. In many cases they represent between half and two-thirds of the total urban population and are growing at twice the rate of the urban area as a whole. Within them live hard working people, many of them holding a range of permanent but low-wage, low-skill jobs. The marked characteristics of these areas are high densities of housing per square mile and of persons per room. Sex ratios are often unbalanced with a higher proportion of males or females, depending on local employment opportunities. There are high proportions of dependents under 15 and over 60 years of age and wide-spread health problems, particularly communicable diseases. Nevertheless, the inhabitants play a very significant role in the social, political, and economic life of cities through direct labour inputs to the modern economic sector and indirectly through the subsistence activities of the informal sectors and should by no means be considered "marginal populations."

Obtaining an overall view of urban housing problems is made difficult because of the lack of adequate and precise data. What seems generally clear is that the conditions of housing do not meet, by and large, a definition of official minimum requirements, namely housing built of permanent materials with enough sanitary equipment, area and facilities adequate to family size and to prevent the transmission of sickness. Most urban housing units are one or two room dwellings in rudely constructed self-built shelters of natural and scrap materials accommodating five persons and without water supply and toilet. For most African countries, things are worsening. Nowhere has adequate housing for all been reached, and no factual improvement is observable at present. But the situation is not hopeless, some countries are embarking on realistic approaches and with increased effort could have a manageable housing situation fulfilling basic standards for all the people in 30 to 50 years, in others this may be achieved in 20 years.

EMERGENT APPROACHES

What now seems crucial is the recognition in many parts of the continent that a large proportion of the demand for residential land is met by slums and squatter settlements. And the greatest resource available for dealing with settlement problems is the creative energy of the people themselves. With effective and positive use of community resources, and with sound planning and sensitive governmental intervention many settlement problems could be turned into opportunities beneficial to communities.

African nations are experimenting with many different approaches to housing problems which can be borne economically. Upper Volta, Uganda and Zambia stress improvement of squatter sites and service schemes through aided self-help. Uganda has sought to aid private sector housing, and Malawi has started national housing and building corporations. Other approaches include erecting core houses and expandable houses, developing mass production methods and using local materials as import substitutes. In general, British-influenced countries like Kenya, Uganda and Tanzania, favour a mixed approach of contractor-built housing with sites and services and the stimulation of the population to help themselves. By contrast, contractor-built housing in urban areas is heavily emphasised in Algeria, Cameroun, Ivory Coast, Gabon, Senegal and Togo, the French-influenced nations.

Meeting housing problems will require innovative approaches. At present the total productive capacity of African nations is still quite low, and the efforts that can be made to produce housing are limited by the urgent need to invest scarce resources in other competing sectors, infrastructure, agriculture, education, industry, among others. Present housing production is under 3 units per 1,000 inhabitants per annum and it is estimated that 10 to 13 units per 1,000 are required to meet current housing needs, without consideration of replacement needs.

Introducing cost control measures is now a widely recognised necessity because costs per square metre of houses, including "low-cost" contractor build housing, recently reached levels higher than those prevailing in Western Europe. The causes which have been identified include increased transportation costs, especially affecting imported building materials, imbalances between demand and supply,

high land prices and construction and labour costs, inflation, the lack of skilled labour and of trained middle
level staff to control the preparation and implementation of
building projects. Introducing proper cost control systems
will provide savings, and require adequate basic data on
house building costs. The establishment of National Housing
Centres in each country, and a permanent Working Group of
Experts on House Building Costs would be an essential step in
the direction of rationalisation and coordination in building.

For low-income earners who are housed, and there is an
unknown but undoubtedly significant proportion of urban
dwellers who are unhoused, the most common methods of obtaining housing is through renting or access to land on which to
build. Probably most new housing is produced by the people
themselves through self-help, barter and communal labour with
the cooperation of friends and relatives. Normally, the
design and construction process is informal, even where the
services of small-scale private contractors are used. Increasingly, however, in urban Africa more people live in
homes they do not build themselves. A large share of new
housing is produced by local jobbing builders using a mixture
of traditional and modern techniques adapted to short-life
materials such as mud, wattle and daub, and sun dried or
kilned mud bricks. As workers become more secure in their
new environment they slowly improve their homes with more
durable materials and fittings indicative of their rising
social status.

Innovative ways of financing housing building are introduced through the "unorganised money market," for example
mutual aid associations like esusu in Nigeria. Generally the
associations convene on fixed dates and all members then pay
specified sum. The whole amount collected is given to one of
the members, who is either drawn by lot, chosen according to
a list of priority, or selected during the meeting itself
after a study of his needs and requests. The person then
reimburses the sum by paying his regular contribution for the
time needed to cancel the debt. Normally no interest is
charged on these loans or paid on the savings contributed.

A rising number of employees of government, commercial
and industrial enterprises would normally seek help from the
organised financial market. However, in urban areas there is
a general absence of facilities to obtain credit for housing,

at least for workers. Mortgage loans are difficult to get
when properties are held communally because of the lack of
proof of "ownership." Repayment periods are as short as 5
years, with down payments as high as 50 per cent.

Housing finance institutions could provide a means to
collect savings and attract capital, and to transform them
into funds placed at the disposal, on reasonable conditions,
of people and agencies who want to rent or build houses.
Indeed, the past decade has been one of remarkable, but un-
even, development in housing finance. Nevertheless, the
ability of housing finance institutions to meet the acute
housing problems of the majority of urban dwellers is severely limited in the face of an overwhelming demand. Furthermore there is a distinct bias toward upper and middle income
housing by private institutions, and an emphasis on middle
income, civil service and "low cost" newly-built urban housing by official institutions.[12]

What is needed, above all else, to help ordinary people
and residents of slums and squatters settlements, are mechanisms for providing credit, loans and finance to support initiative, participation and self-help projects, and to encourage new and labour intensive technologies and the upgrading of the skills of small-scale builders. Though the response by official and conventional private institutions has
been inadequate, the response of slum dwellers and squatters
themselves has been considerable. Self-help building is
undertaken by family and voluntary community action or paid
for by spontaneous mutual savings groups, arrangements
through local stores and post offices, and personal loans and
guarantees. Efforts are being made in Ethiopia and many of
the British-influenced nations to strengthen potential local
sources of housing finance such as mutual aid, church, rotat-
ing credit, and tribal associations.

Sites and services schemes are now a popular method of
dealing with urban housing problems. In the past governments
feared they would lead to the creation of new slums, a fear
which has not yet been fully disproven. Furthermore in some
of the early projects it was evident that housing ministries
lacked the skills to initiate and control sites and service
development. Today they are seen as low-cost and non-disrup-
tive measures and have been introduced in Botswana, Kenya,
Senegal, Tanzania and Zambia with technical and financial aid
from external agencies. Sites and service schemes are nor-

mally phased through various stages. At first land and plots
are allocated, levelled and access ways demarcated; these may
then be connected with water, sewerage and electricity; provision can be made for social and public services and a
school built which can be used as a community centre for
training people how to build and improve houses. Two examples
of this approach are Port Sudan and Lusaka.

Port Sudan on the Red Sea has been the target of huge
migration from rural areas. Its population trebled in the
last two decades, with an average annual growth rate of more
than 6 per cent. In 1970, 60,000 people, or more than half
of the two population of 112,000, were living in squatters
areas, called deims, at densities of 50-100 families per
hectare. Open spaces were used as rubbish dumps, shacks were
made of scraps of wood, cardboard, tin and rags. In 1975,
some six years after the initiation of a resettlement project
40,000 squatters were provided 200-250 square metre plots
with security of tenure and access to basic facilities. This
was considered a necessary investment in the future manpower
required to realise the economic potential of Sudan's only
seaport and key entry and exit serving Khartoum and Gezira.

In Lusaka a declared goal of the city council is the
upgrading and servicing of "spontaneous settlements," adding
new sites and service plots. UNIP, the national political
party, provides leadership and control in these settlements
and runs local project offices and centres for the mobilisation of public participation. Overall planning is undertaken by the city council with the assistance of the World
Bank. Selection of sites for upgrading is made using a
number of criteria: proximity to employment, facilities and
services, suitability of subsoil for eventual sewer installation, and conformity with the Lusaka Development Plan.

Programmes to upgrade existing squatters settlements are
underway in various other cities, among them Rabat, Dakar,
and Dar-es-Salaam. The main features are the improvement of
sanitation, social services, road access, education, and the
provision of security of tenure. Most existing structures,
bad as they may be, are retained but gradually improved by
families on a self-help basis. In this sense the full participation of residents is indispensable, and the organisation and training of residents is an important objective.

The basic elements of self-help are that labour is supplied by the people themselves, thereby saving on building

costs, labour and profits to intermediaries, and enhancing the formation of community spirit. Aid is provided by government with the assistance of external sources and can take various forms: technical and managerial aid in site development, housing design, financing, and arrangements for mutual cooperation between participants. More specifically many governments are considering introduction of aid in the form of loans for roofs, foundations, and sanitary installations, for the supply of materials such as cement, doors, windows, and for the rent or purchase of machines and tools.

Ethiopia, Senegal, Sudan and Upper Volta have begun to build up experience in aided self-help schemes and a number of important requirements emerge from their experience. There must be a team approach involving planners, architects, local builders, and social workers, as well as the residents themselves in the process of self-help. Proposed housing designs should be capable of extension and improvement, simple to construct, and make use of locally available materials. Careful thought should be given to the selection and number of participants and to their organisation and preparation.

AREAS OF AGREEMENT

In conclusion, it is now widely recognised that governments must do more to tap people's resources than merely create programmes and enlist their participation. The people in Africa's slums and squatters settlements have their own ideas of what is needed and their own organisations for fulfilling them. To ignore their accumulated wisdom, their judgement and the social forces at work in their communities is to ignore their humanity. What they require is for government to give sufficient priority to their needs, to cooperate with their popular actions, and to introduce, with assistance from friendly nations and international agencies, new policies, planning and allocation of material and financial resources to aid the resolution of settlement problems.

Major efforts in these directions were called for by delegates to the African Regional Preparatory Conference held in Cairo[13] prior to Habitat: The United Nations Conference on Human Settlements, May/June 1976.[14]

The delegates emphasised specifically the introduction of national human settlement planning policies and the cre-

ation of the institutions, public participation and political
will to implement them; the establishment and attainment of
minimum standards of housing, health, food, education, water
supply, sanitary facilities, and electrification; the recognition of the importance of land as a resource requiring
effective controls on its use for the benefit of the nation
and community; and the initiation of regional international
cooperation towards a new world economic order and monetary
policies. Attaining these objectives will require as well
innovative approaches to investment, trade and finance strategies, organising technical assistance services and management training programmes, and promoting the transfer of
scientific and technical knowledge about human settlements.

There is now general agreement that greater effort and
political commitment is required to end the disadvantageous
policies that lead to the erosion of African life and cultural identity. No less a personage than Professor Adebayo
Adedeji, United Nations Under Secretary-General and Executive
Secretary of the UN Economic Commission for Africa, has
pointed out that two decades after independence the prevailing economic, political and administrative functions of
cities, and their resultant impact on settlements, still bear
a strong legacy of the colonial era. The Dual City remains −
one small, gleaming and modern; the other large, sprawling
and deprived − and there is a persistence of economic under-
development and dependence on external economies. The need
is, he says, for the definition of an alternative policy
approach which will ensure a balanced relationship between
human settlement needs and economic development. One which
will make the benefits of development available to the majority of people.[15]

Professor Adedeji notes the new initiatives formulated
in the Lagos Plan of Action 1980-2000 at a meeting of African
Heads of State and Government in Lagos April 1980, the declaration by UNIDO of 1980-1990 as the Industrial Development
Decade for Africa, and the UN Transport and Communications
Decade for Africa. These are instruments which indicate the
types of support mechanisms required to stimulate Africa-
centred production linked to the provision of effective
transport, public utilities and social infrastructure for the
benefit of the community. Above all, he believes that the
attainment of Africa's settlement and development objectives
rests on creating an authentically African conceptual frame-

work and strategy based on the principles of national self-reliance, democratisation, de-alienation, renascent self-confidence, and continental cooperation among African States.

Acknowledgements

    Significant contributions to the resolution of human settlement problems in Africa are being made by architects, planners, social scientists and policy-makers in many parts of the continent, among whom I should like to mention those who were present with me at various UN Habitat meetings in 1975-76: Dr. Mostafa M. El-Hifnawi, Chairman, General Organisation for Housing, Building and Planning Research, Cairo, Egypt; Dr. Adebayo Adedeji, Executive Secretary, United Nations Economic Commission, Addis Ababa, Ethiopia; Professor S.H. Huzayyin, Director, Cairo Demographic Centre, Egypt; Samir Amin, Director, African Institute for Economic Development and Planning, Dakar, Senegal; George K. Muhoho, Director, National Environment Secretariat, Nairobi, Kenya; Meshack M.L. Shongwe, Chief Health Officer, Mbabane Town Council, Swaziland; H.E. Dr. Henry K. Matipa, Minister of State for Local Government and Housing, Lusaka, Zambia; Mr. Mamadou A. Aw, Deputy Executive Secretary, Economic Commission for Africa, Addis Ababa, Ethiopia; E. Paul Mwaluko, Director, United Nations Centre for Housing, Building and Planning, New York; Professor A.L. Mabogunje, Department of Geography, University of Ibadan, Nigeria; Andrew N. Ligale, Director of Physical Planning, Nairobi, Kenya, and Président, Commonwealth Association of Planners; Hassan Fathy, Architect, Cairo, Egypt; Jean Rafamatanantsoa, SEIMAD, Tananarive, Malagasy Republic; Ngada Tamboura, Direction de l'Habitat, Bamako, Mali; Professor Joseph Ki-Zerbo, Upper Volta. Valuable insights were also gained whilst on a study and lecture tour of Ghana from the work of H.N.A. Wellington on spontaneous urban housing growth in Nima and F.A. Abloh on social and physical growth of towns in Ghana, and from discussions with Professor E.A. Boateng, Head, and Dorm Adzobu, Senior Research Officer, Environmental Protection Council; Dr. J.W.S. de Graft-Johnson, Head, Building and Road Research Institute (CSIR) at Kumasi; Professor P.A. Tetteh, Head, School of Architecture and Planning, University of Science and Technology, Kumasi; and Professor J. Owusu-Addo, President of the Ghana Institute of Architects and Head of Architecture, University of Science and Technology, Kumasi.

REFERENCES

1. UNESCO, "Social Implications of Industrialization and
    Urbanization in Africa South of the Sahara," UNESCO,
    Tensions and Technology Series, Paris, p.50 (1956).
2. Basil Davidson, Africa in Historical Perspective, in
    "Africa South of the Sahara 1976-77," Europa Publi-
    cations Ltd, London, p.3-16 (1976).
3. Basil Davidson, Africa in Historical Perspective, in
    "Africa South of the Sahara 1976-77," Europa Publi-
    cations Ltd, London, p.12 (1976).
4. Paul Oliver, ed., "Shelter in Africa," Barrie and
    Jenkins, London, p.7 (1971).
5. Basil Davidson, "Africa, History of a Continent,"
    Weidenfeld and Nicholson, London, pp.89-94, (1966),
    and Paul Oliver, ed., "Shelter in Africa," Barrie
    and Jenkins, London, p.9 (1971).
6. UNESCO, "Social Implications of Industrialization and
    Urbanization in Africa South of the Sahara," UNESCO
    Tensions and Technology Series, Paris, p.12 (1956).
7. John Collins, Lusaka: Urban Planning in a British
    Colony, 1931-64, in "Shaping an Urban World," Gordon
    E. Cherry, ed., Mansell, London (1980).
8. United Nations, Department of Economic and Social
    Affairs, World Housing Survey 1974: an overview of
    the state of housing, building and planning within
    human settlements, United Nations, New York,
    ST/ESA/30 (1976).
9. United Nations, Economic Commission for Africa, "Human
    Settlements in Africa: The Role of Housing and
    Building," United Nations: Addis Ababa,
    E/CN.14/HUS/15, April (1976).
10. Thomas L. Blair, "The International Urban Crisis," Hill
    and Wang, New York, and Hart-Davis McGibbon Kee,
    London (1974).
11. United Nations, Economic Commission for Africa, "Human
    Settlements in Africa: The Role of Housing and
    Building," United Nations: Addis Ababa,
    E/CN.14/HUS/15, p.28ff (1976).
12. United Nations, Economic Commission for Africa, "Human
    Settlements in Africa: The Role of Housing and
    Building," United Nations: Addis Ababa,
    E/CN.14/HUS/15, Ch.VII (1976).
13. United Nations, Habitat: Conference on Human Settle-
    ments, "The Regional Preparatory Meetings," United
    Nations, New York, A/CONF.70/PC/14, July (1975).

14. United Nations, Report of Habitat: United Nations
       Conference on Human Settlements, Vancouver, 31
       May-11 June 1976, United Nations, New York,
       A/CONF.70/15 (1976).
15. Professor Adebayo Adedeji, "Keynote Address on the
       Impact of Development, Modernisation and Social
       Change on the Style and Quality of Life in Africa:
       An Assessment," a paper given to the International
       School, Town and Country Planning Summer School,
       September 1982, University of Lancaster, and
       published in the Report of Proceedings, Royal Town
       Planning Institute, London (1982).

BIBLIOGRAPHY

"Africa South of the Sahara 1976-77," Europa Publications
       Limited (1976) - sixth edition of a survey and
       reference book of all the countries south of the
       Sahara Desert, including a Who's Who of major
       personalities, information on regional organisations,
       and articles on history, languages, culture and
       political, social and economic development.
"African Social Studies, A Radical Reader," edited by Peter
       C.W. Gutkind and Peter Waterman, Heinemann, London,
       (1977) - the work is organised into sections on
       methodology, history, economics, social structure and
       ideology and politics and presents the writings of
       Africans and non-Africans representing a range of
       views previously buried in narrowly-circulated left
       journals.
H. I. Ajaegbu, ed., "African Urbanization: A Bibliography,"
       International African Institute, London (1972) - a
       comprehensive listing of literature dealing with
       specific towns.
Council of Planning Librarians - Exchange Bibliographies,
       especially "Urbanization, Industrialisation and the
       Development Process," by Robert D. Dean; and "A
       Selected Bibliography on Rural-Urban Migrants' Slums
       and Squatters in Developing Countries," by Aprodicio
       A. Laquian, Monticello, Illinois (1971).
Hassan Fathy, "Architecture for the Poor," University of
       Chicago Press, Chicago (1973) - illuminates the point
       that the vast majority of Africans have to live in
       very poor circumstances and cannot afford to rent or
       buy houses erected with the aid of modern technology.

210 T. L. BLAIR

"Human Settlements: An Annotated Bibliography," prepared for Habitat: United Nations Conference on Human Settlements, Vancouver, Canada, 31 May-11 June 1976, by International Institute for Environment and Development and Pergamon Press, Oxford (1976) - a useful working document for researchers.

Hilda Kuper, ed., "Urbanization and Migration in West Africa," University of California Press, Berkeley (1965) - a collection of articles including the seminal essay by E.P. Skinner, "Labour Migration among the Mossi of the Upper Volta."

Kenneth Little, "Urbanisation as a Social Process," Routledge and Kegan Paul, London and Boston (1974) - an essay on movement and change in contemporary Africa by a professor of African Studies, University of Edinburgh.

Paul Oliver,ed., "Shelter in Africa" Barrie and Jenkins, London (1971) - an excellent collection of articles by architects, planners and social scientists with case studies of traditional and spontaneous housing and squatters settlements.

Horace Miner,ed., "The City in Modern Africa" Praeger, New York (1967) - articles covering various aspects of urbanism in Africa from different standpoints.

Elliot P. Skinner, ed., "Peoples and Cultures of Africa" New York (1973) Published for the American Museum of Natural History by the Doubleday/Natural History Press - an anthropological reader with excellent contributions on African languages, architecture; and on Islamic culture zones.

United Nations, Economic Commission for Africa, "Human Settlements in Africa: the Role of Housing and Building" E/CN.14/HUS/15, Addis Ababa, April (1976) - prepared in collaboration with the Government of the Netherlands as tool for African administrators, technologists, economic and financial planners, in the preparation of national development plans, the implementation of chosen polices and programmes in human settlements, and the establishment of national and local institutions.

United Nations, Department of Economic and Social Affairs, "World Housing Survey 1974: An overview of the state of housing, building and planning within human settlements" ST/ESA/30 New York (1975) - the first in a series of comprehensive reviews of world housing conditions intended to stimulate interest in, and discussion of, international housing problems. Atten-

tion is given to the methodological aspects of
monitoring of the world housing situation as a continuing process essentially inter-related with
national and regional development.

United Nations, "Report of Habitat: United Nations Conference
on Human Settlements" United Nations, New York (1976)
- the decisions and proceedings of a conference called
to consider the problems and solutions related to
world habitation.

United Nations, Habitat: United Nations Conference on Human
Settlements, "The Regional Preparatory Meetings" New
York, A/CONF.70/PC/14, (29 July 1975) - a report of
the proceedings and recommendations of preparatory
meetings on Asian, Latin American, and African problems held in Tehran, Caracas and Cairo.

UNESCO, "Social Implications and Industrialisation and
Urbanisation in Africa South of the Sahara" UNESCO,
Tensions and Technology Series, Paris (1956) - a
pioneering study undertaken by Daryll Forde, of the
International African Institute, and European social
scientists.

Frank Willet, "African Art", Thames and Hudson, London (1975)
- an enthusiastic view of art, architecture, and
sculpture, today and yesterday.

Working Papers of the International Urbanization Survey 1970
-72, "Urbanization in Tropical Africa" Colin Rosser;
"Urbanization in Nigeria" Leslie Green and Vincent
Milone; and "Urbanization in Zambia" Alan F. Simmance,
published by Ford Foundation, New York (c1973) - part
of a well conceived world survey series on urbanization problems.

Urban planning in China

Report of an American Delegation of City Planners

I. Urban Settlement Policies

Leon S. Eplan, AICP

The distribution and form of settlement of a population is recognised as a critical issue for both developing and developed countries. China's pattern of settlement is grounded in history but has also been modified by post-1949 government policies. In conversations with our delegation, China's urban planners were clear about their objectives, and realistic about the problems they face.

URBANISATION

Officials of the State Administration of Urban Construction outlined their efforts to realise national economic and ideological goals through policy directives guiding national and local government planners in investment decisions. The aim of these policies is to enable the country to realise more quickly the Four Modernisations – in industry, agriculture, science and technology, and defence – while remaining consistent with the principles of Marxism. The desire to reduce the disparity between urban and rural areas and to bring these two sectors into closer cooperation was especially strong. Chinese planners stressed the importance of turning cities from centres of consumption to centres of production, in line with policies first enunciated by Mao Tse-tung over thirty years ago.

Population Growth

Settlement patterns in the People's Republic have altered dramatically since 1949, reshaped by a population that in thirty years has grown from approximately 540 million to an estimated one billion. Although China's population remains predominately rural (80 per cent live in the country-side), the major urban regions still attract a significant share of this growth. Most of the large urban places in the eastern areas have doubled their populations during the past thirty years, and the number of urban industrial workers rose from 45 million in 1958 to 95 million in 1978 (New York Times, July 6, 1979).

It is interesting to note that the twenty per cent of the population which is urban nearly equals the entire popu-lation of the United States! Furthermore, China's population lives in a land area just slightly larger than the United States, only eleven per cent of which is arable.

We were told that Beijing in 1949 had a population of 1.5 million people living in an urban area now occupied by 4.8 million people. Shanghai's urban area population has grown from 4.2 million to 5.7 million. Nanjing, with 1.9 million people in its urban area today, has experienced a population increase of 18 per cent during the past thirty years. Guangzhou's population of 2.7 million people is one million more than in 1949.

Family planning and other measures of control have sought to reduce the population of the nation as a whole. Strong social pressures to delay marriages and to limit fam-ilies to one child have led to a substantial decline in the birth rate. While family planning efforts have been rela-tively successful in the cities, they have been less so in the countryside. Overall, the population is estimated to be rising at a rate of two per cent annually (CIA, 1978, P.1), indicating that the effect of such policies will be realised only in the long term.

In addition to family planning programmes per se, all of the cities the delegation visited have set population limits, discouraged industrial expansion in the central areas, re-stricted migration into the city proper, and made plans for the construction of satellite towns to which population growth can be redirected. Thus, Beijing has set a goal of four million persons for its city proper, a decline of 800,000 inhabitants. Shanghai is somewhat less ambitious. The city's regional population - referred to in China as the municipal administrative area - is projected at 12 million

persons by the year 2,000, a slight increase over the present
level of 11.2 million, and Shanghai officials are seeking to
keep its urban population between 5.5 million and 6.0 million
persons, approximately the present level. Suzhou was an
exception. Its year 2,000 population is projected at
570,000, a 12 per cent increase from its present population
of 510,000.

City Size

As a result of its dramatic population growth, China now
has 13 cities with urbanised populations of over one million
persons. There are 29 such places if the nearby agricultural
areas are calculated in the total (Beijing Review, March 17,
1980). Where there were 150 cities in China before 1949,
there are now 216 cities and 3,200 towns of various sizes,
including 2,000 country towns each with a population of
10,000–50,000 persons (Beijing Review, April 21, 1980).

Chinese policy deals directly with the size of cities.
In discussing urban policy, Chinese officials frequently
distinguished between "large", "medium" and "small" cities.
While no firm definition was given to these terms, one writer
has suggested that the distinctions are as follows: a large
city has 500,000 or more people, a medium-size city has
100,000 to 500,000, while a small city has fewer than 100,000
persons (Ma, 1979, p. 838). Some officials in discussions
with the delegation used a population of 200,000 as the
dividing line between medium and small cities.

National planning officials now emphasise the development of small and medium-size cities as an alternative to the
further concentration of people in the crowded eastern cities
where some 65 per cent of the urban population lives, and the
expansion of commune enterprises capable of absorbing surplus
labour resulting from agricultural modernisation. Thus as
farm labourers are replaced by machinery, they are to be
settled in these smaller places rather than in the already
over-crowded larger cities. The objective is not only to
relieve growth pressures on the eastern cities, but to exploit natural mineral and agricultural resources in the western areas. New towns have been developed near natural resources, and several railroad lines have been upgraded to
provide a better east-west linkage for the shipment of farm
goods and extracted minerals from the western interior
regions to the coast. However, there are Chinese planners

who believe that the present emphasis should be on the construction of large and medium-size cities "because cities
cannot truly fulfil their functions if they are too small;"
that output, value, profits and products provided by industries in small cities and towns in the interior lag far
behind the coastal cities. (Beijing Review, March 17, 1980).

In summary one can say that, earlier and more purpose-
fully than many developing countries, China has analysed her
urbanisation process and moved to control it. The difficulties of doing so, however, are well illustrated by the un-
reliability of the very population data we have been discussing. The first and last national census was taken in
June 1953. Although it was an admirable first attempt, its
results have been questioned. The size and distribution of
the Chinese population are known only within very wide
limits. Even the present modernisation-oriented regime has
not succeeded in fully restoring the country's statistical
system which collapsed in the confusion of the Great Leap
Forward (1958-1959). Discrepancies among the estimates of
foreign observers are also wide. Until recently most writers
presented rounded figures; attempts at more precise estimates
frequently differed by 50 to 100 million persons! The data
available on individual cities and the distribution of population within metropolitan regions, is equally vague and
inconsistent.

PLANNING PRINCIPLES

City planning, the delegation was told by officials of
the State Administration of Urban Construction, is tied to
city development, which has two aspects: management and
construction. Development, of course, reflects Party policy,
which emphasises improved production in the cities and improved living conditions for peasants. Six newly issued
principles upon which urban planning in Chinese cities is to
be based were outlined.

City Size and Industrial Infrastructure

Cities should not become too large; they should be well
separated from one another and be individually as compact as
possible. Attempts are being made to limit population growth
in the city proper (the urban core) of the largest cities,

and to redirect increases into small and medium-size
satellite towns. As urban areas and industries should be
planned together, so should industries be placed in these new
towns. While some new towns might be as small as 10,000
persons, the policy concentrates on towns in the
200,000-300,000 range.

The second principle emphasises those considerations
needed for industrial development. Industry requires particular attention to the infrastructure: good roads and
transportation systems, adequate water and electricity, and
sufficient land. Industrial development should also be linked
to cultural development, so that workers enjoy the places in
which they work. Therefore, in addition to industrial jobs,
provisions must be made for theatres, clinics, shops, schools
and other amenities.

Environmental Protection and Civil Defence

A third principle directs local officials to develop
plans which would improve the urban environment "for the
benefit of all citizens." It calls for the dispersal of new
industrial production primarily into small and medium-size
new towns, especially in the interior regions. Existing
polluting industries are also to be relocated, with preference given to dispersal rather than on-site technological
improvements. Within urban areas, no new "heavy" (ie. un-
desirable industry should be placed in residential areas.
Buffers should be established between industries and housing.

A fourth principle focuses on the need and value of
civil defence in the planning of cities. What was learned in
times of war should be incorporated into peacetime plans.
Apparently the efforts to relocate new industrial enterprises
to the interior and to disperse production serves this defence consideration.

Economy, Preservation and Participation

Fifth, national officials emphasised the importance of
making construction projects as economically realistic as
possible. Plans should be practical and affordable. "In our
planning," they stated, "we will consider in order of importance (1) function, (2) economics and (3) aesthetics." Ef-

ficiency should be balanced with preservation values, both of which are important, "We want to restore and redevelop, not tear down. We want to repair and rehabilitate our older cities."

The sixth, and final, principle related to public participation. The masses, the delegation was told, should be mobilised to participate in city planning, especially in the formulation of general plans. Citizens of an affected area should be consulted regarding those measures which directly affect them. Furthermore, advice should be sought from officials of related government agencies, and their ideas worked into the planning of cities.

PRACTICE

Many aspects of the six principles outlined above were framed within a national goal of self-sufficiency for each province or region, a policy which has helped to shape recent settlement patterns. This policy grew out of a national commitment to improve rural conditions and to lessen distinctions between urban workers and agricultural peasants, to overcome inequalities between the city and the countryside. New towns are an attempt to fulfil this goal by integrating industrial and agricultural production, thereby permitting "the fruits of industry to flow to the peasants." New towns should be compact, yet separated by prime agricultural land from existing development.

Beijing's design principles, for example, seek to link the city with its nearby rural area "in order to increase production." City officials are attempting to locate much of the new growth outside the existing urbanised area in such a way as to protect good farm land. "We have invested much to protect these lands. They supply vegetables to the city. Furthermore, this concept also serves the natural ecology."

Shanghai has combined a population limitation policy with one related to developing satellite towns and communes. In its second Five Year Plan, the city mapped out plans for the construction of five new towns, each built around an individual major function or type of production (cultural centre, production or tractors, light industry, manufacture of machinery and generators, and production of petrochemicals). Seven other small production centres, many in-

volving older existing towns, have been established on the
perimeter of Shanghai. (The delegation visited the satellite
city of Jinshan, 70 kilometers to the south, built around one
of the country's largest petrochemical plants, employing
24,000 production workers).

While Nanjing has also sought to restrict its population
and construct three satellite towns, it was unique among
those places visited in its approach to its urban form. Its
plan, still in draft form, conceptualises five land use
zones: at the core, the old city proper; a buffering scenic
zone around the core; a third zone, along the Yangtze River,
dominated by large, basic industry (with the smaller, cleaner
industries still being directed towards the city proper); a
fourth zone of forests and agriculture; and finally, an outer
zone with small towns of 30,000-50,000 persons.

Suzhou's urban concept is shaped by the city's historic
character. Founded in 514 BC, it has experienced little
basic change in location or design. The city has now been
designated a national historic place whose special sites are
protected by the national and provincial governments. The
new plan being drawn emphasises the city's history and seeks
to preserve its 70 historic monuments, clear the canals, and
restore 35 gardens in addition to the seven which have
already been restored. Tourism is a major industry, as well
as small factories (silk, electronic instruments), many of
which are being placed in small towns on the outskirts of the
city. "We want to integrate the city with the countryside,
industry with agriculture - a unified whole," officials there
stated.

Public Participation

In keeping with the planning principles outlined above,
there was evidence that attempts to involve the public in the
preparation of local plans, especially the general plans,
were being made in some cities, although the success of these
efforts was unclear. The planning process outlined by Beijing
officials, for example, involves seven major steps, two of
which include outside experts and the public:

- The preliminary plan is developed by the staff of the
  planning bureau.

- The plan receives approval of a review commission.
- Comments are invited from specialists in several functional areas.
- Comments are invited from the public.
- The plan is submitted, as amended, to the city governing body (the Revolutionary Committee at the time of our visit) and approved (or amended or rejected).
- The plan is submitted, as adopted or amended, to the State Council for review.
- The State Council approves the plan.

Conversations with officials and with citizens in their homes left the visitors with the impression that citizen participation is less than desired. There appeared to be little participation in the formulation of the more conceptualised general plans, while most input was received on short-term projects programmed in the detailed plans. This experience seems to confirm Laurence Ma's conclusions in his study that, "... active citizen's participation in the planning process appears to be negligible, except that in planning multi-story apartment buildings the city's residents are sometimes surveyed to find our about their housing needs and preferences. The department, therefore is quite free to implement its decisions without having to worry about the possible political repercussions that are commonly associated with city planning in a democratic system" (Ma, 1979, p.847).

Nevertheless, when projects affect a specific area, some input apparently is sought through the street and/or the neighbourhood committees. Many of the smaller- and medium-scale public works projects are undertaken by the district government and its outreach office, the street committee, which apparently functions as a public information mechanism as well as the "ears" of the government. In Nanjing, the committee, which is appointed by the district, has the duty of putting the decisions of that level of government into practice - "to solve problems of contradictions among the people." The staff of the street committee is assigned one or more functions (industry, education, health, welfare, construction or security) and it reviews with the neighbourhood committee those projects which will directly affect them.

PROBLEMS

The American urban planners noted a variety of possible problems which may have to be addressed if planning is to prove an effective instrument of public policy in China.

Impact of Diverting Growth to Satelite Cities

The policy of diverting most new growth into the satellite towns has not gone unchallenged. One planner noted that the youth especially have resisted living in the newer, somewhat sterile, agricultural commune centres and industrial new towns. Shanghai officials admitted that "young people still want to live in older areas of the city." To make this policy work in human terms, measures were outlined in Shanghai which might be useful to other Chinese cities, improve living standards in satellite towns, install more cultural and educational facilities, and the like. In Jinshan, officials were interested in devising an optimum (and considerably larger) size for their new town, one which would allow them to introduce more amenities and retain their population.

Without challenging the logic or wisdom of such a policy, it may be useful to indicate some possible pitfalls. When London adopted such a policy of population diversion, for example, the results were far different from what had been expected. The city was left with an aging population, students, visitors and the poor, and relatively few middle-class, middle-aged persons. Industries found it increasingly difficult to find a suitable labour force, while schools hospitals, and utility systems were under-utilised in the central areas and overloaded in the outskirts.

China's current swing to a satellite city policy (and to communal agricultural villages), accompanied by population and economic limits on the central core of the large cities, may be too abrupt. A more evenhanded approach may be needed to assure desirable results.

Deterioration of Built Environment

Faced with extraordinary growth, it is not surprising that the cities visited placed so much emphasis on new construction and so little on maintenance and preservation. The demand for more housing, additional sewer lines, new schools and hospitals, more roads and new facilities is not unlike the response which American urban regions made to the growth pressures of the 1950s and 1960s. Yet this almost total concentration of resources on new construction in the suburbs and satellite cities is apparently leaving in China, as it did in America, few resources for the maintenance of the housing and the upkeep of the infrastructure of the urban core. The result is likely to be an accelerated deterioration of the existing physical environment. Already Beijing is concerned about a shortage of materials to maintain and reconstruct its city proper. In the briefings of the Urban Planners Delegation, only in Shanghai was there an emphasis on maintenance, although in Nanjing too some concern was expressed: "We really do not want to change too greatly; we like slow change. We have been criticised: 'You are building behind a curtain.' We like the old as well as the new. How do we keep up with the maintenance of what we build?" officials asked of the American visitors.

Adherence to National Planning Principles and Standards

The influence of national planning principles on local plans appears to be pervasive. Officials in each of the cities visited by the delegation described similar problems of recent growth - traffic congestion, too many bicycles, housing shortages, air pollution and the like. Yet, despite sharp contrasts in the urban character and form of these cities, they were all experimenting with virtually the same solutions - population limitations placed on the city proper, construction of ring road systems, development of satellite towns, and construction of high-density housing - all responses to national guidelines.

It will become increasingly important that national settlement policies be cast in such a way as to recognise and encourage individual differences among cities and urban regions. Especially when these policies are translated into national standards, American experience suggests that unfortunate results can follow if not enough flexibility is built into the planning process. Nationally established and rigidly held national road standards, for example, often led to the devastation of American cities' core areas. Similarly, road widening in Beijing is now removing housing (2,000 rooms) during a period of housing shortages. In American public

housing experience such guidelines have contributed to monot-
ony and unrest. The row-upon-row of standardised housing in
Beijing, Jinshan and elsewhere, and the rigid site planning
shown to the delegation in Nanjing may also be the result of
uniform policy planning at the national level.

Strengthening the Planning Process

Like many Western countries, China continues to experiment with its urban planning process. Difficulties over
what should be covered in local plans, the problems of recon-
ciling differing views, and of gaining approval of local
decision-makers were all described to the delegation.

Furthermore, once plans have been formulated, apparently
they are not always obeyed, causing local planners to com-
plain (not unlike their western counterparts) of a lack of
vital local support for their efforts. Heads of local departments of urban planning and construction have begun to observe that other departments of local and provincial governments, as well as trades and professions, have often ignored
urban plans, defied regulations governing the selection of
construction sites, and "ruined the unified design" of local
planning and construction. Some of the complaints were attributed to events of an earlier period, when plans were
"undermined by interference and sabotage of Lin Biao and the
'Gang of Four'," but there is also a concern over the present
lack of widespread support for and adherence to local plans.
The department heads have, in a recent report (FBIS, October
15, 1979), proposed five ways to improve the planning process
in China:

- strengthen the leadership over urban planning (ie. sub-
  ordinate other interests to the goals outlined in the
  local plans);

- complete urban plans where these are yet to be finalised;

- Improve the existing system for urban construction by
  establishing an implementation component for the plans
  (ie. by formulating a capital improvements programme);

- establish a system of laws governing urban planning to
  assure the implementation of plans for urban development;

- improve the organisations in charge of urban planning. The report states that, "At present, except for Beijing and a few cities, the departments in charge of urban planning remain weak ... unable to tackle the task they are confronted with." The proposal is, in the larger cities, to place urban planning, designing, surveying and prospecting work under unified control, while in medium-size and smaller places, to place urban planning under the respective capital construction commissions in city construction bureaus.

Absence of Trained Planners

Conversations with city officials and educators indicate that only recently have programmes been devised to train students for planning and management work. There are now three universities offering a distinct planning degree – Tongji University of Shanghai, Wuhan University and Chongqing University. Qinghua University is proposing to offer a graduate-level planning degree. The estimated production of trained planners is about 100 graduates a year for the country. The estimated need is "many thousands." In the absence of university and advanced educational institutes, China will have to reply on the experience of less formally trained specialists to carry out the guidelines being laid down by the State for general and detailed city plans.

Local governments' efforts reflect this absence of trained planners. Only five general plans have thus far been approved by the State Council, according to officials in Zhaoqing, whose plan is one of the five. The questions raised by local officials in the six cities visited reveal their uncertainty regarding alternative solutions, which is perhaps the reason for almost literal use of the national guidelines. In virtually all cities, the planners suggested that "we have not done our work well," and are rewriting their plans. Beijing municipal planners are still struggling to have their plan in a condition to submit to the State Council. Nanjing has had two plans preliminarily approved locally, but have yet to complete and submit a final plan. In Guangzhou, the plan has been revised ten times and is not yet finalised. There is, then, a critical need for trained planners, especially in view of the extraordinary implementation powers possessed by the local government.

II. Administration of City Planning

Martha M. Davis, Edwin A. Winckler, Norman Krumholz,
Israel Stollman for Harvey Perloff, James L. Caplinger

The administrative structure within which the city planning function is performed in China provides insight into the
role of city planners and their concerns. City planning
bureaus perform the traditional function of preparing a
master plan. Their principal source of power is through the
site selection process and, in most cities, through the
building and utility design process. But many bureaus and
commissions of the municipal government and other levels of
government and other levels of government impact the city
planning process. A detailed discussion of the municipal,
district and neighbourhood structure has been written by
Laurence Ma in a recent article in Asian Survey (Ma, 1979).
In this paper we are adding impressions based on our general
conversations with Chinese city planners during the course of
our visit. We also describe in more detail the overall
governmental structure at the national and municipal levels
within which urban policy is formulated. In most cities
visited we obtained an organisational breakdown of construction commissions and urban planning bureaus.

LEADERSHIP

National

At the national level, overall urban policy is set by
the State Council, essentially the cabinet of heads of a
large number of ministries and ministry-level agencies within
the national government. Under the authority of the State
Council, more specific coordinative functions relevant to
urban development are performed by three commissions - the
State Planning Commission, State Economic Commission and
State Capital Construction Commission. This tripartite division of labour is repeated in the provinces and larger
cities. The Planning Commission frames overall economic
goals and resource allocations, the Economic Commission coordinates the different sectors of the economy, and the
Capital Construction Commission coordinates physical planning, design and construction. Until recently most oper-

ational details relating to urban development were handled by appropriate specialists within the State Capital Construction Commission.

A State Administration of Urban Construction has recently been attached to the State Council, evidently as a staff office to assist in processing urban issues. This suggests that urban policy is receiving more attention at the highest levels of government, though whether this is part of an overall filling out of the table of central government organisation, a response to a higher volume of specifically urban decisions, or an actual rise in the priority of urban issues was not clear. The new director of this bureau is Shao Jingwa, formerly deputy governor of relatively under-developed Ningxia province in northwest China. The delegation was greeted by the deputy director, Ding Xiu who formerly performed a similar national urban policy function with the Urban Construction Bureau within the Capital Construction Commission.

The State Council reviews the outline master plan of all provincial capitals and other cities with populations over 500,000. Once the master plan is approved at the state level, the provincial government assumes supervision of the detailed plans. Three cities directly administered by the national government (Beijing, Tianjin and Shanghai) are an exception, however, as the State Council supervises their detailed as well as outline plans. Evidently outline master plans for cities under 500,000 are supervised entirely by the provincial governments in accordance with standards and guidelines set by the national government.

Municipal

At the municipal level, the leading organ in urban policy as in other areas is of course the city government; in 1979 still administered by the municipal revolutionary committee. As at the national level, functions relevant to urban development are coordinated in three commissions – Planning, Economic and Construction. The division of labour among these, the same at the municipal as at the national level, can be inferred from their internal organisation. Under the Planning Commission are bureaus allocating materials, labour and energy. The Planning Commission itself appears to have a strong voice in the allocation of invest-

ment capital. Under the Economic Commission are bureaus
supervising different sectors of the economy - textiles,
machinery, petrochemicals, etc. Under the Construction Commission are bureaus providing public facilities and services
- Construction Engineering, Public Utilities, Housing Administration, etc. Thus the Planning Commission sets the overall economic goals and allocates the resources necessary to
achieve them, the Economic Commission coordinates the different sectors of the economy, and the Construction Commission
provides needed infrastructure and services.

Presumably many specific project proposals arise from
within the expanding industrial plans under the Economic
Commission. However, the Planning Commission has final say
over what can actually be built and when, and the Construction Commission has final say over where within the municipality each project should be built and how. Differences of
opinion among these commissions go to the city government for
resolution. Although such differences no doubt occur, our
hosts stressed that the three commissions, many of whose
members have worked with each other for a long time, are
housed together in the city government's headquarters, and
work together harmoniously on most issues. As a further, and
more formalised form of coordination, representatives of the
three commissions meet weekly under the chairmanship of one
of the vice mayors and with the participation of such other
agencies as are relevant to solving the particular problems
on the agenda. Nevertheless, recent complaints about the
"anarchy" in construction in Beijing suggest that the authority of the Construction Commission vis-a-vis the other two
commissions and vis-a-vis its own bureaus, is less than complete. Among the suggestions for reform is that the nation's
capital city have an authoritative review apparatus with
final say over construction.

The bureaus under one commission may communicate directly with the bureaus under another commission on matters
on which policy decisions have already been coordinated among
the commissions. New policy issues must, however, be referred by a bureau upward to the commission, which would then
raise it with other commissions and other relevant organisations, and notify its own bureau of the eventual result.
Thus, if a factory decides that it needs to expand it would
report its proposal upward to the industrial bureau supervising it, which would in turn report it to the Economic Commission. The Economic Commission would check with the Plan-

ning Commission about the suitability of the proposed plan expansion to the municipality's economic target and resources, and with the Construction Commission about the suitability of its location and the availability of supporting services. If the Planning Commission approves the expansion, the Economic Commission would notify the factory to contact relevant bureaus of the Construction Commission to clear its proposed location, design and environmental impact.

Obviously, the process here is only an abstract and ideal one. In any concrete instance the informal processes surrounding it might mean that initiatives, information or influence flowed in more complex patterns than the bureaucratic channels outlined. Nevertheless, the fact remains that for successful completion the project would have to make it through the official channels. Nor is it obvious that there are alternative channels through which such issues are more likely to be processed. Thus the normative legal/institutional procedures may handle most cases, including many important ones, much as described. Even what happens when these prescribed procedures do not work may be largely prescribed - disagreements go to the city government for resolution.

IMPLEMENTATION

Municipal Construction Commission

The Municipal Construction Commission is the municipal government's means of coordinating physical development and is the link with the construction commissions at higher levels of government - provincial for most cities, and directly to the State Construction Commission in the case of Beijing, Tianjin and Shanghai.

We obtained the most complete information about the Beijing Construction Commission and Urban Planning and Administration Bureau. From our brief conversations in other cities we found both similarities to and differences from the Beijing structure (see Figure 1).

It is our understanding that the Construction Commission in Beijing focused on coordinating planning, design and construction but not on the maintenance of the physical plant. The Urban Planning and Administration Bureau and nine con-

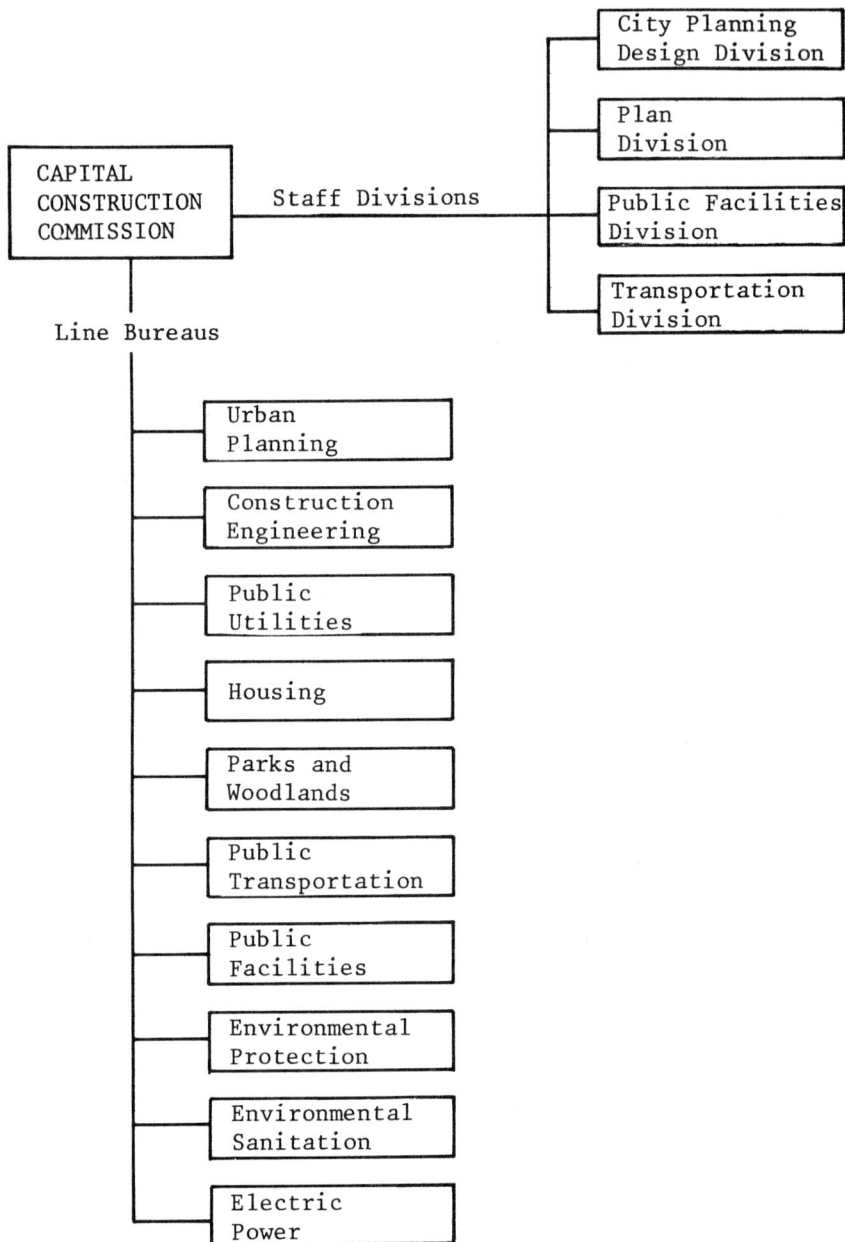

Fig. 1. Beijing Municipal Capital Construction Commission.

struction bureaus are under its jurisdiction. The Commission has four staff divisions which coordinate the activities of the bureaus:

- The City Planning Design Division reviews the work of the Urban Planning and Administration Bureau.

- The Plan Division prepares the annual construction plan.

- The Public Facilities Division coordinates the activity of construction bureaus.

- The Transportation Division reviews the work of the Transportation Construction Bureau.

The construction bureaus are responsible for all construction and do only minor design work, usually involving adjustments needed during construction.

Municipal Urban Planning and Administration Bureau

The Beijing Urban Planning and Administration Bureau has two principal functions: planning and design. Its principal source of planning power is through its responsibility for selecting sites for all approved construction projects. Its two design institutes design all construction projects.

The Urban Planning Bureau is responsible for ensuring the implementation of State-established design standards, developing broad master plans that implement national development policies in the context of local conditions, and developing detailed district plans for implementing policies established by the Municipal Government through its Economic, Planning and Construction Commissions.

To perform these functions, the Urban Planning Bureau has four planning divisions, two design institutes and two technical support divisions and a bureau office to coordinate division activities. These are shown in Figure 2.

- The Master Plan Division prepares a master plan based on principles established by the State Council and the Municipal Government, establishes site requirements for construction projects, reviews development requests, and reviews alternate sites for approved projects for conformity with the general plan.

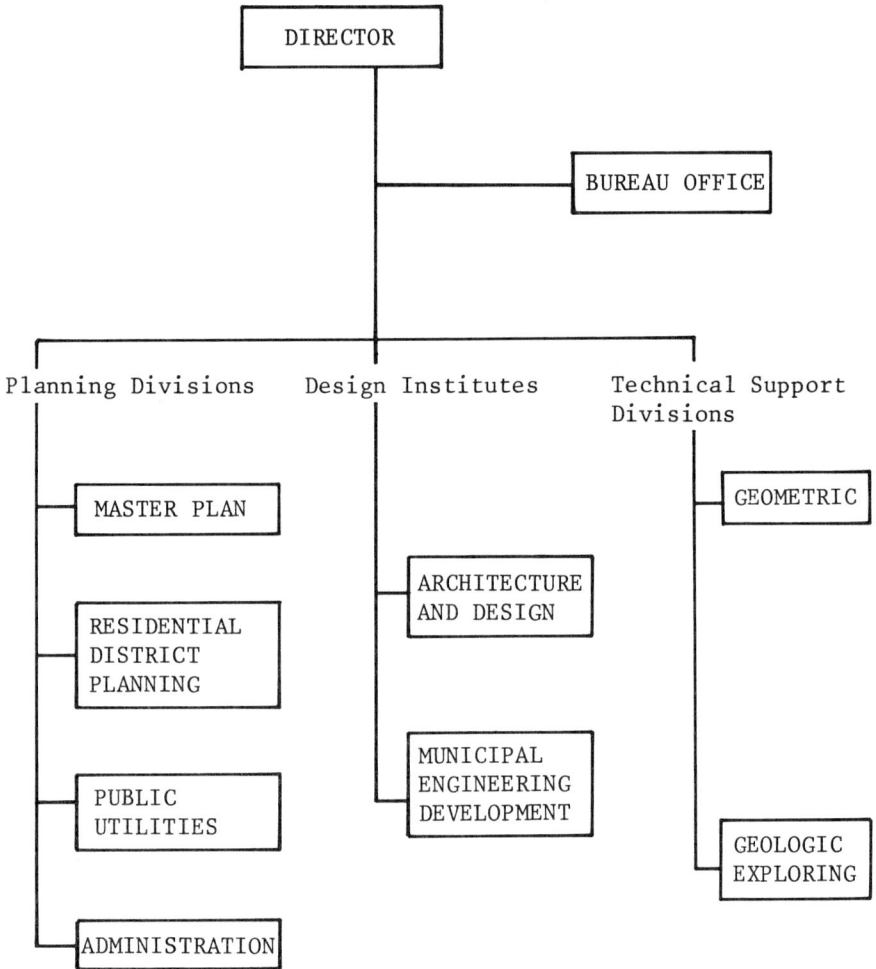

Fig. 2. Beijing Municipal Urban Planning and Administration
         Bureau.

  - The Residential District Planning Division has three
    district teams which develop plans for residential dis-
    tricts, locate sites for housing to be built in the next
    five years and reviews site proposals for conformity
    with the district plan.

  - The Public Utilities Division plans road systems, water
    mains and drainage systems in cooperation with the re-

sponsible bureau and reviews the impact of proposed
sites on water and sewer systems.

- The Administrative Division receives and processes requests for sites from responsible bureaus and coordinates the review with the Master Plan, Residential District Planning and Public Utilities Planning Divisions
  and coordinates with the client and affected neighbourhood.

- The Architectural and Design Institute designs housing
  and other buildings including small factories. The
  Institute works closely with planners in selecting
  building sites so that site design considerations are
  included, makes final decisions on such matters as
  building height and amenities, prepares site plans for
  areas designated in district plans and approves design
  specifications after consultation with designers,
  builders, construction administrators and the client.

- The Municipal Engineering Development Institute designs
  sewers and other public facilities and participates in
  the review of sites and site design.

- The Geometric Division prepares maps of all scales for
  the various divisions of the bureau.

- The Geologic Exploring Division conducts field investigations of geologic conditions.

To coordinate activities of the various municipal bureaus
concerned with physical plant development and maintenance,
the Municipality of Beijing has established four coordinating
groups: transportation, housing, environment and public
utilities.   Representatives from the responsible bureau,
various Urban Planning Bureau divisions and appropriate construction bureau participate.

Some variations in organisation of the urban planning
process in other cities were:

- In smaller cities the construction commission was generally responsible for both new construction and the maintenance of the physical plant.

- In Guangzhou the design institute was independent of the
  urban planning bureau and conversations indicated that

in many cities both arrangements have been tried at
various times.

While we were given no explanation for these variations it is
reasonable to assume that construction commissions concentrate on construction when the volume is great, but when
construction is minimal, it is combined with the maintenance
function. The combining of planning and design in one bureau
probably is a response to coordination problems, whereas
strong independent design institutes may reflect the large
scale of the operation and power of the directors of the
institutes.

Planning officials expressed concern about several aspects of the city planning process. In many cases these
concerns are shared by city planners everywhere and are not
unique in China.

- They have difficulty implementing their long range plans
  because short range plans tend to dominate decision
  making.

- The basic planning objectives and principles have not
  been sufficiently clarified so that they provide guidance to designers of individual construction projects.
  Some of the principles they are interested in developing
  and implementing might include, but not be limited to,
  proper use of land and open space; greening of the city;
  planning of commercial districts; and achieving an ecological balance.

- The objective of relating planning to the "mass line" is
  clear, but the mechanisms for accomplishing it have not
  been created. Chinese planners feel the need to develop
  tools for survey and analysis, convincing the people,
  and working with them during the planning process.

- Planners feel the need to ensure that plans, once decided, are carried out thoroughly. They lose credibility
  with the public when there are many changes.

- Because of the great diffusion of powers and responsibilities related to city planning and development, there
  is need to clarify the roles of different agencies, and
  to coordinate related functions in a more effective way
  through the Construction Commission.

LOCALITIES

The Chinese enjoy the powerful social and cultural cohesion of a people who have lived in the same part of the
world and shared the same language and traditions for 5,000
years. The social organisation of their cities suggests the
extent of this cohesion.

Districts

The Governing body of the municipal government is headed
by a mayor, appointed by the central government in Beijing,
Tianjin and Shanghai, and by the provincial government elsewhere. Municipal boundaries generally encompass rural
counties surrounding the city proper, or the urbanised central area. The city proper is divided into semi-autonomous
units of descending size until everyone is part of some
organisational unit. Regulations enacted in the 1950s set
forth the objectives for creating urban neighbourhood committees, people's mediation committees, social order and
security committees, and subdistrict offices of municipal
agencies. The structure has not been completely implemented,
but there appears to be a renewed emphasis on doing so.

The largest units are districts containing 200,000 to
600,000 people. Each district is sub-divided into neighbourhood committees of 50,000 to 70,000 people. These neighbourhood units make up the basic social unit and the lowest level
of official government. They, in turn, are further sub-
divided into smaller resident or street committees of 8,000
to 10,000 and finally to socialist courtyard committees,
which are frequently led by retired persons who are directly
elected and serve without compensation. It is said that the
Chinese are uncomfortable unless they know who's in charge;
this organisation should dispel such disquietude.

Neighbourhoods

The neighbourhood and smaller units provide the Chinese
Communist Party with a vehicle to disseminate and implement
Party directives. If the Party decides, as it has, to impose
a policy of strict birth control, the street and courtyard
committees hold supportive training and propaganda sessions
and apply powerful peer pressure for conformance.

The Neighbourhood committee's eight basic functions are:
security; family counselling, including pre-natal courses and
family planning; sanitation, mobilising families to clean up
areas; child care services, including operation of nursery
schools and kindergartens and organising children after
school; programmes for the elderly; help in repairing apartments; adjudication of family and interfamily disputes; and
assisting youth returning from the country to find work and
adjust to new conditions. Of course, the well-organised
local units make up an invaluable surveillance and information network for the regime, but they also supply the Party
with information about the needs or concerns of the people at
the "grassroots" level which may then become the focus for
city or national policy.

At the same time, the neighbourhood committee also performs a variety of decentralised services for their people
which in many ways renders them more autonomous than their
American counterparts. They organise production groups and
run small commercial and industrial enterprises whose surplus, along with the relatively small sums they receive from
the city budget, can be invested in jobs or housing or other
ways that benefit their own neighbourhood. They operate
nurseries and kindergartens for the children - a wonderous
national resource - sweep the courtyards and pick up trash,
organise the young, mobilise labour for local projects, and
provide housing and welfare for any indigent elderly. (A
Chinese tradition which persists in this revolutionary culture is the responsibility of children for the welfare of
their aged parents.) They also provide a substantial measure
of social control. Minor cases of juvenile delinquency or
vandalism, while apparently rare, and handled by the neighbourhood committee applying cultural and peer pressure in
public "criticism" sessions. They even run local health
facilities.

In the Fengsheng neighbourhood in Beijing, for example,
the 53,000 residents are divided into 25 resident committees
each of which provides a health station. These are staffed
by three local housewives who receive one month of medical
training and continuous in-service training at the neighbourhood hospital. This health group provides personal, immediate
care for patients with minor illnesses, refers more complicated cases to the neighbourhood hospital and provides
follow-up care at home after a patient has been treated in
the hospital. The technical level of care does not approxi-

mate that with which Americans are familiar, but it is personal, direct and unbureaucratic, and much less expensive.

In sum, the Chinese have developed much autonomy and responsibility to the neighbourhood level, but have included their neighbourhoods as part of their extraordinary pervasive system of political and social control.

III. Future Exchanges

Janet A. Cady

American and Chinese planners alike feel a need for more long-term, in-depth dialogue related to urban administration, planning, and design. Perhaps because of rather than in spite of differences in culture, values, political systems, geography, and history, there is much to be gained from future exchanges. Outlined below are areas of potential joint study suggested by members of this delegation, by other American professionals who have visited China, and by Chinese officials and planners.

ADMINISTRATION

City Planning Process

The Chinese and American City planning processes have many similarities but certain key differences. In the United States an attempt is made to guide and control development through zoning, subsidies and tax policies, and public development through capital improvement programming. In China the city planner's principal tool is his role in controlling site selection for development initiated by municipal agencies, enterprises, and institutions.

The Chinese programme to develop urban master plans is in its early stages. These master plans appear to be principally generalised land use plans showing the pattern for future development such as major roads, clusters of new developments, or rings for different types of development. Each such plan is accompanied by a broad policy statement defining objectives and programme priorities. Chinese officials in several cities expressed concern to the US Urban Planners Delegation about problems with implementing their master plans. Exchanges between US and Chinese planners on

the planning process could focus on evaluating the master
plan as a tool for decision-making, approaches to establishing planning guidelines and criteria for development, the
potential use of zoning and design guidelines as planning
tools in China, and techniques for capital improvement programming.   In addition, a survey of the types of analysis
conducted for developing plans and making resource allocation
decisions would be useful.

Systems Planning

Plans in Chinese cities seem to be formulated after the
fact to accord with and implement policy directives from the
State, and to be based on preconceived ideas about appropriate development patterns. Chinese city planners do not appear
to use systems analysis for planning streets and transit
services. It would be useful for them to learn techniques of
systems planning used in the US which provide a way to design
networks of streets and transit services in coordination with
settlement policy, recognising the human needs of neighbourhood and housing design, as well as the grand ideals of monumental civic design.

URBAN DESIGN

City Size and Patterns

While the size and pattern of a city is determined to a
large extent by its geography, its economic base, and its
environs rather than by any given geometric form or magic
standard, it is a subject to which Chinese officials and
planners give a great deal of attention. All of the larger
cities have undertaken a series of measures designed to influence size and pattern: limiting growth or actually reducing the population of the central city, limiting the expansion of private transportation while encouraging people to
live in close proximity to their place of employment, etc.
American and Chinese planners would benefit from an exchange
of views and experience in this area.

As part of the effort to limit growth, most larger
Chinese cities have built around them a number of smaller
satellite areas (usually called "new towns") during the past
20 years. Despite the many problems surrounding the new

towns, the Chinese experiment has generally been more successful than our own. A whole range of fascinating topics
surrounding the potential and limitations of new towns could
be explored:

> The design of the new towns themselves
>> - city layout
>> - community features
>> - design of service facilities
>> - integration of housing with other amenities
>
> Policy issues surrounding new towns
>> - where to build
>> - size (population) limitations
>> - density
>> - how to attract ("assign") workers and residents,
>>   not only for the major industry, but in service
>>   industries
>> - what should the balance be between new towns and
>>   conservation of the centre city?
>
> Sociological aspects of new towns
>> - do they tend to better serve a certain age group?
>> - do they tend to be more suitable for certain
>>   social or occupational groups?
>> - what accounts for their success or failures?

Neighbourhood Design

In rebuilding older districts in the city proper or in
planning for new satellite towns, Chinese planners attempt to
locate housing close to employment centres, markets, schools,
recreation facilities, and other amenities. There is concern
not only about spatial relationships and physical aspects of
the community, but about social aspects as well. For example,
there has been an ongoing debate among planners about the
social effects of high-rise versus medium-rise housing.
High-rise buildings are more land-intensive and tend to be
more economic and efficient but medium-rise buildings provide
more opportunity for personal interaction and are more consistent with Chinese culture and tradition.

Less attention is given to the design itself, and much
of the new construction is monotonous and monochromatic.
Prescribed design and site layout standards, in some in-

stances, may not provide enough opportunity for flexibility, variety, and visual attractiveness. American architects and housing experts who have visited China have indicated that the mixing of buildings of different heights, more use of colour, and improved site planning could be incorporated into Chinese plans without adding to the overall cost. Better design and planning would also provide better use of interior floor space. Chinese planners would also be interested in exploring ways to minimise the costs of infrastructure. An exchange of experiences in housing design and construction materials would be of great value to the Chinese and might be an area of export potential for the United States.

HOUSING

Housing Design and Construction Techniques

Chinese officials indicated to National Committee Board members during a meeting in November 1980 that housing construction was China's priority need, and the area in which they would be most interested in initiating exchange programmes. They emphasised the need to learn about and acquire new technology but noted that design had been sorely neglected over the past decade. Indeed Chinese newspapers and periodicals are full of reports on the "housing crisis," not only about the shortage of housing but about the lack of planning and coordination that has led to poor quality and waste in the construction sector. In some instances new housing projects have gone up without the necessary water, electricity, and gas lines to service them, so hundreds of thousands of square meters of floor space are reported to be unoccupied. Given this situation, the Chinese indicated an interest in an exchange of information on architecture and engineering design as it relates to external design of housing units as well as the internal technical systems (electricity, ventilation, plumbing, etc.). Although not mentioned by the Chinese, this might encompass site selection and planning, landscape design, energy-efficient design, and interior and component design.

Useful exchanges could be initiated in the field of building construction, especially among building materials manufacturers and contractors with considerable experience in city construction and those involved with the construction of multi-family housing. Possible areas of cooperation include:

- construction methods, materials, and standards
- use of industrial by-products or waste materials for housing construction
- management of construction and maintenance.

The Chinese and US approaches to housing and development are characterised by great differences in financing and policy formulation. To bridge this gap, useful future exchanges could take place involving both national and local housing policy makers, including those who formulate housing policy with regard to finance, construction, neighbourhood renewal, and self-help housing and those who study and analyse housing policy. Americans have indicated a need to explore the following questions on housing and housing construction in China if they are to gain the most benefit from exchanges in this area:

- how are annual housing targets determined?

- what organisations in China deal with housing and construction? what are the responsibilities of each?

- how is housing financed in China?

- how are funds allocated?

- how is rehabilitation and maintenance financed and carried out?

- what is the relationship between rents and maintenance and repair?

- what regulations apply to the private ownership of housing stock?

- how are housing standards established? how have they changed over the years? why?

- how is housing used to achieve other social goals (ie. to limit the size of families, encourage migration from the cities, control the population of the city-proper)?

Seismic Safety

On July 28, 1976 a devastating earthquake, registering 7.2 on the Richter scale, struck the industrial city of Tangshan in northeast China, killing an estimated one million people. Only a few buildings remained standing and those were not habitable. Since that time the Chinese have estab-

lished strict standards of quake-resistance for new structures in earthquake-prone areas and have exhibited great
interest in learning how to build more resilient cities. It
is an area in which an exchange of data, research results,
and technology would be of mutual value. Some exchange relating to seismic safety and earthquake prediction, an area
in which China leads the world, has taken place in recent
years.

TRANSPORTATION

Transportation planning is a subject of vital importance
in both the United States and China. American urban dwellers
are all too familiar with the serious problems of traffic
congestion, noise, air pollution, and inadequate and poorly
maintained public transportation systems. As China moves
toward modernisation, many of the same problems could result
from inadequate attention to transportation planning. Areas
in which American and Chinese transportation planners might
benefit from an exchange of information and experience include:

- policy formation

- transportation as infrastructure

- techniques of collecting basic transportation data to
  assist in predicting future transportation needs

- transportation planning, including systems of streets
  and systems of public transportation facilities with
  attention given to the relationship between population,
  economic productivity, land use, and travel demands for
  the movement of people and goods within urban areas and
  neighbourhoods

- traffic management, including technical methods for
  separating and controlling different types of vehicles
  as well as pedestrians, technical means of improving
  highway safety, and law enforcement

- transit management, concerned with optimum utilisation
  and scheduling of buses and subways

- safety education of drivers, bicyclists, and pedestrians

- statewide or provincial transportation planning, involving the allocation of resources to major road, rail,
  aviation, and waterway systems across states or prov-

inces. This is both a policy and a technical subject, and is receiving increasing attention in the United States.

ENVIRONMENT

Regional Planning and Ecological Design

US planning agencies now require an environmental element within many regional planning studies, developing extensive survey information on environmental conditions, land suitability, carrying capacity, etc. and have developed expertise in policy planning to implement environmental goals. This seems to have progressed beyond the present role of environmental planning in China, and is an area where fruitful exchanges might take place. The PRC's environmental policies are general policies; there is a need for individual cities to integrate environmental objectives within the process of master planning, transportation planning, etc., rather than seeing the site-specific locational studies as the principal tool for implementing an environmental goal.

Since many large Chinese cities are indeed "regions," including rural counties in addition to the built-up urban area, the US counterpart would likely be at the metropolitan or regional level. Within the United States, specific cities and regions which merit study come to mind. These include the Metropolitan Council in the Twin Cities of Minneapolis-St. Paul (Minnesota), Dallas (Texas), Fairfax County (Virginia), and several Florida counties and cities which are required by state law to develop environmental plans and programmes as part of their comprehensive planning. Site visits by Chinese planners to these locations might be supplemented by visits to specific state agencies dealing with common issues, such as power plant siting (Massachusetts and Minnesota, for example), and hazardous waste management (Michigan), since these are relevant current policy issues for Chinese urban planning strategies.

Environmental Research

Staffs of the environmental monitoring station in Beijing and the geographic institute in Nanjing expressed to the US Urban Planners Delegation interest in developing con-

tacts with US colleagues and obtaining results of research in
environmental modelling, simulation, and prediction of impacts from new developments. Research staff in governmental
agencies, non-profit institutions specialising in environmental analysis, and in larger consulting firms providing
environmental planning services in the US could assist in
bringing these research findings to the attention of their
Chinese counterparts, with benefits to both countries. Published materials and personal contacts to discuss the research findings and their applicability in the Chinese setting could be exchanged. While many Chinese officials are
visiting the US on various missions and are thus aware of
what some of the larger US cities are doing, it is not clear
that this information is being received where the detailed
research knowledge could do the most good. Since the research institutes do provide contract research services to
the larger cities in industrial location analyses, there
should also be exchanges at this level.

PRESERVATION/CONSERVATION

The problem of maintaining a country's cultural heritage
while modernising is world-wide. In recent years China has
recognised the importance of preservation; many historic
buildings have been restored and maintenance programmes initiated. Work in Chinese architecture, city building,
ancient construction methods, and garden design have been
resumed since the end of the Cultural Revolution (a time
during which many historic landmarks and cultural relics were
destroyed). In spite of solid accomplishments, much remains
to be done. Areas of cooperation between the United States
and China might include:

- Landmark survey and preservation
  The Bureau of Cultural Relics has undertaken a survey of
  national and regional landmarks, but this does not
  include vernacular architecture or landmark districts.
  An exchange of information relating to the survey and
  registration of landmarks as well as of actual preservation and maintenance methods and technology would be
  of mutual benefit.

- Preservation of vernacular architecture
  Capital improvements such as street widening, building a
  subway system, and housing and office construction have

frequently destroyed many distinctive features of cities. These problems are further aggravated by the lack of attention given to mingling modern buildings with ancient architecture in such a way as to preserve the character of a city. China, as it modernises, is proving to be no exception. An exchange of information on how each country has coped with these problems would be of great interest and value to both American and Chinese planners.

- Rehabilitation
It has not been fully recognised in China that the revitalisation of existing housing stock is a real possibility for helping to ease the severe housing shortage and for helping to maintain existing family and social structures. Americans might share their experience in the rehabilitation of old housing - including self-rehabilitation whereby residents would be encouraged to upgrade the quality of their housing themselves, with labour training, tools, materials, and organisation provided.

TOURISM

Tourism is one of the most rapidly developing enterprises in China. In 1978, 124,000 foreign tourists were received - as many as the total number in the previous 24 years. By 1979 this figure had jumped to 960,000, and in 1980 to an estimated 1.1 million. The value of tourism to China is obvious but it brings a number of problems. Among them, traffic congestion and pollution, overcrowding of landmark buildings and scenic places (sometimes to the point of creating irreversible damage), and eyesores created by poorly designed tourism facilities.

Exchanges in tourism might include:

- the relationship between urban conservation and tourism development

- the tourism plan as it relates to the larger plan of the city

- the design of tourism facilities and placement in the environment

- the preservation of historic and scenic sites.

Hotel Design

As the tourist industry has developed in China, so has the shortage of hotel rooms, especially in those cities receiving large numbers of visitors. A number of new hotels have been built and construction is being undertaken in Beijing, Shanghai, Nanjing and Guangzhou. Unfortunately, the results of these efforts are not always pleasing. Construction has been shoddy, and, in some instances, the hotels have been located in such a way as to detract from the natural beauty of scenic tourist spots. It is an area in which the Chinese would benefit from better consultation with American architects and in which many American firms are interested in establishing useful contact.

LANDSCAPE ARCHITECTURE

Garden and Park Design

Chinese gardens are world famous. They are generally fairly small, but the spatial design and use of materials transport the visitor to another world. Americans could learn a great deal from the Chinese about creating small parks and retreats in urban areas, whereas the Chinese would be interested in research projects focusing on vegetation for landscaping and grass strains that could be used for ground cover in the barren cities of the North, for instance.

Behaviour Science and Design

Chinese may also find of interest results of recent behaviour studies in the US which demonstrate that the social interactions in an area may be strengthened by physical layout. The old courtyard houses in China offer many opportunities for social intercourse among residents. How such interactions can be continued in new housing layout presents another challenge to Chinese architects and planners today, and is an area of increasing interest to American architects and planners.

PLANNING AND DESIGN EDUCATION

Most planners in China today are engineers or construction architects; there does not seem to be any sense of a holistic approach to urban planning. As mentioned earlier in this report, only three universities (Tongji, Wuhan and Chongqing) offer a distinct planning specialty, producing a total of about 100 graduates a year. Courses include construction design, construction theory, structures, transportation, construction equipment, construction economics and geography. Four universities (Harbin, Xian, Liaoning and Chongqing) have institutes that conduct research on design and construction. Each provincial government also has a design institute and construction company, as do the municipalities of Beijing, Shanghai and Tianjin.

Nearly all American planners who have visited China have perceived a need for the Chinese to upgrade the quality of planning and design education. In addition to making certain printed materials available to schools of planning and design institutes, it was felt that an exchange of scholars would be of great benefit. Several Chinese scholars are currently enrolled in Schools of Architecture here in the US or are serving interships in American architectural firms. The University of Minnesota's School of Architecture has begun an informal exchange programme with Chongqing University and has extensive informal contacts with Tianjin University. Surely there are others as well, but much can still be done.

Suggested projects include:

- exchanging faculty members for an academic year

- participating in continuing education programmes or on-the-job training for professionals

- organising joint workshops around specific topics in planning and design education to include both educators and practitioners

- arranging for American educators to give lectures and consult on education-related matters in China

- working with Chinese schools of architecture or planning on specific projects

- assisting in a survey of curriculum needs of schools and in developing programmes.

TRANSLATION AND EXCHANGE OF LITERATURE

Many Chinese read English fairly well, and simply supplying books and periodicals to schools of architecture and planning or relevant state, provincial, or municipal level bureaus would have some impact. The translation of selected design literature, though, would mean a far larger group of professionals and students would have access to it. Certainly there are few Americans who can read Chinese literature without translation. Training translators and interpreters who are familiar with the subject matter is also essential if any exchange projects are to succeed.

REFERENCE

Changes in Cities and Towns, Beijing Review, No. 16, p.27, April 21 (1980).

China Acts to Slow its Rate of Growth, New York Times, July 6 (1979).

"China: In Pursuit of Economic Modernization," Central Intelligence Agency, National Foreign Assessment Center, p.14 December (1978).

Housing China's 900 Million People, Beijing Review, No. 28, p.17-27, November 30 (1979).

The Chinese Approach to City Planning: Policy, Administration, and Action, Laurence J.C. Ma, Asian Survey, Vol. XIX, No. 9, p.836-854, September (1979).

Two Views on China's Urbanisation, Beijing Review, No. 11, p.6-7, March 17 (1980).

Xinhua Correspondents Comment on Urban Planning, Foreign Broadcast Information Service, p.17-19, October 15 (1979).

APPENDIX

Notes on Administration of City Planning, Post-1979.

Since 1979 extensive changes have taken place as a result of major governmental reorganisation. These include a new ministry, and organisation for Beijing (Figs. 3 and 4).

The Ministry of Urban and Rural Construction and Environmental Protection was created in May 1982 as part of a major governmental reorganisation, combining the State Capital Construction Commission, the State Administration of Urban Construction, the State Administration of Building Construction, and the National Bureau of Surveying and Mapping. Similar reorganisations aimed at reducing the number

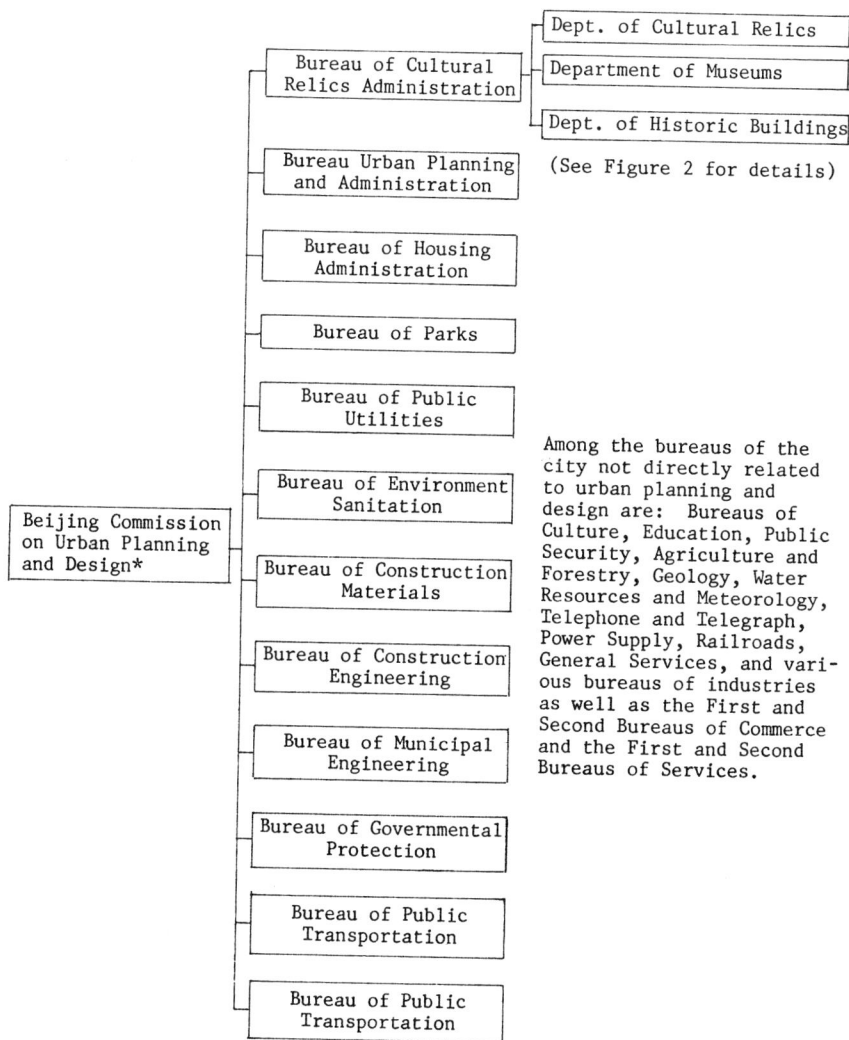

```
                              ┌─ Dept. of Cultural Relics
          ┌─ Bureau of Cultural  ├─ Department of Museums
          │   Relics Administration └─ Dept. of Historic Buildings
          │
          ├─ Bureau Urban Planning    (See Figure 2 for details)
          │   and Administration
          │
          ├─ Bureau of Housing
          │   Administration
          │
          ├─ Bureau of Parks
          │
          ├─ Bureau of Public
          │   Utilities
          │
          ├─ Bureau of Environment
          │   Sanitation
Beijing Commission
on Urban Planning ─┤
and Design*       ├─ Bureau of Construction
          │   Materials
          │
          ├─ Bureau of Construction
          │   Engineering
          │
          ├─ Bureau of Municipal
          │   Engineering
          │
          ├─ Bureau of Governmental
          │   Protection
          │
          ├─ Bureau of Public
          │   Transportation
          │
          └─ Bureau of Public
              Transportation
```

Among the bureaus of the city not directly related to urban planning and design are: Bureaus of Culture, Education, Public Security, Agriculture and Forestry, Geology, Water Resources and Meteorology, Telephone and Telegraph, Power Supply, Railroads, General Services, and various bureaus of industries as well as the First and Second Bureaus of Commerce and the First and Second Bureaus of Services.

*Chairman: Jiao Ruoyu (Mayor). Deputy Chairman: Zhao Pengfei (Deputy Major); Shen Bo (Deputy Chairman, Beijing Basic Construction Commission); Chu Chuanheng (Assistant to Mayor); Zhou Yongyuan (Director, Bureau of Urban Planning and Administration); Tong Zheng.

Fig. 3. Beijing Commission on Urban Planning and Design.

DEPARTMENT & DEPARTMENT HEADS   FUNCTIONS

Department & Department Heads	Functions
Bureau Office Yu Changfeng	Serves the Director of the Bureau
Dept. of Planning Finance Zhang Pinghua	Accounting of all departments
Dept. of Comprehensive Planning Pan Taimin, Qian Ming, Zhu Yanji	Makes master plans and considers the directions of urban development
Department of Detailed Planning Tian Rugeng, Ke Huangzhang	Makes detailed plans for key construction area
Dept. of Transportation Planning Qian Lianhe, Tan Boren	In charge of street planning, public transit, and suburban highway and railroad planning
Dept. of Public Utilities Planning & Administration Pang Erhong, Zhang Tingwu	Planning of water supply, sewage discharge treatment, and energy supply
Dept. of Planning and Administration of Urban Areas Li Yuguang	Planning and administration of all construction projects in the city proper; initial selection of land for construction; issues construction permits after project approval by the Department of Science and Technology
Department of Planning and Administration of Suburbs Cui Yuxuan	Planning and administration of all construction projects in the suburbs; initial selection of land for construction; issues construction permits after project approval by the Department of Science and Technology
Dept. of Administration of Comprehensive Planning Li Xinshu	Drafts regulations for urban planning and administration; investigates and makes decisions on illegal construction projects; compiles land use and construction permit statistics
Dept. of Science and Technology Zheng Zuwu, Zhang Jinggan	Evaluates and approves all construction projects; engineering and architectural research; administers Beijing Institute of Architectural Design, Beijing Institute of Engineering Design for Public Utilities, Division of Geodetic Survey; provides information services

Beijing Bureau of Planning and Administration Director: Zhou Yongyuan

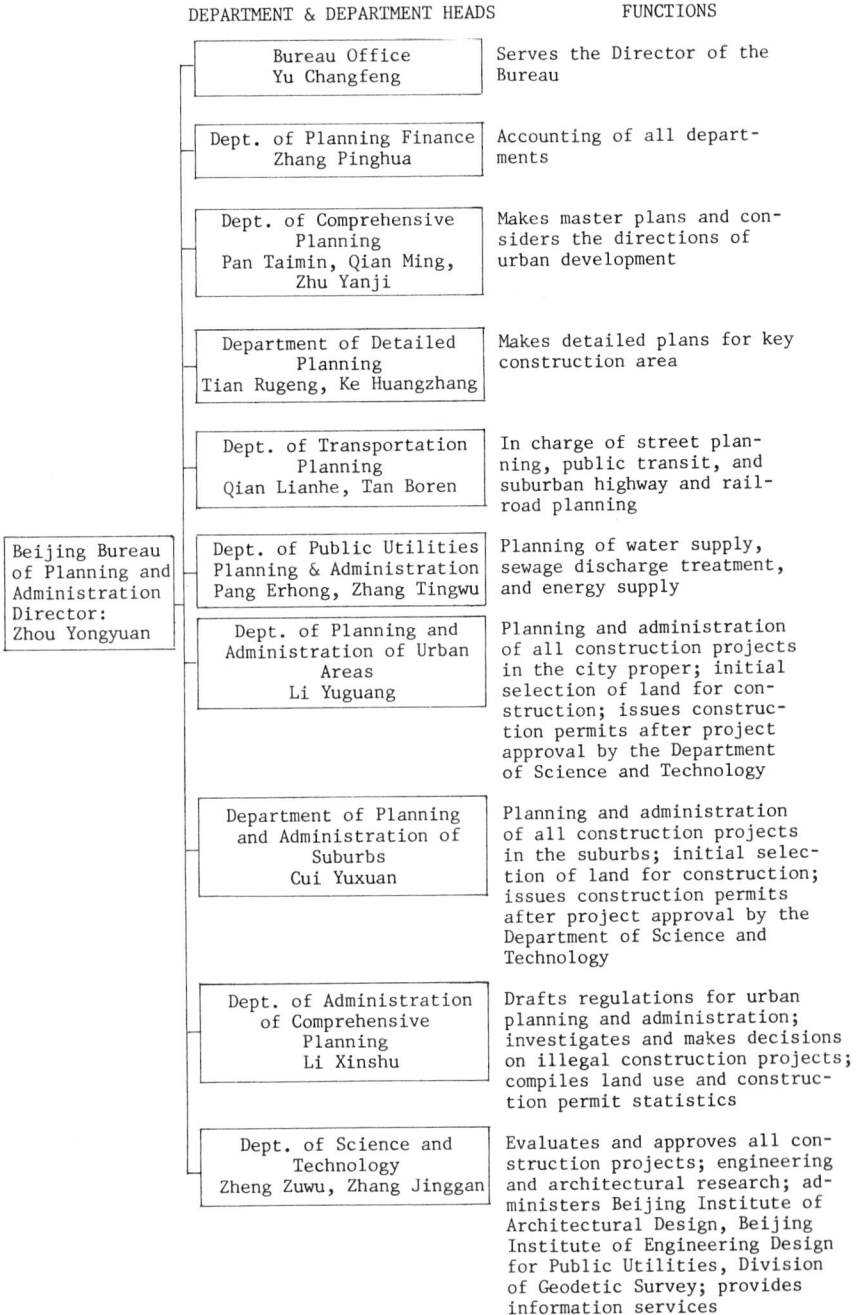

Fig. 4. Beijing Bureau of Planning and Administration.

of organisations involved in planning and construction and eliminating overlapping functions are scheduled to take place at the provincial and municipal levels of government next year. Li Ximing, 56, former vice-minister of Power Industry, was named minister. The new Ministry has the following administrative units:

- Bureau of Urban Planning
- Bureau of Rural Construction (primarily housing construction)
- Bureau of Environmental Protection
- Bureau of Municipal Engineering and Public Utilities
- Bureau of Parks and Gardens (Urban Landscape)
- Bureau of Housing Administration
- Bureau of Architectural Engineering
- Bureau of Design
- Bureau of Science and Technology
- Bureau of Education (primarily in charge of the education of those working in the Bureaus of Urban Planning and of Design)
- Bureau of Surveying and Mapping

MEMBERS OF THE DELEGATION

Harvey Perloff, Dean, School of Architecture and Urban Planning, University of California, Los Angeles, California; James L. Caplinger, Senior Program Officer for the Social Sciences, The Charles F. Kettering Foundation, Dayton, Ohio; Roger L. Creighton, Roger Creighton Associates, Delmar, New York; Martha M. Davis, Special Assistant to the Chairman, Department of City Planning, New York, New York; Leon S. Eplan, Director, Graduate City Planning Program and Professor of City Planning, Georgia Institute of Technology, Atlanta, Georgia; Reginald W. Griffith, Executive Director, National Capital Planning Commission, Washington, D.C.; John E. Hirten, Project Manager, Honolulu Area Rapid Transit, Honolulu, Hawaii; Norman Krumholz, Director, Cleveland Center for Neighborhood Development, Cleveland, Ohio; Elisabeth Ladd, Executive Director, Energy Facilities Siting Council, Boston, Massachusetts; Weiming Lu, Lowertown Redevelopment Corporation, St. Paul, Minnesota; Barbara L. Lukermann, Research Planning Consultant, St. Paul, Minnesota; Neal R. Peirce, Contributing Editor, The National Journal, Washington, D.C.; Robert W. Siler, Jr., Hammer, Siler, George Associates, Washington, D.C.; Arthur P. Solomon, Director, Harvard-MIT Joint Center for Urban Studies, Cambridge,

Massachusetts; Israel Stollman, Executive Director, American Planning Association, Washington, D.C.; Edwin A. Winckler, East Asian Institute, Columbia University, New York, New York; Janet A. Cady, Program Associate, National Committee on United States-China Relations, New York, New York.

Southern Europe:
Urban management and
plan implementation
David A. Rushforth

BACKGROUND

The Joint Activity on Urban Management of the OECD has been concerned with the problems of implementation for a number of years.* Through this time attention has shifted from plans and why they are not implemented, towards decision-making processes and why in urban management these are less effective than they might be. Concern is with better understanding the roles of different levels of government in this process and how all involved parties can participate in an appropriate way in the formulation and execution of policies.

---

* The Organisation for Economic Cooperation and Development (OECD) was set up under a Convention signed in Paris on 14th December 1960, which provides that the OECD shall promote policies designed:
  - to achieve the highest sustainable economic growth and employment and a rising standard of living in Member countries, while maintaining financial stability, and thus to contribute to the development of the world economy;
  - to contribute to sound economic expansion in Member as well as non-member countries in the process of economic development;
  - to contribute to the expansion of world trade on a multilateral, non-discriminatory basis in accordance with international obligations.
  The Members of OECD are Australia, Austria, Belgium, Canada, Denmark, Finland, France, the Federal Republic of

Germany, Greece, Iceland, Ireland, Italy, Japan, Luxemburg, the Netherlands, New Zealand, Norway, Portugal, Spain, Sweden, Switzerland, Turkey, the United Kingdom and the United States, Yugoslavia has a special status.

The OECD provides a broad framework for cooperative efforts which is designed to respond to the changing needs of participating governments. Since 1974 the Cooperative Action Programme of the OECD's Technical Cooperation Service has undertaken a series of projects specifically designed to improve management in urban government. These projects are being carried out and coordinated through the Joint Activity on Urban Management, guided by its Steering Committee representing OECD member countries. This committee meets twice a year at OECD headquarters in Paris to discuss common problems, policies and programmes and for a number of years it has encouraged a project concerned specifically with the difficulties of implementation in urban management. It is this work which forms the basis for this paper.

"Urban Management" has been defined in the OECD as being:

"... the task of organising and carrying out the operational, planning and policy-making functions of city government, involving the participation of professional advisors, political decision-makers, and citizens, and requiring on the one hand, cooperation with the national policies of government, and on the other, sensitivity to the private social goals of citizens."**

Urban management is thus a wider concept than town planning in which it has some of its origins. It seeks to bring into the arena the viewpoints and expertise of politicians, professors, practitioners, and the public. It is concerned with both the public and the private sectors and with procedures as much as institutions. Its problem is its complexity but by distilling some fundamental criteria for improvement, urban management hopes to contribute to making settlements more human - everywhere.

** See "Aspects of Urban Management" by J.R. Thornley and J.B. McLoughlin, Organisation for Economic Cooperation and Development, Paris, 1974, p.21.

A "Joint Activity" is intended first to promote ex-changes of experience between countries with similar prob-lems, and second to foster cooperative action by these countries to develop and operate new institutions, policies and practices designed to overcome these problems. The basic method of work is to obtain, exchange and compare case studies of experience within the subject of each project. These case studies are seen as the record of the learning process of urban management; they report on how particular problems were encountered, tackled, and overcome. Generally they relate to a specific city, chosen for its experience; or they may cover a group of cities or a country.

Once a sufficient number of case studies have been pre-pared for a project, a symposium is organised, often in one of the participating countries, to present, compare and dis-cuss the accumulated experience. This discussion is used to produce proposals for cooperative action between countries to improve existing, or initiate new, practice. Thus, the Joint Activity on Urban Management provides a principal means for the OECD to help member governments to improve the effective-ness and efficiency of their urban management.

A series of symposia on key areas of urban management have been held in various European cities appropriate to the themes discussed. These have included documentation, train-ing, implementation and the management of metropolitan areas. As part of this series, two symposia have been held on the theme of implementation - one in Athens in October 1977 and the other in Milton Keynes in July 1979.

ATHENS SYMPOSIUM

This symposium, entitled "The Implementation of Urban Plans," was held at the kind invitation of the Greek auth-orities in response to the concern that too many urban plans are never implemented or at best are only implemented in part. The general purpose of the meeting was to review the experience so far gained in responding to the problems of implementation in different settings and to bring out any special problems or experience gained which might provide lessons to an international audience.

The fundamental reason for the failure of plans in many cases was seen to be that plan-making and plan-implementation

have been separated as two independent processes, and that
disproportionate attention has been given to the former. The
making of a plan does not guarantee its implementation, and
the reasons for failure may lie as much in the isolation of
the plan-making as in the implementation procedures themselves.

The symposium was attended by over 50 participants from
13 different member countries. As a result of the papers
presented and the discussion which took place some consistent
areas of concern emerged as underlying the problems of implementation in most of the settings represented at the meeting. A specific list of issues was identified by the host
country as being of particular concern in Athens and these
were found to be relevant elsewhere. They included:

- high rises in land values
- insufficient control over land values
- excessive fragmentation of land titles and many
  small sites
- inflationary conditions encouraging speculative
  exploitation of property
- continuing migration from rural to urban areas
- lack of legal powers to enforce decisions
- inadequate administrative systems to support the
  implementation process
- lack of an effective system of local self-govern-
  ment.

At this stage two basic components of the problems of
implementation were seen to be involved:

Physical Aspects: embrace all the problems resulting
from continuing large scale rural to urban migration: growth
of illegal settlements, demand for housing, pressures on
infrastructure provision, problems of control and monitoring
of change, and pressures on land values.

Administrative Aspects: include several recurring themes
such as local accountability, the role of public participation, distribution of responsibilities between central,
regional and local levels of government.

One significant result of the Athens symposium was the
recognition that documented examples or case studies of
actual implementation experiences were very scarce. Many

practitioners were clearly either too busy or disinclined to document or publish their experiences. This prompted an experimental series of case studies of real-life examples of implementation processes to be commissioned by the OECD as an attempt to fill this gap and as a step towards developing a model for wider application. Four of these case studies were compiled using a similar format, two from the United Kingdom and two from Spain.

A preliminary analysis of the various implementation procedures undergone in each of these developments allowed the following summary and comparisons to be made:

(a)   overcoming administrative complexity: A basic problem of management underlies all the difficulties of implementation. Responsibilities must be clearly defined and structured within the implementing agencies and provision must be made for the contributions of all other actors involved by strengthening organisational capacities.

(b)   the need for commitment: Some means of encouraging the political will to implement decisions must be found. This commitment by decision-makers must also be accompanied by local involvement in the early stages of the policy formulation/execution process.

(c)   sensitivity to change: A balance must be found between flexibility and rigidity in order that implementation can proceed on a continuing basis. This requires monitoring, evaluation and adaptation procedures as an integral part of an incremental operation.

(d)   effective control mechanisms: Appropriate techniques and means of enforcement must be available and applicable, especially in terms of land ownership, and land values in order to support the above requirements.

MILTON KEYNES SYMPOSIUM

Some 18 months after the Athens meeting a second symposium on implementation was organised in the United Kingdom at the kind invitation of the Milton Keynes Development Corporation. It provided a forum for the latest developments

and enabled an assessment to be made of the approaches so far
developed both in the implementation process itself and in
the research aimed at improving this process. The symposium
also provided the stimulus to produce a framework for implementation which introduced a valuable checklist and basis
for discussion.

By this time, attention had ceased to focus only on
"plan" implementation and was looking more to the whole
policy and decision-making process. It was realised that the
implementation of decisions in urban management, whether they
relate to plans, programmes or policies, is a remarkably
difficult thing to achieve effectively, and is impossible to
achieve entirely to the satisfaction of everybody involved.

The simple reason for this is that decision implementation in urban management is typically a very difficult and
complex procedure. It is complex because the decisions being
made affect numerous different communities of interest – in
both the public and private sectors. Policy execution, therefore, involves many and varied actors who are protecting a
wide range of interests and who are pursuing many different
and sometimes conflicting objectives.

Because of this complexity, the implementation process
frequently covers lengthy periods of time and must be sensitive to changing circumstances. It must, therefore, be able
to accommodate some uncertainty, yet also be able to ensure
commitment if it is to achieve desired results. Perhaps most
important of all, proposals must remain feasible in political, economic, administrative and technical terms on a continuing basis. This calls for regular monitoring and flexibility so that appropriate modifications can be made as and
when required.

It was at this point of understanding that the Milton
Keynes symposium took place and defined the following objectives:

(a) to examine in some depth, specific implementation prob-
     lems and issues which have been identified as being of
     particular concern;

(b) to evaluate and learn from the findings and experiences
     of the case studies, analyses, and similar research work
     which has recently been undertaken on implementation
     processes;

(c) to provide continuity and follow-up to the interest generated at the first symposium on implementation in Athens; and

(d) to suggest in the light of the discussions, the most appropriate directions for further work in this field by the Joint Activity on Urban Management.

A total of 43 participants from 13 countries took part in the discussions which extended over five days. The symposium was launched with a framework paper which gave a comprehensive view of what might be done to improve plan implementation. This recognised that compared with plan-making, plan implementation has been neglected and is lacking in theory. It was noted that if real progress is to be made, there must be, in addition to institution building, also a clarification of those procedures which will improve the prospects of making a plan more implementable. The thesis was put forward that to improve plan implementability in urban management it is necessary from the outset to improve awareness of the causes of success and failure in the process. The gap between planning and implementation must be more clearly perceived and made evident: the impediments discouraging implementation must be identified so that they can be either removed or avoided.

By applying a checklist of procedures, inter-relation-ships can be identified and the robustness of the plan improved. It was noted that if such a checklist is to be compiled, then two underlying factors must somehow be built into it: the political component and the intrinsic irrationality of the process involved. This is the challenge; if a theory of implementation is indeed possible, then the development of a checklist may well be an important, even essential step towards such an objective. By the end of the proceedings a tentative listing of "laws" or "golden rules" which will facilitate implementation in most circumstances had been identified. This seemed to be a significant step and provides a new point of departure for continuing work on improving understanding of implementation in action. The ten "laws" as stated here will perhaps now become the focal points of future case studies to test their validity and value in different settings.

1   Targeting resources on a single set of beneficiaries (or standards or programmes) is well nigh impossible. Be prepared to spread the wealth.

2   "Coordination" is a central process in implementation
     but the more coordination a goal requires, the more
     likely is failure.

3   Never present decision-makers with only two options.
     They will then accept or reject. Present three and they
     will then debate how to do whatever is being discussed.

4   The more rigid and detailed a statute being implemented,
     the more numerous and artful the ways around it.

5   Programmes requiring long-term shifts must be embedded
     in less radical programmes or they are unlikely to sur-
     vive long enough to change anything at all.

6   Long term changes must often be divided into a series of
     short term projects which fit the political time sense
     of elected leaders and can be pursed piecemeal.

7   Citizen participation is a two-way street. It gives the
     planner a chance to influence the public as well as the
     reverse.

8   Elected bodies cannot be expected to commit themselves
     to large scale, long term programmes or expenditures.
     It reduces their manoeuvrability.

9   It is sensible to limit the comprehensiveness of a plan
     to those items that can be remembered by its users.

10   Effective plans are keyed to budget cycles. But as
     resources for public action decrease, the budgets may be
     those of private developers as well as public agencies.

IMPLEMENTATION IN SOUTHERN EUROPE

There was considerable debate throughout the proceedings
concerning the validity of seeking and applying a single
model or set of "rules" or procedures which can be relevant
and useful in all planning environments. This is, in fact, a
key issue in all work of the Joint Activity which has as a
prime mission the exchange of experiences between member
countries.

It seems that the continuing existence and healthy constitution of the Joint Activity supports the view that a

worthwhile degree of interaction is taking place amongst the various countries represented. This is not to say that the nature of the activity is not constantly under review and subject to regular reorientation. Participants are very aware of the different "realities" with which we are faced in terms of the political, socio-cultural and economic climates prevailing. Common ground is found more often than not but exposure to the significant differences which exist between working environments also helps the important process of adaptation and modification of approaches which have been tested and can be transferred in some hybrid form.

At the Milton Keynes symposium on implementation papers presented from Greece, Portugal, Yugoslavia and Turkey threw into clear perspective the problems of finding a single ideal model or any ubiquitous solutions. Nevertheless, many common problems were identified and by comparing notes on the state of the art of dealing with these problems both with countries with much in common and others with very dissimilar conditions, options in terms of potential solutions begin to emerge.

In the southern Europe context the problems of land-use control and land ownership as pivotal concerns is very evident. The need for standards and regulations which are realistic and able to be effectively policed emerged as a basic need. This in turn reflects the two most essential criteria for policy execution: continuing political support and adequate resource back-up. Both of these pre-conditions imply commitment which in turn reflects the human component of all urban management problems. In any working environment, it is finally the motivation, skills and attitudes of individuals at all levels of responsibility which determines success and how to better generate and tap this human resource becomes the eventual challenge of implementation in urban management everywhere.

New towns - Principles in practice

Abuja: Planning the new capital of Nigeria - Unique symbol or urban prototype

Stephen C. Lockwood

INTRODUCTION

In 1975, the Federal Capital Development Authority of Nigeria (FCDA) was established and charged with the responsibility of developing a new Federal Capital City. The FCDA decree culminated several years of informal consideration and technical studies of the efficacy of moving the Federal Capital out of Lagos.

A detailed design and construction process is now underway which will result in the establishment of Abuja, the largest newly planned city in the world.

The motives behind the capital city move were several. Following independence in 1960, public sentiment in Nigeria began to develop for the establishment of a new national capital city free of colonial associations and emblematic of Nigeria's identity as the world's largest black nation and its leadership in tropical Africa. The emergence from civil war in the seventies strengthened support for relocation of the capital out of Lagos to a new site for both increased security and clear ethnic neutrality.

Most recently the return to an elected civilian government under a US-style federal structure, has provided additional political impetus for a new and central capital city location more easily accessible to the 19 state capitals and Nigeria's 75 million persons.

Reinforcing the political and administrative rationale has been a widely shared desire to escape Lagos. The explos-

Fig. 1. Abuja and the new Federal Capital Territory in the
         National Context, showing also Lagos, the existing
         capital, and the 19 states. All graphics courtesy
         of the author and Wallace, McHarg, Roberts and Todd,
         Inc., The Master Plan for Abuja the New Federal
         Capital of Nigeria 1979.

ive and uncontrolled growth of Lagos (now approaching 4 million) with its associated congestion, squalor, and lack of infrastructure and its steamy land-poor environment have earned it national, if not international, notoriety and added an escapist justification for a capital relocation. Removal of the seat of government and its economic dependents is also calculated to assist in the effort to cool down Lagos' current 9 per cent annual growth.

Finally, it is expected that the new capital city can play an important role in regional development. Nigeria's low primacy index reflects the large size of its economy and its regionalisation compared to most African nations. The Federal system of Nigeria with its anticipated dispersal of power and fiscal autonomy is leading to increased awareness of the need for a parallel spatialisation of national development planning. In such contexts, decisions to relocate capital cities away from the dominant commercial industrial centre have not been uncommon, viz., in Brazil, Pakistan, Tanzania and more recently in several southern African countries. Placement of a large new city in Nigeria's relatively undeveloped Middle Belt Region complements the development of several new state capitals and industry towns as a component of an emerging nationwide growth pole strategy (see Figure 1).

The above rationales for relocation notwithstanding, the post-oil boom atmosphere in Nigeria has, at the same time, forced a new resource realism on the nation's capital programming. This is likely to restrain the capital city development process and require that the new capital city justify itself through more than the bravura architectural display which characterised previous national capitals in less developed countries (LDC's). Thus, while providing a physical seat of government appropriate to Nigeria's national self-conception and in keeping with its international aspirations is the first objective in establishing the new capital city, there are, at the same time, two additional objectives which have been considered important: Nigeria's rapid urbanisation exemplifies the opportunity, if not the need, to demonstrate new and replicable prototypes for various aspects of urban form suitable to the resource constraints and lifestyles of developing countries, additionally, all such urbanisations must be placed within, and supported by, a regional development strategy so that their full potential as a catalyst for growth and diffusion of development is realised.

The appropriateness of the balance in which these three objectives are achieved as the detailed design, construction, and implementation goes forth is a judgment which will doubtless be made. The paragraphs which follow, however, are addressed primarily to the second and third issues: the creation of an urban form and structure appropriate to a poor developing country city and the role of that city in a regional context.

THE CAPITAL CITY MASTER PLAN

The consultants for the master planning of the New Federal Capital City and Federal Capital Territory were selected through an international competition. The brief given the winning team consisted of four major requirements: the new capital should be sited in the Federal Capital Territory; it should be programmed to be ready for relocation of the seat of government in 1986; the city is to be primarily administrative with minimum industry; it should be capable of growing to contain a population of 3 million.

From this point of departure, the consultant team carried out a site selection process, prepared a regional plan, programmed the capital city and developed the capital city master plan, drafted a design and development manual, and carried out a construction logistics analysis. Throughout this 18-month process, findings or plan recommendations were carefully reviewed by the FCDA Board and staff, federal and state ministry personnel, and by panels of Nigerian and international experts.

Throughout the plan development process, the planning team struggled with three major overarching contextual issues which formed the background to the plan decisions: first, it was important to identify the specific phenomena to be avoided and those to be sought through definition of an urban structure and form based on a review of the Nigerian and international urban experience to date; second, it was necessary to adopt a realistic attitude about the role and potential of documentary guidance as a starting point for the urban development process; third, the specific plan decisions which could be transmitted through plan documents with respect to structure and form had to recognise important resource limitations. These issues are discussed briefly below.

Problems of Cities Vs. Problems in Cities

The development process for the New Federal Capital City has been taking place within the frame of reference of urban Nigeria today. The functional and qualitative shortcomings of the existing large cities in Nigeria are well-known and exhibit commonalities with other similar contexts worldwide. Lagos presents only the most dramatic evidence of the diffi- culties of accommodating rapid growth: the same symptoms are present in nearly a dozen other Nigerian cities of over 250,000 where concentrated and visible poverty is endemic and problematic.

In such contexts the provision of suitable employment within a dualistic urban economy cannot keep up with mi- gration and natural increase; development outpaces the pro- vision of infrastructure; land prices condemn the poor majority to marginal land with the least services; and basic needs are met at a very low level, if at all.

To date the most common strategies to deal with those problems - and supported by international development insti- tutions - is to view them as problems in cities, to be at- tacked on a basis of project-by-project additions, up-grad- ings, or retrofits. Given the backlog of unmet basic needs, such an approach is reasonable.

But this "catch-up" approach ignores the speed with which the scale of these problems is growing. In tropical Africa, the rural-to-urban migration which is so central to urban growth is not so much released by rising agricultural productivity or concrete job opportunities in the city as it is produced by rural poverty and boredom and a belief, fueled in part by reality and in part by adapted European values, that city life is better. In Nigeria for example, 50 million additional city dwellers will be generated in the next 25 years - about half of those migrants. Despite attempts to "cool down" migration, in most countries where urbanisation is still less than 20 per cent, urban populations are doub- ling in 10-15 years. Whether planned or not, twice as much "city" will be built in Africa as exists today over the same time period.

The relatively low level of urbanisation in the African context offers an opportunity to discover new strategies for channeling urbanisation into a more viable form and avoid the

second-best strategies which the "catch-up" context of more
highly developed economies might impose. Such a perspective
views the problems of "cities to be" as well as problems in
cities as the appropriate focus of solution generation. An
attack on the problem of cities requires a more complex approach, one which considers ways in which to better capitalise on scale economies in order to conserve scarce social
resources without, at the same time, placing the burden of
externalities on those which can least afford it.

Those solutions must harness the unique potentials of
cities to provide the most cost-effective context for alleviating the problems of the poor through capitalising on the
economies of scale and agglomeration for firms, public services, and households alike. The ability to combine several
urban components like land, service, and transport in innovative and efficient patterns can lead not only to fiscal
economy and improved quality of life but also to minimisation
of unintended impact and maximisation of intragroup subsidies
than can make urban life more equitable. This is more than a
dry theoretical concern. It requires the development of an
urban technology affordable within each nation's resources in
combination with urban forms appropriate to the context of
local culture and free from the preconceptions inherited from
developed countries.

Whether in the form of urban extensions, satellite
towns, urban renewal or restructuring, or completely independent growth centres, there is a desperate need to develop new
responses to the challenges which have to date eluded natural
resolution as large cities in Nigeria and other LDC'c continue to grow. Some of these challenges include:

- Recognition that in LDC cities, the poor are not an
  afterthought to be relegated to the fringe and dealt
  with as an afterthought. The LDC city is the poor.

- Generation of employment opportunities for the unskilled, especially support of the informal sector.

- Capturing scale economies of urban form and structure
  for those who can least afford to overcome spatial
  separation through coordinated public transport and
  land use locational specifications.

- Employment of urban systems which capitalise on abundant indigenous resources (labour and land)and econ-
  omise on scarce resources (capital and technology).

The degree of specificity and detail must be appropriate to the degree of programmatic, technical, and resource uncertainty. It should recognise the role and potential of subsequent detailed planning and design. It must also be consistent with the policy and capability for development control.

In the Abuja plan development process, an attempt was made to respond to major sources of uncertainty – especially sources of variation in population and rate of growth. The program itself was developed through casting alternative growth scenarios and analyzing economic, demographic, and social variables to select a reasonable range of parameters for planning purposes. Abuja has been constrained by current government policy to be primarily an administrative city. Initial policy has been to avoid competing with other centres for scarce major industrial investments. Like other non-primate capitals without major industry, its public sector employment is expected to be about 35 percent of the total formal employment with the construction industry the second largest employer during the first two decades of development.

Low basic/non-basic ratios increasing over time and a large informal labour force component were reflected in employment projections. In addition, careful attention was paid to estimating the informal component of each sector in order to determine both land requirements for employment and the likely labour force participation, headship rate, and total population (Table 1).

Table 1. Distribution of Total Labour Force by Sector and Type for 1.6 Million Population.

	Formal	Informal	Total
1. Public Sector			
Federal Civil Servants	60,300	–	–
Parastatals	65,000	–	–
Other Public Employees	46,000	–	–
Subtotal	171,300	–	171,300
2. Industrial Sector	84,200	31,000	115,200
3. Service Sector	241,850	333,000	571,850
Total Employment	497,350	361,000	858,350

While there is necessarily some uncertainty surrounding the future size of the Federal employment (and to an even greater extent for other sectors, formal and informal), key demographic and economic factors, such as family size and migration rate, which in turn affect overall population and population-based spatial and functional requirements were also problematic. Therefore, ranges were developed for each factor in the demographic and income projections (Figure 2).

In recognition of this programmatic uncertainty, an attempt was made to highlight key issues and make concrete choices where the development process required specificity. Other issues were highlighted but left as more appropriately resolved at a subsequent level of detailed planning or design. This distinction is most clearly illustrated in the plan's attitude towards the "Central Area" (seat of government, CBD, and Federal institution) versus the "Development Corridors" (residential areas and subcentres).

The Central Area has received considerable urban design attention with respect to the relationships among its buildings, spaces, and functional systems. It is expected to be the focus of further area-wide detailed architectural and urban design studies. The development corridors, by contrast, are the subject of more generalised planning with the major infrastructural and public service systems dimensioned and located. However the infill of residential communities has been defined by a discussion of principles and examples only. Not only is there a need for experiment and variety with respect to residential community design, but there is also a recognition that the degree of control exercised over the private sector and individual residential activities in the development corridors must be more schematic. Experience has shown that attempts to impose a high degree of design control in a fast growth context may limit legal development, but not population growth, resulting in overcrowding, peripheral squatter development, and other unintentional effects. The degree of control implied or required by a master plan must recognise realistic administrative capacity limitation in development management.

The actual city as built is thus likely to exhibit a sharp contrast between the formal coherence imposed by FCDA's full design control of the Central Area, infrastructure, and public buildings on the one hand and the less visible and more strictly functional ordering of the informal residential

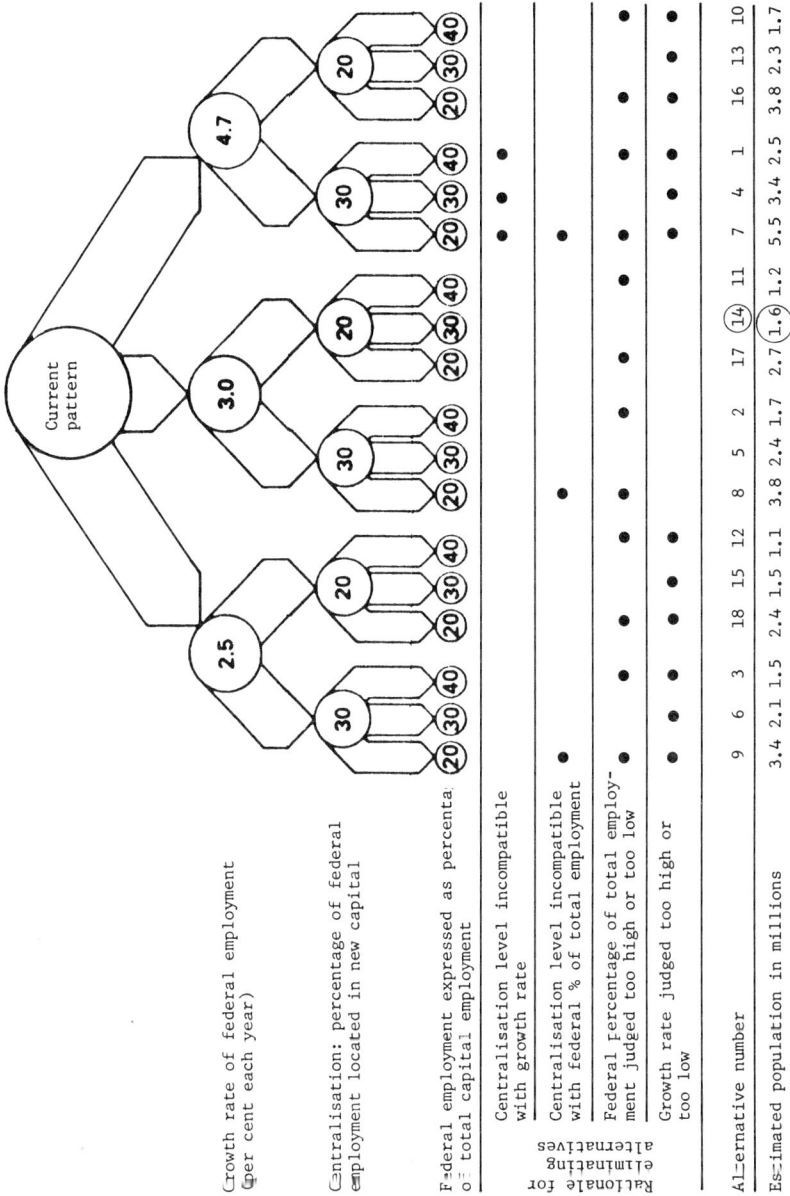

Fig. 2. Assumptions underlying labour force composition alternatives.

developments which surround them. This approach to the role
of the Master Plan requires a painful abandonment of imported
preconceptions of an orderly and architectural city-scape and
an acceptance of an urban image responsive to the more informal reality of a resource-scarce urban development process.

Throughout the master planning process, the consultant
team attempted to modulate the degree of plan specification
through following the advice which is inscribed around a
famous portrait of the 18th century Massachusetts Divine,
Reverend John Lowell which reads, "In necessaries unitas, in
non-necessariis libertas, in utrisque caritas" - that is,
balance among the major functional systems and infrastructure
elements; flexibility for variety and experimentation in the
sub-systems and at the architectural scale; and, throughout
the plan, a concern for equity.

Appropriateness - Technical, Economic, and Cultural

Given a policy decision to build a new capital city in
an undeveloped region, a key responsibility imposed on the
planning team was to develop a response appropriate to the
context - in terms of cost, technology, and cultural expression. The planning team attempted to develop an "affordable city," a city development process, and urban form, and
system technologies which would husband the scarce resources
of the public sector and of the household - in terms of
money, materials, time management, and energy.

The matching of expectations to resource availability
will, in Nigeria, as elsewhere, involve the abandonment of
approaches to city building which cannot, without massive
subsidy, reach the masses. In Nigeria, 80 percent of the
urban households have a household income of less than $3,000
per year while typical current public sector provided low-
cost housing has been offered at $50,000-$60,000! Public
sector planning, design, and the formal construction industry
is not geared to the modesty implied by such resource limitations. The inherited urban imagery of cottage and hedge-
row lined lanes or a phalanx of "Corbusian" apartment blocks
and the plans and standards which accompany it, more often
than not, reflect institutional priorities of elites over-
balancing the needs of the poor.

Closely related to the affordability issue is the much-
discussed question of "appropriate technology." At the urban

scale, this issue becomes critical with respect to key infrastructure issues. High-tech capital, energy and management-
intensive infrastructure systems have no place in development
contexts like Nigeria where land is nationalised, labour
cheap, technology imported and expensive and experienced
management scarce and overburdened. The Abuja plan avoids
the temptation of specifying the "latest" technology fashionable in developed contexts in favour of those which can capitalise on locally abundant resources.

Appropriateness relates not only to the choice of technology but also to more general issues of urban form. A major
shortcoming of past planning for many LDC cities, including
those in Nigeria, has been a failure to recognise and accommodate the indigenous patterns of urban organisation and
adaptation already present in the country - in both traditional and colonial cities. This requires a search for
plan elements which would simultaneously permit the different
segments of the future resident population to maintain an
important degree of continuity with their several social and
cultural traditions while encouraging, where appropriate,
amalgamation of the various stream of urban tradition and
lifestyles with respect to interaction between social life
and physical form, into a new and common context that can
reinforce national commonality.

MAJOR CITY PLAN DECISIONS

Within the above limitations, the overall process of
plan development involved a sequence of choices with respect
to basic functional and formal options. At each step in the
planning process, options were reviewed in a hierarchical
step-wise approach proceeding generally from large-scale to
small-scale decisions. Throughout the process the team was
mindful of the current problems of cities in Nigeria and
similar LDC's so as to minimise their occurrence in the new
city.

Site Selection

The new Federal capital city was to be located somewhere
within a centrally positioned Federal Capital Territory
(FCT), created out of areas donated by three states. The FCT
is 8,000 sq.km of Federally owned land under direct adminis-

tration control of the Federal Capital Development Authority
(FCDA), a specially appointed agency of the Nigerian government, whose chairman holds ministerial rank.

The FCT is situated just north of the humid lowlands of
the Niger/Benue Rivers trough, but south of the driest
Sahelian portions of Nigeria, in an area called the Middle
Belt. The central location and topography of the FCT combine
to produce a significant variation in climate as one goes
from southwest to northwest to northeast parts of the territory. The climate is tropical and exhibits distinct wet and
dry seasons. The rainy season is shorter and temperatures
somewhat lower in the northeastern areas. Monthly precipi-
tation is estimated to range from negligible in the November-
January period to a peak of 300mm.

The FCT is generally characterised as a tilted plain
rising slowly in elevation from southwest to northeast.
Several ranges of low mountains and numerous rocky knobs rise
above this plain. These rocky knobs are particularly prominent in the northeastern portions of the FCT, providing a
strong visual image and distinctive landmarks for the site of
the new capital. These landmarks play a strong role in the
proposed city plan, providing a setting of appropriate variety, interest, and image for Nigeria's new capital.

The choice of city site was based on a systematic analysis of the natural and manmade resources of the FCT. An
ecological synthesis was developed based on an inventory of
10 basic environmental factors. Preemptive criteria were
then used to screen land unsuitable for urban development.
The remaining area was comparatively rated on positive and
quantifiable environmental criteria. Finally, these ratios
were sieved with subjective judgments about man-made constraints, visual elements, and the site capacity. The Gwagwa
Plains in the northeast quadrant of the FCT were judged to be
the most suitable location for major urban development.

Overall Urban Form and Structure

The general overall form of the city "footprint" was
determined by both natural and functional considerations.
The site selection process involved finding the most suitable
site for urban development within the Federal Capital Territory that could ultimately handle up to 3 million people.

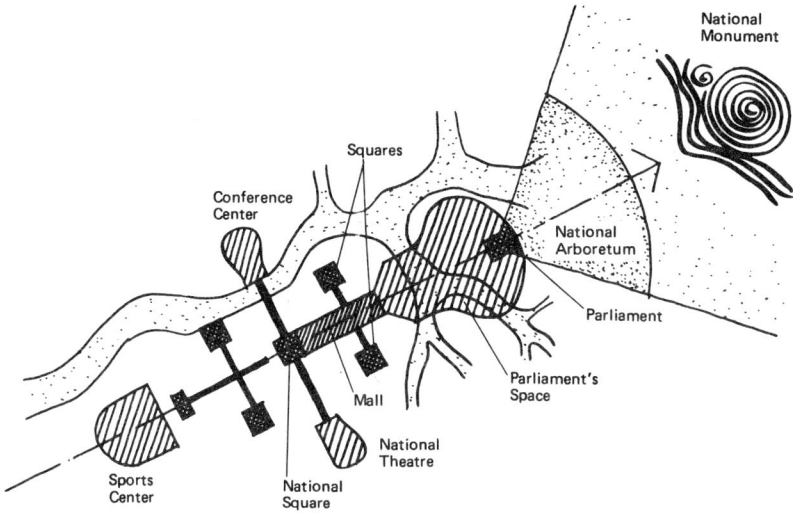

Fig. 3.   Monumental Core of the Central Area.

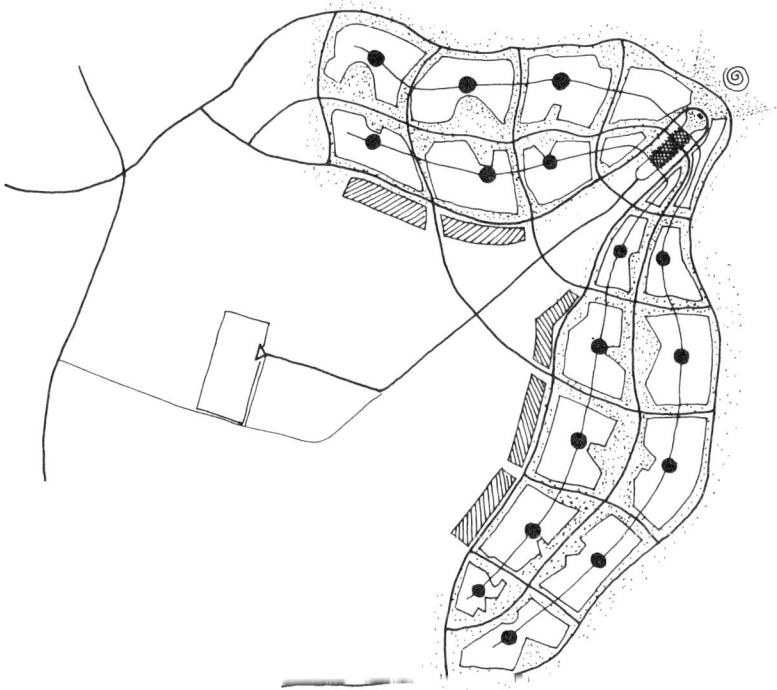

Fig. 4.   Development Corridors.

The importance of climate and view and the location of geo-
technically developable land led to the selection of a con-
tiguous banana-shaped segment of the Gwagwa Plains above 400
meters in elevation. This site - 16 miles by 3 miles in
extent - lies under the escarpment of the Also Hills which
provide a dramatic backdrop and natural boundary.

The elongated footprint area was consistent with the
concept of staged linear growth out from a centre in two
directions. Linear distribution for transport, power, and
water supply supports incremental growth and minimizes trunk
costs. At the same time, however, the entire development was
located in a single drainage shed. This resulted in counter-
posing to the linear geometry of man-made distribution systems a transverse branch-like network of sewer and drainage
system following the natural slope and drainage course. While
these geometries contrast dramatically each responds to the
requirements of the most efficient layout appropriate to its
function.

The overall form of the city was also influenced by the
desire to capitalise on the natural beauty of the site. The
stream valley and water course network has been preserved for
aesthetic as well as drainage purposes and, along with the
escarpment of hills and inselbergs which jut up through the
Gwagwa Plains, forms the visual backdrop to the city and its
major focal point.

The overall urban structure of the city within the footprint area consists of two major elements: the Central Area
consisting of the Seat of Government, the Federal Administration, the Central Business and Commercial Districts and
National institutions; and the Development Corridors of residential areas and employment-service sub-centres strung out
in a linear fashion for staged growth along the major infrastructure systems (Figures 3 and 4).

Centrality and the Seat of Government

As the Federal Capital and administrative centre, it was
deemed appropriate that Abuja should have a clear physical
focus centring on the location of the Seat of Government and
Federal administration. Thus, a dramatic placement was chosen
using the most prominent natural feature, Aso Hill, to emphasise the uniqueness of these functions.

A series of alternative Central Area plans were developed and discussed in detail in the Master Plan. The
selected plan carefully capitalises on the hills and stream
valleys of the central area as well as the impressive backdrop formed by the Aso Hills. The key government and ministerial buildings, major office and commercial services, and
national cultural and sports institutions were closely integrated in an urban design scheme that attempts to blend symbolic location, functional efficiency, and design constrasts
with the rest of the city. The full range of urban design
tools have been employed to achieve a dignified setting responsive to the natural landscape in which the requirements
of efficiency are met with relationships structured to balance efficient governmental functioning with a hierarchy of
building, spatial, and landscape treatment contrasts.

Special efforts were made to blend normal urban activities in with government functions at the edge of formal
government precincts to avoid the sterility characterising
government centres on many new capital cities. Similarly,
the balance between monumentality and pedestrian scale and
accessibility was a trade-off carefully considered. Elements
of the urban space and building patterns evident in historical Nigerian capitals were built into the plan to provide and
appropriate continuity with the indigenous urban tradition.

Finally, consideration was given to the stageability of
the central area, recognising that it may be under construction for a generation or more. The possibility of a sense of
completeness at several stages was achieved by building-space
relationships and by providing separate precincts or squares
for successive additions of government buildings.

Emphasis on the symbolic importance of the Central Area
within the overall urban area was carefully balanced by deliberate decentralisation of employment to minimise the central congestion and long commutes for the poor that characterise most large monocentric LDC cities. Non-essential
ministries were decentralised into special sub-centres. A
large proportion of the formal non-headquarters commercial
employment and the majority of informal service employment
will also be in the development corridor described below.

Development Corridors

Abjua is designed for staged growth in the form of a
pattern of linear development extending in two directions

- Recognition in the design of institutional and legal arrangements for city development of the scarcity of public administrative capacity.

- Blending indigenous rural and small-town traditions with new requirements of urban organisation so as to maximise continuity between traditional and modern urban form and culture.

- Accommodation of uncertainty with respect to forecast of land and service demand-related population and migration pressures.

- Respecting the potential and problems associated with the natural environment as it becomes urbanised.

- Achieving supply-demand balance and self-sufficiency of infrastructure and service vis-a-vis population through all stages of growth.

- Avoiding unreasonably rigid spatial separation of activities and sacrificing symbiosis to zoning pre-conceptions.

- Employment of affordable and replicable facility standards with the flexibility to upgrade capacity and quality as economic capability increases.

- Provision of basic service in an accessible form and avoidance of over-investment in unnecessarily specialised facilities.

These problems of cities constitute an agenda of objectives around which the master planning process has been taking place. While the development of a new capital city is itself hardly prototypical, it occasions the opportunity to search for new solutions that can be more generally applied in the context of existing or other new urbanisations.

The Impact of Program Uncertainty

Master plans as development guidance tools in LDC contexts have illustrated characteristic shortcomings which have limited their usefulness and discouraged their preparation. Their utility depends on avoiding the extremes of either over-rigidity or vagueness which have hampered many well-known capital city and new town plans.

from the central area. The major components of this pattern
include:

- A central linear park which, by responding to geo-
  physical features, organises growth into two parallel development corridors.

- A linear transportation system consisting of dual
  transit lines each forming the central spine of a
  development corridor and intersecting the Central
  Area.

- A peripheral highway system flanking each development corridor and defining their outer limits connected with a parkway in the central park by transverse parkways.

- Growth modules in the form of development sectors -
  self-contained mini cities of 100,000 to 250,000
  focused on internal secondary employment centres and
  subdivided into residential districts.

- Sector centres straddling the busways to provide
  high accessibility to the City core and for inter-
  and intra-sector travel.

- Separation of sectors from each other by the central
  park and transverse parkways to lend individual
  identity and to avoid the disruptive "continuous-
  extension-under-construction" dust, noise, and
  visual chaos which for such a long time has characterised other large planned cities.

- A sector road system designed to provide easy access
  to centres from the periphery but designed to dis-
  courage traffic through residential areas.

- Residential districts of 40,000-80,000 focused on a
  hierarchy of commercial, community, and utiltiy service centres and organised into a hierarchy of
  small-scale residential communities.

- A mix of residential options in terms of income and
  housing type concentrating high densities directly
  adjacent to transit corridors and lower densities on
  the periphery.

- Industrial estates along the lower peripheral highways for larger scale light industry not located
  directly in residential areas.

 -   Complete infrastructure systems to the residential
     community scale - water, power, sewer, drainage, and
     telecommunication.

Major elements of the development corridors are highlighted
below.

Transportation

Fragmentation of daily life is a key feature of the
existence of the urban poor in LDC cities. Land prices place
the poor in marginal areas on city peripheries which are also
usually the least and most expensively serviced area and
farthest from employment. This locational disadvantage is
compounded by immobility. In most poorer LDC cities, the
poorly operated public bus systems and rather better para-
transit compete disadvantageously with the subsidised private
automobile for inadequate road space in a chaotic and un-
managed fashion.

The traffic congestion of the larger LDC cities in
Africa and Southeast Asia is legendary despite relatively low
automobile ownership rates. A shortage of road space and the
absence of traffic control systems in combination with an
aggressive driving population leads to anarchy and paralysis
on the road. Nowhere are the "go-slows" more dramatic than
Lagos, the current capital. The real victims of this situation are the population majority with no car.

Less than 35 percent of the future households in the New
Capital City are projected to have a vehicle in the year
2000. The effective functioning of the new city and the
degree to which it represents a substantial improvement over
existing cities will thus depend on its public transport
system. Here the choice of appropriate technology is crucial. The only alternative to growing and chaotic congestion
in which transit riders suffer is banning automobile use or
separating transit from general traffic. In a de novo context
and where the automobile is the leading system of economic
success and social modernity, the latter approach is substantially more acceptable.

The use of separate bus rights-of-way provide an effective solution. With their simple and known technology, their
stageability, upgradability in degree of exclusiveness and
grade-separation, their on- and off-line operational poten-

tial, their high capacity, their relatively low capital costs, and simple management, exclusive busways seem to offer a perfect solution. The are being proven in both advanced and developing country contexts, especially in Latin America.

In Abuja, the busway application has been configured to provide express service between the various sector centres (for which the busway serves as a central spine) as well as off-line distribution which offers short-walking distances and no transfer service from residential areas. The complete family of transit vehicles which comprise public transit in Nigeria can be accommodated, including the city bus, minibus, van, and mammy wagon.

A highway system was also developed, including peripheral bypass highways enclosing the developed area of the city, a scenic central parkway, an industrial highway, and a network of arterials designed to bypass sector centres and eliminate through traffic from residential communities. A controlled access airport expressway has been designed to facilitate high speed, friction-free exit from the city.

An important part of the transport system design activity of the master planning process was the sensitivity testing of both the transit and roadway systems for their adequacy and balance under substantially different conditions of income, car ownership, and employment concentration than those assumed in the year 2000 projections. The recommended system is sized and configured to handle a doubling of the forecast traffic.

Service Hierarchy and Residential Communities

The key to sector, district, and residential community organisation and dimensions is the hierarchy of employment opportunities and service systems. Special studies were made of existing and emerging service delivery patterns for each system: health, education, libraries, cultural, recreation, post and telegraph, police, fire, religious, maintenance, and administration. In each case, emphasis was placed on the location of the lowest level of service at the residential community level.

The residential district is the basic module of city organisation and growth, consisting of 6,100 to 10,000 house-

282   S. C. LOCKWOOD

holds in the form of a series of residential communities or
"neighbourhoods." Each district is conceived of as a town
containing all but the most specialised community service
such as post-secondary education and referral hospitals.
Through density controls, the opportunity is provided for a
broad range of income groups in each district - especially
given the FCDA control over land-lease price.

Three or four districts are organised into a sector.
Each sector focuses on a commercial/institutional/service
centre straddling a transit corridor. All the services
through specialised post secondary education and referral
hospitals, as well as recreational and cultural facilities
(short of those necessarily city-wide), are contained within
each sector. Both modern and traditional commercial facilities are accommodated. The sector centres are also designed
as locations for formal governmental and business activities,
especially those sectors most immediately adjacent to the
Central Area.

Thus through income mixing, at least at the district
level, through decentralising formal governmental and commercial employment and by a bottoms-up priority for community
services, the locational disadvantages at which the poor
majority otherwise would find themselves, have been minimised.

At the district and sector levels, a broad range of
planning factors has been designed to reinforce local identi-
fiability - the service hierarchies, the locations of sector
and district centres, the sector-district transport network
the open space systems, physical boundaries formed by natural
features, as well as the areal extent based on walking distance, etc.

Below the level of the district it is expected that the
focus of communal social identity and the scale of provision
of household-related service will be the local residential
community of 500 to 1,500 households. This conclusion was
not reached without considerable hesitation. While the
"neighbourhood concept" has a long and honourable tradition
in European and North American planning, little evidence was
available in Nigeria about the relationship between a sense
of local residential community and its physical, social, and
administrative manifestations. Special research was carried
out in the relationships among physical and social factors in

their several indigenous urban manifestation - both traditional and modern.

The traditional pattern was found to be in evolution
with some elements having been replaced by modern counterparts with social services and amenities (mosques, churches,
primary schools, markets) now playing a greater role as the
social focus within a subarea. Often, these foci have even
taken the name of the ward.

These investigations suggested that while the activity
foci of local community life varied among the various re-
gional-ethnic urban traditions in Nigeria and while kinship
ties were especially important, it was reasonable to expect a
strong sense of neighbourhood identity to evolve around
shared facilities and service reinforced by modern social
homogeneity, physical identity, and administrative
designations.

It would be a mistake to assume that the classic neighbourhood model based on service-sheds are completely applicable. For example, universal primary education, the basis
for use of the neighbourhood school as a point of community
organisation, is only 5 years old in Nigeria. The local
traditional markets or mosque are considerably more central
to the daily life of an urban family in Nigeria at the present time. The low degree of development of service delivery
systems, the mix of traditional and modern, formal and informal service systems emerging in urban Nigeria may result in
an as yet-unimagined amalgam. Thus, at the local residential
community level, the Plan does not impose the "garden city"
model of introverted neighbourhoods focusing on schools and
separated by open space buffers and major streets. Indeed,
interaction among neighbourhoods has been encouraged by
suggesting the use of major residential streets as lines of
interaction rather than as boundaries.

There is a danger at this scale of planning, of imposing
a provider rather than a user perspective because of the
anonymous and evolving nature of the actual resident client.
Obviously, the type of social affinities and cohesion in
these communities will, in the future, be defined by a complex interaction of inter-household relationships, cultural
heritage, occupation service facility and income use patterns
as well as physical features of the area. While no master
plan can guarantee a given social mix, the intention of the

"loose fit" approach taken at this level of the plan is to
provide the maximum flexibility to accommodate a broad range
of socio-economic, cultural, and local facility use patterns.

Housing

Housing is more than merely the dwelling unit. It is a
complex product made up to a combination of attributes:
indoor living space, land, utilities, locational situation
(with respect to work and services), outdoor living space,
and relationships with family, friends, and neighbours. As
such, housing is a basic need and represents the closest
point of contact between the City residents and the new city.
In addition, housing is also the largest land consumer and
the major cost element. The success of the new city will, in
the eyes of its residents, be judged not just on how the
organisation of the City fits everyday needs but also on the
quality of the residential environment.

The existing housing situation in Nigeria exhibits the
classical symptoms of policy neglect. The majority of the
urban households crowd into rented one-room quarters without
services. Housing costs and land pricess are high, and even
the rich and upper-level bureaucrats are served by an inefficient and import-dependent building industry. Obviously,
institutional problems are key: the need to mobilise savings,
reasonable site and structure standards, access to credit,
limited dependence on foreign contractors and imported technology.

Provision of satisfactory housing in sufficient quan-
tities at an affordable price is a test which few newly planned cities have met. The poor, who are the majority residents
of such cities, have either been relegated as an afterthought
into remote squatter towns not deemed worthy of the planners
attention, or conversely jammed into limited varieties of
expensive high standard units not likely to meet their individual life-style or economic needs. Only the land problem
has been clearly resolved for Abuja since the Federal capital
territory is in unencumbered Federal ownership.

While recognising that a housing program for the new
capital city cannot be developed in isolation from national
policy (indeed part of the Master Planning Team is now developing such a policy), the major principles of the housing
program have been laid out to strike a balance between the

improved standards which the government might wish to provide (especially in the "showcase" context) and the costs which the city's residents can afford. The proposed housing program is built around several principles:

- Efficient plot layout and modest standards of infrastructure which permit upgrading of standards and environment as economic capacity - government and/or household - increases.

- Housing options for all income groups ranging from detached housing and flats, to traditional compounds, rooming houses and shared service accommodations with overall density varying from 175-225 people per net hectare.

- Increased reliance on affordable standards, local construction materials, reduced level of finish, etc.

- A variety of approaches to individual and cooperative provision of housing, including sites and services provision with core houses, use of shared services, and self-help/self-contracted construction to lower costs.

- A broad range of housing programs have been tested aimed at providing a range of size/quality/type/ infrastructure/ financing combinations for each income level. For each programme, different combinations of housing and infrastructure standards and subsidies were mixed to bring payments within the affordability limits of each income group. Fifty different housing/infrastructure combinations were tested. Selected combinations were used to "test" the Master Plan although no final program has been selected.

Within this framework, overly rigid requirements for settlement are to be avoided in order to minimise the establishment of cheaper rival squatter settlements which have typically characterised other planned new cities in developing countries. Low cost serviced plots must be made available to attract potential squatters to the city itself. Since density cannot therefore be completely controlled, a preservicing strategy has been adopted with infrastructure sized with ample reserved capacity.

Just as the rate of population growth and density cannot be completely controlled, so the design and construction process will likely be relatively informal as necessary to provide a range of affordable housing for all income groups. In Abuja, small-scale private contractors are likely to be the main builders for most of the population. If low-cost housing is to be produced, only a modest degree of standardisation is realistically compatible with their capabilities and those of their clients. The centrally-controlled design and construction process of large-scale housing projects exhibited in several earlier capitals is not expected to play a substantial role in housing the population since it cannot provide housing affordable to the bulk of the population. Thus, the combination of sites and services layouts, core houses, and low-use compound-type rooming houses which are likely to characterise an affordable residential area is not likely to sit well with the "townscape" crowd or those whose preconception of residential areas are based on developed country images. Here one may expect a substantial conflict between supporters of a "dignified" vs. an affordable new capital city.

THE REGIONAL DEVELOPMENT PLAN

A Regional Development Plan for the 8000 sq.km Federal Capital Territory was developed as an integral part of the master planning process. The plan recognises that the new capital will serve as the focus for a wide range of city-building as well as city-support-service activities that will have a major impact on the population and economy of the entire Middle Belt of Nigeria.

While city support needs were taken as the paramount land use, a suitability analysis and regional development/ settlement strategy were used as the basis for preparation of a regional plan to develop and restructure the settlement pattern and economy of this heretofore remote section of the country.

City support requirements in terms of natural resources - water, agricultural forestry products, and building raw materials - were dimensioned and tested against regional capacity. The short run water supply needs are to be met by impounded surface water requiring extensive and careful watershed protection. But in the long run, water will be imported by aqueduct from the Shiroro hydroelectric project 120km from Abuja. Similarly, the projected demand for food and fuel has been measured against the productive advantage of agricultural and forestry land in the FCT compared with adjacent states. Clearly the FCT will not be self-sufficient in food and large food deficits form the basis for an important market for the superior farmland to the west and south.

While the FCT is not prime farm land, the need for reliability and self-sufficiency in fresh produce led to a proposed program for irrigated truck and fruit farming, cattle grazing, and irrigated firewood forestry. This agricultural development program was developed recognising the productivity limits of the FCT environment and management options reviewed in that light. For cropping and grazing the recommended approach builds on the existing subsistence patterns but encourages centralisation in irrigated areas in combination with modest technical assistance. Similarly the forestry program is designed to rely on Taungya production with some plantation development in irrigated areas.

An important aspect of the agricultural program for the FCT has been the careful attention paid to the possibilities of urban/agricultural/recreational symbiosis. With respect to irrigation, the agricultural and forestry program has been closely integrated with the city river-based wastewater treatment scheme, with suitability for cropping and grazing related to effluent quality improvements with downstream distance. Similarly, the forestry program has been designed not only for productive purposes (lumber and firewood) but also to serve the protective function of soil preservation, erosion prevention, surface water retention and recreation development. The regional recreation program itself consists of major setasides for conservation, national parks, and monuments. National monuments and wilderness protection areas have been designed to protect sensitive watersheds, unique and prominent visual features, and unusual wilderness areas from development. The potential for major national park-game preserve has been studied and a promising semi-enclosed plains area proposed for a multiple-use wildlife conservation unit.

Also supportive of the city building process are the opportunities to develop a combined extractive industry/ building material production activity in the region. The FCT is rich in certain building materials - clay, sand, dimension stone, etc. An extractive industry program has been identified for development in close conjunction with regional infrastructure provisions.

The regional infrastructure program has been developed to support the capital city's direct needs for access, power and water. It is recognised that the capital's success as a growth pole will depend in part on the competitiveness of its access and infrastructure. In addition, the plan must provide the appropriate sectoral linkages for the FCT agro-industrial and building materials industry to insure production support-ive of the city's development. Major highway improvements linking Abuja to the national grid have been planned and are currently under construction. The proposed system will make a dramatic difference in Abuja's accessibility to the rest of the nation. The Abuja International Airport is under design and is expected to become a major hub along with Lagos and Kano. A special study indicated that a rail connection was not economically justified during either major construction phases or for continuing operations. Connections into the national power and telecommunications grids are also indi-cated in the plan along with suitable locations for liquid fuel and water storage facilities.

It is possible that the original government policy of restraining industrial development at the Capital may prove to be suboptimal in light of the major infrastructure invest-ment which Abuja requires. Therefore, the Regional Plan, while primarily focused on city support activities and rural development, does admit a later amendment to accommodate a more aggressive industrial development strategy.

The second major element of the Regional Plan is the settlement strategy. The strategy is designed to reconfigure the existing settlement pattern in coordination with the city support economic activities described above and to set a general framework for an FCT-wide rural development program.

The FCT is located in the park savannah and upland for-ested plateaus which characterise much of Nigeria's underde-veloped Middle Belt. This region was largely by-passed by the export-oriented agriculture induced by the British col-onial regime and includes hundreds of villages largely un-touched by any aspect of economic development. A FCT popu-lation of about 300,000 is located in 500-600 small villages evenly spread at very low density throughout the major plains supported by a small-scale cash cropping characterised by the slash-burn crop rotation farming. Few villages have any service or vehicle access. While the Government originally intended to clear the entire territory to eliminate tenure-

claim problems, they have now been convinced of the enormous
magnitude of this task. The long-run population relocation
program will be confined to the city footprint, reservoir
watersheds, airport and ultimately the proposed game preserve. Even this limited program will involve up to 50,000
people over a 20 year period.

The regional settlement strategy has three components.
First, an economic development/service delivery corridor is
to be established along the new north-south highway (A-2) and
supplied power grid connections. (Figure 5) The three largest
villages have been designated as "satellite towns" to serve
as the focus for the development of the agro-industrial and
extrative-related building industry to support Abuja. In
addition, they will serve as the highest level service delivery centres outside Abuja itself. The early employment and
service opportunity project make the satellite towns logical
relocation targets and will reduce somewhat the squatter
problem. Should the government reverse its policy on limitation on "dirty" industry in the FCT, these towns could
become industrial centres, close to, but not in, the new
capital.

Second, other smaller settlements in the development
corridors will also be reinforced as service delivery centres
for the adjacent smaller towns within 10-15 km of the corridor. A building control policy for the zone is being discussed as part of this program.

Third, the remaining smaller villages more than 10 km
from the corridor which are not affected by relocation will
be subject to a policy of "benign neglect." Too far to service and too small to aggregate, they will be allowed to
attrite.

The overall Regional Plan recognises the interdependence
of the FCT and the surrounding states. Watershed preservation
and water supply, relocation impacts, and food requirements
suggest the need for close cooperation and joint planning.
Additionally, unwanted urbanisation may be induced just
across FCT borders along access routes. For these reasons
the FCDA is undertaking joint planning consultation with
adjacent states and may establish formal Joint Planning Districts to develop and administer such institutional measures
for cooperation and control as they deem mutually desirable.

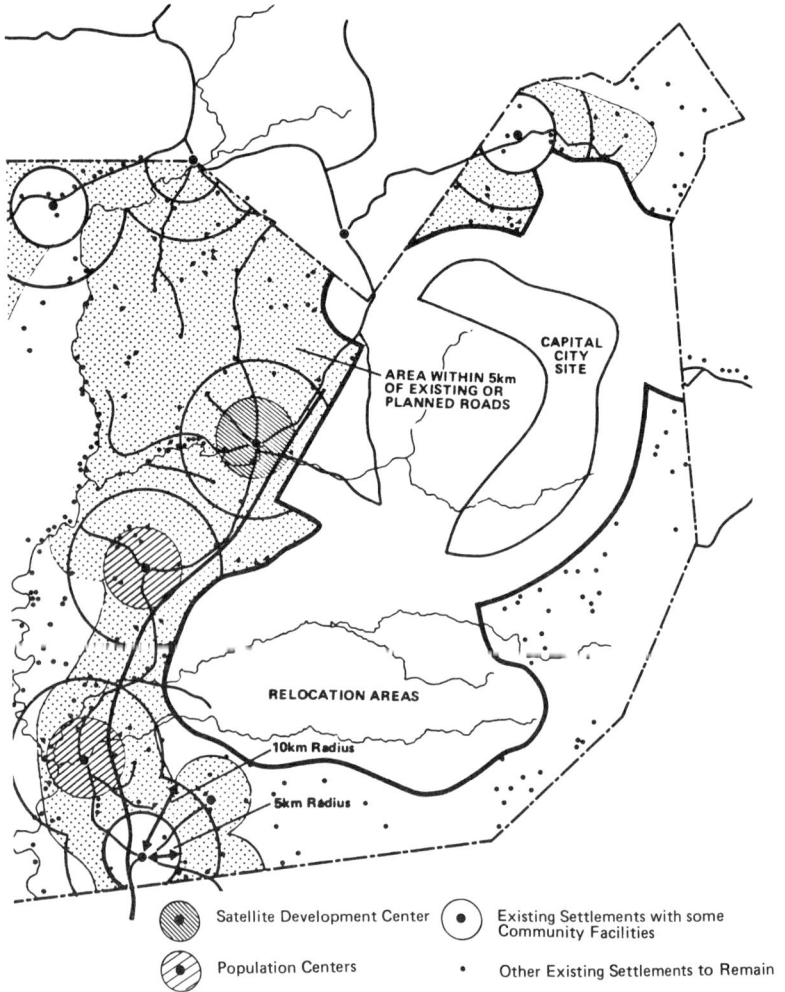

Fig. 5.   Recommended settlement pattern and service provision

IMPLEMENTATION PROGRAMME

   The development of Abuja is just beginning with the
official adoption of the Master Plans and the Design and
Development Manuals. The urgency of the 1986 deadline will
require that design and construction activities normally
sequenced be overlapped and compressed under a "fast track"
approach. For example, a base camp has been constructed and

early action infrastructure projects begun prior to completion of the Master Plan. A so-called "Accelerated District" has been selected for initial design and construction
even while additional base technical studies procede.

This process is being guided by the Logistics Plan which
was carried out by the consultant team to ensure that the
1986 target of initial occupancy for 150,000 was technically
feasible. The Logistics Plan detailed the fast track strategy
to meet the time schedule and provided an estimate of the
labour, materials, equipment and facilities necessary to
construct each project over the eight-year period.

A two-stage strategy was developed which concentrates
initially on building the Accelerated District prior to
undertaking major building or infrastructure construction.
This initial development will provide permanent housing for
FCDA staff and the construction labour force leaving maximum
time for detailed design of government buildings and infrastructure, which constitute the second phase. It also mini-
mises a potential squatting problem and allows time for the
organisation of the FCT building materials industry.

Special attention has been paid to the rate of build up
of labour force during the first stage in order to avoid the
necessity for the "temporary workers housing" which, in new
LDC developments, characteristically become permanent problems. The first worker group will temporarily occupy nearby
abandoned villages while completing the low cost sites-and-
services, rooming houses, and compounds of the accelerated
districts housing supply that they themselves will subsequently occupy. Thus the labour force is essentially constructing its own housing and financing their occupancy
through their construction jobs. Throughout the remainder of
the second stage, the construction scheduling has kept housing completion parallel with estimated total construction
labour force and dependents. This approach, aside from reducing squatting will eliminate a very large daily labour
transportation cost and will improve control of the work
force.

Squatting, of course, will be a perennial problem. In
the long range, affordable housing located near employment
opportunities is the key to its minimisation. Migrant recep-
tion centres and transitional lodging have also been recommended.

The Logistics Plan has carried out an analysis to anticipate and offset major material and transport bottlenecks through identifying specific components of the required building materials industry and preparing an access programme. Each component of the 8-year construction programme has been related over time in terms of a strategy, critical path activities and requirements in terms of individual contracts.

Contracts were scheduled and sized to minimise precontract time. A special effort was made to mix large contracts for efficiency with small contracts to maximise participation of Nigerian construction firms.

Finally, recommendations were made for the organisation and staffing of the Development Management and Materials Management organisations as well as the information systems required to support their operations. It is expected that the Logistics Plan, like the Master Plans, will be evolving documents, updated with changing conditions or increased information.

CONCLUSION

Abuja is just beginning its development trajectory. Only the passage of decades will reveal the degree to which it fulfills the aspirations of its sponsors. Clearly much further thinking, plan development, and plan revision will take place over the next decade. The development of a new national capital city is a relatively rare event. Comparison with earlier similar occasions provide an opportunity to determine if there is something more than simply change – like progress – in the development of urban form and structure concepts and the city development process itself.

Acknowledgements

The author wishes to express his appreciation for the helpful remarks of Mr. Thomas A Todd of Wallace, McHarg, Roberts and Todd and Mr. Walter G. Hansen and Dr. Andrew T. Lemer of Planning Research Corporation.

The consultant team for the master planning of the New Federal Capital City and Federal Capital Territory is a joint venture of Archisystems International, Inc., a division of Summa Corporation; Wallace, McHarg, Roberts and Todd; and Planning Research Corporation. Graphics credit: Wallace, McHarg, Roberts, Todd.

Dodoma: Provisions for cultural preservation and development in urban planning in Tanzania

Richard May, Jr.

INTRODUCTION

Arts and handicrafts have historically played a significant role as indigenous expressions of predominantly rural African societies. Urbanisation, on the other hand, is a 20th century phenomenon, particularly in East Africa. Programmes for cultural preservation and development, though strongly supported by many African governments, have not been implemented in urban settlement programmes, except where such plans relate to cultural buildings and spaces such as schools, museums, parks, plazas, theatres and stadiums.

The process of urbanisation has not occurred as rapidly in central Africa as in other underdeveloped regions, such as Asia and Latin America, where more people have been driven to urban areas in search of economic and social opportunities. For those who do migrate, the transition from rural to urban life is difficult and their survival during this period requires continuity in their social institutions and the opportunity to maintain themselves with subsistence gardens and livestock. Provision for the continuity of these indigenous cultural patterns of which traditional arts, crafts, dance and rituals are inseparable expressions, is an essential aspect of successful urban planning in developing countries. Unfortunately, most urban plans have been conceived with insufficient attention to local tradition and culture and, therefore, lack adequate provision for easing the transition to urban life. As a result, in most cases, new residents have had to build their own settlements, usually in the shape of informal shantytowns or favelas surrounding the formal city, which houses only the wealthier, already integrated members of urban society. Avoiding or at least minimising this phenomenon remains the greatest challenge facing urban planners in developing countries.

In Africa, the distinction between artists, crafts people and artisans does not exist as it does in European societies. Houses and settlements and production of tools, utensils and other artifacts have traditionally involved the application of design and decoration in the process of fashioning the basic structure and form of these objects. Therefore, in considering the role of arts and crafts in African urban development, one should not separate the role of skilled building artisans from the production of indigenous building materials, especially since both are in short supply.

Sensitive planning can anticipate the vital subsistence needs of urban migrants and the role of cultural preservation and development in the settlement process. However, there are some serious problems to be overcome. The city, as a Western institution, is not easily adaptable as a setting for indigenous rural ways of life and traditional cultural institutions. In fact, many African government leaders recognise this dichotomy and have decided to emulate foreign planners and urban designers for guidance in designing new settlements. This dichotomy is sometimes further complicated by certain disparities which can occur between established cultural institutions and newly adopted national, political, economic and social policies. The planner who designs settlements fostering both ideals may face problems difficult to resolve within the framework of essentially Western urban design forms and institutions.

The urban plan provides only the physical setting for urban life. Although experience has shown that people can adapt to almost any physical setting to serve their cultural needs, sensitive urban planning should make such adaptation unnecessary, or at least facilitate the process. To achieve maximum success in the integration of indigenous culture and the arts within urban plans, calls for more detail than found in most new settlement plans. Planners must do more than create potential for the survival of customs and the development of new institutions. They should also suggest governmental and social organisations and resources necessary to institute and continue the various human activities envisaged

for each area in the urban plan. However, in the final analysis, it is the government's and the people's responsibility
to activate the mechanism necessary to achieve their aims.

The above comments apply, to some extent, wherever urban
development is taking place within the African continent. As
an example, this article will focus on cultural policies and
the status of the arts in the United Republic of Tanzania,
and the role of indigenous culture and the arts in the design
and development of the new national capital at Dodoma.

NATIONAL CULTURAL POLICIES AND PROGRAMMES OF THE UNITED REPUBLIC OF TANZANIA

Tanzania's rich culture has its roots in the varied
natural environment of the Republic which stretches from the
Indian Ocean on the east to the great chain of inland lakes
of its western and northern borders. The terrain and climate
change radically from the exotic off-shore islands of
Zanzibar and Pemba, to hot and humid coastal plains, and to
the great central plateau, over 1,200 meters in altitude.
This inland plateau is Savannah covering most of the country
and is drier and cooler than the coastal areas. The northern
region is dominated by the towering extinct volcances of
Kilimanjaro (6,000 meters), Meru (4,800 meters) and other
lower peaks only 300 kilometers south of the Equator.

At the time of national independence in 1961, there were
123 tribes throughout the country, in addition to the island
and coastal population, which was strongly influenced by
several centuries of Arab domination. The range of cultures
reflect their varied physical environments. The Chagga grow
coffee and bananas on the slopes of Kilimanjaro, and the
Masai herd cattle on the arid plains. In the centre of the
country, the Gogo, Hehe and Lugura struggle under the constant threat of famine due to drought. The largest group is
the Sukuma, numbering one million peasant cotton growers,
south of Lake Victoria. Second largest are the Nyamqazi in
the west with 400,000. Several other tribes near Lake
Tanganyika number 300,000 people. Each has its unique
customs, language or dialect, and distinct building forms,
arts, crafts and dances.

The most prominent evidence of cultural differentiation
among the groups are the many unique forms they have devel-

oped in their buildings and settlements. The houses of the
Gogo in the vicinity of Dodoma are known as tembes. Their
rectangular buildings surround a cattle corral and have walls
of woven or upright wattles with flat mud roofs resting on
forked uprights. These buildings are quite low with interior
floors slightly below ground level.

The Iraqu and Gorowa, who live in the north on Lake
Manyara on top of the Rift wall, build their houses on a
slope with the back wall underground and the other walls of
stone or wattle and daub. The Nyakusa in the southern Rungwe
mountains near Malawi build their homes of bamboo with intri-
cately designed reinforcing. The doors have striking geometric designs made of ochre mud and are painted white. The
Masai herdsmen, who inhabit the Rift Valley in Southern Kenya
and Northern Tanzania, have perhaps one of the strongest
cultures in the region, retaining their simple red dress,
ornaments and traditional settlement patterns. Their mud and
wattle houses have distinctive low rounded shapes to resist
the wind. The settlements are circular, surrounded by dry
thorn hedges for protection, and the interior of the circle
is used as a livestock corral at night.

In addition to these purely African building forms are
those contributed during the period of Arab domination.
There are a number of ancient mosques and other buildings of
more permanent construction distinguished by their excellent
design and exquisite decoration, particularly in their carved
wooden doorways.

Early art forms which have survived include pottery,
wood sculpture, bark cloth printing, mat plaiting, black-
smithing, painting, wood carving of stools, combs, spoons,
dishes and domestic tools, weapons, drums and other musical
instruments. Although many of these art forms have faded
with the introduction of manufactured implements during the
colonial era, several do still thrive. Principal among these
is the wood sculpture known as Makonde, which is the name of
the village near Dar es Salaam, the traditional centre of
this art form. Makonde uses ebony (and ivory where permitted) and is frequently characterised by very intricate human
forms intertwined in pillars, or abstract figures of satyrs
and shetani (devils). Makonde's origins may lie in traditional religious figures characteristic of most African
sculpture. However, it is also possible that this art was
influenced by the skills developed in the elaborately carved

wooden doors still gracing many of the old Arab houses in Zanzibar. Makonde is a thriving industry today as a result of a growing tourist demand. In recent years, individual creative artists have developed more original abstract designs in ebony as a new form of Makonde.

Other surviving art forms are:

- Pottery with traditional and new decorative motifs. The Sukuma and Nyamwezi produce the best and Asian-type pottery is made in and around Dar es Salaam.
- Mat-plaiting. Mats are primarily used for baskets, floor and wall coverings, but also as prayer carpets and for burial shrouds. There is great variety in the materials and decorations.
- Bark-cloth printing is the work of two major groups – the Haya and the Yakyusa. The printed pattern is always black and the colour of the cloth varies from light to dark brown. The motifs are usually stylised represen- tations from nature – the sun, plants, birds, people and animals. Originally used as clothing, bark-cloth was formerly used by the Haya for bedding and burial shrouds.

Other art forms such as painting, music, dance and the theatre have not survived as well as the handicrafts men- tioned above. Despite government support for their develop- ment, it is difficult to overcome the foreign stronghold in these fields. Colonial rule, and particularly the colonial education system, deliberately disrupted the foundations of traditional cultures in order to replace them. The situation is aggravated by imports from Europe and North America. As President Nyerere put it:

"When we were at school we were taught to sing the songs of the Europeans. How many of us were taught the songs of the Wanyamwezi or of the Wahehe? Many of us have learnt to dance the rumba or the cha- cha, to rock and roll, and to twist, and even to dance the waltz and the foxtrot. But how many of us can or have even heard of the Gombe Sugu, the Mangala, the Konge, Nyang'umuni, Kiduo or Lele Mama? Lots of us can play the guitar, the piano or other European musical instruments. How many Africans in Tanganyika, particularly among the educated, can play the Nnanga or the Zeze or the

Marimba, the Kilanzi Ligombo, or the Mangale? And
even though we dance and play the piano, how often
does that dancing - even if it is "rock and roll"
or "twist", how often does it really give us the
thrill we get from dancing the Mangala or the Gombe
Sugu - even though the music may be no more than
the shaking of pebbles in a tin? It is hard for
any man to get much real excitement from dances and
music which are not in his own blood."[1]

NATIONAL CULTURAL POLICY AND THE ARUSHA DECLARATION

In establishing the Ministry of National Culture and
Youth in 1962, President Nyerere summarised the aims of
Tanzania's policy as follows:

1   A selective revival of our traditions and customs.

2   Promotion and preservation of our cultural heritage.

3   Our culture as an instrument of national development and
     unity.

4   The development of our tribal cultures into one national
     culture.

5   The contribution of our culture towards the development
     of mankind and the contribution of other cultures to our
     own development.

6   The necessity of overhauling the educational systems
     inherited from the former colonial powers and the need
     for all Tanzanians to remove the influence of the col-
     onial mentality from their minds.[2]

In 1965, the Ministry of National Culture was reorgan-
ised as the Ministry of Community Development and National
Culture, whose functions and responsibilities have been
gradually expanded to include the supervision of the national
museums in Dar es Salaam and Zanzibar; the village museum of
traditional tribal houses near Dar es Salaam; the National
Stadium, the National Film Censorship Office, the National
Festivals and State Celebrations; the Department of Swahili
Language and Literature, the Department of Traditional Music,
the Department of Theatre and Drama, and the University of
Dar es Salaam.

In combining community development and national culture under a single ministry, the government has created a great opportunity for cooperation to assure maximum consideration of cultural preservation and artistic expression in the development of new communities.

In establishing a Ministry of National Culture, Nyerere did not merely aim toward the revival of indigenous Tanzania cultures. He also stated that the Republic would borrow selectively from other cultures: "Mankind would not progress at all if we refused to learn from each other. But to learn from each other's cultures does not mean we should abandon our own."[3]

The Arusha Declaration of 1967 provided the government and people of Tanzania with principles, policies and a national commitment to the building of Socialism. A major element of the policies set forth in the declaration is that of self-reliance to be achieved by maximum utilisation of available national resources - namely land and manpower. However, the doctrine of self-reliance does not mean rejection of foreign aid or unwillingness to borrow and use foreign skills, methods, techniques and tools. It does not preclude, for example, the adoption of modern architectural skills and materials in preference to traditional practices.

Recognition of the need for foreign assistance and skills in national development and more specifically in the design and development of buildings and human settlements is therefore held by the government to be consistent with the principles in the Arusha Declaration. This is, of course, realistic in view of the overriding urgency for increasing the limited supply of technically qualified personnel to support this programme. The government has instituted a variety of training programmes to overcome these manpower deficiencies. For example, the ARDHI Institute in Dar es Salaam has a very successful training programme for architectural and town planning assistants, land and quantity surveyors, and other para-professional personnel in housing and construction. International assistance to this training programme is provided by the United Nations Centre for Human Settlements and the Government of Denmark. Regrettably, Tanzania has no university level programme for the training of architects and town planners. Students seeking such training go to universities in Kenya, the Sudan, or Europe and North America, where in some cases there are courses es-

pecially designed for students from developing countries.
Many do not return and the nation suffers a "brain drain" in
the loss of qualified personnel who have received government
or international scholarships for oversea training. Hopefully, these problems will be overcome by increasing employment opportunities and offering higher wages as the rate of
general economic and human settlement development increases.

Meanwhile, during the transition period, both government
officials and their foreign consultants face the challenge of
developing settlements designed to achieve the aims of the
Arusha Declaration and national cultural policies. To achieve
success requires: (1) the development of a sensitive knowledge and understanding of the country's culture and policies
by the foreign consultants; (2) the most careful review of
settlement plans and designs by Tanzanian officials and professional personnel to assure compatibility with Tanzanian
culture and government policies; (3) maximum effort to build
up a Tanzanian counterpart in staff to allow their rapid
takeover of planning, design and construction supervision;
and (4) the creation of mechanisms and programmes for acti-
vating the cultural, political and artistic aspects of settlement plans.

An outstanding example of this process is the government's programme for the development of the new national
capital at Dodoma.

DODOMA, THE NEW CAPITAL OF THE UNITED REPUBLIC OF TANZANIA

In 1973, Parliament and President Nyerere, designated
Dodoma as the new capital city of Tanzania. It lies in the
heart of the country, in scenic highland boasting an excellent temperate climate and at the intersection of Tanzania's
major railway and highway routes. Dodoma will be a capital
city with 350,000 people in eleven separate residential communities connected to its centre via transit loops and an
arterial road network. Future extension areas provide for an
eventual growth to 800,000 people in eleven additional communities.

Immediately following the official decision to move the
national capital, the government established the Capital
Development Authority (CDA) to select the site for the city
and coordinate its development. Dodoma was chosen because it

is in the centre of the country and also to stimulate growth in the surrounding region, one of the least developed areas of Tanzania. Already an established regional centre, Dodoma's 75,000 people provide a nucleus for the development of the new capital.

The Master Plan

In his foreword to the master plan report, President Nyerere said:

"We have to build in a manner which is within our means and which reflects our principles of human dignity and equality as well as our aspirations for our development. We have to take advantage of the opportunity to make Dodoma a good place in which to live and work, and to bring up children as good Tanzanians. The town must be integrated as a so- ciety as a whole; it must be neither an ivory tower nor a new version of our existing towns. It must draw upon the lessons of other specially built cities throughout the world but it must not be a copy of any of them. Dodoma must be a town which is built in simple style but with buildings which reflect the light, air, and space of Africa. It must reflect the future and their must be room to grow, but it must not be futuristic in the sense of symbolising passing and individualistic emotions...

The buildings should conform to the circumstances and needs of Tanzania. For example housing must have a low capital and maintenance cost. Public buildings must be designed to serve the people in a socialist society... For we are a poor country, building a new capital city in a nation committed to the principle of Ujamaa.*

I believe this Plan, as it stands, is consistent with the ideology of Tanzania... Dodoma will be built as a series of connected communities, each having a population of about 28,000 people. Within these communities people will be able to cooperate for joint activities of a productive, educational, and social nature while remaining part of the larger towns.

The Master Plan Report sets forth the following aims
with respect to social and cultural policies.[4]

The two basic purposes of the City are to function
as the new Capital of Tanzania and to provide the
necessary impetus and infrastructure for a strong
programme of regional improvement and development.
The plan will accommodate the National Government's
ministries and related agencies, parastatals and
institutions, as well as the industrial, commercial
and social establishments of a modern city which
must serve the needs of a large urban and regional
population.

The recognition and maintenance of the traditional
life styles and social structures of the Tanzanian
people was another major basis for the design of
the Master Plan. The national heritage of people's
relationship to the land, the importance of the
family, personal contacts among neighbours, the
integration of outdoor and indoor activities in the
daily life at home, and the fact that most
Tanzanians have always lived in small rural communities, were taken into account in the design of
the new city's housing types and residential environment.

The TANU** policies of self-reliance and self-help
dictate that the urban residents must be given
ample opportunities to participate in the construction of their homes and to augment their food supplies. The plan is therefore based on the need to
ensure that sufficient land is set aside near the
homes for gardens and shambas. And the housing

---

* The Ujamaa (family) village programme is a system of developing cooperative villages based on the African concept of
the extended family. The concept was extremely popular at
its inception, and by mid-1975, it was estimated that 70%
of the mainland population lived in Ujamaa villages.

** Tanganyika African National Union, the national political
party founded under the leadership of President Nyerere in
1954. Now known as the CCM (Chama cha Mapinduzi - Party
of the Revolution).

policies and programmes must encompass cooperative and other self-help action.

The Capital City form and design should respect and reflect the Tanzanian heritage and customs and the characteristics of the local climate and landscape. While the Master Plan incorporates positive features and values of other cities in the world, it should result in the growth of a Tanzanian and African city which will allow the future generations to develop in the spirit of the contemporary Tanzanian nation."

The National Capital Centre[5]

The master plan for Dodoma located the Capital Centre in the southeast quadrant of the inner city within a ring road, the hub of the region's main roads. The National Capital Centre (NCC) is both the new seat of Tanzania's government and Dodoma's new town centre. The NCC will eventually contain 21 national ministries, hotels, department stores, shops and restaurants, transport terminals, churches and mosques, and apartments for over 5,000 persons.

The NCC site comprises 150 hectares on a slope forming a fine natural background, toward the spectacular landmark, the Mlimwa Hill. Within walking distance of the old city centre, the site provides ample land for the foreseeable future. A new commercial centre between Old Dodoma and the ministerial area will form a bridge between the two.

To reflect the lively atmosphere of a Tanzanian town centre it was decided the NCC should integrate shopping, housing and cultural facilities to achieve the bustle of a village market day. Tanzanians prefer low buildings in the centre, reflecting the landscape and the traditional habitats of the country, to Western skyscrapers.

The Capital Centre forms an immense stairway symbolising Tanzania's progress (Fig. 1). Built on a slope facing north, the energy of the hill is harnessed by forming the site into seven terraces. On each terrace is a mixture of activities: government, shopping, restaurants, offices and housing (Fig. 2). The great staircase leads to the Ujamaa Square containing the most important buildings and the nation's symbol of Ujamaa, the monumental "tree" (Fig. 3).

304 R. MAY

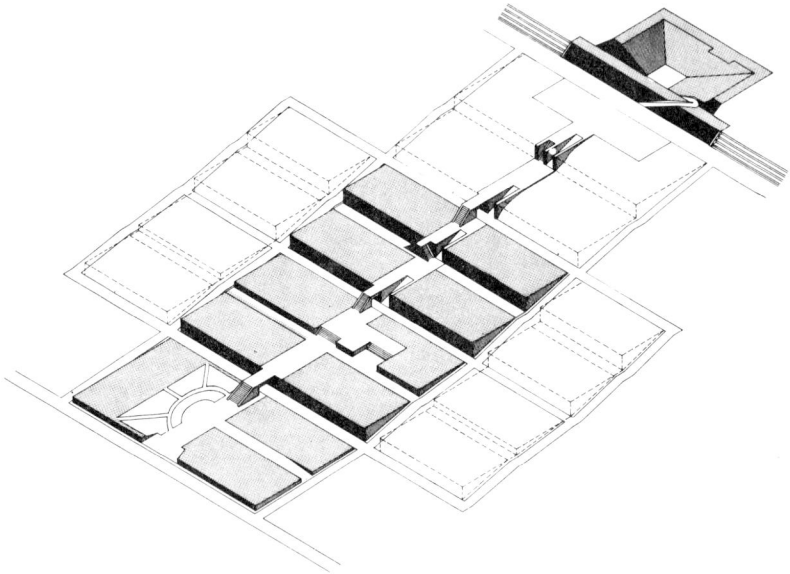

Fig. 1. Schematic Plan of Stepped Terrace, National Capital
Centre, Dodoma, Tanzania.

Museums, arts and crafts galleries, and theatres are
interspersed among the shops and offices of the Capital
Centre (Fig. 4). The Museum of Social and Political History,
the National Library, and the Museum of Science and industry
will all be in Uhuru (Freedom) Park at the base of the first
terrace. West of the NCC, adjacent to a central park is the
site of the National Theatre Complex for drama, dance, and
music, with an outdoor informal amphitheatre within the park
itself. Immediately east of the NCC will be the 60,000 seat
National Stadium and Sports Complex and a 2,000 seat amphitheatre to be used for a variety of social and political
events.

ACHIEVEMENT OF THE SOCIAL, POLITICAL AND CULTURAL AIMS OF THE DODOMA PLAN

The Capital Development Authority (CDA) and its consultants have clearly striven to plan for the development of
Dodoma as a Tanzanian city embodying the nation's political

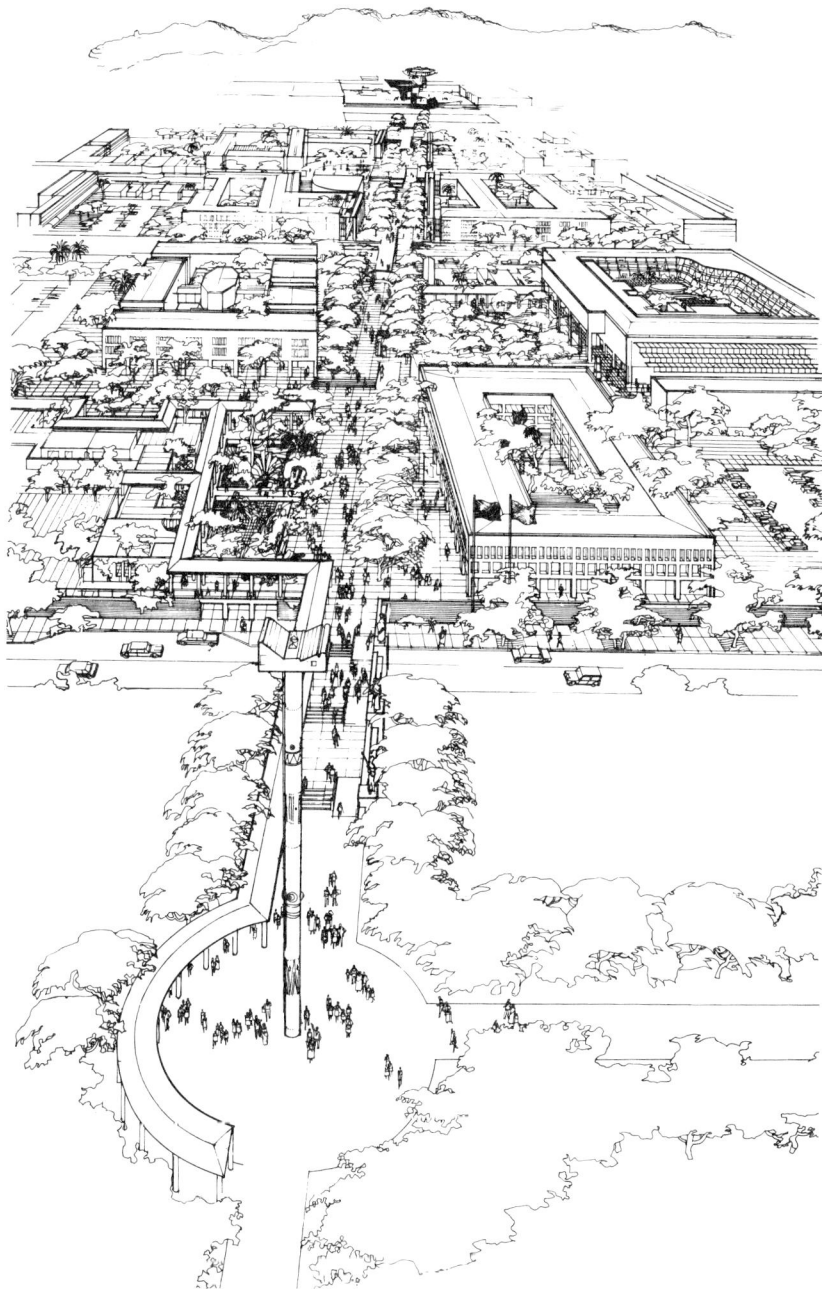

Fig. 2.   Perspective of the National Capitla Centre looking
          south.

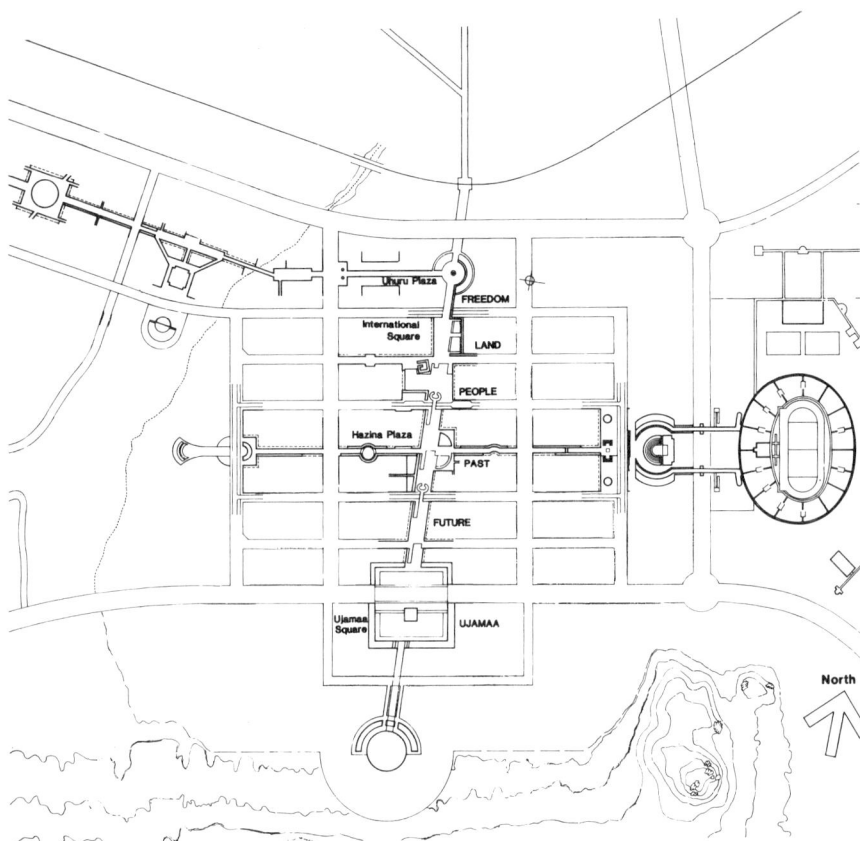

Fig. 3.   Major pedestrian ways of the National Capital
          Center.

and social aims and providing an environment for the varied
cultures of the nation to survive and develop. In considering
the potential success of this endeavour one should bear in
mind the varied purposes of the Government in moving the
capital and developing a new city as its seat: to improve
the effectiveness of the national government in its primary
role of governing and directing the nation's development; to
provide the stimulus and base for the economic development of
central area of the country which has lagged behind that of
other areas; to support the gradual transition of the nation
from its predominantly rural economy to a more balanced   so-

Fig. 4.   Hotel Galleria, Dodoma, Tanzania.

ciety with an increased industrial base and greater social
opportunities, which can only take place in urban areas.

It should therefore be recognised that the main purpose
underlying the commitment of huge efforts and resources to
the development of the new capital is the raising of living
standards and improving the health and well-being of the
national as well as the regional population. Yet, for the
majority of people moving to the capital, the transition from
a predominantly rural to an urban society is neither possible
nor desirable in one quantum jump. For this to occur, the
new city must create an environment which supports the continuation of traditional familiar and social and economic
opportunities. The mere provision of a physical setting for
the effectuation of this transition is insufficient. Even
the building of physical facilities in the form of housing,
schools and working places will not achieve these ends. The
transition can only take place through Government and CCM,
the National political party, sponsorship and operation of
programmes to assist the new residents in adjusting to their

new environment. Encouragement of native craftsmanship and
support of traditional arts can play an important role in
this process. The need for community organisation to make
this process come about was foreseen by Nyerere in saying
that "Within these communities people will be able to cooperate by joint activities of a productive, educational, and
social nature while remaining part of the larger town."[6]

National Policies in the Master Plan

In reviewing the Master Plan and the CDA's development
programme it is clear that the Government has given the
highest priority to the development of Dodoma as a means for
modernising Tanzanian society, and only secondarily is it to
serve as the national symbol and model for cultural preservation. For example, the President's foreword to the Master
Plan stresses political and social aims more than cultural
aspects.[6] It would also appear that the decision to retain
foreign consultants was made with the conscious intent to
build a modern world capital emulating non-African urban
forms.

Yet, the Government has also stressed the need for the
city to accommodate the basic needs of traditional Tanzanian
society and to feature cultural and political elements and
ambience which symbolises the nation's traditional cultures
and its policies for Socialism and self-reliance embodied in
the Arusha Declaration.

Despite the handicap of their being neither Tanzanian
nor representative of Socialist societies, the planning consultants under the direction of the CDA and its advisors have
made great efforts to interpret both aims in the plans for
the new capital.

For example, with respect to the overall concept and
major plan elements:

1   The plan shows great sensitivity to the national geo-
    graphic setting and the varied landscapes of the
    country. The basic structure of the city embodies care-
    fully selected axes for views and circulation reflecting
    the national geography of Tanzania.

2   The city is shaped by the topography of the region and the site, dramatising and capitalising on its major natural features.

3   In accord with the predominant character of human settlements in Tanzania the overall and net densities of population are low in comparison with most urban models.

4   Ample open spaces permeating all areas of the city provide intimate contact with the natural landscape and allow for private gardens and livestock grazing.

5   The nuclear pattern of communities provides a feeling of scale familiar to the people which can permit the continuation of traditional social units and customs. The circular form of these communities and the neighbourhood units within them is reminiscent of traditional Tanzanian settlement patterns.

6   The emphasis on low horizontal scale in the National Capital Centre is more attuned to the national character and more befitting the site than higher building forms which usually tempt the urban designer.

7   The plan provides for the natural growth of the existing city of Dodoma to allow for its gradual evolution into the new city, thus permitting the continued functioning of many familiar elements such as the railroad station, market and business centre.

To fulfill the political and social aims of the Government the plan:

- Places great emphasis on improving the environment and the economy of the surrounding region;

- Provides for a hierarchy of settlement levels and unit sizes corresponding to the national political structure of CCM - the Cell, the Branch and the District; thus facilitating the organisation of community development programmes;

- Provides for activation of the principle of self-reliance in shambas, grazing compounds and neighbourhood commercial spaces for informal sector activities;

- Provides the physical setting for social development in sites for community facilities (schools, health centres, etc.);

- Calls for social integration in the provisions for varied types and sizes of housing units within each community;

- Provides many monuments, forms and symbols in the National Capital Centre reflecting the nation's cultures and aspirations.

The Role of the Arts and Crafts in Dodoma's Development

Other than general references and the designation of sites for monuments, museums, galleries, and market for the sale of crafts, there is little mention in the Master Plan or the National Capital Centre plan report on the role of the arts in Dodoma's development.

However, this should not be taken as an indication that the vital role of the arts in the City's development has been neglected by the CDA. As stated earlier in the Introduction, it is difficult in African societies to draw a line between artists, craftsmen and building artisans since indigenous forms and decoration are intrinsically involved in the traditional building process.

To build the capital it has been necessary for the CDA to mobilise and train a huge work force on the site and to even organise the local manufacture of certain building materials so as to reduce the necessity of importing and/or shipping from the main coastal industrial areas. It has also become apparent that conventional construction and finance methods cannot produce housing within the means of the vast majority to Tanzanians who will live in Dodoma. Their needs can only be met through self-help construction on sites with services provided by the CDA. A special staff has therefore been set up to organise this process and to assist and train people in the building of their houses. The UN and the ARDHI Institute are assisting in this programme.

This programme is however, only the first step in a much larger programme of community organisation as envisaged by President Nyerere to assist residents in making the transition from their rural customs to becoming full participants in the new urban society. As the city develops and attracts increasing migration, strong positive measures will be needed to prevent the development of squatter settlements in the surrounding area such as that which occurred in Brasilia and is the characteristic pattern around growing urban centres throughout the developing world. Merely negative development controls to prevent such development have proven unsuccessful in countless examples.

Although it devotes sufficient space in designed residential districts, the Dodoma master plan is deficient in not devoting sufficient attention to the problem of settling the new population and in not suggesting specific measures for dealing with this problem. In organising the community development process the CDA will require the cooperation of CCM and various government agencies responsible for aspects of social welfare and foreign technical assistance in this field. First, a joint task force might be charged to prepare a plan and programme for community development including estimates of the human and material resources required. In view of the scarcity of resources, the maximum effort must be made to transfer the responsibility for carrying out the programme to the people themselves as rapidly as possible by the early identification of community leadership.

The cooperation of the Ministry of Community Development and National Culture is essential to the success of community development as well as the planning of the national cultural facilities to be built in the capital. Its participation can assist in the preservation of traditional culture as an essential element of the city's development as the social as well as the political and governmental capital of Tanzania. A significant portion of community development programmes can be constructively devoted to training in arts and crafts related to the building of dwellings, community buildings and the making of furniture and floor mats and other essential home furnishings and objects. If settlement patterns in Dodoma follow those experienced elsewhere, people will tend to group with others from their own region and tribe, thus permitting the continuation of the customs, music, dances and festivals characteristic of each region. Such activities will need support and in turn will contribute to the authenticity of the national pageants, theatrical and musical presentations to be staged in the National Capital Centre.

Through this programme Dodoma will realise President Nyerere's hopes when he said:

".....Dodoma has the possibility of becoming a unique 'man-centred city - one designed to serve

the people who live in it, and the nation which
decided to develop it as the Capital."[7]

Acknowledgements

Grateful acknowledgement is given to the government and
authorities of the United Republic of Tanzania whose publications are quoted herein; to Conklin and Rossant, Architects
and Planners, of Dodoma and New York, and designers of the
National Capital Centre, for use of their illustrations; and
to EKISTICS, Volume 48, Number 288, May/June 1981 in whose
pages certain portions of the author's original work
appeared.

REFERENCES

1. J. K. Nyerere, in Tanzania National Assembly Official
    Reports (1962).
2. The Cultural Policy of the United Republic of Tanzania,
    L. A. Mbughum, The Unesco Press, Paris, p.18 (1974).
3. The Cultural Policy of the United Republic of Tanzania,
    L. A. Mbughum, The Unesco Press, Paris, p.17 (1974).
4. Master Plan for Dodoma, Project Planning Associates,
    Toronto, Canada, Chapter III, p.39-40 (1975).
5. Based on Urban Design for the National Capital Centre,
    Conklin and Rossant, Architects and Planners, Dodoma
    and New York (1980).
6. Foreword to Master Plan for Dodoma, Project Planning
    Associates, Toronto, Canada, p.vi (1975).
7. J. K. Nyerere, Foreword to A Portrait of Dodoma, Capital
    Development Authority (1975).

BIBLIOGRAPHY

African Traditional Architecture, Susan Denyer, Heinemann
    Educational Books Ltd., London (1978).
Crafts, Small-scale Industries and Industrial Education in
    Tanzania, Karl Schadler, Weltforum Verlag, Munchen
    (1968).
African Furniture and Household Objects, Roy Sieber, Indiana
    University Press (1980).

All figures are by courtesy of Conklin & Rossant, Architects
and Planners.

New towns in Malaysia: Problems, failures and achievements

Haji Mohamad bin Haji Abdul Rahman

INTRODUCTION

The study of new towns development and urbanisation in Malaysia is important because like other areas all over the world this phenomenon is the cornerstone of rapid social change. To some experts, urbanisation is the progenitor of growth. Today, scholars have become less optimistic about it.

Historically, Malaysia although relatively the most urbanised nation in the ASEAN region, apart from the city state of Singapore, and the fifth in Asia after Hong Kong, Japan, Singapore and Taiwan, experienced rapid urban growth only after the Second World War. The towns that grew were in response to a set of social, economic and security conditions that prevailed during that particular period. Very few of these towns were consciously planned and deliberately developed. The number would be further reduced if we attach the concept of "a complete social and functional structure with sufficient jobs to make it self-supporting, spaciously laid out to give light, air and gracious living and surrounded by a green belt that would provide both farm produce and opportunity for recreation and relaxation to the residents", or a complete community development to the definition of a town. (H. Evans, ed., New Towns: The British Experience. London: Charles Knight 1972).

Demographic statistics continue to show rapid growth in urban population. In Peninsular Malaysia, about 54% of the population is rural, while for the whole of South East Asia,

the figure is 80% in 1970. These statistics, although providing an indication of recent trends, do not give the full
picture.

In the wake of a new realisation, jolted too suddenly by
the May 13 Incident 1969, the government embarked on a new
strategy for social and racial conflicts of the national
development through its New Economic Policy (NEP). The
launching of the Second Malaysia Plan (1970-1975) can thus be
considered as the watershed of planned urban development in
Malaysia. Among other policy variables, the NEP adopts urbanisation as a development strategy to rectify both racial
and a real imbalance in Peninsular Malaysia. The development
of new towns has been a major instrument aligned towards this
objective. The growth of new towns development and urbanisation can be enhanced by sound development planning, for
development planning in Malaysia has become synonymous with
the government's commitment to the socio-economic restructuring as much as the purely economic progress of the country.

BACKGROUND TO THE GROWTH OF TOWNS IN MALAYSIA

Urban development in Malaysia can be said to have been
originated with the expansion of British influence in the
beginning of the 20th Century. As has been stressed earlier,
therefore, the growth of towns was a response to a set of
social, commercial, economic and security conditions prevailing at a particular time. The towns and settlements that
emerged and which Malaysia are building can be classified
broadly into the following:

Commercial/Administrative Centres - These were initially
built to meet the needs of exploiting the countries' natural
resources and plantation development, the most important
being tin mining, rubber cultivation, and were located in the
tin rich and fertile western coastal plain of Peninsular
Malaysia. To provide adequate manpower in tin mines and
rubber plantations, Chinese from mainland China and Indians
from the Indian sub-continent respectively were encouraged to
migrate to Peninsular Malaysia. It was only later that administration, military and religious functions were attached
to these commercial centres.

New Villages - There were about 400 in number and were developed to accommodate half a million inhabitants, mainly

Chinese in the rural areas after declaration of the "Emergency" in 1948 and were mainly in the West Coast of Malaysia.

<u>Satellite Towns</u> - These were built to serve the long and short term needs of overspill of other existing towns; Petaling Jaya (1953) and Shah Alam (1967) come under this category.

<u>"Agropolitan Settlements"</u> - These are the latest in the concept of new towns and are built within agriculture hinterland and are located mainly in the Regional Development Areas like JENGKA, 1966; Johor Tenggara (KEJORA), 1972; Pahang Tenggara (DARA), 1972; Trengganu Tengah (KETENGAH), 1973; and Kelantan Selatan (KESEDAR), 1978.

<u>New Urban Growth Centres</u> - These are growth centres located near four designated national growth poles of Kuala Lampur - Petaling Jaya (Bangi New Town), Georgetown - Butterworth (Bayan Baru New Town), Kuantan (Gebeng New Town) and Johor Bahru (Pasir Gudang New Town).

PROBLEM AREAS

Rural-Urban Drift

        Rural-urban drift in the first half of the 20th Century has been characterised by the preponderance of push factors and the absence of a conscious balance between deceleration of urban growth and guiding the natural course of rural-urban migration. The push factors include a broad range of better paying occupational opportunities, the greater security in times of war and insurgency, the facilities for storage, exchange and redistribution, the availability of health, education and other social facilities, the low status accorded to farmers and the constraints imposed by traditional society on the individual combine to push rural dwellers to urban areas. The urbanisation rate was, however, faster than the facilities and services could accommodate.

Imbalance of Distribution of Population by Race

        The origin of the commercial centres and new villages was by far the most important factor that caused the dominance of Malay population in rural areas and Chinese and

Indian in urban areas. In 1970, the urban population was
2,527,900 or representing 28.7% of the total population of
8,801,400. In the case of Malays only 14.8% live in urban
areas in 1970, compared to their dominant share of 52.7% of
the total population. They, however, are almost equally
distributed among the metropolitan towns (6.8%), large towns
(8.0%) and small towns (6.8%). The Chinese comprised 47.0%
of the urban population in contrast to their 35.8% share of
the total population. They are heavily concentrated in the
metropolitan towns (29.0%) and are relatively lesser in both
the large towns (18.0%) and small towns (25.1%). The Indians
whose share of the total population is merely 10.7% have
substantial numbers living in the urban areas totalling 34.4%
of the urban population. They, too, are heavily concentrated
in the metropolitan towns (24.1%) though much lesser in the
large towns (10.3%) and small towns (10.1%).

Disparity of Income between Races

The better commercial and occupational opportunities in
the urban areas afforded a better level of income to urban
population consisting of mainly Chinese settlers, thus
resulting in imbalance in income level between ethnic groups.
In 1970, the income per household in the urban areas was
$428.00 per month and in the rural areas was $200.00 per
month. The average household income was $264.00 per month.
The breakdown in terms of racial group is as follows:

Racial Group	Average Household Income ($ monthly)
Malays	172
Chinese	394
Indian	304
Others	813

In 1970, out of the 900,000 Malay families, 65% were
poor; 26% out of 525,000 Chinese families and 39% of the
160,000 Indian families were poor. Out of the total poor
families, 74% consists of the Malays, 17% of Chinese and 8%
of Indians and 1% others as can be seem from the following
table:

	No.of House-hold (000)	No.of poor Household (000)	Poverty Rate (%)	% of poor Household
Malays	901.5	584.2	64.8	73.8
Chinese	525.2	136.3	26.0	17.2
Indians	160.5	62.9	39.2	7.9
Others	18.8	8.4	44.8	1.1
	1,606	791.8	49.3	100.00
No. in rural areas	1,166.7	683.7	58.6	86.3
No. in urban areas	439.3	108.1	24.6	13.7

Note: For purpose of this assessment, poverty line is income per household below $264.00 per month.

Culture of Poverty

The better opportunities in urban areas draw rural popu-lation to migrate. The flow of migration, however, is faster than the new requirements for labour surplus and the develop-ment of services in housing, health and education. Aspir-ations are racing far ahead of the potential for their achievement; housing shortages are forcing people to live in squatter areas and a new class of urban poor is being created. The pressures of urban poverty resulting from low wages, under-employment and unemployment give rise to crime. Manifestations of the good life, but restricted by financial affordability induce some to resort to theft as a way of life. In Kuala Lumpur alone the number of reported crimes rose from about 8,000 in 1974 to nearly 11,000 in 1975; robberies and burglaries topped the list.

Squatter population in Kuala Lumpur metropolitan area is in the region of 250,000 or constitutes 0.23% of the popu-lation. The rise of squatter population can be correlated to the pace of industrialisation. In a sense industrialisation induces the acceleration of the squatter situation and the problem of 'Culture of poverty' which it intended to alleviate.

Related to the problem of culture of poverty is deviant
behaviour manifesting in drug addiction, robbery, extortion,
prostitution, incest, etc.

The Urban Conflict – from Race to Class

The urban population 'transplosion' or sudden expansion
of urban society has also had decisive impact on the social
ecological structure of the cities in Malaysia, as well as in
other South Asian cities. Urban society was formerly divided
into watertight compartments of a plural social structure,
where interaction and integration of various ethnic and cultural group was lacking. It was not an integrated social
structure but rather a combination of small societies.
Clifford Geertz (1965) in referring to this situation in a
small Javanese town used the term "hollow town". In Malaysia
a parallel to this situation was the prevalence of "China-
towns" in the cities of Kuala Lumpur, Ipoh and Penang and
compartmentalisation on ethnic line in residential areas. It
is also interesting to note that even amongst similar ethnic
origin, the Malay for example, there were divisions along
regional or parochial line. The existence of "Kampung Jawa"
in some towns in Malaysia bears testimony to this situation.
(This term refers to an enclave of Malays of Javanese
origin).

Industrialisation and modernisation, parallel with the
process of urbanisation, is also breaking down monopolisation
of occupations along ethnic lines. Occupational opportunities
are in theory open for members of all ethnic groups. At the
same time rising unemployment rates reduce the actual opportunities of upward occupational mobility. The potential for
open conflict is enhanced, because competition for jobs between members of ethnic groups is now combined with competition for living space. Moving into a residential area or
an occupational area that was formerly monopolised by a
particular ethnic group is interpreted in the social con-
sciousness as invasion and leads to defense reactions.

The conflict situation is enhanced by the consolidation
of a multi-ethnic upper class which is an object for envy to
all ethnic groups in the lower class. One may not feel as
envious and frustrated to see a member of one's ethnic group
becoming prosperous as seeing a member of another ethnic
group in that position. Again one would feel restrained to

channel expressions of conflict against members of the same
elite group living in the same residential area.

The situation would be totally different in the case of
persons of different ethnic origin competing for the same
territory and for the same jobs. This would lead to frus-
tration riots in the lower class areas themselves. By contrast, it was observed that during the May 13th Incident in
Malaysia no conflict occurred between members of the upper
class.

Rural remains rural

The migrants to urban areas are mostly the young and
educated who have marketable skills. The old and uneducated
remain in the rural areas employed in traditional occupations. Many villages have suffered shortage of manpower to
till the agriculture land. At the same time the mentality
remains traditional-mystical as against modern-rational associated with urban mentality.

Self-containment and Self-Sufficiency

Under the modern town concept fashioned along British
towns, a town should be self-contained and self-sufficient.
However, this principle of self-containment and self-
sufficiency were not achieved in the planned town of Petaling
Jaya for example, which became a dormitory town for the
middle class who commute daily to work in Kuala Lumpur.

Social Balance

The principle of social balance was also not achieved in
some new towns. The social composition of Petaling Jaya is
preponderantly weighted to high income earners. Low income
earners for whom the town was planned, became the minority
group. Industries in the new town had to depend on workers
who reside elsewhere in the surrounding rural areas to obtain
full complement of their labour requirements.

The principle of social balance developed further from
Ebenezer Howard's social mix should ideally cover a diversity

of employment and housing to provide freedom of choice; balanced physical development between built-up areas and open spaces; a population heterogeneity with respect to age, occupation, income, ethnicity and class. This omission is particularly striking in the new villages which were hurriedly built.

National Language as Unifying Factor

In a multi-racial society like Malaysia one of the unifying forces is the common language or the National Language. To achieve national unity, mere acceptance is not adequate; this acceptance must be manifested in the practical use of it in all communications. The overwhelming display of signboards in characters reflective of ethnic ownership of properties in towns certainly does not bear the spirit for unity. It is to be hoped that future towns in Malaysia, including also existing towns, should give due respect to the National Language in the interest of national unity, whether through voluntary effort in the spirit of true loyalty or by force of law or administrative injunctions.

Community Development

Community development as defined by a UN publication refers to "the processes by which the efforts of the people themselves are united with those of governmental authorities to improve the economic, social and cultural conditions of communities into the life of the nation and to enable them to contribute fully to national progress."

There are two important factors to the concept of community development; these are the progress of the individual as a member of the community and the community development itself as a whole. The individual members are expected to participate in all activities and efforts for the development of their community. From time immemorial, the spirit of community help, or gotong royong, finds expression in the collective efforts in all activities of life of the Malay community, ranging from such activities as marriage and engagement ceremonies, funeral rites, khatam Quran (completion of the reading of the Quran) and feasts to other village activities such as building of individual houses, construction of roads, drains, community centres and so on.

Community development in the more formal form had its roots in Rela, or the collective efforts of the people for protection and security against the Communist terrorist after the Japanese occupation. This activity was undertaken purely on a voluntary basis and was limited to a few settlements only especially those that faced serious threats from Communist infiltration and atrocities.

The spirit of gotong royong has been seen to be more effective in the earlier days and in the rural setting. In a plural society sentiments abound along racial or religious lines. The complexities of city life perhaps are not always conducive to better social interaction. The participation of all races in some voluntary activities has been found to be lacking in the bigger cities and towns of the country. One perhaps can argue against the merits of gotong royong in such development projects as construction of roads or bridges or community centres. To the business-minded individuals, participation in such efforts is a waste of time. Considering the opportunity cost of the time spent in participation in such efforts as against the financial benefits that could accrue within the time span, it is a time loss to him. One can argue therefore that such efforts could be more costly considering the time lost by the many individuals who participate in such efforts. Such efforts may be more expeditiously and efficiently carried out on contract basis.

It is also to be observed that equal participation of all races is not reflected in such voluntary bodies as the Womens Institute. The formation of the National Advisory Council for the Integration of Women in 1976 adopted as one it its objectives, the unity amongst the peoples of Malaysia and international understanding and harmony.

With regard to Rela, participation has not been equally spontaneous not only from people of all races but from people from all walks of life. The enforcement of Rukun Tetangga Scheme under the Emergency Ordinance in 1969 can be viewed as a reflection of the erosion of the spirit of gotong royong especially in the bigger cities of the country. The objective of Rukun Tetangga is to enable people residing in cities and towns to involve themselves directly to preserve peace and maintain security within the neighbourhood. Generally, the scheme is intended to foster goodwill amongst neighbours and amongst people of all races and all walks of life throughout the country. However, the many legal actions taken against those who fail to report for duty reflect to a certain degree the reluctance of certain groups of people or certain individuals towards this group effort.

DEVELOPMENT AND MANAGEMENT OF TOWNS

Unlike British towns, towns in Malaysia were not planned and developed by separate authorities like the Town Development Corporations in the United Kingdom. Instead, the planning and construction were undertaken by several government departments and or agencies responsible to the various State Governments, for under the Malaysian Constitution local Government comes under the state jurisdiction. Only after the passing of the Local Government Act in 1976 was there a uniform management machinery for all local authorities in Malaysia. Thus, therefore, the development of town and town board administration have shown a lack of sound planning and administrative control. Perhaps, the late passing of the Local Government Act, 1976 was due to the fact that in 1952 when local councils first started, the government then felt that it was too early to adopt democratic practices in local council. The suspension of some local authorities and municipalities by the government reflects its concern in the efficient management of the authorities.

The task of development or redevelopment of existing towns is a massive one especially with the objective of restructuring society. This task may not be best carried out by the government departments and or agencies who have not direct responsibility and control over the planning and development of towns. In Malaysia, the Urban Development Authority which was created under Act of Parliament No. 46 in 1971, has been specially charged with the function of urban redevelopment in line with the twin objectives of New Economic Policy. UDA, within the framework of the Third Malaysia Plan, will continue to contribute to the creation of a dynamic commercial and industrial Malaysian community consisting of a new breed of Malaysians living and working in unity. UDA will also try to increase the property ownership of bumiputras through land development, besides increasing the business participation of bumiputras in urban areas. (Bumiputra refers to "son of the soil" ie. Malays and other indigenous races.)

It is relevant at this juncture to mention the satisfactory increase of bumiputra business ownership in Kuala

NEW TOWNS IN MALAYSIA 323

NEW TOWNS IN MALAYSIA 323

Lumpur. In the long term, the equitable sharing of business and residential ownership especially in the Federal Capital as well as in other big towns would provide a sound and healthy footing in the social fabric of Malaysia's cosmopolitan society. Another successful example worth mentioning is the creation of Shah Alam, the state capital of Selangor, which was first started in 1968, which was initially developed by several government agencies but later due to sluggishness in its growth, the sole responsibility of developing the new town was transferred to State Economic Development Corporation (PKNS).

The Regional Development Authorities such as KEJORA, DARA, KESEDAR, KETENGAH and JENGKA are the closest vehicles to the New Town Development Corporation in United Kingdom in terms of organisational set-up. Thus, in Malaysia the establishment of separate authorities solely responsible for the development of new towns would certainly exert more cohesion and expedite development.

URBANISATION WITHIN THE CONTEXT OF THE NEW ECONOMIC POLICY

The New Economic Policy is a socio-economic policy designed to achieve national unity through two complementary and mutually reinforcing objectives of eradicating poverty irrespective of race, and restructuring society to eliminate the identification of race with economic function and geographical location. The poverty eradication programmes are aimed at improving economic conditions and quality of life of the poor by directly increasing their access to public facilities, and indirectly providing opportunities to participate in economic activities; while the programmes for restructuring society are aimed at creating a just socio-economic environment by assisting all Malaysians to find employment, secure participation and acquire ownership and control in all economic sectors.

What is sought under the New Economic Policy, therefore, is not only the improvement in economic welfare of every Malaysian, but also the visible reflection of the multi-racial composition of Malaysian society in its countryside and towns, farms and factories, shops and offices. Their achievement would ensure socio-political stability in a plural society.

The New Economic Policy which is to be the basis of subsequent development plans up to 1990, introduced new dimensions and meanings that extended further the scope and substance of Malaysian development efforts. Among other policy variables, it adopts urbanization as a development strategy to rectify both racial and a real economic imbalance in Peninsular Malaysia.

Urbanization and urban development in Second Malaysia Plan (1971-1975) is reflected in the following policy measures:

(a) Urbanising the rural areas by way of industrial dispersal in areas which have been almost exclusively devoted to agriculture and mining.

(b) Establishing "new growth centres" in agriculturally based areas.

(c) Exposing the rural inhabitants to urban environment by providing urban type services to check excessive urban drift.

(d) Improving facilities in existing urban centres to accommodate influx of rural migrants.

Under the Third Malaysia Plan, this strategy for urban development is reinforced by a policy of developing both existing towns and "new growth centres" designed to break up the polarisation of urban development in particular regions and spread it out to all regions. The aim is to ensure that the greatest number of people possible would benefit from urban growth through the opportunities created for an expanded range of jobs, services and amenities which large urban regions tend to provide.

MALAYSIA'S EXPERIMENT

Development of New Population Concentrations Within the Concept of New Growth Centres

For purpose of easier identification in the organising process of the regional development urban programme, it is seen appropriate in this part of the discussion to classify them into three levels of population organisation each of which corresponds directly to the levels of physical settlements:

(i)   Organisation of hierarchy of new towns within the
      context of the development project region.

(ii) Organisation of urban elements within a new town.

(iii) Organisation of physical elements within residential
      areas, commonly known as neighbourhood units.

      With this in view, Malaysia's experiment in organising
population concentration within the development region may be
seen through the three levels of organisational structure,
ie. firstly at Regional Level which is more related to the
economic and political objective of the government and should
reflect the objectives of the five year National Planning
(Malaysia Plan) and the New Economic Policy; secondly at
township level which is more of meeting urban programme objectives in providing urban environment to the primarily
agricultural population and thirdly at localised neighbourhood level which is primarily concerned to meet the sociological desires of the potential settlers into the region.

Population Organisation Within Regional Context

      A series of Regional masterplan studies has been carried
out during the last ten years in Malaysia, which have come up
with regional development Masterplans among which are the
Johor Tenggara Region (KEJORA) and Pahang Tenggara Region
(DARA); each occupies approximately 750,000 acres and
2,500,000 acres of land respectively and to be developed by
primarily public development agencies - DARA, KEJORA, FELDA
(the Federal Land Development Authority), MAJUTERNAK (the
National Livestock Development Authority), either direct or
by joint ventures and private sectors. Through years of
implementing these Masterplan proposals, much has been
learned about the relationship of this regional planning to
both national and urban planning. Techniques and methodology
of regional planning appropriate to Malaysian conditions has
slowly evolved, and it has been recognised through the five
year Malaysia National Plan that these three levels of planning cannot be separated. It has been identified that the
pattern of national development depends a great deal on the
outcome of regional development and at the same time regional
development depends upon the urban structure and its system
of development growth poles.

The opening of these new regions for agricultural, forestry and mining development has led to a comprehensive
organisation of population concentration through its urbanisation programme, for example, establishment and creation of
centralised settlements, new urban centres, tourist and industrial centres. The urbanisation strategy employed in
these primarily agricultural regions is to concentrate all
hinterland population in otherwise scattered and isolated
agricultural villages into centralised villages and new townships, where all urban amenities and facilities will be provided. It is a strategy to provide an urban environment most
attractive to the potential migrants into these regions from
other areas outside the project regions to fill up all the
employment opportunities created within the agricultural,
manufacturing, commercial and administrative sectors. Such
concentration of population will ultimately provide enough
support population for establishment of the new townships.
At what size and which level of socio-economic activities and
services expected to be established for the new townships,
together with how many of those townships can be established,
are some of the questions where definite answers have to be
found. Although each Masterplan has identified and proposed
these urban growth centres and villages, inevitably revisions
have to be made from time to time corresponding to changes in
agricultural development patterns, financial and manpower
resources and political decisions.

The Pahang Tenggara (DARA) and Johor Tenggara (KEJORA)
Master Planning Studies have identified and proposed a series
of urban growth centres and concentrated settlements aimed at
providing accommodation for the workers of surrounding plantations, consisting of the existing villagers scattered within
the region and the in-migrating rural population from outside
the region. This agricultural population base forms the
nucleus which will ultimately draw other types of population
in the form of generated workers as a result of development
of wider economic opportunities in secondary industries and
tertiary (services and adiminstration) sectors. The process
of organising the expected population within these regions
may be more easily clarified here physically in terms of
settlements.

Within the KEJORA region, the Masterplan proposed three
types of population concentration by 1990, ie. (i) two major
Service Centres (each with 14,000 and 30,000 - 50,000 popu-
lat:on); (ii) six large central villages (each with population between 1,500 and 5,000), and (iii) 30-40 large vil-

lages (each with less than 1,500 population). On the other
hand, Pahang Tenggara Region (DARA) by 1990 will have 36 new
towns consisting of a one regional centre of 50,000 - 100,000
population; ten centres having a population concentration of
15,000 - 50,000 each and 16 centres with 5,000 - 15,000 population and nine centres with less 5,000 population. The
ultimate total population is expected to reach 500,000 by
1990 and these figures are derived from total employment
opportunities which are expected to be in the range of
180,000 jobs to be created within the Pahang Tenggara Region
by 1990. These include 90,000 jobs in the primary sector,
and another 90,000 jobs in secondary and tertiary sectors.
Within the Johor Tenggara on the other hand, by 1990 its
population is expected to reach 400,000. This ultimate population includes population increase within existing towns,
namely, Kluang and Kota Tinggi located within the fringes of
the Johor Region and which has been foreseen by the Masterplan study to be potential regional and sub-regional centres
for the region with an expected 1990 population to be around
180,000 and 30,000 respectively.

The number, location and size of these population concentration centres have been determined by a prime concern
that distances to work should not be unduly long. This has
led to a certain reduction in the size of each settlement
hinterlands and thereby settlements with smaller population
size were inevitable. Comparatively, there is a great difference in the hierarchy of settlements in terms of size and
number between DARA and KEJORA settlement. This is due to
the different techniques in identifying each town's agricultural hinterlands which form the economic base of the centralised settlements, differences in the strategies of its
urbanisation programme, differences in the initial land
development programme by the implementing agencies and to a
large extent there are two different study groups undertaking
the two regional studies and again at different periods.

However, during the implementation period of those
Masterplan proposals, some revisions as to the number and
size of population settlement centres have been made. Some
settlements have been amalgamated to form larger towns, some
settlements have been deleted from the urban structure programme, and some new centres have been created. This is in
consequence of the various detailed urban studies undertaken
in formulating and establishing the detailed urban form of
settlements enumerated in the second part of this discussion.
(See Table 1).

Table 1. Population Concentration Centres Within Johore and Pahang Development Regions

1990 Projected Population	Pahang Region			Johore Region		
	Original proposal	Revised proposal	Not yet re-examined	Original proposal	Revised proposal	Not yet re-examined
Less 1,500	9	3	3	35–40	2	28
1,500– 5,000				6	6	
5,000–10,000	9	5	4	–	8	–
10,000–15,000	7	4	2	1	1	–
15,000–20,000	6	3	4	–	–	–
20,000–30,000	3	–	2	(1)*	–	1
30,000–50,000	1	1	–	1	1	–
50,000+	1	1	–	(1)*	–	1
Total number of towns	36	17	15	45–50	18	30

*Existing towns at fringe of the project region
Source: (i) New Towns – A Malaysian Perspective, Ho Khong Ming, 1977
        (ii) Town Planning Dept., KEJORA, Johore, 1979

The number of population settlements within the region, sizes of each settlement in terms of its ultimate population by 1990 and the functions of each settlement within the urban hierarchy depend largely upon (a) respective catchment areas of the hinterland, and its primary resources which determine the total workers to be concentrated, and (b) the size of its sphere of influence that it is able to command in order to support its urban components. The bigger its sphere of influence in terms of population thresholds, the higher the standard of its urban components that can be established. Its capability to command as wide a sphere of influence as possible depend upon its accessibility in terms of transport-ation and road network. In this context of new development projects all these factors are to some extent dictated by national policies. As the region was originally virgin jungle, the small scattered existing population is not an influential factor in determining the regional transport network.

(a) Hinterlands as used here refers to productive land resources capable of creating employment opportunities once exploited. Most of these resources whether primarily pro-ductive for forestry, agricultural or mining development are alienated into smaller units to various agencies. As such, most of the hinterland is delineated to contain a number of these alienated parcels of land and at times partly defined by geographical features like rivers, existing tracks, or swamps. Each hinterland so delineated is large enough to provide an economic base to establish a new town and not small enough to support establishment of a centralised settlement or a new urban centre. Daily need to travel from place of residence to the hinterland constitutes a major factor too in determining the location of the settlement. The acceptable maximum time to work is half an hour and this represents a distance of 7-15 miles by a normal motorised vehicle like trucks or motorcycles and through normal metalled roads. Travel distance from settlements to hinter-land will not normally be direct and this constitutes an element to be considered. This consequently will determine the size of hinterlands and thereby the size of population concentration in a particular settlement.

(b) Capability to command wider spheres of influence or attraction than any other settlement will determine the settlement's ultimate functions and its level within the urban hierarchy. Its strategic location along a regional or

sub-regional road for example will be able to command and
support regional or sub-regional activities such as supply of
luxury goods, wholesaleing, and a higher level of administrative, educational and social services like technical schools,
colleges, hospitals or district office. In such a case, in
addition to the resource-based population and the local
induced population, the town will be able to attract a more
complex regional and sub-regional induced population. A
study conducted by the Consultants for Pahang Tenggara
Masterplan provides a picture on the occupational structure
of some Malaysian towns as shown in Table 2.

Theorctically a great bulk of population in a town of
less than 5,000 would still primarily be engaged in resource-
based activities and this provides less opportunities for
creating non-resource based employment. Such a town can only
support, for example, a primary school and lower level of
health facilities. Only a town of 10,000 population would be
able to support a secondary school. It seems also that threshold level for a complete range of urban activities could
only be supported by a town with a population range of not
less than 15,000.

ii)   Second Level of Population Concentration - Township

While the first level of population unit is identified
physically through the distribution of settlements within the
context of the overall region, the second level here concerns
more on how this population within the concentrated unit
should be organised in such a manner that will permit optimal
provision of amenities and services. This involves organisation of every physical component of the settlement where the
ultimate population will be accommodated. Again here there
is an evidence of an identifiable hierarchy of population
concentration units where each and every level of population
unit is organised around the catchments of particular functions. Each unit will have its own entity in respect of its
function as illustrated in Table 3.

The Organisation and design of the 'housing cluster' and
'village' has been geared to emphasize creation of a strong
sense of local community identity. Within a housing cluster
of say 20 families, much of the social activities will be
focussed in and around the incidental open space or common
courtyard. Similarly, at a wider unit of population concen-

Table 2. Percent of Employed by Town Size and Economic
Activities in Malaysian Towns

	Less than 5,000	5,000-14,999	15,000-29,999	30,000-49,999	50,000+
Agricultural & other primary occupation	72.8	45.5	24.6	14.2	10.9
Secondary processing	2.8	6.6	6.3	8.2	4.4
TOTAL RESOURCE BASED:	75.6	52.1	30.9	22.4	15.3
Manufacturing	2.9	3.2	7.9	7.9	13.4
Utilities	0.4	1.0	1.7	2.0	2.2
Commerce	6.5	13.8	19.0	21.4	21.2
Transport/Storage	2.1	4.1	4.9	6.1	6.4
Services	10.0	22.2	31.3	34.6	35.7
Construction	2.3	3.5	4.7	5.5	5.8
Residual	0.2	0.1	-	0.1	-
TOTAL OTHER ACTIVITIES:	24.4	47.9	69.5	77.6	84.7

Source: New Towns - A Malaysian Perspective, Ho Khong Ming, 1977.

tration, a number of community facilities, like kindergarten, corner shops, surau (religious building) provide a focus for social and local community activity at a wider range of community. Location of a kindergarten would be such as to form a local focus close to local shopping facilities, open space and play areas and requires a catchment of 200-300 families.

At neighbourhood unit, a more comprehensive provision of shopping and social amenities is provided within the local

Table 3. Type of Settlement, Function and Population Size

Unit	Function	Population Size
1. Housing Cluster	cul-de-sac, incidental open space common courtyard	20 families 100 people
2. "Kampung" (Village)	surau, kinder-garten, corner shops, village centre	300 families 150 people
3. "Desa" (Neighbour-hood)	primary school, police post, local centre	850- 1,000 families 4,500- 5,000 people
4. "Pekan" (Smaller town)	town centre secondary school, health centre, mosque, post office, police and fire stations	1,700- 2,000 families 9,000-10,000 people
5. "Bandar"	town centre government offices, post office, mosque, police and fire stations, health centre, or hospital college	2,000+ families 10,000+ people

centres for a bigger catchment of community. Such facilities and amenities include provision of a primary school,community hall, adequate parkland, police station, etc. are located within the neighbourhood centre, which is generally not more than ½ mile from the outer limit of surrounding housing areas. Provision and location of these facilities is cen-tralised within the settlement to minimise journey lengths and its proximity for community use can be fully exploited.

Within the town and large village, sites for the pro-vision of principal administrative, religious, recreational

and social facilities for the community as a whole are provided. These will include government offices, secondary
schools, town mosque, health centre, library, post offices,
etc. A wider range of commercial facilities in addition to
basic shops and stalls, like market area, cinemas and shops
of specialised nature will be provided in the town centre.

The distribution and location of the various levels of
the above mentioned community centres in corresponding to
respective population catchment areas are such as to enhance
their role as the focal points of either commercial, social,
religious and administrative activity for the various levels
of the community. Each of the centres is located in the most
geographical centre of each community and closely related to
any roads serving the principal residential areas.

(iii) Third Level of Population Concentration-Neighbourhoods:

A third or lowest level of population concentration or
settlement corresponds more to organising a much smaller unit
of population settlement constituting from a localised residential area with say 20 families to larger units of 300-
1,000 families which may be termed as neighbourhood and sub-
neighbourhood units. A balanced organisation between physical components of the settlement and the sociological desires
and needs of the human elements within the settlement is a
prime concern to planners in achieving effective physical
plans for the urban programme.

Before contemplating any particular form of development
and the type of environment most appropriate and attractive
to the community, it is of prime importance for the planners
to know firstly the type of community likely to settle within
the settlement, secondly what are their needs, attitudes and
preferences, and thirdly, how can the settlement be designed
to match their needs, attitudes and preferences.

A number of social studies has been undertaken by the
Masterplan groups and it has been identified that the population of the new urban settlements within these two regions
will primarily consist of migrant population who are
villagers from existing rural villages outside the region.
They are either smallholders working on their own land or
agricultural labourers working on someone else's land earning
below $200.00 a month and majority from young Malay families
with 2-3 children.

These rural population are pressured to migrate either
to existing urban areas or to the new settlements, due to
lack of security in their own villages in terms of monthly
income, housing, land for small holding and wider educational
opportunities for their children. They have to leave their
villages in search of opportunities that provide better
income, and hopes for their children's education.

Their attitudes and preferences towards new settlements
are tied up with their close network of social and kinship
ties of a village community and the long tradition of living
in informal and low density settlement. Although they are
attracted with all the basic urban amenities like piped
water, electricity, paved roads, community facilities within
walking distances like health clinics, primary schools, shops
and markets, but the type of urbanised residential buildings
which consist of concrete, terrace or other regularised types
of buildings common in urban areas are something that they
are completely unfamiliar with.

Economic opportunities like additional income by participating in small business activities, engaging in poultry
and fruit farming besides working in the plantations, and the
physical environment with all the basic urban amenities and
facilities provided are the incentives most attractive to the
migrants. But the immediate social impact from their long
traditional rural environment to the unfamiliar urban
environment is something that they have to cope with and
something that planners have to be aware of in designing
proper residential settlements within the new town.

The above awareness has led to a concern for providing
an appropriate and balanced environment between recreating
the traditional rural village and eventual transformation of
urban settlement, most suitable to the new migrants. This
leads to the identification of the basic guidelines in the
planning of residential development at localised level:

(a) The need to maintain the original social characteristics
of rural societies by providing wide opportunities for face-
to-face relationships among each settler families. This
leads to a preference for cluster type of housing or grouping
of houses into units. Each cluster or unit comprises of
about twenty dwelling units at the most which enable each
settler family to know one another. The houses may be laid
out around a cul-de-sac, open space or common courtyard

instead of the traditional layout of a row of identical houses commonly fronting a street. Such a layout of grouping houses around a common space will provide a wider scope of immediate social, communal activity among the residents and create a sense of total belonging to the neighbourhood.

(b) The need to maintain the pursuit of traditional spare-time social activities common in villages. This can be achieved by the provision of spaces around the houses, where each house lots are large enough to allow for poultry farming, fruit and vegetable cultivation; this will help the migrants to supplement their diet as well as incomes. The sizes of housing lots range between 2,100 sq.ft. for terrace type, 3,500-4,000 for semi-detached type and 5,000-10,000 for detached type.

(c) The need to maintain the traditional marketing and shopping patterns as well as close and constant social interaction among housewives. Village housewives have to make daily trips to market because of the lack of any storage facilities like refrigerators available in the house, and it is in the market area that they have frequent contact with other members of the community. They also make frequent social visits to one another during their leisure time especially during the late afternoon. In order to facilitate such a need, houses are grouped as near as possible to the others and shops, schools, markets and other daily-used facilities are sited within proximity and walking distances. Here pedestrian and bicycle paths are strongly emphasized in the layout to provide easy, convenient and safe movement of the residents.

(d) The need to match the taste and preferences of the migrants towards the types of houses they preferred. From a number of social studies undertaken, it is found that preference for detached houses is more than other types, and those of a traditional Malay architecture, particularly on stilts than those on the ground level type. Thus, this leads to the building of more detached timber and semi brick-timber type of houses. Each regional authority is also contemplating building houses on high stilts especially in areas of steeper slopes.

The preferences of the future community in the new settlement mentioned above are not regarded here as planning constraints in the process of designing appropriate form of

residential settlement, but should be regarded as opportunities for creating an environment that is potentially
urban and at the same time to capture the character of a
traditional rural commuunity.

FELDA'S SETTLEMENT

Felda settlements are new villages built by Federal Land
Development Authority (Felda) in association with the opening
up of undeveloped land for agricultural development. This is
in response to the government objectives of providing the
landless rural population with a 1/4 acre house plot and
10-15 acres of agricultural plantation to each family either
for rubber or oil palm cultivation. The objective of Felda
is more of land settlement rather than urbanisation as in the
case of other Regional Authorities (KEJORA, DARA, KETENGAH)
etc. As a result, Felda settlements are naturally very rural
in character, with a fairly low residential density, lower
standard of physical infrastructure, and very limited employment opportunities.

Within the Felda settlement, each settler house is built
on a 1/4 acre lot of 1 chain by 2½ chains in dimension. Such
large house plots are provided so that the settler can engage
in other activities like poultry rearing, vegetable and fruit
cultivation during their spare time. This can supplement
further his sources of income. When his economic situation
improves, he can rebuild a bigger and better house on the lot
itself. Rebuilding and extension of original timber house to
a more superior type by the settlers is evident now within
the older and most established Felda settlements like those
in the Bukit Besar Complex in Johor.

Felda settlers are selected from those heads of family
who are married, 18-35 years old, up to 40 years for ex-
personnel of armed services, having no criminal records, and
owning not more than two acres of rural land or one lot of
urban land. These qualifications may have changed from time
to time depending on need and suitability. Suitability and
need are based on such criteria regarding health, educational
qualifications, special skills, occupational backgrounds and
family size. By the end of 1975, Felda had settled 35,000
families in its land schemes, and is expected to settle
around 5,000 families per year during the Third Malaysia
Plan. By the end of Second Malaysia Plan (1971-1975) Felda

NEW TOWNS IN MALAYSIA

had developed 721,000 acres of cropland in 167 land schemes and 110 village settlements. 80% of the areas developed are located in three states of Pahang (45%), Johor (23%) and Negeri Sembilan (12%).

Felda villages have been developed as isolated schemes and scattered throughout the country. Each village has an average population of 3,000 or 500 settlers. Each settler or head of the family selected to participate in the scheme is allocated ten to fifteen acres of agricultural plantation and a 1/4 acre house lot and a standardised timber house. The agricultural plantation allocated to the settlers within a scheme is at an average of 5,000 acres in total.

Characteristically, Felda villages are non-urban in nature by population size and by the standards of infrastructure provided which consist of laterite roads, provision of piped water by communal taps at one side of the road for the use of general houses and provision of toilets of pit latrine type. Electricity and solid waste or garbage disposal facilities are not readily available. Social services like primary schools, clinic, sporting facilities, shopping facilities are provided but limited to a lower level.

Because of a small population which is limited to between 200 and 300 families within each individual village, the development of higher levels of commercial and social services are therefore also limited. Most Felda villages become hinterland villages to nearby existing towns which may not be more than 8-10 miles away and connected by regular bus services. In such instances, Felda villages help to increase the growth rate of the existing towns and more specialised social and commercial facilities and services emerged within the existing towns. Felda villages on the other hand are not expected to grow to a stage where they can support higher type of tertiary services.

However, in recent years Felda has remodelled development of their settlements, especially those within the regional development areas of Pahang, Johor and Trengganu regions, in line with the government's policy of creating new growth centres in such areas. Examples of such settlements are the town 22 (Keratong) in Pahang Region and Bandar Mas in Johor Region. Each of these townships is an agglomeration of a number of Felda villages which ultimately will give a population of 5,000 to 10,000 which is capable of supporting the

338   H. MOH. BIN H. ABD. RAHMAN

urban amenities and services normally available in a town and
to generate employment opportunities in secondary and
tertiary sectors.

Prior to above urban strategy, Felda also endeavoured in
the development of new towns but this is confined to the idea
of servicing a number of Felda villages contiguously developed within their bigger project area like Jengka Triangle.
Jengka Triangle is a Felda land development project area
where typical individual villages of 300-400 families each
were established separately and distributed within large
acres of agricultural plantations. Each village has its
agricultural hinterland of around 4,000-5,000 acres. The
village is located in the centre of each agricultural hinterland. The advantage of these isolated and scattered villages
within the region is the convenience cf the settlers of not
having to travel a long distance to their plantation.

CASE STUDY: BANDAR TENGGARA

New Towns development in so far as it has evolved in
Malaysia and in other countries, has been primarily concerned
with providing overspill and regional development functions.
It is a concern to reduce congestion in existing large cities
and decentralise urban programmes to a lesser developed
region. Within the Malaysian context of new town development, it has gone further into the creation of what is known
here as new growth centres. These new growth centres were
established primarily to fulfil the requirements of the New
Economic Policy besides the above two roles.

Bandar Tenggara (South East New Town) is planned to meet
the above objectives and has been geared to the need of urbanising the rural people by exposing them to the urban environment. Located within the Johor Tenggara Project region, it
will perhaps be the first new growth centre to emerge from
virgin jungle in this southern part of Peninsular Malaysia.
It is planned to accommodate an estimated population of
15,000 by 1990 and ultimately its design is to cater and
service a population capacity of between 40,000 to 50,000.
It will be an administrative, commercial, cultural and distribution centre for the northern region of Johor Tenggara.
Its position as a regional centre will nevertheless be
strengthened with the recent State Government's intention to
designate Bandar Tenggara as an administrative centre for the
proposed new district of Kulai.

The urban structure and concept of the proposed Bandar Tenggara is focussed on the proposed regional road. This main regional road was used as a development spine for the new town. Connected at three points from this main regional road are the two main town distributory roads which form the main linkages between major land uses of the town. The town centre which will accommodate all the major social, commercial, and administrative facilities, is located at the intersection of the two town distributory roads and within immediate access to the regional road. A series of residential distributory roads radiate from the main town distributory road to serve the various residential areas and local centres throughout the town.

Foot and bicyle paths, well separated from vehicular routes, provide another system of access routes linking the residential areas to the town centre, local centre and major institutions like schools, clinics, hospital, and the 336 acres of industrial area. The industrial area is located to the northern periphery of the town separated from housing areas by a stretch of green belt and a main road.

River and stream valleys running through the town site were retained as much as possible in their natural state and continuously linked to the major town parks, playing fields and to the areas of jungle as well as the oil palm plantations surrounding the town site.

Housing requirements of the town were to cater for three settler groups consisting of those employed in the surrounding oil palm estates, the Felda workers employed in the Felda Oil Palm schemes, and those generated workers engaged in the industrial, commercial and administrative sectors. The housing areas will contain approximately 8,800 houses comprising of various dwelling types in a ratio of 37% detached houses, 17% semi-detached houses, 31% terrace and 13% flats the type of housing plots and its area are as shown in the accompanied table. These ratios are bound to change, and that in the early stages at least the greatest proportion of housing will be detached, with little higher density accommodation.

Varying dwelling types and plot sizes were to cater for the different social and economic levels of the town population to correspond to the differences in their capability to pay, and preferences for house types. This helps to diversify the community preferences for house types, and types of accommodation and living environment.

340 H. MOH. BIN H. ABD. RAHMAN

The pattern of residential development throughout the town is generally distributed in smaller groups of dwellings clustered around a particular function, as mentioned earlier. Residential Area Phase II as shown in the following illustrations provide the perspectives to the above idea:

Bandar Tengarra:
Illustration of Residential Area Phase II

Housing Units	Lot Size	Total Units	Acreage
Terrace	22' x 80'	2,749	110.0
Semi-detached	40' x 80'	1,692	125.0
Detached	80' x 100'	2,186	400.0
Flats (1 block)	40' x 200'	1,125	65.0
Total:		7,752	700.0

Housing Units and Services Allocation	Acreage
Residential	700.0
Educational	130.0
Town Centre	160.0
Local Shopping Centre	47.0
Industrial	320.0
Open Space/playing field	200.0
Parks	750.0
Roads (exclude Regional Road)	400.0
Other (cemetries, refuse disposal area)	64.0
Felda settlement	503.0
Total:	3,274.0

The first housing area programmed for development started in early 1976 where a total of 150 units of timber houses were built. Another 826 units of detached houses will be completed by the end of the year. At present there are about 1,200 people in the town, some living in temporary houses in the town and on the fringe of the town. Under the Third Malaysia Plan a total of 1,265 housing units are planned to be constructed. Ultimately these houses will be owned by the settlers themselves.

Initially the settlers in the town are workers in oil palm plantations in the nearby agricultural hinterland and in the timber complex. These workers are attracted to migrate and settle in our new towns because of the good prospects for earning higher income, ownership of shares in the KEJORA subsidiary companies they are working for, home ownership and better amenities for education and health, shopping and better physical environment. The environment of service and other industries will on the other hand provide new opportunities especially for their children, who will therefore not necessarily have to emigrate elsewhere to find jobs.

A family, where the husband and wife work in the oil palm plantation as estate worker and harvester can earn an average income of M$350.00 a month initially. Worker incomes will of course vary depending upon the price received for product and yields obtained. However, given the prevailing market price of palm oil and oil palm products and projected yield, the annual income of worker is expected to remain high, around M$7,200 per annum or M$600.00 average per month per family. (1 US dollar equals 2.2 Malaysian dollars).

Bandar Tenggara is our experiment in the application of a modern town concept, essentially based on British town concept. Bandar Tenggara is a town where initially occupational opportunities are agro-based and later on ancillary and other industries are expected to be established. New migrants are provided with a choice of job opportunities as the town grows. Through our system of home-ownership of various types of houses, the settlers would be residing and working in the town. Bandar Tenggara in this respect is self-supporting.

With regard to the age structure, the initial settlers are between the ages of 19 and 47. Most of them have an average of 3 children between the ages of 1 and 14. Although initially, the average settler's income is low but later with additional income that can be earned by other members of the family including wife and children who are anticipated to work in the industrial sector, the family income would be in the region of M$600.00 per month which is equivalent to salaries earned by clerks in government or private sector firms in towns in Malaysia. In fact some Felda settlers cultivating oil palm are earning an average of M$1,200 per month. They thus can be regarded as belonging to the lower middle class in the hierarchy of classes in Malaysia.

Although our first batch of settlers consists of Malays from
the more depressed areas of Johor, the list of candidates
whom we are now selecting consists of many non-Malays from
other parts of Johor. The application for establishment of
industries that we are now processing have both come from
companies owned by both Malays and Chinese or by Chinese-
Malay joint ventures. Allocation of houses, shop-houses and
industrial buildings is intermingled such that there would
not be any segregation among ethnic groups. With these programmes, it is hoped that Bandar Tenggara would have a
socially-balanced community.

As regards to the people's participation in the town
development, this has been limited to areas where it is most
economically feasible to undertake. Infrastructure facilities
and housing have been contracted out to private contractors.
The settlers will participate in the beautification programme
whereby they will be planting trees on a voluntary basis and
making their town beautiful according to plans prepared and
approved by the Authority. The 'Kelantan-style' to be adopted
in KESEDAR whereby settlers would be building their own
houses should merit further study. As this is a new project,
and evaluation of its merits and demerits is deemed to be
premature.

The management of the town demands a two-way flow of
communication between the authority and the beneficiaries who
are the settlers themselves. Their sociological desires and
their attitudes will have to be taken into consideration.
This communication has been effected through the establishment of the Town Committee which consists of the elected
members of settlers in the town.

Their activities range from organising social functions
to economic activities. It is also our policy that migrants
to the town should be able to improve their income level and
their standard of living from time to time. As their present
income is still low to enable any surplus income for investment directly and individually, they are now in the process
of forming a co-operative society for purposes of undertaking
business projects. These projects include managing a petrol
kiosk and workshop in the town and sundry goods store. They
are also contributing towards the running of a kindergarten
and have contributed some money towards the building of a
'surau' which is financed by KEJORA. The community is also
organising 'Rela' type vigilante corps to ensure security

within the town area. All these efforts are within the spirit
of 'gotong royong' and in the interest of community development. While we are certainly adopting western modernisation,
we are unfailing in preserving indigenous culture and morals.
This scheme can be likened to the concept of the Japanese
modernisation efforts after the Second World War which adopted western modernisation but at the same time preserving
their national moral values and traditions.

ADMINISTRATIVE PROCESS

As can be seen from the preceding outline, the nature of
the growth of towns in Malaysia, very few of which were consciously planned, has contributed, to a greater or lesser
extent, towards the imbalances in the disparity of income in
the regional context and along racial lines. The Government
is therefore under its New Economic Policy, endeavouring to
rectify these imbalances and to re-structure its society of
many races, which has hitherto been identified with vo-
cations. Urbanisation and the building of new towns commonly
known as "growth centres" form part of the strategy towards
achieving this objective.

The process of urbanisation, however, would require a
more intensified co-ordination between physical planning,
which is concerned with the design, growth and management of
the physical environment, with that of social and economic
planning. In this regard co-ordination between the three
levels of planning processes which are the national level,
the regional or state level and sub-regional or local level
would be complementary and imperative. At the national level
physical planning policies and programmes must conform to
national economic and financial constraints and social objectives; at the regional or state level development plans
(structure and local plans) must conform to and reflect
national economic and social objectives through a hierarchical network of related settlements; and at the sub-regional
or local level development plans, considered in much greater
detail, and principally urban in character must make provision, not only for the official development programme and
projects, but for all forms of human needs and activities,
much of it often informal, of a self-help nature, initiated,
planned and carried out by the people themselves. Towards
this end the Government in 1976 passed the Town and Country
Planning Act 76 which would place about 100 local authorities

spread over an area of 51,000 sq. miles in Peninsular
Malaysia by 1990 under proper planning and development control. The restructuring of local authorities in line with
the provisions of Local Government Act 1976 has been effected
in respect to some local authorities in some states in Peninsular Malaysia.

The enforcement of Local Government Act 1976 did not
include the new growth centres within the regional project
regions which are being planned, implemented and administered
by the Regional Development Authorities themselves. By virtue
of State Enactments passed in 1972, the authorities have been
vested with powers to administer and perform functions of
Town Boards apart from their multifarious functions including
the undertaking of agricultural, residential, industrial and
commercial activities. This was done with a view to expediting the processes of not only the planning and constructions
of the new towns but also the promoting and undertaking of
activities that provide the economic base for the towns.
However, in the process due adherence has been given to the
requirements of the Town and Country Planning Act 76 with the
co-operation of and in conjunction with the Department of
Town and Country Planning and State Planning Committee. In
this manner, it is hoped, that the objective of expediting
the implementation of the Regional Masterplans and the restructuring the local authorities will both be met in line
with the government's strategy for urbanisation.

CONCLUSION

In conclusion I might recall that the earlier direction
in the growth of towns was a contributory factor to the divisions prevailing in the social and economic structure of the
country. This is a problem of considerable magnitude and of
grave concern to the government. The May 13 Incident was
regarded as not just a manifestation of racial conflict but
of class conflict. In its effort to rectify this delicate
situation a new strategy for urbanisation was adopted. Under
this strategy a conscious balance is planned between the
processes of natural rural-urban growth and deceleration of
urban growth. The new towns or growth centres within Regional
Development projects form an integral part of this strategy.
Thus it is hoped that within the next decade or so the Malaysian society will have been restructured and fully integrated, strengthening further the foundation that will place
Malaysia amongst the more advanced countries of the world.

BIBLIOGRAPHY

Evans, Hazel, ed., 1972, New Towns: The British Experience,
    Charles Knight, London, for The Town and Country
    Planning Association.
Turner, Alan, 1978, "New Towns in the Developing World:
    Three Case Studies (Venezuela, Angola, Malaysia)", in:
    International Urban Growth Policies: New Town
    Contributions, Gideon Golanyi, ed., John Wiley, New
    York.
Second Malaysia Plan 1971-1975 (Kuala Lumpur, Government
    Printers 1971)
Public and Private Housing in Malaysia, 1979, Tan Soo Hai and
    Hamzah Sendut, eds., Kuala Lumpur: Heinemann
    Educational Books, Asia, Ltd.

Milton Keynes: Plan implementation - Lessons from experience

Lee Shostak and David Lock

It is now widely appreciated that the preparation of a "master plan" does not in any way guarantee the implementation of that plan. This understanding is manifest in a growing public awareness that the fate of many urban plans is a library shelf rather than an action programme. It is also apparent in the increasing frequency with which professional planners, and scholars, attend conferences to discuss the problems of plan implementation.

The purpose of this paper is to contribute to the debates which are underway in academic, professional and political circles about why plan implementation does or does not happen. It draws on the first twelve years of the efforts of the Milton Keynes Development Corporation to stimulate and manage the rapid urban development of a new city in North Buckinghamshire. In offering this contribution Milton Keynes is clearly an abnormal case from which to generalise. It is being developed under the auspices of the New Towns Act, which is implementation oriented legislation. Moreover, the new city is being developed in an extremely attractive location: sitting astride the M1 Motorway; served by the main-line railway from London to the North; and midway between London and Birmingham in the prosperous South East region of England.

Nevertheless, we maintain that there are important messages which can be drawn from the efforts to implement the Plan for Milton Keynes. In this paper we argue that rather than ignoring the New Towns Act analysts and professionals concerned with improving the implementation of plans in the

UK should look again at some of the salient features of this legislation. We also suggest that the nature of the Plan itself is an important factor in understanding why Milton Keynes is being developed rapidly, and successfully, today. Finally, there are factors which can be best regarded as style or philosophy which are aspects of the Milton Keynes Development Corporation's approach to the task of city building and we suggest these are also important.

We must emphasise from the outset, that we are not attempting to argue that Milton Keynes type planning solutions, or even new towns are appropriate responses to the problems resulting from rapid urbanisation in the Third World. That is a debate for another time with a very different agenda. We are suggesting, however, that there are lessons which can be drawn from the process of implementing the Plan for Milton Keynes which are of relevance to efforts to guide rapid urbanisation in many countries. Hence, the paper is structured as follows:

First, we consider the key characteristics of the legislative/administrative framework for Milton Keynes, particularly the New Towns Act, 1965. Second, we turn to a brief assessment of the Plan for Milton Keynes as a basis for an implementation programme. Third, we describe the impact that Milton Keynes Development Corporation's style or philosophy has had on the pace of implementation. Then we turn to consider the value of bipartisan political and financial support for the implementation programme and some of the characteristics of the financial framework for the new town which attract this bipartisan support. We than emphasise the importance of location among the reasons why implementation of the new town has proceeded at a steady pace.

We then describe a few of the major difficulties associated with the implementation machinery being utilised for Milton Keynes. Finally we outline criteria for the assessment of implementation machinery which could be utilised in the appraisal or establishment of implementation processes elsewhere.

THE LEGISLATIVE/ADMINISTRATIVE FRAMEWORK

Any appraisal of the key factors which have led to the implementation of the Plan for Milton Keynes must start with a discussion of the main characteristics of the institutional framework set up under the New Towns Act, 1966. The characteristics are as follows:

The Creation of a Special "Sunset" Organisation to Guide Implementation

When Central Government takes the decision to create a new town, the first task is to designate an area of land for development and offer ample opportunities for individuals to object. Normally, a public inquiry is called to consider objections that certain land is included in the "designated area". After the "designation order" is confirmed, (with the appropriate modifications), a special agency, called a new town development corporation, is created with the express "purpose of securing the laying out and development of the new town". Development corporations, with the consent of the Secretary of State, can generally "do anything necessary or expedient for the purposes of the new town and for purposes incidental thereto".

This special agency, therefore has no other responsibilities. Hence the agency attracts a particular calibre of individual who is interested in development activities. Their attention is not diverted by the problems of urban governance - delivering municipal services or even long term asset management as is the case with local government agencies. The development corporation staff concentrate all of their energies on actually guiding the development of the new town. This breeds a level of spirit perhaps even vision and certainly commitment which, in the opinion of many observers, actually helps to explain the success of development corporations. We shall return to this theme later in this paper.

The development corporation is a "sunset organisation". When the development of a new town is substantially complete, the development corporation is dissolved and the Corporation's remaining asset management responsibilities are transferred to "normal" local government agencies or the New Towns Commission, a publicly owned management agency. Thus, the development corporation has no vested interest in preserving its own future - it concentrates on the task of guiding the growth of the new town.

Land Acquisition and Disposal Powers

A new town development corporation has the power to acquire all land inside the area designated for the new city at existing use values. The development corporation can issue a Compulsory Purchase Order; in practice, the use of this power rarely proves necessary. Thus, the development corporation acquires the freehold of all land in the designated area suited for development. This places the Corporation in an extremely strong position when decisions are made about the land use, timing, and details of any development proposals. Of course, the Development Corporation does not actually perform the developer role in all circumstances; private housing, commercial and industrial developers often acquire sites from the development corporation. Nevertheless, it is almost impossible to proceed with a proposal for development in a new town without the agreement of the development corporation.

Without land acquisition and disposal powers, the development corporation's ability to guide the growth of a new city would be seriously limited. Yet, as we see in examining the rest of the characteristics of the new town development system, land acquisition and disposal powers are a necessary requirement to ensure effective implementation but not sufficient in themselves. The Community Land Act of 1976 for example, gave local authorities in Britain similar land acquisition and disposal powers. This legislation omitted several related powers, and diffused others and the Act was a failure.

Strategic and Detailed Planning Powers

One of the first tasks which a development corporation undertakes is to prepare a master plan. Planning consultants are usually commissioned. Before the plan is approved by the Secretary of State, it is normally necessary to hold a public inquiry to consider objections to the proposed pattern of development.

When the plan is eventually approved by the Secretary of State, it provides a firm basis on which detailed plans can be prepared. The development corporation then uses its power to apply for detailed planning permission for each project direct to central government and this is normally granted if

the proposals are in accordance with the plan. In Milton
Keynes, the net effect of these procedures is that the development corporation has the power to grant itself, and other
developers, detailed planning permission. Thus, the length
of time required in the normal cycle of consultations and
approvals for detailed planning proposals is dramatically
shortened. For example, an industrialist seeking to build a
factory in Milton Keynes has reached agreement with the development corporation, he can confidently proceed with detailed design work and commence construction without worrying
about whether land political considerations will delay or
abort his project.

In the exercise of these strategic and detailed planning
powers, the Corporation works closely with the local demo-
cratically elected councils. Agreement is almost always
reached before development proceeds. In considering these
arrangements, the most important factor is that the balance
of initiative is with with Development Corporation.

Powers to Capture the Increases in Land Value

The land which is acquired by the new town development
corporation is acquired at existing use, normally agricultural value. When the land is sold, or leased, the basis of
disposal is current market value for the proposed use. Thus,
this increased land value is not reaped by the individuals
who happened to own land in the designated area at the time
when the decision to build the new town was made. Instead
this "unearned income" is used to finance the basic fabric of
the city. Until recently, development corporations were
generally required to retain the freehold of non-residential
land in the new town and thus secured the further increase in
land values.

Powers to Borrow Funds for Development from the Exchequer

It is this power to finance the basic infrastructure of
the city with this increase in land value which provides the
security against which the development corporation borrows
funds from central government. Thus when allocating funds to
the new town, the funds are not simply public expenditure but
public investment in servicing land. Assets are being
created.

In the long run, although most certainly not in the short run the development of the new town normally provides a satisfactory rate of return on Exchequer investment. The basis of financial structure for the new town is the opportunity to capture the increased value of the land. Without this provision, it would prove to be extremely difficult to secure the long term finance which is so necessary for the successful development of the town.

The Location of Industrial Investment is Controlled by Central Government

The rapid development of Milton Keynes, as most new towns, has been fuelled by a steady stream of employment growth. In Britain, the location of large-scale "footloose" industrial and commercial operations is steered by Central Government as part of Britain's regional development policy. Generally, postwar regional policy has encouraged job-creating private investment to locate in the "development" areas in the North West and North East regions of England, Wales, and parts of Scotland. If companies could demonstrate that investment in these areas would be commercially or financially foolhardy, then the companies are allowed to invest in other specified growth centres elsewhere in the country, subject to detailed community plans. Those companies which can demonstrate that commercial/financial factors dictate a location in the South East, are encouraged to locate in Milton Keynes or in the other new and expanding towns in the region rather than in areas not scheduled for growth.

The substantial efforts made by new town development corporations in their attempts to attract industrial and commercial investment must not be minimised. Nevertheless, corporations are greatly aided in their efforts by central government's influence over the location of job-creating investment and the priority which the new towns have received. Without the policies restricting industrial development to selected locations, the rate of employment growth in Milton Keynes hence the rate of overall growth would be much slower.

The Board of the Development Corporation is Accountable to the Secretary of State, Not Local Vested Interests

The Secretary of State appoints a Chairman of the development corporation and between eight and ten other Board

members. This Board is accountable to the Secretary of State.
The Board includes members who, in their individual capacity,
are drawn from local government authorities involved with the
new town. Normally, however, the majority of the Board members are selected for their breadth of vision and experience
at guiding large scale activities.

Hence the Board of the Milton Keynes Development Corporation presently includes five local members and five members
drawn from outside the area including two international
bankers, and the leader of the Greater London Council. The
Board is an non-executive Board. Members normally spend one
or two days a month, on average, involved with the activities
of the Corporation. They concentrate on strategic policy
decisions and leave matters of tactics and execution to the
full time technical officers. The Chairman however, is more
fully involved; at Milton Keynes, the Chairman normally
spends at least two days per week on Corporation matters.

The Board is not required by law to gain the consent of
the local authorities to all major policies and programmes
for the new city. In practice, the Board and the senior
technical officers find it sensible to ensure that an effective working consensus exists between the Development Corporation and the surrounding local authorities. The creation of
this consensus, which is discussed further below, is something which is greatly helped by the fact that the Board is
appointed by the Secretary of State and acts generally with
his authority. Local vested interests, particularly the
property owners have considerably less power when a development corporation is created.

The Development Corporation Acts as a Catalyst

The Development Corporation acts as a driving force for
the development of a new city. It is a catalyst and does not
attempt to undertake all the development itself. For example,
in Milton Keynes, water and drainage services are the responsibility of the Regional Water Authority, schools and
roads are the responsibility of the County Council, leisure
facilities are the responsibility of the Borough Council, the
health services are the responsibility of the Oxford Regional
Health Authority etc. etc. Private industry provides the
bulk of the new employment in the area.

The Development Corporation's task is to create the confidence that the City's development will actually happen. In one sense, it is a big confidence trick, in that it is explaining to the main utility agencies that the demand for housing and industrial sites exist, explaining to the new industrialists that there are large numbers of people anxious to move to Milton Keynes, explaining to the new residents that there are plenty of jobs awaiting them when they arrive and cajoling the local government authorities to organise themselves to provide schools, health centres, and hospitals and the other facilities in anticipation of all the growth that is going to take place. All this must be done simul- taneously.

Thus, the legislative/administrative framework provides a strong basis for implementation. This framework relies heavily on the New Towns Act, 1965, but is nicely comp- lemented by the strands of industrial location policy. Yet, successful development requires many more ingredients.

QUALITIES OF THE PLAN FOR MILTON KEYNES WHICH EASE IMPLEMENTATION

Development plans can be evaluated from many perspec- tives - internal consistency, sensitivity to cultural and functional requirements, cost, political acceptability, and comprehensibility. We suggest that there is another criterion which can be utilised - whether the plan aids implementation. Neither of the authors of this paper were, in any way, re- sponsible for the preparation of the Plan for Milton Keynes; hence, we have no vested interest in defending its strengths and weaknesses. However, in our experience, and that of most of our colleagues at the Development Corporation, the Plan for Milton Keynes is highly "implementable".

The principal element of the city-scale structure is an irregular grid of dual carriageway roads intersecting at approximately one kilometre spacing. The roads run roughly in vertical and horizontal lines responding closely to the land form within a reservation of between 60 and 100 metres. With the exception of the city centre the Plan disperses employment areas throughout the designated area. Thus, the low key non-hierarchical road network complements a dispersed pattern of traffic-generating locations for industrial and office developments.

There are two other main structuring elements of the
city, both dictated by the existing topography and geography
but, nevertheless emphasised in the Plan. A system of linked
parkland follows the River Ouzel and the Grand Union Canal,
and extends for some ten miles through the east side of the
City and wraps around the entire northern boundary. Second,
the three existing towns, (Bletchley in the South, Wolverton
and Stoney Stratford in the North) provided the base of early
developments which was extended like the horns of a crescent
toward the centre in the first decade of the City's life.
The eleven existing villages in the area provided additional
foci for new development.

The Plan posited relatively low residential densities –
generally between 20 and 45 dwellings to the hectare. Rather
than impose a rigid hierarchy of neighbourhoods, "activity
centres" were dispersed throughout the City, generally adjacent to grid roads, at which were located local shopping,
schools, and health centres. Central Milton Keynes was planned as the "heart" of the City with major commercial and
office developments and a new railway station.

What are the characteristics of this Plan which aids
implementation? First, the Plan is pitched at the right
level; it is a strategic plan. It is a broad brush plan, in
current British terminology, more akin in its form of presen-
tation to a county structure plan than a detailed local plan.

The Plan outlines broad strands of the development
framework. Clearly the most important characteristics are
the citywide grid road network, the relatively low housing
densities, and the dispersal of employment areas. But the
Plan does not specify detailed design guidelines nor does it
demand a particular form of detailed implementation.

The strategic quality of the Plan strongly complements
the fact that it is also a flexible strategy. The Plan is
not arrogant; it is not tied to a particular set of economic
or social circumstances. This is important because Britain's
economic fortunes have taken a dramatic downturn between the
initial conception of Milton Keynes and today.

The Plan was prepared in an optimistic atmosphere. It
was expected that there would be dramatic increases in real
disposable incomes. Practically all families would own at
least one car, many would own two, and Milton Keynes would be

built during a period when the demand for more space, both inside and outside the home would be increasing rapidly. However, even with the apparent salvation being offered by North Sea Oil, none of these predictions have proved true. At best, the country has a sluggish economic future and the expectations about real increases in disposable incomes have, to a large extent evaporated.

There have been dramatic changes in social policy as well. When the City was designated, and during most of the 1970s, Labour Governments were in power. The Labour Governments emphasised the importance of rented housing and ensuring that Milton Keynes provided ample opportunities for the housing and employment needs of disadvantaged residents from inner areas. When the Conservative Government came to power in mid 1979, Government's concern with the problem of the disadvantaged gave way to a far greater emphasis on maximising owner-occupation and the use of private finance in development. Notwithstanding these fairly dramatic shifts in the economic and social environment in which Milton Keynes is being built, the Plan for Milton Keynes has proved sufficiently flexible to respond and accommodate these changes. It is this strategic flexibility which has made the process of implementing Milton Keynes considerably easier.

This flexibility is often manifest in the capacity of the Plan to accommodate minor, but significant changes in land use. The grid road system is not hierarchical and presumes relatively even distribution of traffic generating activities throughout the City. When combined with the relatively low density of Milton Keynes and the dispersal of employment areas, it is possible to change a particular grid square or a part of a grid square from one land use to another without disrupting the integrity of the Plan. This is an extremely valuable attribute. It means that the Development Corporation can adjust the land use patterns to reflect the demands of the industrial marketplace, detailed investigation of site requirements, or the changing economic environment.

The best example of how this flexibility is utilised is the way that the land use proposals for the sites around the attractive Linford Wood area have evolved. Initially, these sites were seen as housing areas. However during the early years, it became clear that the demand for campus office sites might be substantial and that these areas overlooking

the Wood but easily accessible to both Stantonbury Education
Campus and shopping in Central Milton Keynes might be extremely attractive locations. Hence they were earmarked for
office development. However, the demand for campus offices
has not materialised and the current thinking is that these
sites should be used for higher quality purpose-built industrial developments, and possibly, advance factory units.
Part of the site may actually be developed for housing as
well.

The third characteristic of the Plan which has eased
implementation is the fact that the Plan is policy based. At
the outset, the Development Corporation and the consultant
planners organised a series of goals seminars. These seminars
about housing, education, social development, leisure, transport, etc. served as a focus for a reasonably systematic
examination of the policies on which the Plan for Milton
Keynes was based. The results of each of these policy analyses was published along with the Plan for Milton Keynes in a
volume of detailed studies.

For example, the analysis of housing policy concluded
that the objective of building a city which reflected the
national balance between owner-occupation and rented accommodation was desirable. However, in the early years of the
City's growth it would prove extremely difficult, because
many of the City's new families, being young and with little
savings, could not afford to purchase their own home. Yet,
as a result of this examination of housing policy, an important policy commitment emerged: that all housing built in the
City should be suitable for eventual owner-occupation. Similar analyses covered transport, retailing, leisure, employment, community facilities and several other subjects.

These policy analyses acted as a firm basis on which the
physical development strategy could be prepared. Moreover,
these studies served as a useful basis for an on-going programme of policy review to ensure that detailed development
plans were modified as expectations about the future changed.
Again, this policy framework eased the process of implementation because the Development Corporation did not have to
respond to winds of social and economic change. Instead it
has had a reasonably clear, and up to date understanding of
the social and economic basis of urban life in Great Britain.

The fourth characteristic of the Plan for Milton Keynes
which has eased implementation is that the Plan minimised the

firm commitments which the Development Corporation would have
to make in the early years. Obviously, as soon as the preliminary earth moving contract is let for the first roads and
drainage works, one is embarking on commitments which are
difficult, or at least expensive, to override. Yet the Plan
for Milton Keynes held the number of these preliminary commitments to a minimum.

For example, the Implementation Strategy dictated that
three major east-west lengths of grid roads and two major
north-south grid roads would be constructed as early as possible. However, after this "ladder" was complete, the pace of
additional road construction could be directed solely by the
intensity of demand for new sites. If the Plan had a hierarchical structure, it is likely that the Corporation's commitment to further construction would have been far greater.

Finally, the Plan has certainly facilitated implementation in that it has provided a firm basis for a sustained
Government covenant behind the development of Milton Keynes.
If the Plan had been too conservative in tone, or too socialist, changes of government might have prompted a call for a
reappraisal or fundamental review of both the policy framework and the physical development proposals for the new city.
This, of course, would have been extremely disruptive and
could have easily injured the successful development of the
city.

Throughout this paper we contend that the major task of
the Development Corporation is to create, and sustain confidence of all authorities concerned that the City is actually
going to be developed. Part of the effort to sustain this
confidence entails sustaining the commitment of central
government both at a political and a technical level. An
important ingredient in the confident working relationship
between the Corporation and Central Government has been their
agreement that the Plan for Milton Keynes is a firm basis for
developing the City.

This was particularly apparent in the discussions which
took place between the Development Corporation and the Labour
Government in 1976 and 1977 following the increased political
concern about the inner city. The discussion resulted in
Peter Shore's modification of the long term population target
for the city from 250,000 down to 200,000 but asked the Corporation to maintain the rapid rate of development. The Plan
for Milton Keynes was acceptable to the Labour Government in

ideological terms, and was sufficiently relevant ten years
after the designation of Milton Keynes to provide the Corporation with a firm basis for the debate with the Government.
Without the basis of a firm and clearly acceptable Plan, it
would have been much more difficult to justify the sustained
rapid growth of Milton Keynes.

Yet, in expressing admiration for the "implementability"
of the Plan in this way, we must differentiate between the
Plan for Milton Keynes and the substantial efforts that the
Development Corporation mounts in the preparation and updating of what is called the City Implementation Programme. In
fact, it is the recognition of the difference between the
issues appropriate for inclusion in the Plan, and the much
more detailed matters considered in the City Implementation
Programme which is a key ingredient in the effectiveness of
the planning of Milton Keynes. The first City Implementation
Programme prepared in 1970 provided detailed completion targets, and site by site, scheme by scheme schedules, for every
road, drainage, industrial and housing scheme in the following seven years of the City's development. This programme
required constant updating and rolling forward. A new seven
year programme was prepared in 1977/78.

This City Implementation Programme provides the firm
basis for the detailed planning, design, and construction
process. Without the Programme or techniques which performed
a similar role, the pace of the City's development programme
would be considerably reduced. In practical terms, the City
Implementation Programme has had as great an influence on the
development of the City as the Plan itself.

THE MILTON KEYNES DEVELOPMENT CORPORATION'S "DEVELOPMENT
PHILOSOPHY"

In our view an "implementable" plan, and a legislative/
administrative framework which encourages rapid implementation do not, in themselves, explain why Milton Keynes is
being built today.

We suggest that it is also useful to draw attention to
another set of institutional factors which are not outlined
in the New Towns Act 1965, or in the administrative codes, or
in the Plan. For lack of a better term, we shall describe

these factors as the Development Corporation's "development philosophy".

The Milton Keynes Development Corporation's "development philosophy" has several important strands:

1 The prime objective of the Development Corporation is "to get the place built" as quickly as possible and to the highest possible standards;

2 The Corporation undertakes development, whenever possible, in a way in which the initial investment in infrastructure and buildings can be recaptured and a profit earned but financial objectives are not paramount;

3 Whenever possible, development policies for Milton Keynes emphasise politically (or ideologically) "centrist" or neutral values;

4 The Corporation finds it effective to build a consensus with the other Government Agencies - conflict or confrontation strategies really do not work;

5 Multi-disciplinary professional teams are effective;

6 The Corporation believes it must build an informal but real "partnership" with the construction industry in Milton Keynes;

7 The Corporation believes it must create a confident environment for private investors -

Together, these strands of the Corporation's "development philosophy" summarise the hidden rules which guide how the Corporation approaches the task of guiding the development of Milton Keynes. Each of these strands is briefly described below.

At first it appears unnecessary to note the prime objective of the Corporation is "to get the place built as quickly as possible and to the highest possible standards" but this point must be emphasised for two reasons. First, many large urban developments are undertaken by organisations with many other tasks in addition to building a new town. We would suggest that this inevitably results in a less effective approach. Second, MKDC is single-minded in another way:

maintaining the momentum of the development programme is paramount. From time to time, this emphasis on the programme means that corners are cut in design, or the financial terms offered by a private investor are not as favourable as they could be if the Corporation went back out to the marketplace to secure a new offer. Yet the overriding principle is that the pace of the city's growth must be maintained at a steady rate.

It is also important to emphasise that MKDC undertakes development in a way in which the initial investment in infrastructure can be recaptured and a profit earned but financial objectives are not paramount. The facility to borrow long term funds (not grants) from the Exchequer enables the Development Corporation to maintain high standards of industrial and commercial construction and landscape even if this restricts the financial return on a particular scheme.

This tempering of commercial responsibility with social and environmental concerns is most apparent of course, in the new shopping area at Central Milton Keynes. The justification for this strand of the Corporation's development philosophy is quite straightforward - the physical environment being created in the new city will exist for at least a century. Whenever possible it was felt that the standards of the new development should not be compromised to maximise short-term financial gains.

Any new town development programme is based on a set of social and economic policies which, in turn, are based on a set of values. These policies/values may be socialist or capitalist, egalitarian or inegalitarian, oriented to maximising public goods or private goods etc. etc. From the outset, the Milton Keynes Development Corporation has pursued centrist and neutral policies. Thus maximising social balance, using a mix of public and private investment for industrial and commercial development, securing a balance between housing for sale and housing for rent are all "middle-of-the-road" policies which the Corporation pursues. This enables the Corporation to respond to changes in central government policy extremely effectively and quickly without either appearing to be inconsistent or jeopardising the pace of development. Conversely there is little room in the Corporation's policies for extremism either toward the left or the right.

A clear, and important part of the Corporation's development philosophy is the belief in the need to build and sustain an effective working consensus with all of the other public agencies which contribute to the development of the new town. Thus cooperation is required from the County Council, the District Council, the Regional Water Authority and the Regional Health Authority, and many other smaller agencies.

In the mid 1970s the Government permitted the Development Corporation to reimburse the County Council for the costs resulting from the "undue burden" which the rapid development of Milton Keynes places on the services, particularly education, provided by the County Council. The facility to make these payments, of course, contributes to an effective working relationship with the County Council, as does the rapidly expanding base for local taxes (rates) created by the new town.

In practical terms, without the effective cooperation of the other public agencies, Milton Keynes would prove difficult to build. While the Corporation has direct access to Exchequer funds, and has strong planning powers, progress of the development programme can be delayed by the County Council, the Regional Water Authorities, and the local District Council if they choose to do so. Thus, conflict or confrontation strategies are not very effective and the Corporation rarely, if ever pursues head-on confrontations with other public agencies. This strand of the Corporation's development philosophy is compatible with the overriding importance of maintaining the momentum of the growth of the city.

The advantages of consensus building strategies are also reflected in the Development Corporation's internal organisational structure as well. While many development agencies are divided according to professional disciplines, at Milton Keynes, multi-disciplinary project or area teams have been created. These teams are then each asked to assume responsibility for a particular part of the city. Thus, inter-professional conflict is normally "internalised" within these professional teams. More constructively, this method of working enables the architects to better understand the commercial surveyor's problems and vice versa. This emphasis on multi-disciplinary project teams has been sustained through several changes in Corporation structure.

Another strand of the development philosophy is that it
is necessary for the Corporation to establish an effective
working, albeit "arms length", relationship with a series of
private construction companies. In fact, the Corporation has
to encourage the formation of a contracting resource and
labour force in the area. While private construction companies are required to tender for practically all capital
projects in the new city, the Corporation draws up selected
tender lists, and endeavours to ensure that contractors which
have made a commitment to Milton Keynes are offered the
opportunity to bid for a steady stream of projects. Also,
construction workers, both skilled and unskilled, who wish to
settle in the area are offered priority in the allocation of
housing.

The final strand of the Corporation's "development philosophy" is that it is necessary to create a climate of confidence for private investors and private companies to invest
in the new towns. In a mixed economy like that of Great
Britain in the 1970s and 1980s, the private sector normally
provides the bulk of the investment for commercial, industrial, and leisure facilities. While it is easy to conclude
from the Corporation's public relations brochures, that the
Corporation assumes responsibility for all aspects of urban
life in Milton Keynes, this would be the wrong conclusion.
Without massive investments from industrial and commercial
companies seeking to expand in Milton Keynes, the City would
fail.

The creation of this confident climate in Milton Keynes
for private investors has taken several years. This effort
entails striking the right balance between publicity and
performance. It is, of course, easy to raise expectations
about the quality of life in Milton Keynes, and then fail to
provide the homes, factories, and leisure opportunities. In
fact, it is also possible to "underpromote" the City and not
attract the variety and diversity that private investors
bring to a new city. There is no simple formula for the
creation of a confident environment for private investment.
Yet, it is a bit like an elephant - you know when it walks in
the door.

BIPARTISAN POLITICAL AND FINANCIAL SUPPORT

A strong legislative/administrative framework, an excellent strategic plan, and a Development Corporation with an

action style are important ingredients in the formula which
has led to the implementation of Milton Keynes. Yet, this
success must be seen against the backcloth of bipartisan
political and financial support which the British new towns
movement has earned over the past three decades.

It must not be assumed that this support for new towns
has always existed; the designation orders for many of the
first generation of new towns were often surrounded by heated
public controversy. Even today, many British citizens find
the notion of living in a new town a slightly distasteful
idea. Substantial professional debates have also raged about
the quality of architecture and planning in the new towns as
well.

Notwithstanding the early controversy, the new towns
acquired and maintained a substantial degree of bipartisan
political and financial support. As long as both natural and
planned decentralisation of population and industry from
Britain's cities was an idea in good currency, both Labour
and Conservative Governments found that the balance of advantage lay with the support of the new towns. Of course, in
the late 1970s the apparent stabilisation of the size of
Britain's population, and the sluggish economic future (notwithstanding North Sea Oil) caused both parties to start to
question the need for a continued large programme of investment in new towns.

In the current climate, the task of ensuring the continuation of bipartisan support for the new city has fallen
firmly on the shoulders of the Development Corporation itself. It is important to emphasise that in a period when
both political parties are mounting strong efforts to reduce
public expenditure, the task of maintaining public support
for Milton Keynes (or any public project) often consumes
considerable energies.

Thus, stressing the role of Milton Keynes as a centre
for national economic growth dominates the discussions with
Conservative Government Ministers. While the Labour Government was interested in the city's role as a centre for employment growth, they also sought assurances that London's
disadvantaged were also given every opportunity to move to
Milton Keynes.

Quite naturally, the extent of political support often
dictates the extent of financial support which the Government

offers new towns in general, and Milton Keynes, in particular. The relationship is however, two sided. Substantial
financial support often brings a commitment of strong political support. Ministers are normally quite reluctant to withdraw support quickly from a project which has received substantial public funds.

The financial framework which has evolved for new towns
like Milton Keynes is a particularly appropriate vehicle for
attracting bipartisan political support. A (relatively)
steady stream of Exchequer capital is made available to each
development corporation on the basis of one-year and five-
year capital expenditure bids. While there may be periodic,
and substantial hiccups in the availability of Exchequer
capital, development corporations' normally have a reasonably
clear idea of how much cash is likely to be available over a
two year period. This obviously aids forward planning for
development projects.

While space does not permit a detailed review of the
financing of Milton Keynes, it is important to note that, in
certain circumstances, the financial structure for a new town
can ensure that development is "self-financing". With land
being acquired at "existing land value" and then sold or
leased at "market value", there is scope for the development
corporation to recapture the full costs of providing services
sites. Of course, when land acquisition and infrastructure
costs are rising and property values remain stagnant, the
scope for full cost recovery may be dramatically reduced.

In fact, the 1970s have been dominated by just those
conditions and the short and medium term financial prospects
for Milton Keynes have dramatically worsened as a result of
the stagnation in land values relative to construction costs.
The difference between a new town like Milton Keynes and a
privately developed new town is that in such an economic
climate, the private developer would have terminated his
operations. Yet with the complete financial and political
support of the Government, the Development Corporation has
continued to develop Milton Keynes even though the "break-
even point" has receded.

One reason, of course, that central government is not
overly concerned about the Development Corporation's short
and medium term financial prospects is that every individual
industrial and commercial project is, in its own right, mod-

erately profitable. Every advance factory and office development must, from the outset, show a satisfactory return on
the capital invested. A second reason is that the bulk of
the Corporation's capital is borrowed over sixty years from
the Exchequer at interest rates prevailing at the time the
loan is taken out. Thus, the Treasury reaps the subsequent
benefit of repayments of loans with high interest rates long
after market rates fall. Nevertheless, during periods of
high inflation and low economic growth, a long term perspective on new town finance is essential.

LOCATION, LOCATION, LOCATION

    It should be clear by this point that the institutional
system, the plan, and the politics are all conducive to the
development of Milton Keynes. However, without its favoured
location midway of London and Birmingham and astride the M1
motorway, the mainline railway to the North West, (and the
Grand Union Canal) the implementation of Milton Keynes would
have occurred at a much slower pace. The Development Corporation's General Manager, Fred Roche often stated that "we
have to be bigger fools than we are, not to have made a success in our location."

    Located on the edge of one of Europe's most prosperous
regions, and within four hours drive of over half of the
population of England and Wales, it would have been difficult
to find a more attractive location for the construction of a
new city. Yet, as an indication of the Corporation's concern
about the need to make a good location perfect, the Corporation is anxious to remedy a serious weakness - access to
Heathrow Airport. Thus, an application has been made for a
direct helicopter service between Heathrow Airport and Milton
Keynes.

    Most of the Corporation's publicity brochures enthuse,
in great detail, about the locational advantages of Milton
Keynes and we have no wish to duplicate those messages here.
Let it suffice to say that the city's location is excellent,
and it will be even better if the direct link to Heathrow
Airport "takes-off".

PROBLEMS WITH THE CURRENT IMPLEMENTATION MACHINERY

    The first, and most important problem with the current
development system is that, in a slow growth economy, the

momentum of the city's development is extremely fragile. Without a reasonably sustained, sometimes frenetic, effort to maintain the consensus on the need for further development, the pace of the city's growth could quickly slow down to a crawl. Building this consensus amongst central government, the various local authorities, private financial institutions, and the market place at large, proves to be extremely expensive. A substantial proportion of the senior officers' time in the Development Corporation is spent on building and maintaining this consensus.

This is surprising. One would expect a high proportion of time would be spent on this task in the early years of the city's growth. However, twelve years after Milton Keynes was designated one would expect that other agencies would accept that the future growth of Milton Keynes is a fact of life. Unfortunately, when public sector capital and revenue resources are extremely scarce, there are many factors which mitigate against other public agencies or private institutions accepting the continued need for more investment in Milton Keynes.

Moreover, when there is little real growth in the industrial and commercial sectors of the economy, the task of continuing to attract new employment to Milton Keynes is also expensive. By early 1980, over 26,000 additional jobs had been created in Milton Keynes, and there was a reasonable level of awareness about the new city throughout the country. Nevertheless, it was still widely felt in the Corporation that a sustained effort would have to be mounted through at least the mid-1980s to continue to attract new industrial and commercial employers to the City. Without this constant, and substantial, promotion effort, it was felt that the flow of employment creating investment which is necessary to fuel the continued population growth of Milton Keynes would be reduced.

Thus the political consensus necessary to secure continued public sector investment in Milton Keynes is fragile and the market place confidence necessary to fuel future employment growth in the City also requires constant attention. While in themselves the costs of this effort seem high, when considered against the overall costs of mounting a development like Milton Keynes the "consensus maintenance" and promotion costs seem reasonable. Perhaps this is not a

problem with the development system per se, but is inevitable
in a stagnating economy verging on an era of de-industrialis-
ation.

The second main problem follows from the first. From
time to time the Corporation fails to encourage other public
agencies to make the necessary capital investments sufficiently early enough in the life of the city. The most
conspicuous delay in Milton Keynes has proved to be the District Hospital and, for many newcomers, the absence of the
hospital has been of immense concern. As a result of sustained pressure at the highest levels of Government, the
construction of the hospital has commenced. Nevertheless, a
key weakness in the implementation machinery as it now stands
is that when another public agency fails to construct an
important facility, or delays construction it is normally
impossible for the development corporation to fill the gap.

The final weak link in the development machinery as it
now stands is that the quality of life in a new city, as in
most communities, depends as much on the quality of health,
education, welfare and transport service provision as on the
quality and amount of capital investment in the facilities
from which these services are provided. Obviously, quality
of service and capital investment are related but a high
quality service does not necessarily follow from a high level
of capital investment.

For example, in Milton Keynes, the public transport
service is still regarded as quite inadequate notwithstanding
the substantial investments in new vehicles and depot facilities. Moreover high operating speeds/low operating costs are
also being achieved on the grid road system. Staff-management
relations in the bus company serving Milton Keynes are not
good (as is the case in the bus industry generally) and this
is felt to be the major reason for the unsatisfactory level
of service.

From our perspective, such weak links in the implementation machinery for a new town like Milton Keynes are inevitable. The alternative, asking a development corporation
to assume more direct responsibilities for the development of
facilities and the delivery of services, is both politically
unacceptable, and probably, unworkable.

CRITERIA FOR THE ASSESSMENT OF IMPLEMENTATION MACHINERY

In the introduction to this paper, we suggested that there are important messages which can be drawn from the efforts to implement the Plan for Milton Keynes. We have not attempted to argue that Milton Keynes-type planning sol- utions, or even new towns are appropriate responses to the problems resulting from rapid urbanisation in the Third World. Rather than summarise the messages which can be drawn from the Milton Keynes process, we feel it would be more helpful to draw out a set of criteria which can be used to appraise or establish implementation processes elsewhere. These criteria are as follows:

a)   Does one agency have prime responsibility for guiding implementation?

b)   Is the prime implementation agency (PIA) responsible for:
     - Land acquisition and disposal?
     - Basic infrastructure?
     - A programme of residential and industrial/commer- cial development?

c)   Is a steady stream of "public sector" capital available to the PIA as long term loan finance?

d)   Is the PIA allowed to capture the increased land value resulting from urban development in order to repay long term loans?

e)   Is the strategic plan guiding development:
     - Flexible?
     - Policy based?
     - A basis for a government covenant?

f)   Are the social and economic policies governing the de- velopment attractive to the major political interests?

g)   Is it the right location?

We would suggest that both analysts and practising plan- ners might use these criteria in considering the strengths and weaknesses of implementation processes in rapidly devel- oping countries.

Britain's New Towns:
How riches and success confound
communication

Ray Thomas

This paper is about the failure to translate many of the
benefits of Britain's new town experience for urban planning
elsewhere in Britain and the rest of the world. It gives a
diagnosis of the causes of this failure and attempts some
prescription. Finally, it aims to discuss the implications
in terms of the need for decentralised information systems as
a background to training programmes for people involved with
human settlement development.

I have no apologies for concentrating on the British
experience. One reason is that I only know in any detail
about the experience of this country. But more important,
Britain's experience appears to be parallel to that of other
countries. Like Britain, other countries also have appeared
to have rejected new towns after experiment and experience.

This rejection is puzzling. New town development is, or
should be, about rapid orderly growth. Most countries in the
world face the problems of accommodating rapid growth, and
would like to make it orderly in form. Why, then, is the new
town experience rejected? Usually, we learn from experience.
So what are the implications for urban education and training
if experience is rejected?

My answer is that this failure reflects the public image
of the new towns. This image in turn reflects the fact that
building new towns is a confidence trick. Building new towns
requires cooperation and coordination in the activities of
many different kinds of agencies, both from the public and

private sector. If everybody believes it will happen, then
it will happen (see Roche, "Building A New Town").

The image building activities of development corporations and the supporters of new town building stress therefore the prestige aspects of new town development. So there
is emphasis on a high standard of planning, good architecture, high income housing, environmental concern, social
balance and so on. The image builders or communicators of
new towns derogate or ignore other aspects of new town development such as, site development, drainage, sewerage, centralised planning, planning combined with implementation and
most important of all, economics.

This process of selective image building began even
before any new town in a modern sense had been started. The
first edition of Ebenezer Howard's book in 1898 was entitled
"The Peaceful Path to Real Reform." The next edition in 1902
was called "Garden Cities of Tomorrow." The change in title
is reflected in the balance of the content. The original
edition is predominantly concerned with urban economics, land
reform and transport and how these reforms could be achieved
without a revolution. The emphasis had shifted away from
these matters sufficiently in the second edition for it to
become a blue-print for physical development.

Figure 1, The Vanishing Point of Landlord's Rent, is one
of the diagrams which was included in the 1898 edition but
not in the 1902 and subsequent editions. It shows how Howard
envisaged that the new town would act as a means of redistributing income and wealth from landlords in the city to
residents of the new town through communal ownership of property in the new town. Furthermore, the new town itself could
become an agency for providing welfare state benefits such as
old-age pensions. This example illustrates that one of
Howard's major concerns is fairly independent of income level
or stage of industrialisation. The ideas expressed in this
figure are more relevant to the experience of many third
world countries than to Britain of the 1980s.

In 1976 Britain, among other nations of the world, approved a series of recommendations for national action formulated at the United Nations Habitat Conference on Human Settlements, one of which stated:

Fig. 1. The Vanishing Point of Landlord's Rent from "Tomorrow: a Peaceful Path to Real Reform," 1898.

"... The unearned increment resulting from the rise in land values resulting from change in use of land, from public investment or devision or due to the general growth of the community must be subject to appropriate recapture by public bodies (the community)..."

There was no apparent acknowledgement in approving this Resolution that the new towns had been successfully capturing the "unearned increment" resulting from change in use of land, from public investment and from population growth over a period of thirty years. Yet, in the same period, there were in Britain at least four major unsuccessful attempts to capture this "unearned increment" by legislation and machinery operating outside the new town areas. At the same time as Britain's representatives were approving this Resolution in Vancouver the new town programme in Britain was being cut back, the designated populations of existing new towns was reduced, and it became apparent that it was unlikely that any new new towns would be designated in Britain in the foreseeable future.

The new towns themselves have also played down their economic achievements. You don't get anything for nothing, and the fact that new town development corporations acquire land at near agricultural land prices is the counterpart of the necessity for heavier infrastructure than would normally be undertaken with development at the periphery of existing urban areas. It is pertinent to note, therefore, that even in the financial accounts of the new towns development corporations, matters like sewerage and drainage are often kept separate. There may be good administrative reasons for this separation, but it is difficult to avoid the suspicion that development corporations don't really see such schemes as part of their prime function of building new towns.

If the central government and new town development corporations play down some aspects of their development it is hardly surprising that other commentators and publicists do likewise. Alonso, for example, managed to write a quite influential study "What Are New Towns For?" without mentioning their economic or income redistribution functions. The Town and Country Planning Association, the main propagandists for new towns in Britain, also missed out these aspects in their book entitled "New Towns: The British Experience."

There is no need to pile example upon example from the experience of Britain or that of any other country in the industrialised world. The distortion of the new town image has also influenced the nature of the export of the new town idea to third world countries. Because the prestige aspects of new town development are emphasised in Britain, the most common application of the new town idea in the rest of the world has been in the construction of prestige capital cities like New Delhi, Brazilia, Chandigarh, Islamabad, Dodoma in Tanzania, and Abuja in Nigeria. The construction of these capitals with their grand public buildings, their high income housing for civil servants and their slow and costly growth has, at least in the past, been associated with a rejection of the new town idea as a solution to the main urbanisation problems of the countries in which these capital cities are situated.

It would not be true of course to suggest that there has been no transfer of knowledge from the experience of building new towns to the benefit of other forms of urbanisation. Staff in development move easily from new town organisations to other kinds of agencies concerned with urban development or planning, both within countries and between countries. There have also been many attempts to transfer or sell knowledge derived from the practical aspects of new town development. Many planning consultants in Britain have obtained contracts in other parts of the world partly on the basis of expertise developed in the context of new town development in this country. The British Urban Development Services Unit (BUDSU) was an attempt to institutionalise such an export of new town knowledge. BUDSU's successor, the New Town Consortium (NTC) is another attempt to follow the same pattern. I understand that one of the ways in which the work of the NTC will be carried out is to facilitate planners from other countries learning of the British experience by working in the offices of new town development corporations. The International New Towns Association (INTA) appears to be a mainly French inspired attempt to internationalise the export of new town knowledge from the industrialised world to third world countries.

But in all these examples, the main emphasis is on the practical aspects of development. INTA actually goes to the extreme of restricting control of the organisation and its programme to persons working in new town development. It specifically excludes academics and non-government bodies

such as the Town and Country Planning Association from having
any say in its programme.

The value of this emphasis on the practical aspects of
new town development is very questionable. Practice without
theory can be just as useless and counter productive as
theory without practice. One reason is that the practice of
new town development is heavily tinged with the emphasis on
prestige which, as has been pointed out, gives a very distorted picture of the nature of new town development. It is
difficult for anyone wholly involved in new town building to
escape these image building aspects. One consequence is that
anybody standing on the sidelines who opens his mouth to make
some qualification, reservation or criticism about what is
said by the practitioner is likely to get a kick in the
teeth.

The result is that some aspects of new town development
have been completely neglected. No study of substance for
example has ever been made of the economics of new towns.
High quality academic studies of new towns are rare. The New
Towns Study Unit in the Open University is the only body in
the United Kingdom with a specialised interest in the area
and as far as I know, is one of only two such bodies in the
world.

Without any attempt to make wide scale generalisations,
or formulate theory of any kind, it is difficult to separate
out those aspects of the new town experience which are transferable from the environment of one country to that of
another from those which are not so translatable. This
severely impedes the international flow of information on new
towns. Attempts to export this knowledge like that made
under the auspices of INTA will fail for that reason alone.

The lack of theory has led some educational bodies concerned with planning in third world countries to more or less
reject the new town experience. There is little emphasis on
new towns in the programmes of the Development Planning Unit,
University College London, or in the Bouwcentrum International Education in Rotterdam. These bodies appear to be
following policies almost at the other extreme to those by
INTA. Broadly speaking, DPU and BIE concentrate on bilateral
trade in the dissemination of information. They admit the
new town idea only in the context of an established channel
for the exchange of information between Britain and Holland
on the one hand, and a third world country on the other.

In my view there is room between these two extreme pos-
itions. The export knowledge position (typified by INTA)
will fail, partly because of the lack of theory, but also
because a one way flow of information on new towns or on any
other form of urban development is unrealistic. But the
bilateral exchange of information (typified by Bouwcentrum)
is too modest and unnecessarily restrictive. There are ideas
in the new town area which do have general application.
There is scope, therefore, for multilateral exchange of
information as well.

I would like to see the PCL-Habitat Forum or some new
body play a major part in promoting multilateral exchange of
information of this kind. There is a need for some kind of
centre of information with a special interest in rapid urban
growth which would aim to specialise in the preservation and
dissemination of knowledge on new towns, and other attempts
at rapid planned urban development which are not labelled as
new towns. This centre would be a point of reference for
individuals from any country in the world with an interest in
dealing with rapid urban growth.

REFERENCES

Alonso, W., 1970, What Are New Towns For?, Urban Studies, 7,
    pp. 37-55.
Bouwcentrum International Education, Annual Report, 1977,
    Rotterdam, Netherlands.
Evans, H., 1972, "New Towns: The British Experience," Charles
    Knight, London, for The Town and Country Planning
    Association.
Howard, E., 1898, "Tomorrow: A Peaceful Path to Real Reform,"
    Sonnenshein, London; and later as "Garden Cities of
    Tomorrow," paperback edition by Faber and Faber,
    London, 1965.
Roche, F. L., 1977, Building a New Town, paper given at the
    International New Towns Association Conference,
    Teheran, Dec.
Thomas, R., 1978, Britain's New Town Demonstration Project,
    "International Urban Growth Policies: New Town Con-
    tributions", Gideon Golany, ed., John Wiley, New York.
Thomas, R., 1969, "London's New Towns: A Study of Self-
    Containment and Balance," PEP, London.
Report of Habitat: United Nations Conference on Human
    Settlements, Vancouver 31 May-11 June 1976, United
    Nations, New York, A/CONF. 70/15, especially p.65.

Validity of new town principles
for the developing countries
Gideon Golany

Until recently, most of the new town principles were
imported by the developing countries with little or no adjustment to different and unique social, cultural, economic,
climatic or other conditions. A good example of this is
Chandigarh, capital of Punjab, a new town planned for a motor
vehicle system in a society that is pedestrian or, at most,
bicycle oriented.

This paper discusses the relevance of new towns principles as developed and implemented in the Western industrialised and technologically advanced countries, and their
applicability in the developing countries, especially those
of Asia and Africa.

The Western new town principles have achieved much success in their homelands because they generated growth and
improved socioeconomic and environmental conditions. Public
opinion was prepared to be receptive to the concept. More
importantly, the new town concept was prepared for and introduced primarily, if not absolutely, to the middle income
society, the dominant group. In the developing countries,
however, the majority consists of low income people, living
under entirely different circumstances. The planners/design-
ers who were of Western origin or Western educated, including
Le Corbusier, were brought to a different social climate.
Also, the developing society lacked indigenous design theor-
ists, able to integrate their ideas with an understanding of
the historical evolution of society and settlement forms.

Colonial design was a Western concept and was implemented by the foreign ruler to strengthen his self-image
and dominance. After political independence was won, Western
oriented leadership in design remained. The lack of local
theory and principles, the tendency to show the West that "we
can do it as well", the desire to imitate the West, the
denial of heritage, the lack of confidence, all contributed
to the importation of Western design principles to the developing society. Sometimes good Western designers were caught
in the crunch between their desire to develop designs suitable for the particular society and the desire of their
client to imitate the West.

DISTINCTIONS BETWEEN WEST AND EAST

To support our discussion it is necessary to outline
major distinctions between the developed countries, where new
towns have been highly advanced, and the developing
countries, where the new town movement is beginning, in terms
of factors which are relevant to our new town discussion and
I suggest that there are differences in:

Social values: mutual cooperation and attitude toward
extended family and community, rural vs urban values,
tribal and kinship relations, social vs materialistic
values, attitude toward privacy and toward space requirements, societal closeness, family management within
space, density, tolerance toward religious attitudes.

Technology: absorption of technology within the overall
socioeconomic system, understanding of the comprehensiveness of the system, degree of industrialisation and
manufacturing.

Commuting pattern: transportation system, attitude
toward pedestrian use and the acceptable commuting patterns, change in standard of living, private or public
mass transportation, distance between place of work and
home.

Economic values: acceptable standard of living, distribution ratio among socioeconomic classes, role of the
middle income class, attitude toward segregation or
integration of land uses by different socioeconomic
classes, investment, and employment.

378   G. GOLANY

Pattern of settlement: ratio of rural to urban, pace of
urbanisation process, attachment to agricultural land,
land ownership pattern.

Management, Implementation and Maintenance: mechanism,
attitude, public or private developers, historical attitude toward foreign rulers and toward public property,
energy use system and consumption, attitude toward
saving and financing systems, vision of national goals.

Public policy: local, federal or central government
power structures, possibilities for long term commitment
to urbanisation or regional development.

We have only scratched the surface of this matter, but
it is impossible to discuss each item in detail here. This
review will serve as a background to the following analyses
of new town principles.

NEW TOWN PRINCIPLES

The idea of creating new towns is nearly as old as human
settlements, and the formulation of its modern theory and
practice is now almost a century old. In this century, the
United Kingdom has been in the forefront in the theory and
practice of the new town concept. The basic principles introduced by Ebenezer Howard in 1898 have gone through some modifications with wide application since the 1946 New Towns Act,
culminating in development of thirty new towns. Now many
industrialised and technologically advanced countries in
western and eastern Europe, the USSR and North America have
established new towns, using the British concept as a model.

Some developing countries have tried the new town idea
when building capital cities, but it is only recently, since
the acceleration of urbanisation and an increasing concern
for rural society and its economy, that the new town idea has
been gaining momentum. The growing interest in new towns in
developing countries is hampered by limited experience and
leads to the following questions:

Are the Western new town principles and policies valid
in the developing countries and to what degree? What
are the prime national and regional problems to be
solved?

With the absence of experience in the developing
countries, is there a serious and real danger of importing the new town concept without proper adjustment and
modification to suit the needs of a developing society
and economy? The author has observed that much of the
planning and design of the new towns in the developing
countries has been carried out by Western planners,
designers and architects who are sure of their new town
success in the West but lack understanding of conditions
in the developing countries.

The traditional new town principles, as envisaged by
Ebenezer Howard and later practiced in the UK, can be outlined as follows:

1   Public or unified land ownership
2   Public as main developer
3   Site selection considerations
4   Strong planning control
5   Sound economic base with self-contained and self-sus-
    tained community
6   Urban design form
7   Place of work close to place of residence
8   Confined green belt and intersecting green open spaces
9   Combined town and country atmosphere
10 Balanced community with neighbourhood units
11 Implementation process, maintenance and management.

The Western new town movement has responded vaguely to
some of these principles, but they are important issues in
new town implementation in the developing countries.

Let us then attempt to evaluate the applicability of
these principles to the unique and different conditions of
the developing countries. To be brief and practical, the
analysis of each principle is introduced in two sections –
assumptions and recommendations.

NATIONAL SETTLEMENTS POLICY

One of the basic distinctions between the developed and
developing countries is that most of the developed countries
have become urbanised through industrialisation, advanced
technology and modern transportation methods. Most of them
are almost or completely self-reliant in food production.

The emerging countries are still basically rural-agricultural societies, with very limited industrialisation, limited technology, and poorly developed skills among the citizens.

In the developed countries, new town construction has become part of the national policy for future urban growth. It has been concerned mainly with urban congestion. In developing countries the relatively new urban growth is a result of neglect of rural problems. The majority of the population is still rural and agricultural.

Assumptions:

Rural population will constitute the bulk of the population in the foreseeable future.

Agriculture is the basic economy of the developing countries. Improvements are essential to increase food production.

Agriculture and a rural way of life have introduced social cohesiveness, social order and equilibrium, mutual aid, self-employment and self-reliance. Disruption of this social balance causes an increase in urban problems and disturbs the rural, social and environmental balance.

Dominance of rural-agricultural or regional rural-urban settlements is desirable to retain cultural identity and social values.

Urban growth will continue in uncontrolled forms.

Recommendations:

Policy for future urban growth should be comprehensive and focus on rural-regional communities as well as on large urban centres.

Employment for the spillover population in the rural communities should be found in new jobs, not necessarily depending directly on local resources, and in agriculture related industries.

National policy and strategy for future urban growth should be tied to economic values as well as to the desired social values of the nation. The Western new towns should not be introduced in their conventional

form but rather in the form of "new urban-rural settlements". The focus of the new settlements should be
rural-regional as well as inter-urban.

The new settlements can take a variety of forms:

- Accelerated growth centres in rural ragions,
  based on one existing village.
- New regional-rural growth centres.
- New urban-rural settlements which combine agro
  and urban functions.
- New freestanding urban settlements with new
  rural-regional development in regions to be developed.
- Company town to lead to self-contained communities with sound economic base.
- Development of towns, based on the expansion of
  existing ones.
- New town in-city, to be developed as a self-contained, self-employed and self-governed form to
  encourage growth within the city itself.

New urban settlement types should be introduced primarily to meet the need of low income people in rural-
regions or in congested urban centres.

SITE SELECTION CONSIDERATIONS

Assumptions:

For the majority of the population in rural areas, agriculture is still the basic economy

Agriculture will absorb new techniques and yet continue
to contribute to migration from rural to urban areas

Urban problems will increase as migration from rural to
urban centres continues. New jobs in the rural region
can hold back part of this migration, but not all of it

Rural to urban migration hastens urban deterioration and
the development of uncontrolled urban settlements in the
form of shanty towns. First to move are unskilled,
single persons, followed by families.

Population growth will continue in rural as well as in
urban regions and the need for new housing will increase. The cardinal question remains: Where should
growth occur and what are the best forms of settlement
to be introduced to absorb this growth?

Recommendations:

In terms of location, three types of new towns should be encouraged:

- New town in-city: this concept calls for the implementation of new town principles within sections of large cities where deterioration has become severe. This method can be urban renewal, slum clearance and the like and a new way of achieving the goal of self-help, self-reliance and self-support. The scale should be small enough to make it feasible for and effectively manageable by the people of the developing country. The new town in-city concept should be planned and implemented in an individual way to suit the conditions of the particular developing country.

New urban settlement in rural regions: This should be the first choice in new town development. It has the advantage of serving the majority of the population and the potential of improving regional services, transportation and infrastructure. It can generate local and regional employment, improve marketing of farm produce and create jobs which rely on local manufacturing and industries related to local natural resources. It can facilitate implementation of a national policy, stabilise population mobility and absorb surplus population. New urban settlements in rural regions can be:

- Regional growth centres.
- Transportation centres.
- Self-sustained communities with a sound economic base and provisions for employment.
- A means of upgrading services of the region: education, social services, health, training needs, etc.

Satellite new town: This type of new town is adjacent to major cities, yet can be independent in terms of government and service. It should not be a bedroom town but rather a self-contained community with a sound economic base so that the majority of the population can live and work there. Its prime goal should be to ease congestion in the adjacent large city, absorb rural to urban migration or migration from the city and function as an alternative economic pole to the adjacent large city.

Western cities have failed in the management of large
urban centres. It is doubtful that the developing
counties can do better.

Agricultural land is precious and will continue to be an
essential national resource. Neither a new urban centre
nor the existing one should take over farm land or land
suitable for agriculture.

LAND OWNERSHIP AND LAND USE CONTROL

Assumptions:

Land ownership in the developing countries is characterised by two patterns:

- Much of the non-urban land is owned by public
  authorities (this is especially true in arid and
  semiarid countries);
- Few persons own large tracts of the land used for
  agriculture, while a large number of farmers own
  very small tracts or rent their land.

Land reclamation for agriculture is taking place in the
developing countries and is expected to continue.

Families have a strong attachment to the land and to
their home. Housing for rent is not very common, especially in non-urban centres.

Compulsory purchase (or eminent domain) is occasionally
used by the government for road construction and other
public needs and is tolerated by the average citizen.

Land use control has always been weak in the developing
countries. Much improvement will not take place in the
foreseeable future. Government machinery is slow and
inefficient.

Recommendations:

A public corporation (semi-government agency) should own
and develop the land.

Public land ownership is a strong tool in site selection
and land use control and should be retained by the new
town.

Housing can be offered for sale, but the land should be owned by the public and leased to the house owner with renewal option under specific terms and with a yearly fee in order to retain and strengthen land use control.

The responsibilities of New Town Corporations should be to:

- Own and lease land for development.
- Plan land use development and control.
- Construct housing for sale and for rent.
- Develop the infrastructure, roads and transportation system.
- Provide basic daily services such as education, health care, and social welfare.

ROLE OF PUBLIC AND PRIVATE ENTERPRISE

Assumptions:

The average citizen sees the central, regional or local government as the appropriate provider of public services, utilities and mass transportation. This image has been reinforced by international bodies. The attitude will continue to exist, unless future development of the free market system, public awareness of common needs, acceptance of democracy as a way of life, modern administrative development, or rise of the middle-income class should change the situation.

Any development introduced by the public is expected to complete the circle of policy and goal initiation, planning, investment, implementation and maintenance. Changes in this pattern may occur gradually with the introduction of new factors: self-sufficiency and economic self-reliance, change in the socioeconomic classes, especially the middle income class, and the emergence of local private developers equipped to take over and manage large scale developments. Yet the existing public involvement in any such project will not be changed dramatically.

Recommendations:

Improvement in delivery of services, utilities and mass transportation can occur when the national economy (GNP)

improves, when tax collection becomes more effective and
when average per capital income increases. New town
development can contribute to these changes and should
receive support in view of the desirability of these
changes.

Diversification of the economic base of a new town will
lead to greater social choices. New towns can support
the upgrading of low income groups and the rise of a
middle class. However, public incentive is constantly
required to attract new employment opportunities.

Under the existing unique social, economic, and political circumstances in the developing countries, construction of new towns is and will continue to be primarily a
matter of public enterprise and public control. The
private enterprise contribution can be introduced gradually when the ability of the people to manage large
scale developments has gained strength.

It is important that the development of the new town be
a joint venture by public (in the form of the government) and private enterprise. Pioneering efforts should
not be viewed as profit-making ventures. It is our
opinion that private developers, who are primarily pro-
fit-oriented, should join a project only when it has
reached a secure state.

Public contribution is expected to be introduced in:

A. - Planning, implementation and maintenance of the
      following:

    1 Site selection for the new town, consistent
      with national or regional policy.

    2 Land assembly and financing (and if necessary
      compulsory purchase legislation). Public
      land-use control, especially when private
      developers become involved at a later time.

    3 Development of the basic infrastructure,
      transportation network.

    4 Provision of the basic structure for community
      services such as health care, education and
      social welfare.

B. - Incentives to private developers as well as to
      individuals or families: free or low fee land
      lease: access to the site; tax reduction or tax

relief for a specified period; loan with low
interest or none at all; grant, or standing loan;
other forms of incentives which also can be rated
according to numbers of jobs to be created by the
private investors. Newcomers and families should
also be eligible for incentives in order to attract the desired diversified socioeconomic
groups.

Private enterprise is usually attracted when the pros-
pect of profit seems secure. Private investors are not
concerned with social cost and are not expected to take
on national policy needs. Private developers of industries, of services, of shopping centres, or of housing,
will want to find the infrastructure, access and road
network developed by the public.
Major parts of housing developments can be taken over by
private enterprise on a profitable basis yet still under
terms to ensure that public needs are met. Subsidies in
the form of mortgages with low or no interest may be
given directly to the families.

Planners of the new town should make special efforts to
strengthen the tax base of the community in order to
upgrade services and support the development of local
government. My observation is that there are sequential
chains of planning which support the growth of the tax
base: variety in job opportunities leads to socioeconomic diversification, and this leads to increase in
demand for upgrading services and shopping and to improvement of the tax base. Basic industries can also
contribute to a better tax base.

Efforts should be made to support local small and middle
sized private developers who can jointly or separately
take the responsibility for land development and housing
construction. The new town project can be a tool in
implementing such a policy.

ECONOMIC BASE

Assumptions:

The economic base of the rural settlement has traditionally been agriculture. This tendency will continue
despite minor changes in the level of technology.

Existing urban centres were historically developed as marketing, transportation and, to some extent, administrative centres. They will, expectedly, be centres for industry and services as well.

Improvement of the economic base and diversification in employment will eventually create a wide middle class and improve the condition of the low income class.

A developing society is not motor vehicle oriented and will remain this way because of the size of the local economic base.

The traditional concept of a sound economy in the developing society has been strongly related to self-sufficiency as a means of security and safety for the family.

Recommendations:

New town development should be self-contained, with a diversified and sound economic base (and not a company town), to suit the commuting patterns of a pedestrian oriented society.

A sound economic base reduces the need for commuting, generates local employment, introduces a variety of job opportunities, supports social diversification and community balance, stabilises migration, upgrades local and regional infrastructure and services (especially in rural regions), improves marketing and supports economic growth. For these reasons, it is most desirable for the developing society.

Especially in rural regional new towns, the economic base should include industry, manufacturing and services for the town itself as well as for the region. Economic diversification leads to variety in employment opportunities (age, sex and degree of skill), in land use and in housing demand.

URBAN DESIGN

Assumptions:

Urban growth has been uncontrolled, and without policy and strategy this will continue in the future. The result is shanty towns.

Contemporary planned urban forms in developing countries have been imitations of the Western model: wide straight avenues, large monuments, great open spaces and huge public buildings.

Much of the current development is a continuation of the colonial style, without taking into account the indigenous forms and heritage or the need to respond to climatic stress.

Recommendations:

The city in a developing country should:

- Be compact, but not increase the density of the housing units. This form shortens all utility lines and improves the tax base.
- Adopt the local tradition of integrated land uses for services and jobs within the residential area. Major industries which have a negative impact on the environment should be segregated. The basic concept should allow walking or use of bicycles.
- Introduce clustered housing along the streets or at a dead end to strengthen social interaction among residents and to support contact among extended families.

Energy consumption will be increased by new-town development, and energy resources are limited in most of the developing countries (non-Middle-Eastern ones). Therefore, the overall design of new towns should minimise energy use and reduce the length of utility networks. Compact urban design form is one way to achieve such results.

National and local historical heritage should find expression in the architecture of the new town and in the construction of its housing and its public buildings. This will contribute to a feeling of continuity, identity and pride among the inhabitants.

PROXIMITY AND TRANSPORTATION SYSTEMS

Assumptions:

Private car ownership is limited to a very small portion of the population. Future increase will be minimal.

A developing society is a pedestrian or bicycling one
and will continue to be so in the foreseeable future.

Recommendations:

Urban and neighbourhood development should be clustered
and compact with minimum sprawl.

Service centres should be provided within walking distance of residential areas.

Special pedestrian and bicycling networks should be the
prime "roadway" of the new town.

Public mass transportation should be subsidised to meet
the needs of low income people.

Jobs should be spread all over the new town if possible
in order to minimise commuting. Except where industry
has strong impact on the environment, land use integration has priority.

All transportation and pedestrian networks should be
designed to eliminate dust pollution.

GREEN AND OPEN SPACE

Assumptions:

In contrast to the traditional Western view, green space
and open space are two different issues which do not
necessarily have to be combined in developing countries.

Climatic conditions (arid and semiarid) and scarcity of
water may not make possible the introduction of green-
ery. The open space, however, is still a social and
health necessity for the new settlement.

Maintenance of public space requires skill and financial
resources, which are not always available in developing
countries.

Large tracts of open space of the traditional Western
type require much design and management.

Open space is an essential element in the developing
society and usually attracts people. Moreover, the
limited space in the typical urban modern house makes
open space more important for all age groups. To be
used frequently, it should be close by.

Recommendations:

Open space or green open space should be broken up into
small units and spread among the neighbourhoods close to
each housing cluster. This will intensify its diurnal
use.

No open space should be left unused unless it is tree
covered or paved, or both. Any open space should be
designed to require minimal or no maintenance.

Public open space should meet the needs of all age
groups and of family gatherings.

Small rather than large tracts of open space should be
introduced within the urban area, especially in a cli-
matically stressed region.

TOWN AND COUNTRY ATMOSPHERE

Assumptions:

Developing countries have a long rural tradition which
left its marks in art, music, folklore, leadership,
production and the national economy. The average person
has a strong attachment to the rural and country atmosphere. Although this image will be weakened, it will
continue to be dominant.

Country and rural environment has supported the extended
family setting, so rooted in the developing society;
loyalty to blood relations has been the strongest of all
loyalties.

The extended family form has great merit: mutual cooperation, security (especially for the elderly), social
and economic protection, identity, pride, and leadership. These elements can be utilised positively, for
example in self-help housing, when an adequate plan is
introduced.

In spite of rural-to-urban migration, rural culture and
tradition have viewed urban life as evil and rural life,
seen as honest, with pride. Historically, the village
came into existence in order to protect the collective
interest of the tribal society; therefore, continued
social values were essential. The city, on the other
hand, is created by many individuals of different origin
and for economic reasons.

Urban villagers find themselves in a stormy personal conflict: the old inherited social-rural values conflict with the new urban materialistic values. A true conflict of two 'cultures' exists for the rural to urban migrant.

Recommendations:

The traditional new town concept of 'combining urban and country' environment seems to be suitable for the developing society.

New urban settlement within rural-agricultural regions can help decrease rural to urban migration. Such new towns in rural regions should have a sound economic base, service its region in all its facets and act as a regional growth centre.

New rural types of settlements in different forms should be introduced to retain rural values, rural cooperation and rural economy.

New urban settlements, different from the various contemporary new town types, should be introduced in the rural region. One such new urban type is the agro-urban settlement.

BALANCED COMMUNITY AND NEIGHBOURHOOD UNITS

Assumptions:

Historically, the neighbourhood concept evolved in a traditional society and within the tribal and kinship community, the extended family or in blood related groups.

The Neighbourhood was a physical entity and retained a social identity. It represented safety and security, social harmony, a balanced power structure, and mutual cooperation.

The contemporary village society of the developing countries and in some cases urban neighbourhood units, also based on the extended family and blood related persons, have social cohesiveness, harmony, community balance and a variety of age and sex groups. Elderly persons provided security and continuity.

The modern neighbourhood in Western society usually developed as a service unit without much of the social cohesiveness found in the historical neighbourhood. Exceptions are neighbourhoods made up of migratory groups of the same origin. Yet the modern neighbourhood does not retain the community features of the developing society.

The traditional neighbourhood is a conglomerate of socioeconomic groups, living in harmony side by side.

Social interaction, intimacy, informality, and closeness are very acceptable characteristics of the developing society.

Recommendations:

The neighbourhood and the balanced community are acceptable concepts in the developing society and should be retained.

The neighbourhood in a new town for a developing society should have:

- Integration rather than segregation of land uses.
- Proximity of land uses, essential for all uses.
- A pattern of walkways and bicycle paths with minimal provision for motor vehicles.
- Fragmented open space, close to all housing units, for community interaction. The availability of public open space should make up for the shortage of space in individual houses.
- Daily services should be provided within walking distance from homes: shops, school, playground, social places, etc.

The house (or the apartment) for the basic family unit should have these features:

- Residential units should be close to each other in a clustered, compact form without a high density per residential unit.
- Apartment units should not exceed a height of three floors to avoid elevators and to save energy, management, maintenance, and financial costs.
- Housing units or apartments should be designed and constructed for low income people, who con-

stitute a majority in the population. Local materials should be used.

- Features that are expandable and improvable in the future are recommended in order to meet changes in the standard of living and in family space requirements.
- Interior space planned with much flexibility - perhaps with mobile walls.
- High-rise apartment buildings should not be used because they require special management and main- tenance which the developing society is not ready to offer.

IMPLEMENTATION, MAINTENANCE AND MANAGEMENT

Assumptions:

Implementation of planning is not a strong skill in the developing countries; this weakness applies to techno- logical as well as to management aspects.

The absence of a large middle class and of skilled workers is evident in most of the developing countries; a new town project can be used to support local devel- opers (in a cooperative or other system) for housing construction, road building, infrastructure and the training of low-income labour.

Maintenance is among the weakest skills in the develop- ing countries, and this is a factor no matter how good the quality of planning, design and implementation may be.

Low quality maintenance applies to the infrastructure as well as to common high rise apartment buildings.

There has been little awareness of public needs and therefore little cooperation between the local auth- orities and the average residents. Some expressions of these weaknesses are litter in the streets and in public spaces and inefficient tax collection.

Recommendations:

High rise buildings should be avoided; apartments should not exceed three floors. Fewer units in a cluster make

local management possible. Open spaces should be paved
to minimise the need for maintenance.

It is necessary to train developers and community
leaders in management and maintenance.

The development of a local power structure and of community leaders is essential for self-motivation.

Education for good citizenship should be provided widely
for adults as well as for the young.

Public awareness of the importance of taxes is essential
in order to create an attitude of shared responsibility.

CONCLUSION

In conclusion, the specific characteristics of the developing society require careful attention when importing new
town theory and practice. Most of the traditional Western
new town principles can be used in general by the developing
countries, but there is a need for modifications and adjustments to the demands of unique cultural, social, and economic
settings.

It is certainly evident that developing countries have
their own socioeconomic and political characteristics. This
distinction will continue for many generations to come and
will dictate the need for a unique design and management
system for their new settlements. The new town principles
can be valid for a developing society if proper professional
adjustments are considered in the procedure and detail of its
planning. If not, the new town principles can defeat their
purpose. Under any circumstances, the need is vital for a
deep and real understanding of the specific nature of a developing society, in non-Western terms. The comprehension of
its economic and climatic condition is also important. Importation of Western standard solutions, usually done with
superficial adjustments to impress the client, is dangerous
and socially and economically destructive. Another problem
must be faced: the client himself often has been seeking
imitation of Western society and technology, without much
reliance on indigenous achievements in design, scale, pattern
and building materials. There are encouraging signs that
this tendency is diminishing. Attitudes based on local roots
and increasing self-reliance and pride are taking shape.

New towns in developing countries can improve conditions of low-income groups, can generate new employment opportunities, and can serve as effective tools for implementation of national policy in regard to future urbanisation and economic growth. They can be used to retain and develop social and rural values.

New urban settlements in developing countries should be located in rural regions as well as in existing large urban centres. They should be introduced in a variety of forms.

Finally, large scale new town developments of a million or more inhabitants are rarely planned or implemented in the Western industrialised world. This is the case in spite of no lack of ability to manage such a large scale project. The developing countries, however, with their limited resources, skills and management ability, should aim for small scale new town developments.

NOTES

The paper follows the author's recent visit to India and its new town of Chandigarh and to a conference/seminar in Ahmedabad, attended by leading Indian planners, architects, educators and policymakers. It is a summary of personal research and observations and is intended to add to the understanding of the possible role of new towns in developing countries and the need for further development and research on this subject. The attempt here is to focus on the practical rather than on the theoretical aspect of new town planning and development.

The idea for this paper took form during my stay as a visiting professor at the New Towns Study Unit of The Open University, located at the new city of Milton Keynes, England. Ray Thomas, director of the Unit, suggested that there is a noticeable gap in the understanding of how new towns can fit the needs of developing countries. I am thankful to him and to Dr. Stephen Potter for reading the first draft and offering their comments.

Contributors

Thomas L. Blair is a sociologist/planner, researcher and public policy analyst and Polytechnic professor. He is author of "The Poverty of Planning" and "The International Urban Crisis" and numerous articles, and advisory editor of "Cities," a new quarterly journal on urban policy. He has served many international agencies and consultancy groups in the fields of urban planning, human settlement development and implementation, and architectural and planning education and curriculum development.

Charles L. Choguill is a senior lecturer in development planning, University of Sheffield, Department of Town and Regional Planning, with recent consultancy experience in Bangladesh and Brazil.

Abhijit Datta and Gangadhar Jha are, respectively, Professor of Urban Administration and Development and Municipal Finance, and Training Associate at the Centre of Urban Studies, Indian Institute of Public Administration, New Delhi, India. Professor Datta was educated at Calcutta and London universities and served as a United Nations expert, consultant to the World Bank, and fellow at the Institute of Local Government Studies, University of Birmingham, and the Habitat Forum, School of Environment, the Polytechnic of Central London. Their joint work will also appear in a volume of Habitat International Journal.

Luis Sanchez de Carmona y Lerdo de Tejada was born in Mexico City, has a degree in Architecture from the Ibero-American University and a Doctorate in Urbanism in preparation at the University of Paris. He was Founder Member and President of the Administration Board of the Centre of Housing; Director of Urbanism and Operations of the Urban Institute of the State of Mexico; Head of the Master Plan Office of Mexico City; Coordinator of the Advisory Board on Human Settlements for the Government Plan 1976-1982; and is Director-General of Ecological Development of Human Settlements in the Secretariat of Human Settlements and Public Works.

His co-author Edwin Sours Renfrew was born in Mexico
City, studied at the National Autonomous University of Mexico
and obtained his Bachelors degree in 1974 with a major in
Biology. His academic studies include work on a Masters
degree in Ecology with a thesis entitled "Environmental Planning in Mexico: A Methodological Approach". He has been
concerned with the subject of Urban Ecology in Mexico for 10
years, and is Deputy-Director for Ecological Development for
Human Settlements. He is author of 22 studies and various
journal articles in his field, and is a much-travelled lecturer and conference participant in Mexico and abroad.

Ukwa Agbai Ejionye is lecturer in the Department of
Sociology and Anthropology, University of Benin, Nigeria. He
holds degrees from the University of London, Brunel University, and a Ph.D. from The Open University, England, and was
Commonwealth Foundation Fellow in the social and environmental aspects of development planning at the Habitat Forum,
School of Environment, the Polytechnic of Central London in
1982.

Gideon Golany is Professor of Urban and Regional Planning at the Pennsylvania State University, and has taught at
the Virginia Polytechnic Institute and Cornell University. A
specialist in new-town planning and development, his publications include: "International Urban Growth Policies: New-
Town Contributions" (1978); and "Innovations for Future
Cities" (1976).

Haji Mohamad Bin Haji Abdul Rahman is General Manager,
Kejora, Johore Bahru, Malaysia.

Gloria D. Knight is General Manager of the Urban Development Corporation, Kingston, Jamaica. She has studied at
the University of the West Indies, Oxford and McGill universities, and was Commonwealth Foundation Fellow in urban planning, management and implementation at the Habitat Forum,
School of Environment, the Polytechnic of Central London in
1982. Mrs. Knight holds an award of distinction for work in
urban development and served as the Jamaican representative
to the United Nations Habitat Conference on Human Settlements, Vancouver, Canada 1976.

Stephen C. Lockwood was, at the time of this study,
Vice-President, PRS Voorhees, Division of PRC Engineering
Inc., and Director, PRC (Nigeria) Ltd. He served as resident
general manager for the Abuja Master Plan.

Richard May, Jr. is Chief Urban Planner for Tippetts-Abbett-McCarthy-Stratton, a firm of engineers, architects and urban planners. He holds a degree in urban planning from Columbia University, has worked as technical advisor to the United Nations Centre for Human Settlements in Nairobi, Kenya, and has extensive experience in planning in the Eastern Caribbean, Libya and Korea.

Elpidius Mpolokoso was until recently with the Zambia National Housing Authority. He is now Associate Director of Studies at the Mindolo Ecumenical Foundation, Kitwe, Zambia. He was a participant in the Urban Habitat Programme of the Habitat Forum, School of Environment, the Polytechnic of Central London.

Gilbert J. Njau is Director of the Housing Development Department, City Council of Nairobi and is responsible for coordination of planning, design and implementation of housing projects, with especial reference to low-income communities. He was educated at the University of Toronto and received the Masters degree in Civic Design from Liverpool University. He is a corporate member of the Architectural Association of Kenya, Town Planning chapter, and has held fellowships at the Economic Development Institute of the World Bank and at the Habitat Forum, Polytechnic of Central London.

David Pasteur is a staff member of the Development Administration Group in the Institute of Local Government Studies, University of Birmingham, England. His major Lusaka study, "The Management of Squatter Upgrading: A Case Study of Organisation, Procedures and Participation", was published by Saxon House, Teakfield Ltd., England 1979, from which the figures used here were taken and gratefully acknowledged.

Report of an American Delegation of City Planners. The contributions by Leon S. Eplan (Urban Settlement Policies), Martha M. Davis et al. (Administration), and Janet A. Cady (Future Exchanges), are extracts from "Urban Planning in China," by the National Committee on US-China Relations, E.A. Winckler and J.A. Cady, eds., New York, 1980.

David A. Rushforth is a consultant to the Joint Activity on Urban Management, Organisation for Economic Cooperation and Development, Paris, responsible for projects concerned with improving the implementation of urban policy and the management of urban research. He is a graduate of the School of Town Planning, University of Auckland, New Zealand, a member of the World Society for Ekistics, and has lived and worked as an urban and regional planning consultant in Brazil, Greece and Saudi Arabia.

Lee Shostak was educated at the Massachusetts Institute of Technology and Syracuse University, and worked as a planning consultant in the USA. He has held posts at Brunel University and Trent Polytechnic, and served as Planning Director of the Milton Keynes Development Corporation (MKDC). David Lock, his associate and joint-author, was planning manager of MKDC. Both are now with the Conran-Roche firm in Milton Keynes as Director, and Associate, respectively. Their joint work has also been reported in "New Towns in National Development", published by the International Federation of Housing and Planning, The Hague, with the assistance of The Open University, Milton Keynes, Dudley Leaker, ed.

Ray Thomas is Senior Lecturer in Economics and Director of the New Towns Study Unit, Open University, Milton Keynes. He is author of "London's New Towns: A Study in Self-Containment and Balance" (1969), joint author with Peter Hall et al., "The Containment of Urban England" (1973), and a contributor to "International Urban Growth Policies: New Town Contributions", Gideon Golany, ed. (1978).

Habitat Forum

The Polytechnic of Central London

The Polytechnic of Central London, a major British educational institution located in the heart of metropolitan London, has an established record of excellence in the provision of national and international education through undergraduate, post-graduate and mid-career courses and research facilities.

The Habitat Forum, 35, Marylebone Road, London, NW1

The Habitat Forum, as an academic centre within the School of Environment of the Polytechnic of Central London, is directly concerned with the inter-disciplinary study of the planning and management problems faced by human settlements and the education and training of personnel qualified to deal with these problems.

The Forum's activities include the provision of national and international education through short courses, conferences, seminars, curriculum development, and research, publications, and facilities for visiting scholars and officials studying human settlement planning topics.

The Urban Habitat Course

A major emphasis of the Forum's activities is a mid-career short courses programme, Urban Habitat: New Skills and Perspectives for Urban Managers, offered annually for urban administrators from developing countries. The three main subject areas are: Urban Management; Urban Development Operations; Urban Policy Integration and Implementation. Each subject/ course is a distinct unit of study within a unified training perspective under the leadership of senior persons of wide international experience.

Index